KINGS IN
DISGUISE

KINGS IN DISGUISE

James Vance and Dan Burr

With an introduction by Alan Moore

W. W. Norton & Company
New York London

For information about permission to reproduce selections from this book, write to Permissions,
W. W. Norton & Company, Inc., 500 Fifth Avenue, New York, NY 10110

Manufacturing by Courier Westford
Production manager: Anna Oler

Library of Congress Cataloging-in-Publication Data
Vance, James, 1953–
Kings in disguise / James Vance and Dan Burr; introduction by Alan Moore
p. cm.
Originally published: Princeton, Wis.: Kitchen Sink Press, 1990.
ISBN-13: 978-0-393-32848-6 (pbk.)
ISBN-10: 0-393-32848-1 (pbk.)
1. Graphic novels. I. Burr, Dan, 1951– II. Title.
PN6727.V36K56 2006
741.5'973—dc22   2005058549

W. W. Norton & Company, Inc.
500 Fifth Avenue, New York, N.Y. 10110
www.wwnorton.com

W. W. Norton & Company Ltd.
Castle House, 75/76 Wells Street, London W1T 3QT

1 2 3 4 5 6 7 8 9 0

This book is dedicated with thanks to Brenda, who was there at the beginning; with pride to our daughter, Brigid, who made life during its writing a joy—and with all my heart to the memory of Kate, whose love remains my greatest reward for having written *Kings in Disguise.*

—J. V.

I want to express my thanks to my wife, art assistant, and valued critic, Debbie Freiberg, who provided the excellent coloring for the color illustration, and who continues to inspire and encourage me; to Dave Schreiner and Denis Kitchen for their support, patience, and belief in me; and to James Vance for his special vision and hard work, and for providing me with a wonderful script to interpret.

—D. B.

INTRODUCTION

Here we all are, us tramps, us yeggs. We're standing on a draughty corner of the centuries, right where the rusted sign says 20th runs into 21st. Take a look down the street, a squint back up the track, the muddy and meandering at-times-precarious route by which we got this far, out past the rust and creeper of the rail-yards and across a rope-bridge over a ravine, beyond civilization's ragged Neolithic edge, where all the hungry people are. Look down the beaten path of history and ask yourself if those corroded train-lines look like gold beneath their overgrowth of weed, or if the hawsers that support the wooden crossing, swaying there above its chasm, look as though they're made from ermine. Or do they instead seem built from lowlier yet sturdier materials, and set in place by those of humbler means?

The histories that we were taught in school were gold and ermine histories, the self-penned chronicles of church and state, of kings and generals, of misjudged wars, successful persecutions, hamstrung dynasties, that all too often seemed like a list of mankind's stumbling blocks more than a proud recounting of its progress. When we look back at our culture's high points, at its noblest achievements, we do not in general count coronations, bloody feuds or holy wars amongst that company. The things we generally cherish as a species, unsurprisingly, seem not to be the grand and glorious campaigns that waste us in our thousands, in our millions, but instead the things that make the often-gruelling human trail sweeter: music and art and writing, medicine and learning, and those fruits of science that are not poisonous and do not too severely disadvantage us. The breakthroughs and the triumphs that allowed those fields to exist and to grow are for the greater part not those achieved by government or royalty, nor yet the fabulously wealthy. When we search for names to make us proud of our humanity and of our heritage, the likelihood is that the name we seize upon will be a person born to modest circumstance.

The poor, we're told, are always with us, although one would never think so from the recon-structed dramas we call history. History turns the poor into a nameless herd of unpaid and uncredited film-extras with no speaking part, to cannon fodder or to scabby Bastille mobs, to people whose lives came and went and never merited a cameo from Winslett or DiCaprio. To peo-ple like our parents or our grandparents or great-grandparents or however far one has to scram-ble arse-first down the family tree before one reaches hard black dirt. Didn't their lives, their sto-ries, count for anything? Are they to be excluded from the homo sapiens account simply because they were not born into a noble lineage most likely founded upon murder, incest, treachery, decapitation? Shall we overlook all those who never had the pocket-change to even think of annexing Sudetenland? The lazy good-for-nothing workshy bums who never had to find the cash to overthrow a foreign tyrant that their dads had helped install?

Instead, perhaps we should attempt a different history, a different narrative where even those not blessed by ruthlessly acquisitive blood-genealogies may be included. We should count small human victories as dearly as we count the sinking of armadas, and elect our own dishevelled heroes and aristocrats, our monarchies without a pot to piss in, our own vagrant kings.

In this astonishing and heartfelt graphic novel, James Vance and Dan Burr have rescued a lost butt-end of discarded history, an edited-out sequence from the Souza pageant of the great American success tale. Rags to riches, that's an arc the movie audiences understand. Riches to rags, now that's more problematical but it could still be done if it was something European and depressing. Rags to rags, however, that's a different story, in that it's no story whatsoever, or at least no story that would play within our current entertainment culture's scheme of things. "What, they just start poor and they go on being poor? What's that about? Where's all the con-flict? Where's the payoff? Where's the Liam Neeson part?"

In fact, the whole lives of the dispossessed are conflict, and each meal successfully obtained a payoff. All the dramas of the world are magnified by poverty so that the loss of a few coins might mean the difference between life and death, as surely as the loss of crowns or empires might. Finding the means to feed your offspring or yourself can be a struggle quite as valiant as the pros-ecution of a great colonial campaign, and the achievement of your ends just as miraculous, as great a cause for celebration.

In America, the moment that has come to be iconic as an image of rock-bottom destitution is the Great Depression of the 1930s: sepia lives, dust-saturated, frozen into sepia pictures, news-reel breadlines, but of course that's only half the story. How the math of poverty works out is that if everybody has an equal share, then there should be no rich, no poor. If someone gets rich, then someone else is made, by the same token, poor. If someone should get very rich, then it may be that many people are made poor. This works both ways, of course. If many, many people are made poor then it's a safe bet the money's going somewhere. During the Depression, quite a lot of it was going to the entertainment industry, especially those sections of the entertainment industry that dealt in fantasy. *Snow White* broke the box office records of its day, people prepared to spend the money on an hour or two of carefree Technicolor heaven that they might have spent prolong-ing their more fraught and colourless existence here on earth, just by a meal or two. And then of course there were pulp magazines, be they the spicy or the spattery variety. And then of course there were the comic books with their superheroic symbols of success, men clad in blazing primaries and able with a single bound to leap above their grey trudge through the jobless tenements.

Kings in Disguise closes the circle, the direct descendant of an industry whose boom years were those times that people were most desperate to escape from into dreams of romance and empowerment, using comic strips to tell a story that portrays the grim realities that underlay the times when comic strips were born.

James Vance writes with a naturalism, with an honest voice that doesn't wear its research on its sleeve, and with a finely tuned eye for the human nuances on which his story rests. The careful sense of character and period and texture he conveys is all the more impressive in a medium that all too often revels in the overstated and the overblown. Dan Burr's compelling art, as masterful and unassuming as the best of, for example, Harvey Pekar's worthiest collaborators, is the writing's perfect complement. It has an earthy strength and functionality, just as the writing has, that doesn't leave room for the least manipulative smear of sentiment, but which leaves all the open space for poetry that anyone could wish.

It is a poetry of beans and boxcars, smoking hops and smuggled hopes and is expressed here in the most sublime and lucid terms conceivable, in ringingly clear lines of ink and lines of dialogue, in solid blacks beyond the firelight's edge and moral half-tone greys that threaten to engulf the best intentions. This is simply one of the most moving and compelling human stories to emerge out of the graphic story medium thus far.

It's a hard life, and, as Jack Black assured us, You Can't Win. Pick up this mud-stained masterpiece of raindog regents and their unsung histories, however, and be sure to get, for once, an even break. Good People Here. No Dogs. Be Lucky.

Alan Moore
Northampton, England
July 2005

PREFACE

In the waning years of the Eisenhower administration, I used to spend my preschool summers in the small town where my grandmother lived. From time to time, shabby strangers would come to her back door asking for food or money. She would order me from the room in the same tone of voice she used to warn me away from stray dogs. Then she would pass something portable like a sandwich through the door and send them on their way. Even at the age of five, I couldn't help wondering about the combination of fear and kindness she exhibited toward these strangers, who never returned. I didn't know it, but by witnessing and wondering about these little dramas, I'd taken the first step toward writing *Kings in Disguise*.

It was about twenty years later, in the summer of 1979, that I took the next step. I'd just written a typical first play; that is, one concerned with how fascinating and tragic it was to be me. It was a traditional small-cast drama that scrupulously observed the classic unities. I was beginning a second, and having proven that I could work within Aristotle's restrictions to at least mediocre success, I was ready to cut loose and see just how far imagination could carry me when an ancient Greek wasn't breathing down my neck.

The result was a bizarre pastiche of Depression-era leftist melodrama called *On the Ropes*. Set in 1937, it was crammed with characters drawn from the icons of that period: WPA artists and performers, labor agitators, messianic Communists, sociopathic strikebreakers, and the inevitable tough-but-tender-hearted female journalist. To make things more frenetic, I threw in an escape artist with a death wish and more onstage violence than any two Jacobean tragedies.

It worked. Over the next year, the play was revived and toured so often in regional and college theaters that I grew good and sick of it. The play had a decent run that resulted in recognition for some brilliant performers, and a national playwriting award that led to some lucrative commissions for me. But my God, I was sick of that play.

The only part of it that still appealed to me was a secondary character named Fred Bloch. Fred was an eighteen-year-old orphan of the road who'd found a new family in the dream of brotherhood espoused by the Communist Party. Physically maimed and emotionally scarred, he was little more than a plot device at first—the necessary angry young radical—but soon developed into an endearing and complex character whose dread of loneliness had forced him even further outside the mainstream of society.

For a few months, I tried to write a new play that would allow me to explore what had intrigued me about Fred Bloch. Eventually, I gave it up and went on to other projects. Then, in 1981, *Ropes* received an unexpected revival in Los Angeles, and this time, despite some good performances, it didn't work. Out of my dissatisfaction came the impetus to throw away what I'd done and make a fresh start on the abandoned play.

I'd originally intended to center it around Fred some fifteen years after the events of *Ropes*, but now I found myself going in the opposite direction, inquiring further into his past to discover just who he was, and how he'd gotten to the point where I'd first encountered him. Now, instead of a middle-aged man scrambling to restore a shattered life, he was a boy on the verge of adolescence, caught in the act of running away from home. A brother obliquely referred to in *Ropes* became three-dimensional, followed by a father, then a hometown. . . . The result was the one-act *Kings in Disguise*, which premiered on stage in 1984.

A year or so before that, I'd wandered into a comic book shop, looking for pop-culture material for another play that would remain unwritten. As I'd expected, many of the comics of my childhood were still being ground out by the same old sausage factories. What I hadn't expected to find was a small but impressive amount of work being done for literate, mature audiences, and I found myself being drawn to it. I was bored with the commissions I was getting at that time, and I began to wonder what challenge might be found in writing for this rediscovered medium. At the urging of my friend and fellow writer John Wooley, I prepared a proposal for a comics "novel" based on *Kings in Disguise* and took the final step toward creating this book.

I can no longer remember if those summers at my grandmother's house were on my mind when I wrote *On the Ropes*, but I know for certain that they were when I outlined this new project. The "plight of the homeless" hadn't yet been bumped from the public consciousness by whatever cause of the week that would follow it. Ronald Reagan had just made his infamous statement about the number of people who *wanted* to sleep on steam grates, and it was only natural that my mind would turn back to the prototype of Reagan's administration, the years of Ike, and those strangers who came to the back door for a handout. *They* were whom I would be writing about, every bit as much as young Fred Bloch; the refusal of society to aid them as much my theme as a young boy's rite of passage.

Far luckier than I knew, I came to an agreement with Kitchen Sink Press, a comics publisher (now sorely missed) with arguably the most prestigious catalog in the business. We began auditioning artists, that process coming to an abrupt halt when we saw the work of Dan Burr. A number of these characters have been performed onstage and over radio by strong actors, some of them friends of mine—but whenever the characters come to mind now, I invariably think of them as Dan has drawn them. His half-starved, homely, fallible human beings strike me as the perfect and only way one could represent these characters I've lived with for so long. His Freddie, I think, is as good as cartooning gets. Many artists can draw people leaping or punching or baring their teeth, but Dan's Freddie *thinks*, and in a story that often hinges on a young boy's epiphanies, what Dan has brought to it is pure gold. The skyline of Detroit on a lonely night, the high-spirited bustle of a survivalist commune, the anger and sadness of a woman whose lover is dying—I've asked for the moon throughout this story, and Dan has delivered it every time. Working with him has been exhilarating and deeply satisfying.

The contents of this volume originally appeared in serial form, with a series of gorgeous covers by Burr, Steve Rude, Mark Schultz, Jack Jackson, and the inimitable Harvey Kurtzman (in tandem with Peter Poplaski). An additional ten-page segment appeared in the anthology periodical *Dark Horse Presents*, thanks to a supposedly rival publisher's enthusiasm for the *Kings* material. (Like Freddie, I seem to have experienced the charity of strangers a few times along the way.) Despite the patchwork history, this volume has always been the intended final result, the definitive version of a story I've been telling in a number of media for a long time.

Neither film nor stage, with their necessary restrictions of time, could have accommodated the many small moments that make up this story; and though the strained quality of Freddie's narrative voice could have been made sufficiently palatable for straight prose, the visual element that I find essential to his story would have been missing. *Kings in Disguise*, however elegantly bound, is and should be a comic book.

I'm over a quarter-century older than when I began writing about Fred, and he's five years younger. Even so, I've gotten the better end of the deal. The playwriting awards and the comics awards that *Kings* has received have been gratifying; even more so has been the experience of telling his story.

Most important of all, it was this book that brought Kate into my life. The writer of the acclaimed comics series *Omaha the Cat Dancer*, Kate Worley and I met at a gathering of Kitchen Sink creators. One of those rare meetings of true equals (if I can flatter myself), our friendship developed into a romance and a marriage that lasted for the final decade of her short life. During a time when circumstances often led me to dismiss my own abilities, Kate would hold this book up as proof to the contrary. This new edition would have pleased her immensely. For the memory of her smile and the years I was privileged to see it, I'm grateful to Freddie and everyone who gave me a handout or shared the journey along the road to telling this story.

James Vance
Tulsa, Oklahoma
1990 and 2005

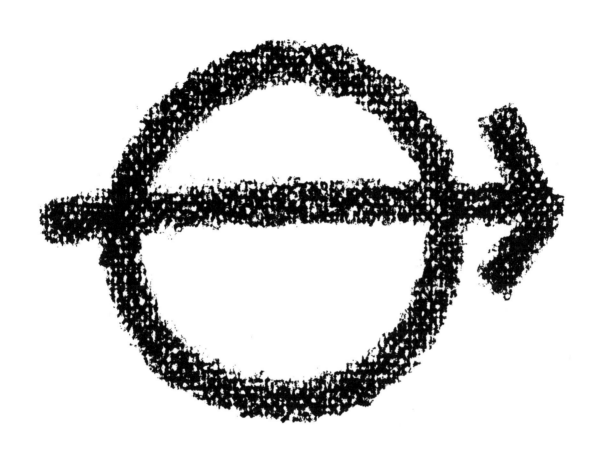

THIS IS A STORY ABOUT DREAMS:

PROPHETIC ...

HEROIC ...

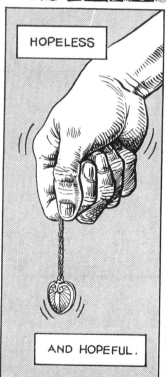

HOPELESS

AND HOPEFUL.

AND DREAMERS, TOO -- OH, YES, THIS STORY'S ABOUT US: THAT ABSURD TRAVELLING TROUPE STILL PERFORMING THE STORY OF MY YOUTH IN THE NIGHTLY ARENA OF MY SKULL.

CALL THEM QUESTERS, WOULD-BE'S, HAD-I-BUT-KNOWNS ... I KNOW WHAT *I* INVARIABLY CALL THEM AS I PEER DOWN FROM THE PRECIPICE OF MEMORY:

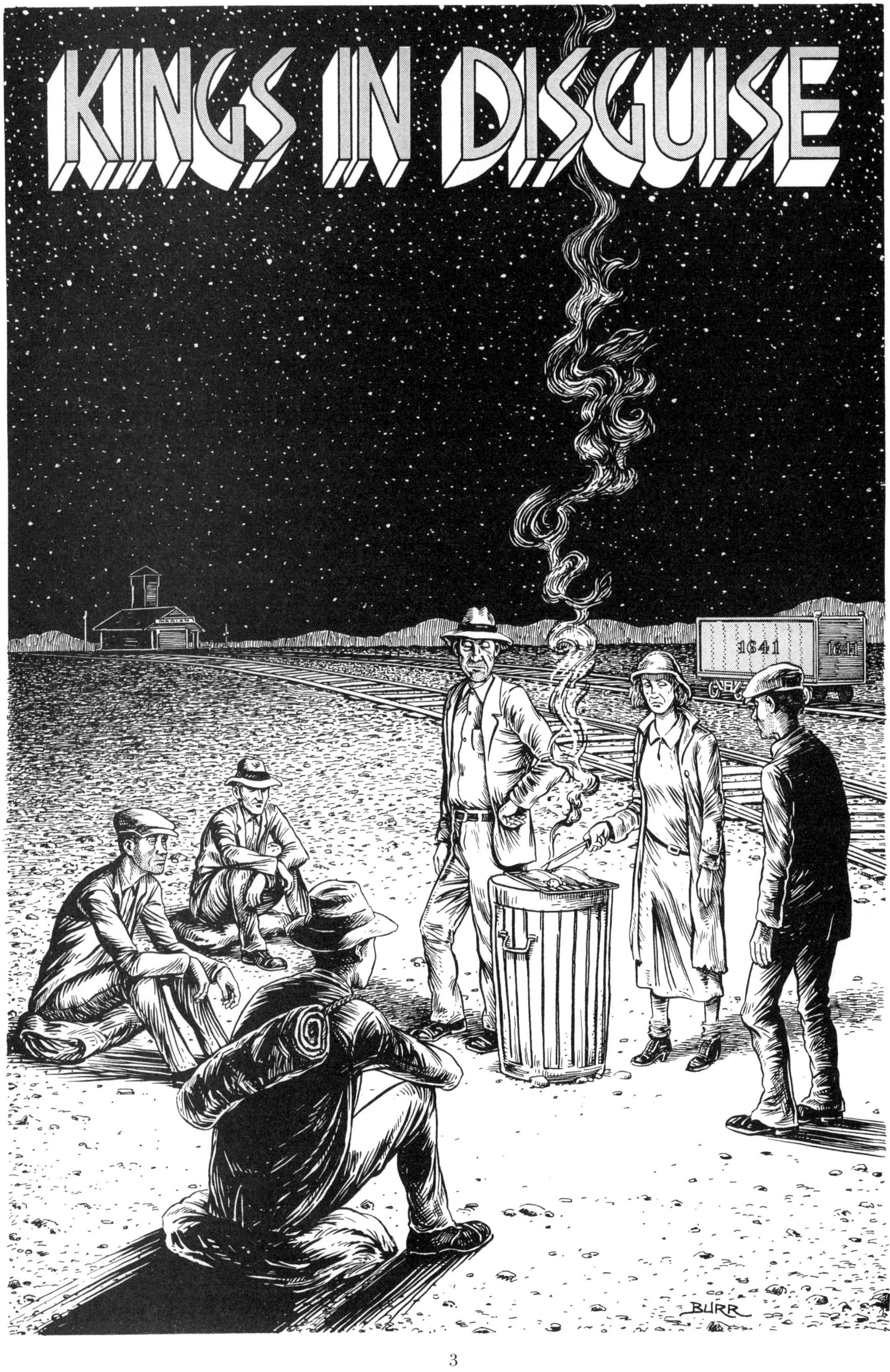
KINGS IN DISGUISE
1641
1641
BURR

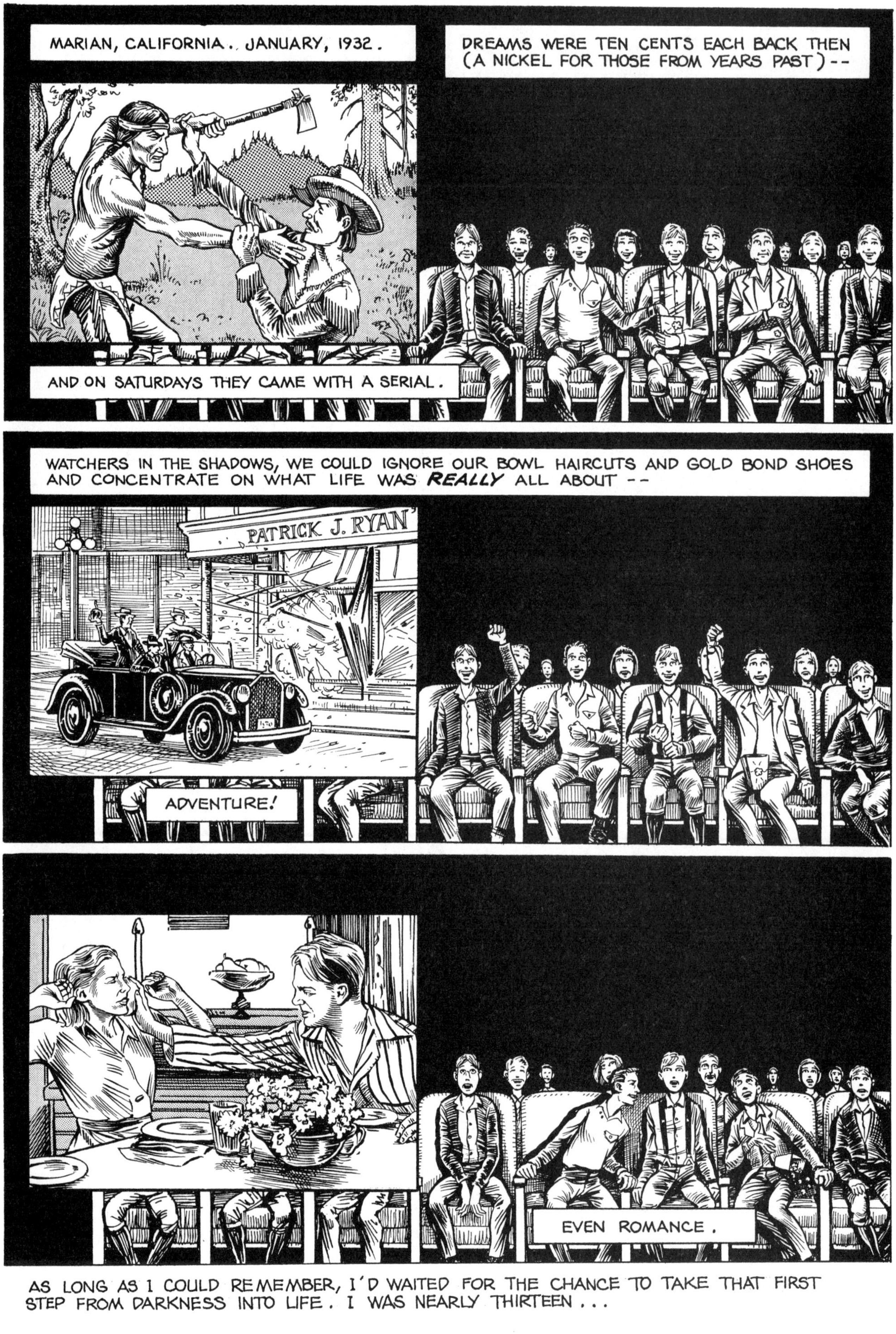
MARIAN, CALIFORNIA.. JANUARY, 1932.
DREAMS WERE TEN CENTS EACH BACK THEN (A NICKEL FOR THOSE FROM YEARS PAST)--
AND ON SATURDAYS THEY CAME WITH A SERIAL.
WATCHERS IN THE SHADOWS, WE COULD IGNORE OUR BOWL HAIRCUTS AND GOLD BOND SHOES AND CONCENTRATE ON WHAT LIFE WAS *REALLY* ALL ABOUT--
PATRICK J. RYAN
ADVENTURE!
EVEN ROMANCE.

AS LONG AS I COULD REMEMBER, I'D WAITED FOR THE CHANCE TO TAKE THAT FIRST STEP FROM DARKNESS INTO LIFE. I WAS NEARLY THIRTEEN...

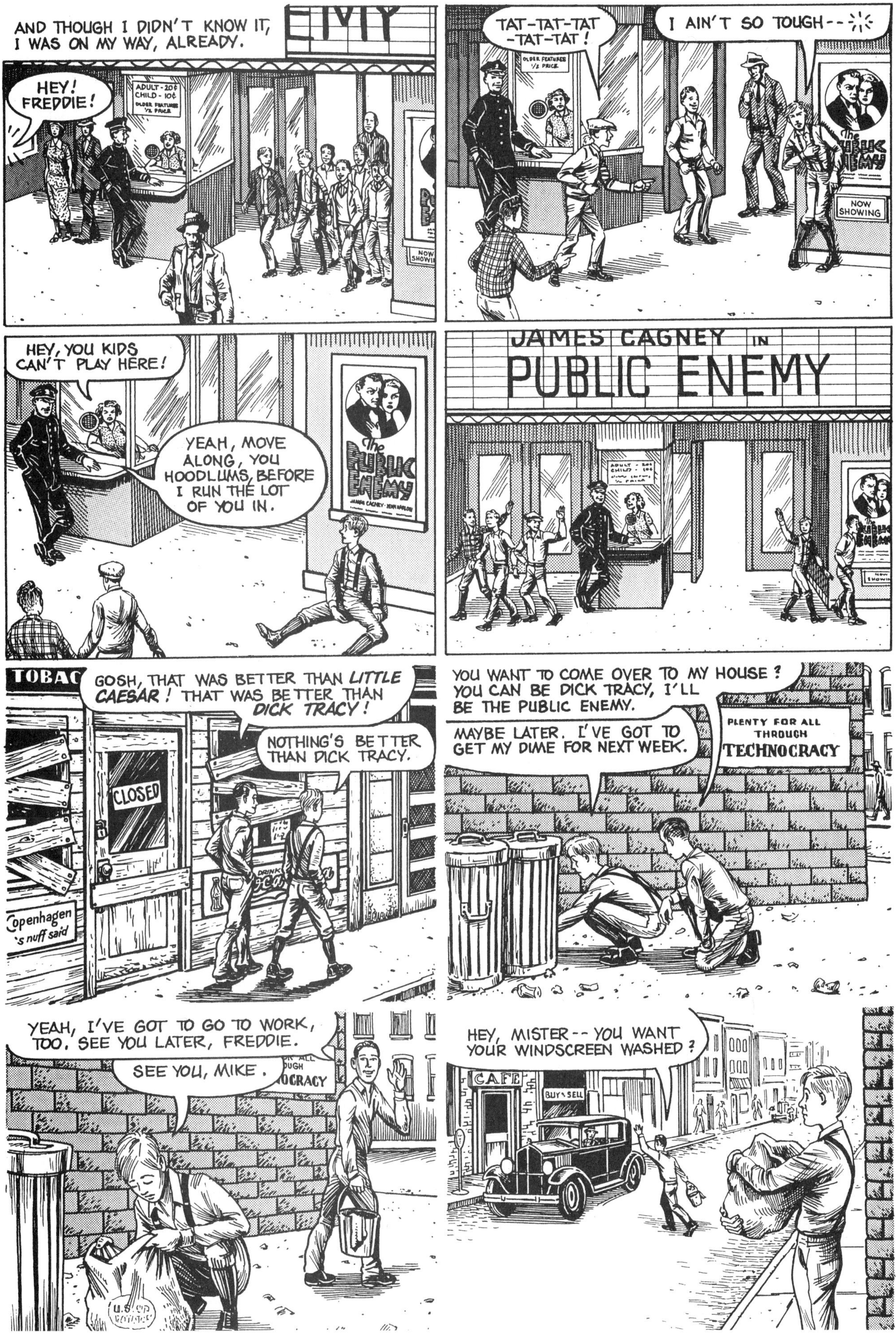
AND THOUGH I DIDN'T KNOW IT, I WAS ON MY WAY, ALREADY.
HEY! FREDDIE!
ADULT - 20¢ CHILD - 10¢ OLDER FEATURES ½ PRICE
TAT-TAT-TAT -TAT-TAT!
I AIN'T SO TOUGH--
NOW SHOWING
HEY, YOU KIDS CAN'T PLAY HERE!
YEAH, MOVE ALONG, YOU HOODLUMS, BEFORE I RUN THE LOT OF YOU IN.
The PUBLIC ENEMY
JAMES CAGNEY IN PUBLIC ENEMY
TOBAC
GOSH, THAT WAS BETTER THAN *LITTLE CAESAR*! THAT WAS BETTER THAN *DICK TRACY*!
NOTHING'S BETTER THAN DICK TRACY.
CLOSED
Copenhagen 's nuff said
YOU WANT TO COME OVER TO MY HOUSE? YOU CAN BE DICK TRACY, I'LL BE THE PUBLIC ENEMY.
MAYBE LATER. I'VE GOT TO GET MY DIME FOR NEXT WEEK.
PLENTY FOR ALL THROUGH TECHNOCRACY
YEAH, I'VE GOT TO GO TO WORK, TOO. SEE YOU LATER, FREDDIE.
SEE YOU, MIKE.
HEY, MISTER-- YOU WANT YOUR WINDSCREEN WASHED?
CAFE
BUY & SELL

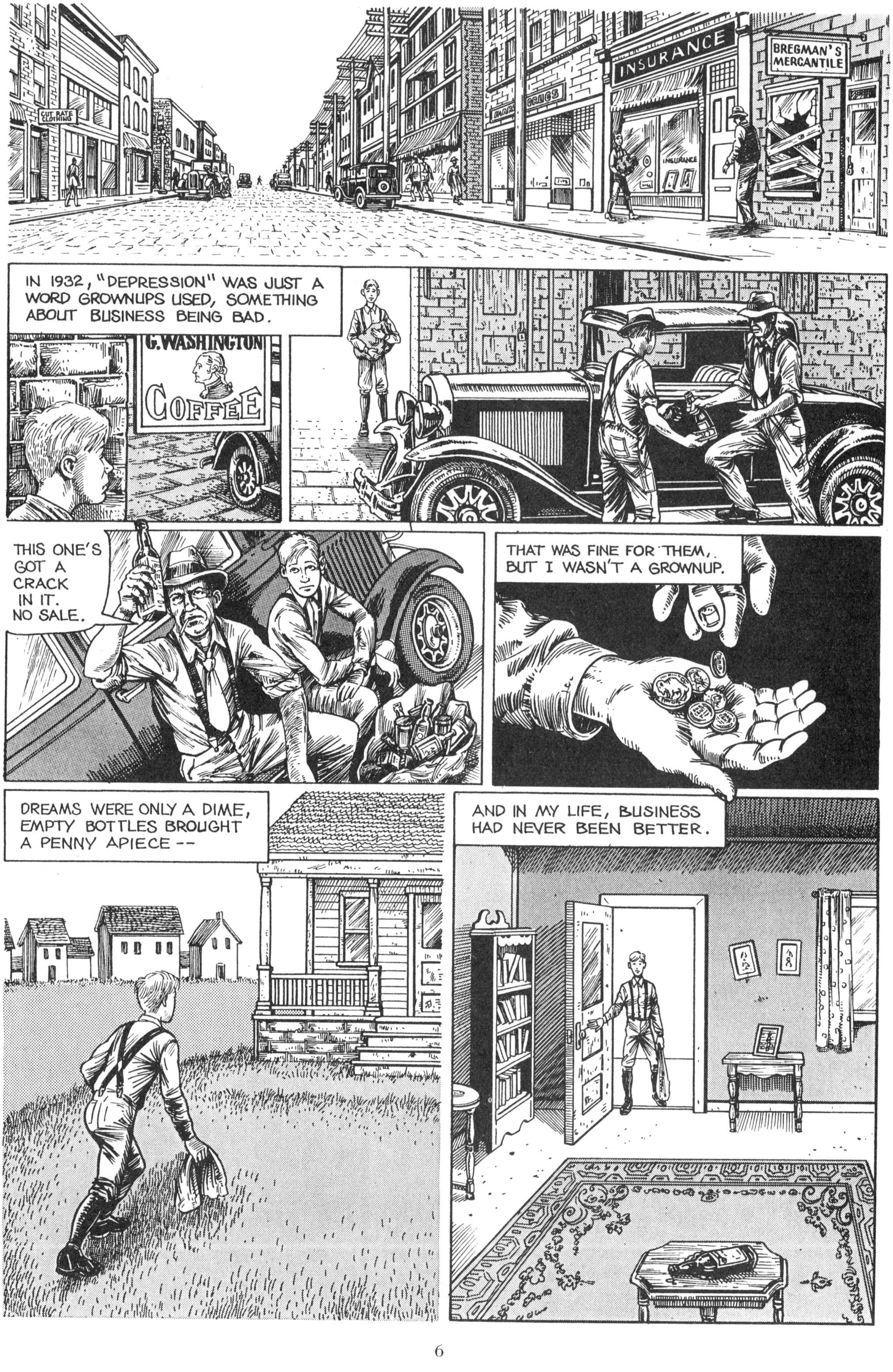
CUT RATE CLOTHING
DRUGS
INSURANCE
BREGMAN'S MERCANTILE
IN 1932, "DEPRESSION" WAS JUST A WORD GROWNUPS USED, SOMETHING ABOUT BUSINESS BEING BAD.
G. WASHINGTON COFFEE
THIS ONE'S GOT A CRACK IN IT. NO SALE.
THAT WAS FINE FOR THEM, BUT I WASN'T A GROWNUP.
DREAMS WERE ONLY A DIME, EMPTY BOTTLES BROUGHT A PENNY APIECE --
AND IN MY LIFE, BUSINESS HAD NEVER BEEN BETTER.

~TALK~ME~THAT WAY

~WAY I WANT~ DAMN RUMMY

~STILL~ FATHER, BOYCHIK!

~DO, SPANK ME?!

DAMN IT, THAT MONEY DIDN'T JUST WALK OUT OF OUR ROOM BY ITSELF! AND THIS HOOCH WASN'T HERE YESTERDAY-- DON'T YOU THINK I CHECK?

MY SON DOESN'T TALK TO HIS FATHER THIS WAY, DO YOU HEAR ME, AL?

MY SON SHOWS HIS FATHER SOME RESPECT! LIKE HE'S GOT COMING!

RESPECT FOR WHAT? DRINKING UP THE GROCERY MONEY SO YOUR FAMILY CAN STARVE? WHAT HAVE **WE** GOT COMING? DON'T YOU THINK FREDDIE MIGHT LIKE A DIME FOR A SHOW OR SOME CANDY ONCE IN A WHILE?

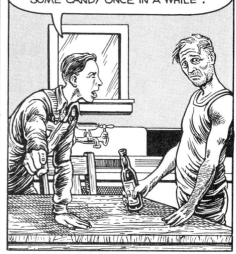

FREDDIE- COME HERE TO YOUR PAPA...

GET THE HELL AWAY FROM HIM!

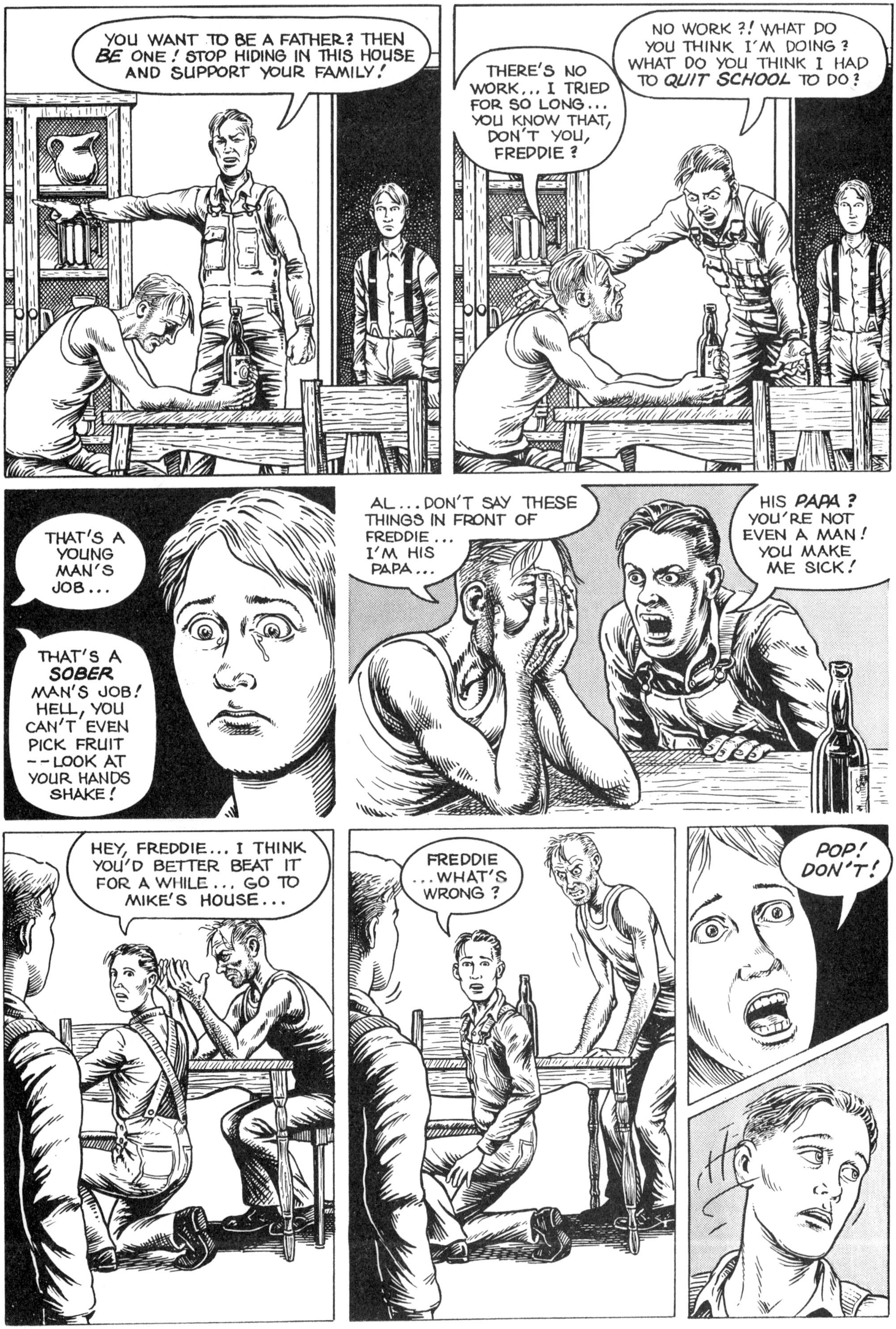
YOU WANT TO BE A FATHER? THEN BE ONE! STOP HIDING IN THIS HOUSE AND SUPPORT YOUR FAMILY!
THERE'S NO WORK... I TRIED FOR SO LONG... YOU KNOW THAT, DON'T YOU, FREDDIE?
NO WORK?! WHAT DO YOU THINK I'M DOING? WHAT DO YOU THINK I HAD TO QUIT SCHOOL TO DO?
THAT'S A YOUNG MAN'S JOB...
THAT'S A SOBER MAN'S JOB! HELL, YOU CAN'T EVEN PICK FRUIT --LOOK AT YOUR HANDS SHAKE!
AL... DON'T SAY THESE THINGS IN FRONT OF FREDDIE... I'M HIS PAPA...
HIS PAPA? YOU'RE NOT EVEN A MAN! YOU MAKE ME SICK!
HEY, FREDDIE... I THINK YOU'D BETTER BEAT IT FOR A WHILE... GO TO MIKE'S HOUSE...
FREDDIE ...WHAT'S WRONG?
POP! DON'T!

AL! DON'T HURT HIM --

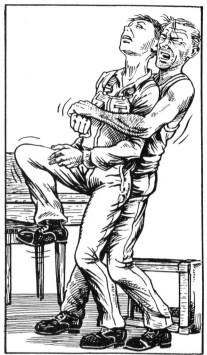

CRUNCH

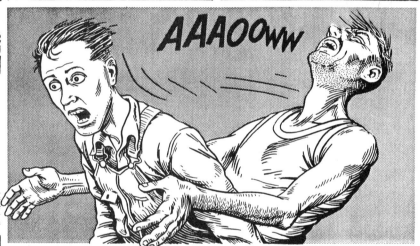

AAAOOww

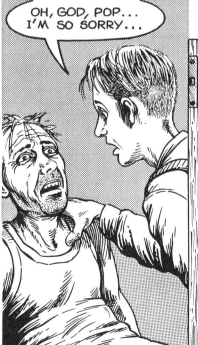

OH, GOD, POP... I'M SO SORRY...

I NEVER DID MAKE IT TO MIKE'S HOUSE THAT DAY.

THAT NIGHT I HAD A DREAM:

IT WAS THE DAY OF AL'S BAR MITZVAH, AND THE MINYAN OF ORTHODOX, CONSERVATIVE AND REFORM THAT MOM HAD ROUNDED UP FROM THE NEIGHBORING TOWNS WERE ALL SHOWING UP AT ONCE.

WE'D MADE FUN OF POP FOR CRYING THAT DAY, AS HE DID AT EVERY IMPORTANT OCCASION... MOM ALWAYS SAID THAT WAS ONE OF THE REASONS SHE LOVED HIM --

BUT IT WAS DIFFERENT IN MY DREAM.

AND THEN I SAW WHY HE WAS CRYING -- AND IT WASN'T FUNNY ANY MORE.

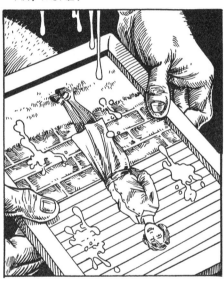

POP HIMSELF HAD CONDUCTED AL'S BAR MITZVAH, BUT FOR SOME REASON HE WAS GONE NOW. IT WAS THE MAN WHO HAD LED THE KADDISH AT MOM'S FUNERAL WHO HANDED ON THE TORAH...

AND RECEIVING IT IN TREMBLING HANDS, I REALIZED THAT AL WAS GONE, TOO.

UNPREPARED, AND NOT A LITTLE AFRAID, I BEGAN TO READ. THE ANCIENT WORDS ECHOED FROM THE WALLS OF THE EMPTY ROOM.

AND THEN THE SLEEPING PART OF MY DREAM WAS OVER.

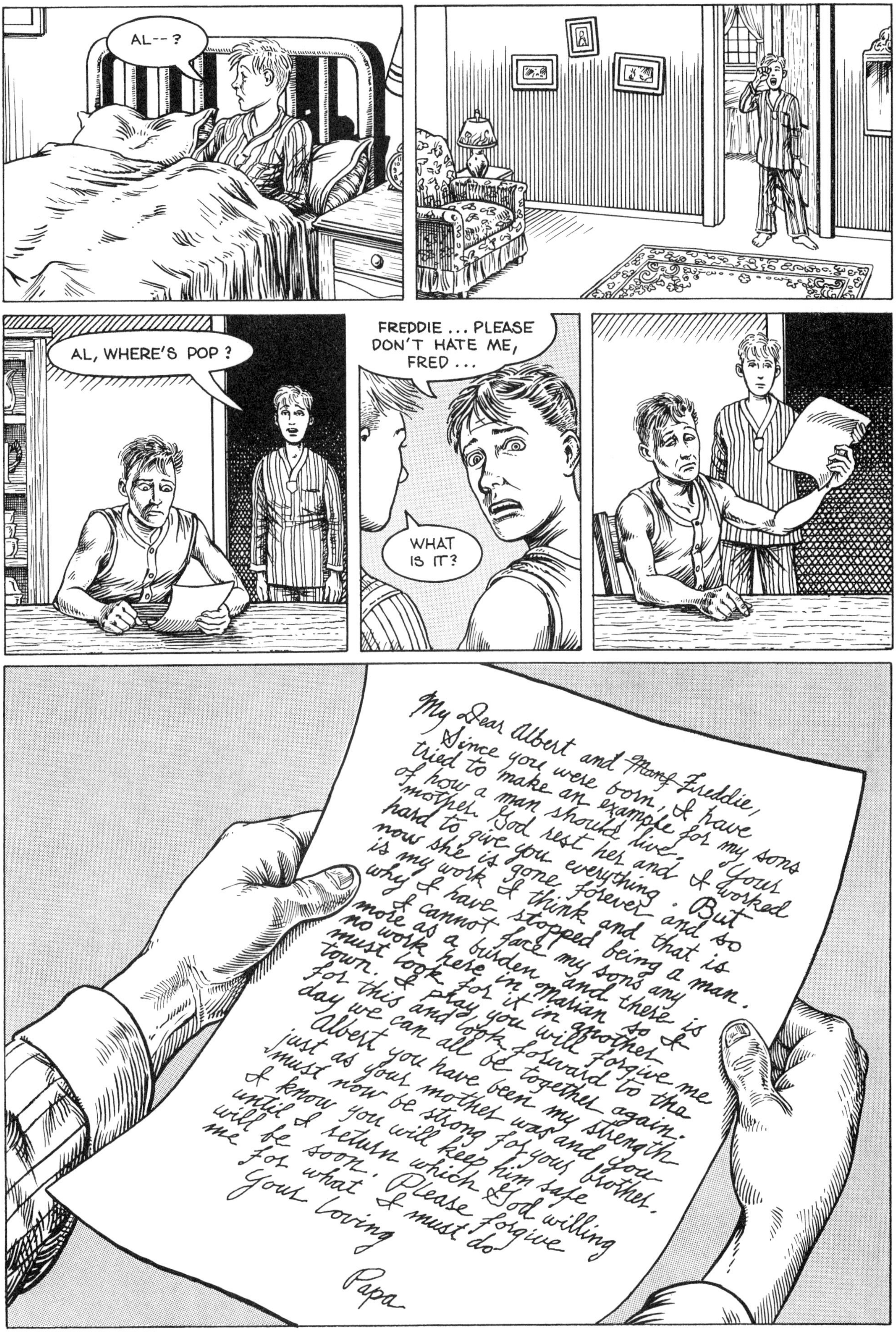
AL--?
AL, WHERE'S POP?
FREDDIE ... PLEASE DON'T HATE ME, FRED ...
WHAT IS IT?
My Dear Albert and ~~Manf~~ Freddie,
Since you were born, I have
tried to make an example for my sons
of how a man should live. Your
mother God rest her and I worked
hard to give you everything. But
now she is gone forever and so
is my work I think and that is
why I have stopped being a man.
I cannot face my sons any
more as a burden and there is
no work here in Marian so I
must look for it in another
town. I pray you will forgive me
for this and look forward to the
day we can all be together again.
Albert you have been my strength
just as your mother was and you
must now be strong for your brother.
I know you will keep him safe
until I return which God willing
will be soon. Please forgive
me for what I must do
Your Loving
Papa

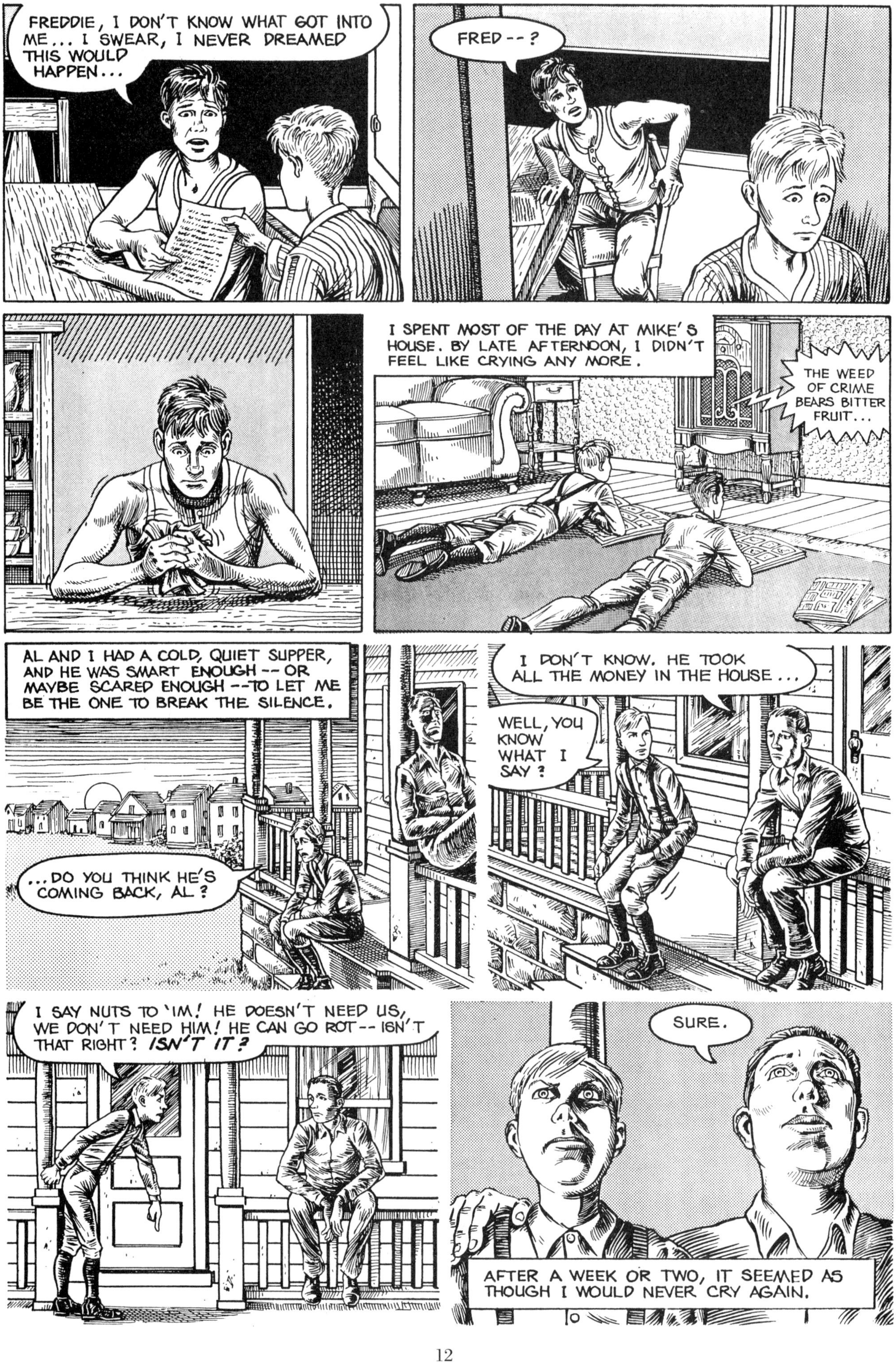
FREDDIE, I DON'T KNOW WHAT GOT INTO ME... I SWEAR, I NEVER DREAMED THIS WOULD HAPPEN...
FRED--?
I SPENT MOST OF THE DAY AT MIKE'S HOUSE. BY LATE AFTERNOON, I DIDN'T FEEL LIKE CRYING ANY MORE.
THE WEED OF CRIME BEARS BITTER FRUIT...
AL AND I HAD A COLD, QUIET SUPPER, AND HE WAS SMART ENOUGH--OR MAYBE SCARED ENOUGH--TO LET ME BE THE ONE TO BREAK THE SILENCE.
...DO YOU THINK HE'S COMING BACK, AL?
I DON'T KNOW. HE TOOK ALL THE MONEY IN THE HOUSE...
WELL, YOU KNOW WHAT I SAY?
I SAY NUTS TO 'IM! HE DOESN'T NEED US, WE DON'T NEED HIM! HE CAN GO ROT--ISN'T THAT RIGHT? ISN'T IT?
SURE.
AFTER A WEEK OR TWO, IT SEEMED AS THOUGH I WOULD NEVER CRY AGAIN.

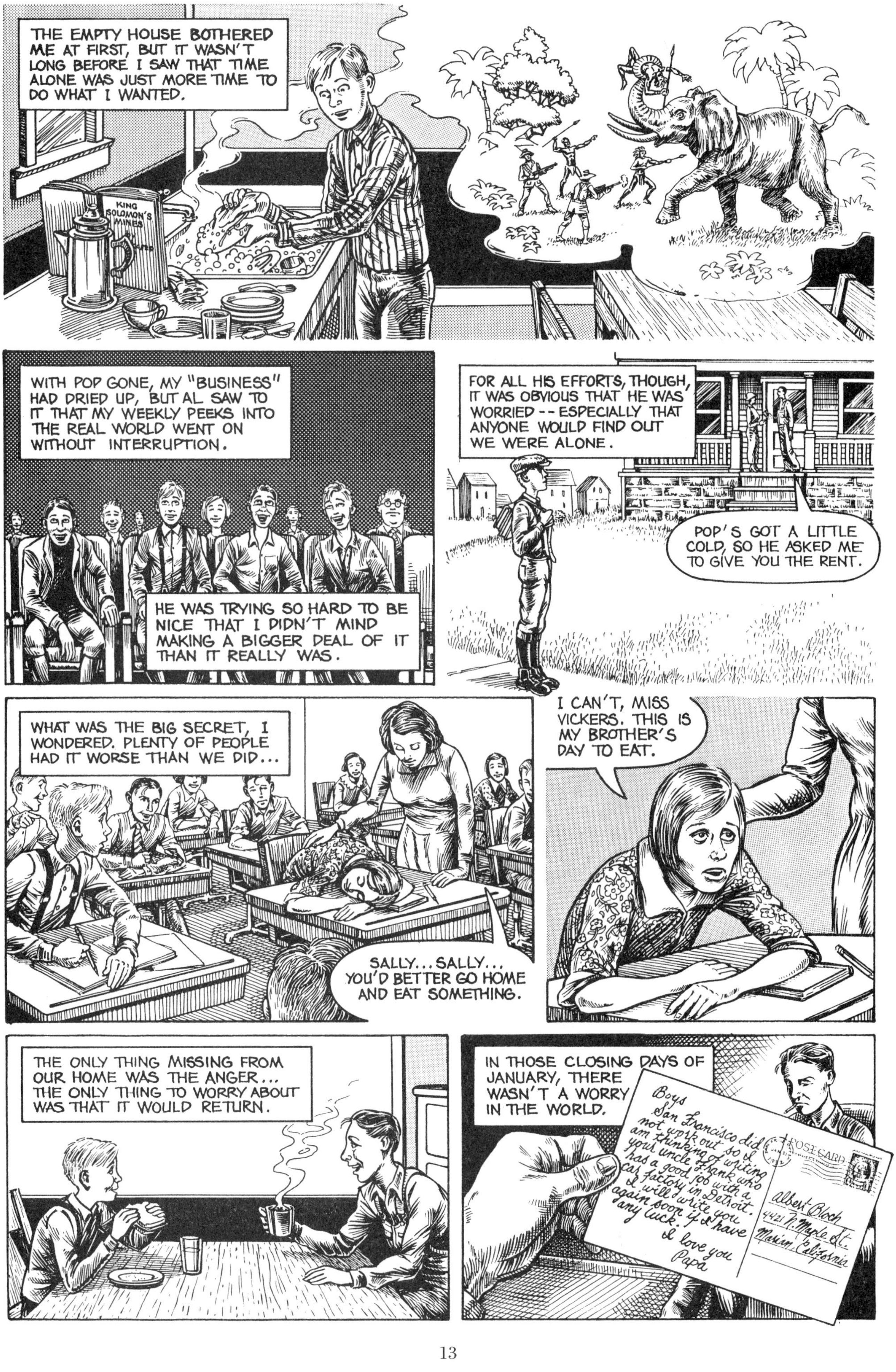
THE EMPTY HOUSE BOTHERED ME AT FIRST, BUT IT WASN'T LONG BEFORE I SAW THAT TIME ALONE WAS JUST MORE TIME TO DO WHAT I WANTED.
KING SOLOMON'S MINES
WITH POP GONE, MY "BUSINESS" HAD DRIED UP, BUT AL SAW TO IT THAT MY WEEKLY PEEKS INTO THE REAL WORLD WENT ON WITHOUT INTERRUPTION.
HE WAS TRYING SO HARD TO BE NICE THAT I DIDN'T MIND MAKING A BIGGER DEAL OF IT THAN IT REALLY WAS.
FOR ALL HIS EFFORTS, THOUGH, IT WAS OBVIOUS THAT HE WAS WORRIED -- ESPECIALLY THAT ANYONE WOULD FIND OUT WE WERE ALONE.
POP'S GOT A LITTLE COLD, SO HE ASKED ME TO GIVE YOU THE RENT.
WHAT WAS THE BIG SECRET, I WONDERED. PLENTY OF PEOPLE HAD IT WORSE THAN WE DID...
SALLY... SALLY... YOU'D BETTER GO HOME AND EAT SOMETHING.
I CAN'T, MISS VICKERS. THIS IS MY BROTHER'S DAY TO EAT.
THE ONLY THING MISSING FROM OUR HOME WAS THE ANGER... THE ONLY THING TO WORRY ABOUT WAS THAT IT WOULD RETURN.
IN THOSE CLOSING DAYS OF JANUARY, THERE WASN'T A WORRY IN THE WORLD.
Boys
San Francisco did not work out so I am thinking of writing your uncle Frank who has a good job with a car factory in Detroit. I will write you again soon if I have any luck.
I love you
Papa
POST CARD
Albert Bloch
4421 N. Maple St.
Marin, California

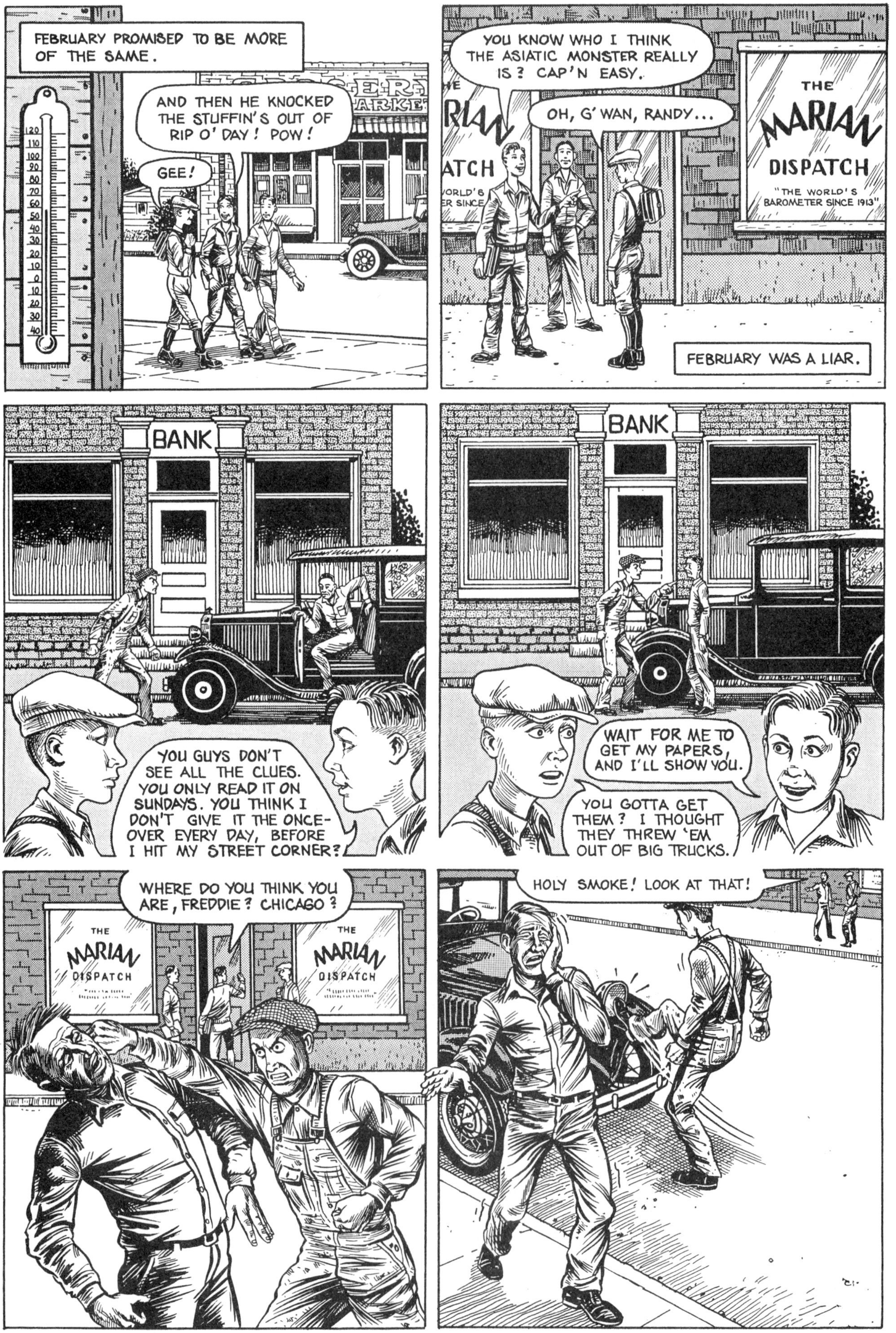
FEBRUARY PROMISED TO BE MORE OF THE SAME.
AND THEN HE KNOCKED THE STUFFIN'S OUT OF RIP O' DAY! POW!
GEE!
YOU KNOW WHO I THINK THE ASIATIC MONSTER REALLY IS? CAP'N EASY.
OH, G'WAN, RANDY...
THE MARIAN DISPATCH
"THE WORLD'S BAROMETER SINCE 1913"
FEBRUARY WAS A LIAR.
BANK
YOU GUYS DON'T SEE ALL THE CLUES. YOU ONLY READ IT ON SUNDAYS. YOU THINK I DON'T GIVE IT THE ONCE-OVER EVERY DAY, BEFORE I HIT MY STREET CORNER?
BANK
WAIT FOR ME TO GET MY PAPERS, AND I'LL SHOW YOU.
YOU GOTTA GET THEM? I THOUGHT THEY THREW 'EM OUT OF BIG TRUCKS.
WHERE DO YOU THINK YOU ARE, FREDDIE? CHICAGO?
THE MARIAN DISPATCH
THE MARIAN DISPATCH
HOLY SMOKE! LOOK AT THAT!

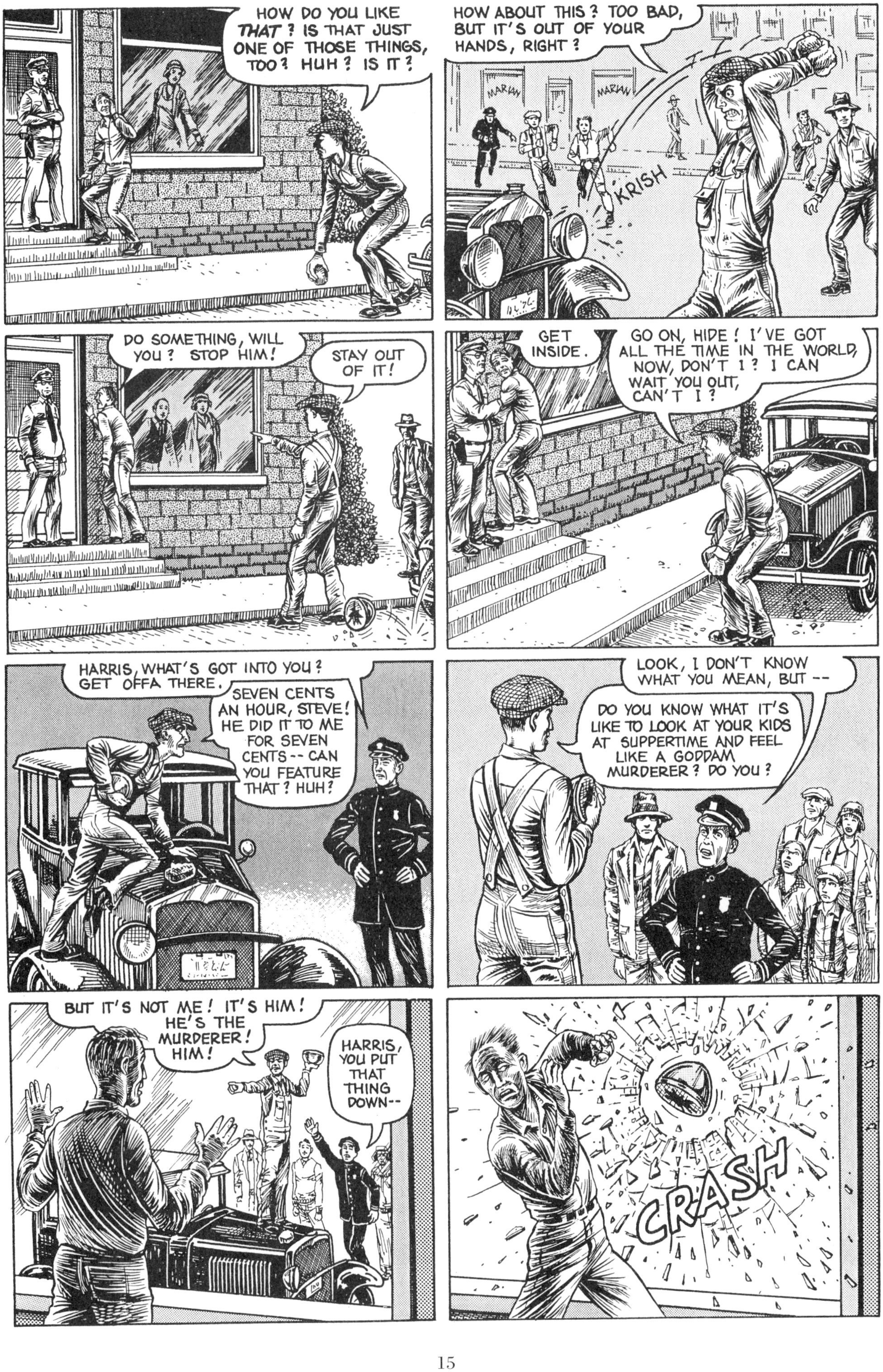
HOW DO YOU LIKE *THAT*? IS THAT JUST ONE OF THOSE THINGS, TOO? HUH? IS IT?
HOW ABOUT THIS? TOO BAD, BUT IT'S OUT OF YOUR HANDS, RIGHT?
KRISH
DO SOMETHING, WILL YOU? STOP HIM!
STAY OUT OF IT!
GET INSIDE.
GO ON, HIDE! I'VE GOT ALL THE TIME IN THE WORLD, NOW, DON'T I? I CAN WAIT YOU OUT, CAN'T I?
HARRIS, WHAT'S GOT INTO YOU? GET OFFA THERE.
SEVEN CENTS AN HOUR, STEVE! HE DID IT TO ME FOR SEVEN CENTS -- CAN YOU FEATURE THAT? HUH?
LOOK, I DON'T KNOW WHAT YOU MEAN, BUT --
DO YOU KNOW WHAT IT'S LIKE TO LOOK AT YOUR KIDS AT SUPPERTIME AND FEEL LIKE A GODDAM MURDERER? DO YOU?
BUT IT'S NOT ME! IT'S HIM! HE'S THE MURDERER! HIM!
HARRIS, YOU PUT THAT THING DOWN--
CRASH

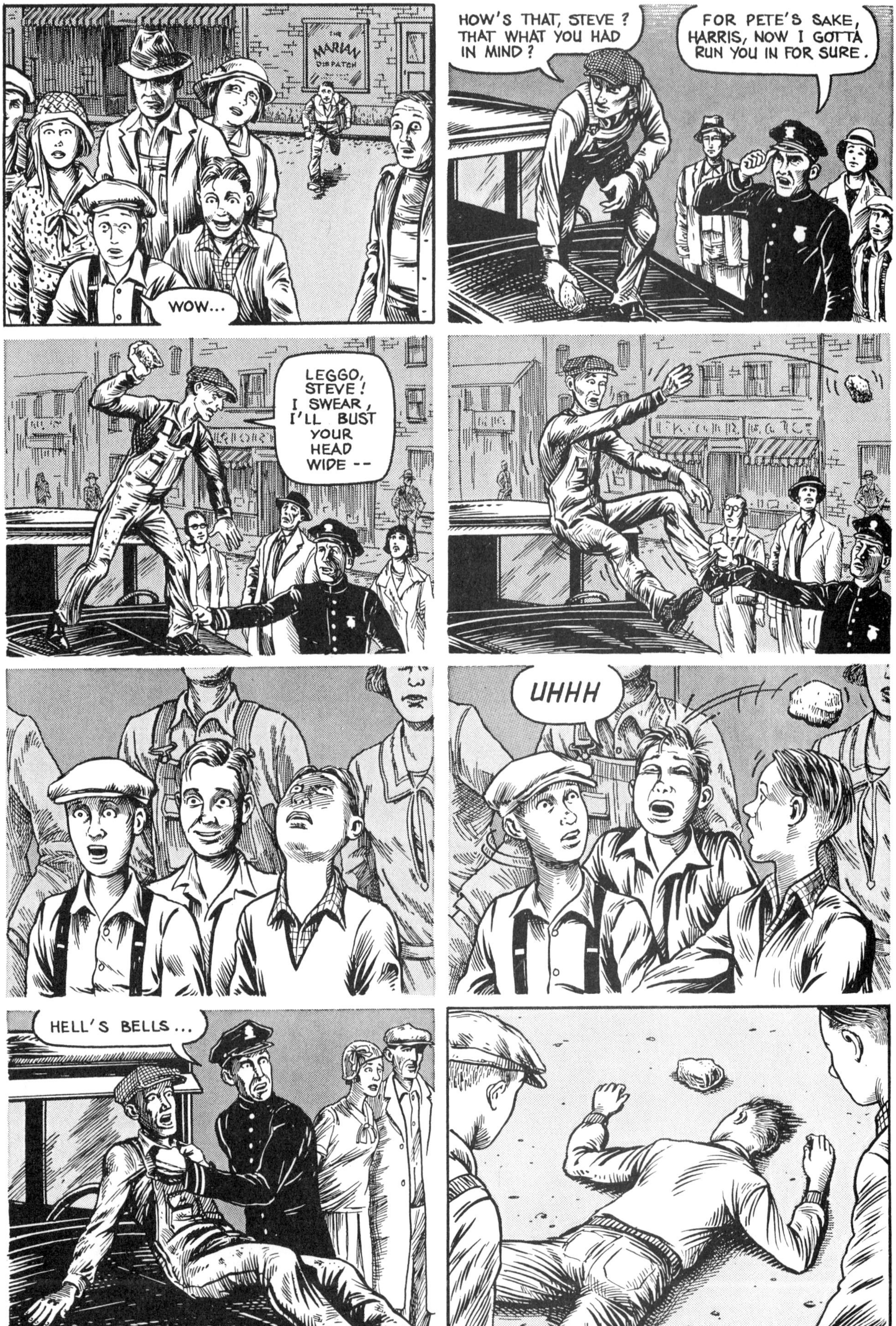
WOW...
HOW'S THAT, STEVE? THAT WHAT YOU HAD IN MIND?
FOR PETE'S SAKE, HARRIS, NOW I GOTTA RUN YOU IN FOR SURE.
LEGGO, STEVE! I, SWEAR, I'LL BUST YOUR HEAD WIDE --
UHHH
HELL'S BELLS...

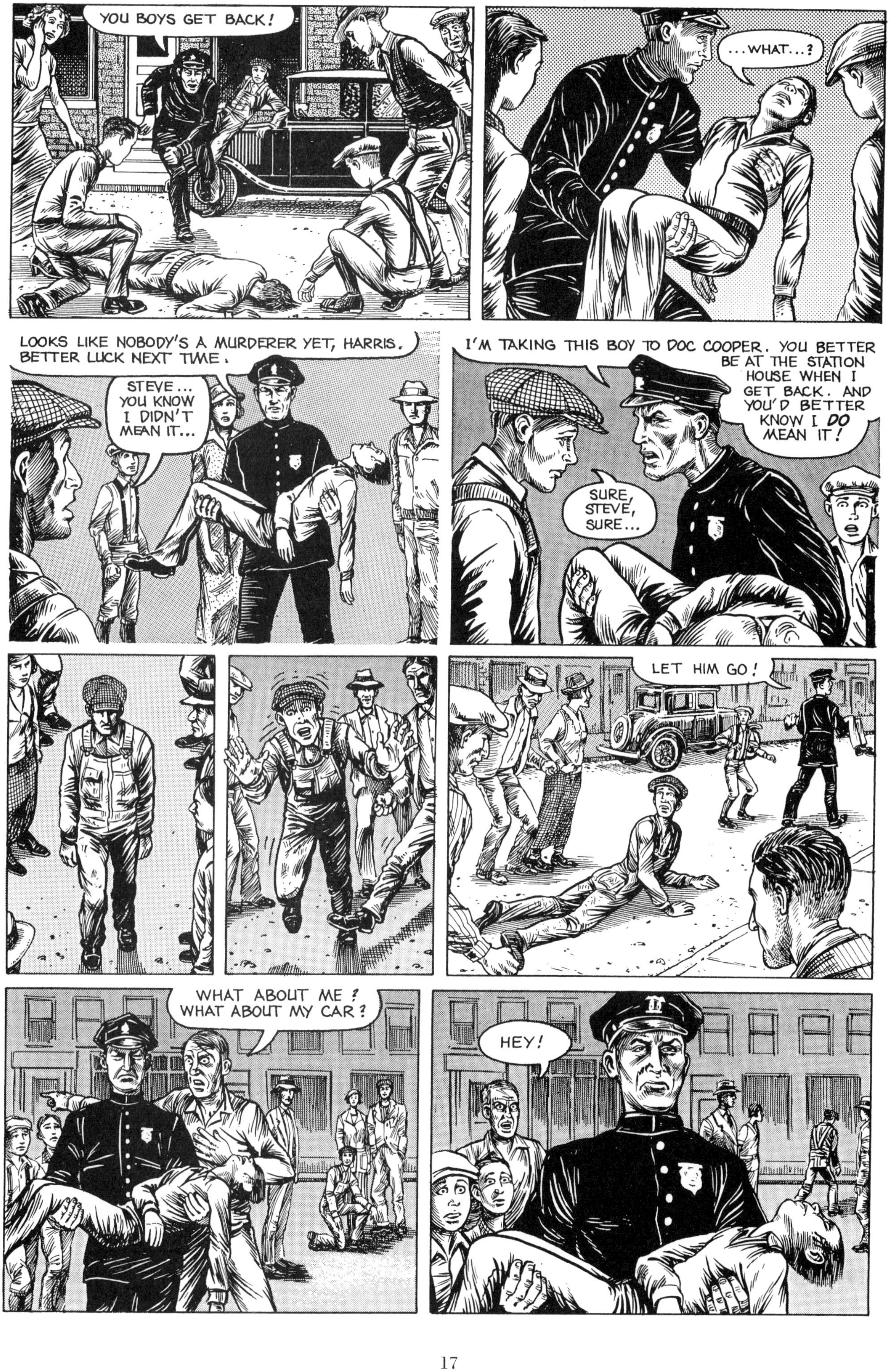
YOU BOYS GET BACK!
...WHAT...?
LOOKS LIKE NOBODY'S A MURDERER YET, HARRIS. BETTER LUCK NEXT TIME.
STEVE... YOU KNOW I DIDN'T MEAN IT...
I'M TAKING THIS BOY TO DOC COOPER. YOU BETTER BE AT THE STATION HOUSE WHEN I GET BACK. AND YOU'D BETTER KNOW I **DO** MEAN IT!
SURE, STEVE, SURE...
LET HIM GO!
WHAT ABOUT ME? WHAT ABOUT MY CAR?
HEY!

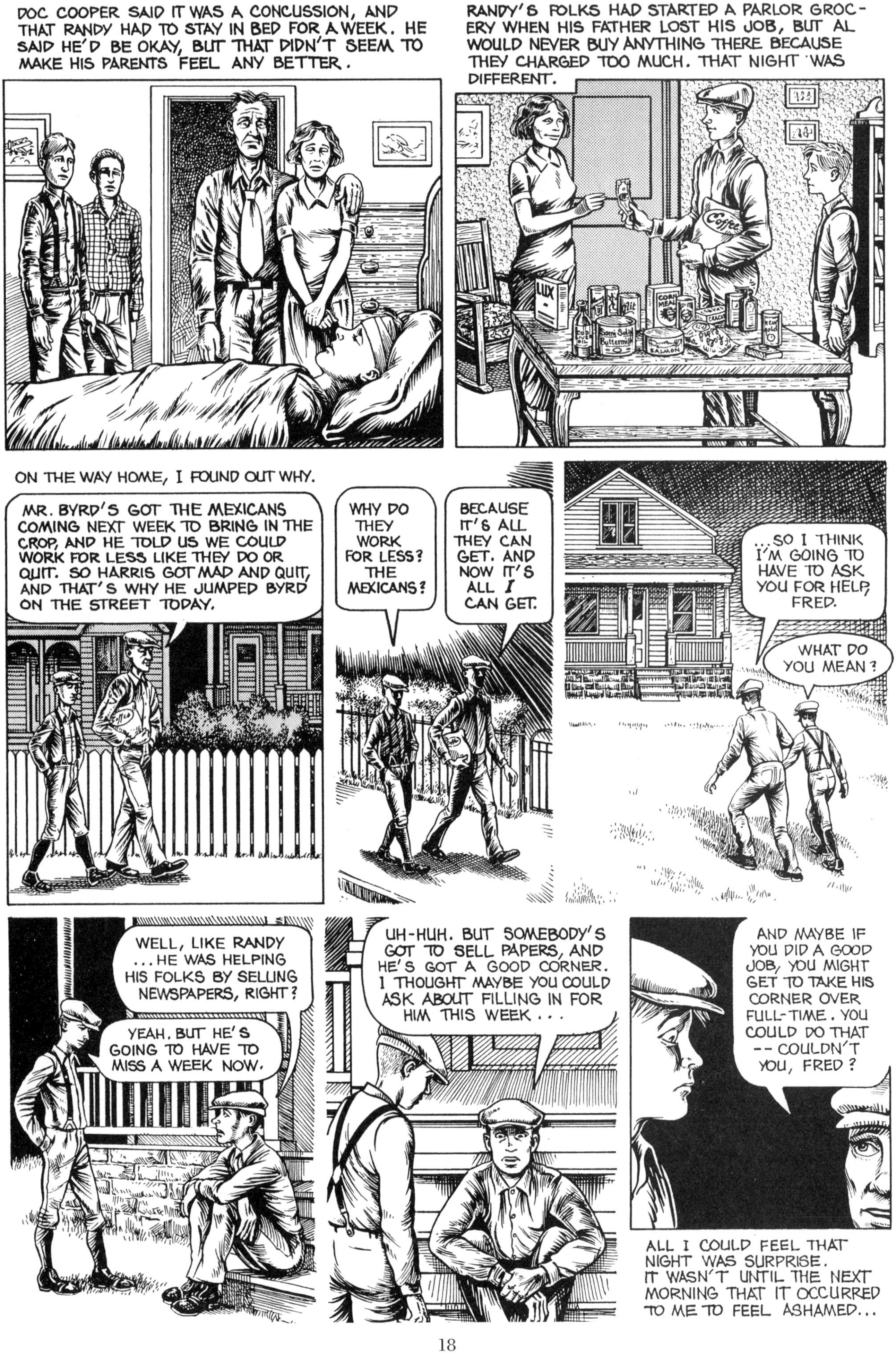
DOC COOPER SAID IT WAS A CONCUSSION, AND THAT RANDY HAD TO STAY IN BED FOR A WEEK. HE SAID HE'D BE OKAY, BUT THAT DIDN'T SEEM TO MAKE HIS PARENTS FEEL ANY BETTER.
RANDY'S FOLKS HAD STARTED A PARLOR GROCERY WHEN HIS FATHER LOST HIS JOB, BUT AL WOULD NEVER BUY ANYTHING THERE BECAUSE THEY CHARGED TOO MUCH. THAT NIGHT WAS DIFFERENT.
ON THE WAY HOME, I FOUND OUT WHY.
MR. BYRD'S GOT THE MEXICANS COMING NEXT WEEK TO BRING IN THE CROP, AND HE TOLD US WE COULD WORK FOR LESS LIKE THEY DO OR QUIT. SO HARRIS GOT MAD AND QUIT, AND THAT'S WHY HE JUMPED BYRD ON THE STREET TODAY.
WHY DO THEY WORK FOR LESS? THE MEXICANS?
BECAUSE IT'S ALL THEY CAN GET. AND NOW IT'S ALL I CAN GET.
...SO I THINK I'M GOING TO HAVE TO ASK YOU FOR HELP, FRED.
WHAT DO YOU MEAN?
WELL, LIKE RANDY ...HE WAS HELPING HIS FOLKS BY SELLING NEWSPAPERS, RIGHT?
YEAH. BUT HE'S GOING TO HAVE TO MISS A WEEK NOW.
UH-HUH. BUT SOMEBODY'S GOT TO SELL PAPERS, AND HE'S GOT A GOOD CORNER. I THOUGHT MAYBE YOU COULD ASK ABOUT FILLING IN FOR HIM THIS WEEK...
AND MAYBE IF YOU DID A GOOD JOB, YOU MIGHT GET TO TAKE HIS CORNER OVER FULL-TIME. YOU COULD DO THAT -- COULDN'T YOU, FRED?
ALL I COULD FEEL THAT NIGHT WAS SURPRISE. IT WASN'T UNTIL THE NEXT MORNING THAT IT OCCURRED TO ME TO FEEL ASHAMED...

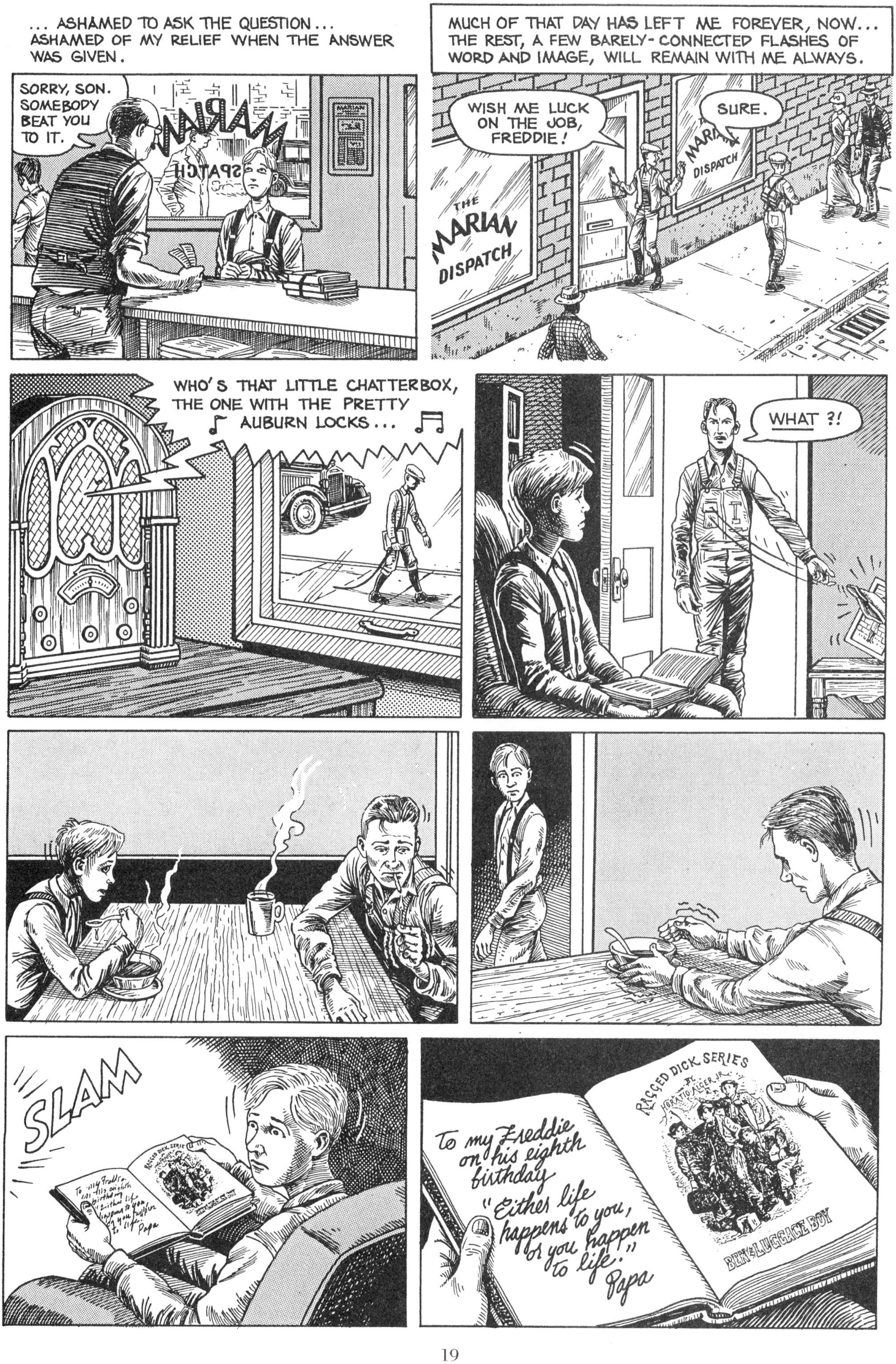

... ASHAMED TO ASK THE QUESTION... ASHAMED OF MY RELIEF WHEN THE ANSWER WAS GIVEN.
SORRY, SON. SOMEBODY BEAT YOU TO IT.
MUCH OF THAT DAY HAS LEFT ME FOREVER, NOW... THE REST, A FEW BARELY-CONNECTED FLASHES OF WORD AND IMAGE, WILL REMAIN WITH ME ALWAYS.
WISH ME LUCK ON THE JOB, FREDDIE!
SURE.
THE MARIAN DISPATCH
WHO'S THAT LITTLE CHATTERBOX, THE ONE WITH THE PRETTY AUBURN LOCKS...
WHAT ?!
SLAM
To my Freddie on his eighth birthday "Either life happens to you, or you happen to life." Papa
RAGGED DICK SERIES
BY HORATIO ALGER JR.
BEN THE LUGGAGE BOY

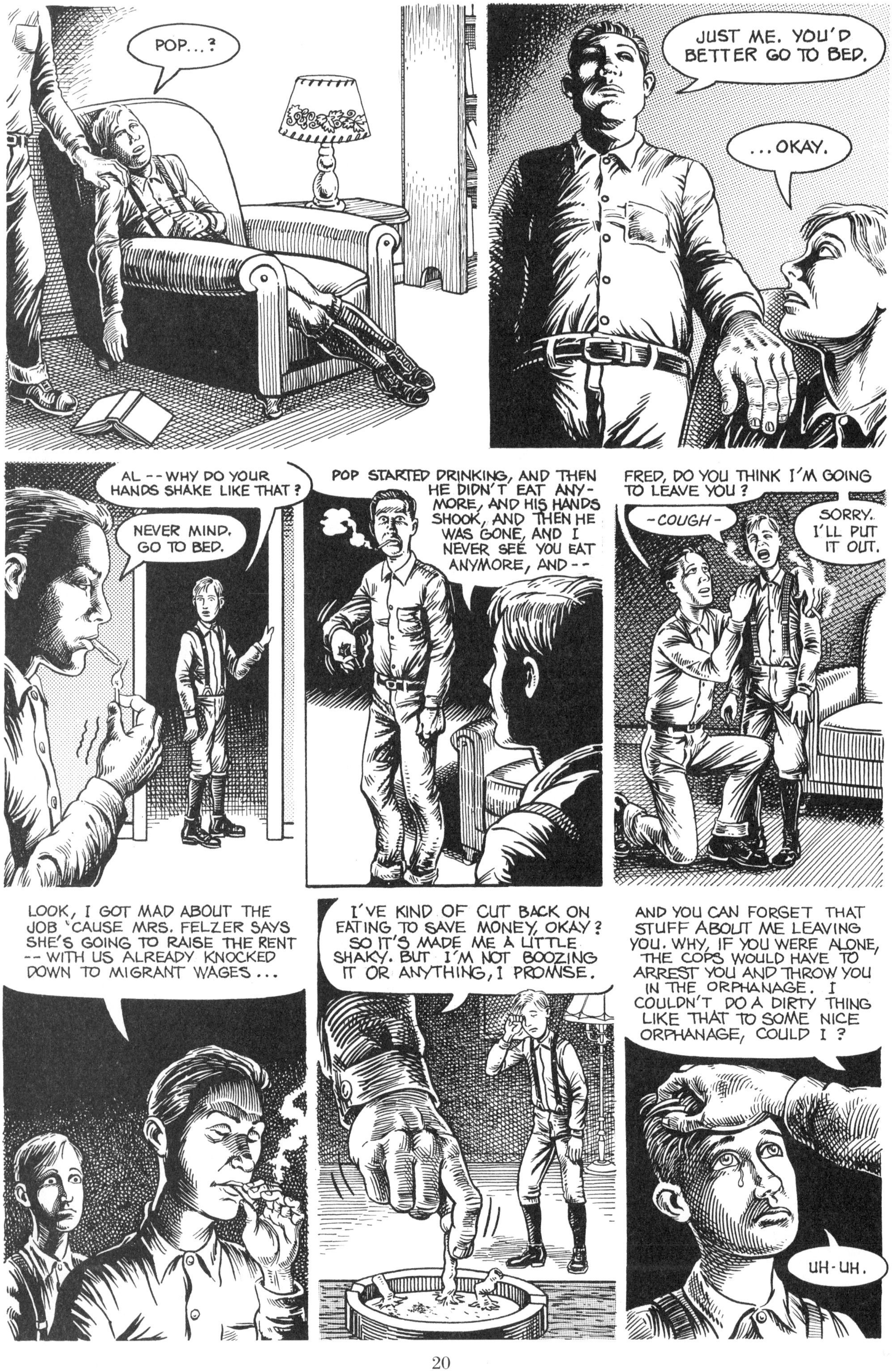
POP...?
JUST ME. YOU'D BETTER GO TO BED.
...OKAY.
AL--WHY DO YOUR HANDS SHAKE LIKE THAT?
NEVER MIND. GO TO BED.
POP STARTED DRINKING, AND THEN HE DIDN'T EAT ANYMORE, AND HIS HANDS SHOOK, AND THEN HE WAS GONE, AND I NEVER SEE YOU EAT ANYMORE, AND--
FRED, DO YOU THINK I'M GOING TO LEAVE YOU?
-COUGH-
SORRY. I'LL PUT IT OUT.
LOOK, I GOT MAD ABOUT THE JOB 'CAUSE MRS. FELZER SAYS SHE'S GOING TO RAISE THE RENT --WITH US ALREADY KNOCKED DOWN TO MIGRANT WAGES...
I'VE KIND OF CUT BACK ON EATING TO SAVE MONEY, OKAY? SO IT'S MADE ME A LITTLE SHAKY. BUT I'M NOT BOOZING IT OR ANYTHING, I PROMISE.
AND YOU CAN FORGET THAT STUFF ABOUT ME LEAVING YOU. WHY, IF YOU WERE ALONE, THE COPS WOULD HAVE TO ARREST YOU AND THROW YOU IN THE ORPHANAGE. I COULDN'T DO A DIRTY THING LIKE THAT TO SOME NICE ORPHANAGE, COULD I?
UH-UH.

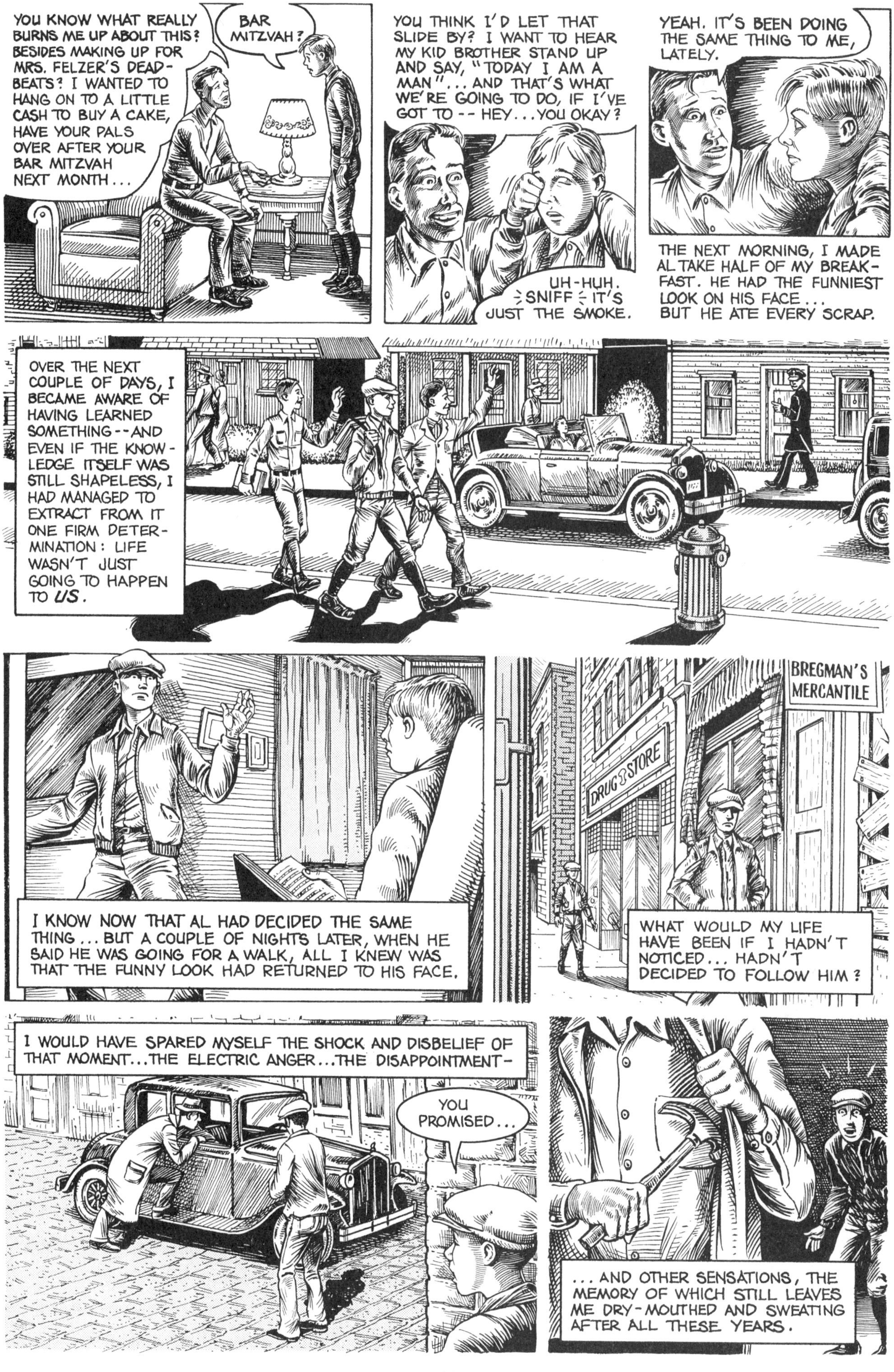
YOU KNOW WHAT REALLY BURNS ME UP ABOUT THIS? BESIDES MAKING UP FOR MRS. FELZER'S DEAD-BEATS? I WANTED TO HANG ON TO A LITTLE CASH TO BUY A CAKE, HAVE YOUR PALS OVER AFTER YOUR BAR MITZVAH NEXT MONTH...
BAR MITZVAH?
YOU THINK I'D LET THAT SLIDE BY? I WANT TO HEAR MY KID BROTHER STAND UP AND SAY, "TODAY I AM A MAN"... AND THAT'S WHAT WE'RE GOING TO DO, IF I'VE GOT TO -- HEY... YOU OKAY?
UH-HUH. ≷SNIFF≶ IT'S JUST THE SMOKE.
YEAH. IT'S BEEN DOING THE SAME THING TO ME, LATELY.
THE NEXT MORNING, I MADE AL TAKE HALF OF MY BREAKFAST. HE HAD THE FUNNIEST LOOK ON HIS FACE... BUT HE ATE EVERY SCRAP.
OVER THE NEXT COUPLE OF DAYS, I BECAME AWARE OF HAVING LEARNED SOMETHING -- AND EVEN IF THE KNOWLEDGE ITSELF WAS STILL SHAPELESS, I HAD MANAGED TO EXTRACT FROM IT ONE FIRM DETERMINATION: LIFE WASN'T JUST GOING TO HAPPEN TO US.
I KNOW NOW THAT AL HAD DECIDED THE SAME THING... BUT A COUPLE OF NIGHTS LATER, WHEN HE SAID HE WAS GOING FOR A WALK, ALL I KNEW WAS THAT THE FUNNY LOOK HAD RETURNED TO HIS FACE.
BREGMAN'S MERCANTILE
DRUG STORE
WHAT WOULD MY LIFE HAVE BEEN IF I HADN'T NOTICED... HADN'T DECIDED TO FOLLOW HIM?
I WOULD HAVE SPARED MYSELF THE SHOCK AND DISBELIEF OF THAT MOMENT... THE ELECTRIC ANGER... THE DISAPPOINTMENT-
YOU PROMISED...
...AND OTHER SENSATIONS, THE MEMORY OF WHICH STILL LEAVES ME DRY-MOUTHED AND SWEATING AFTER ALL THESE YEARS.

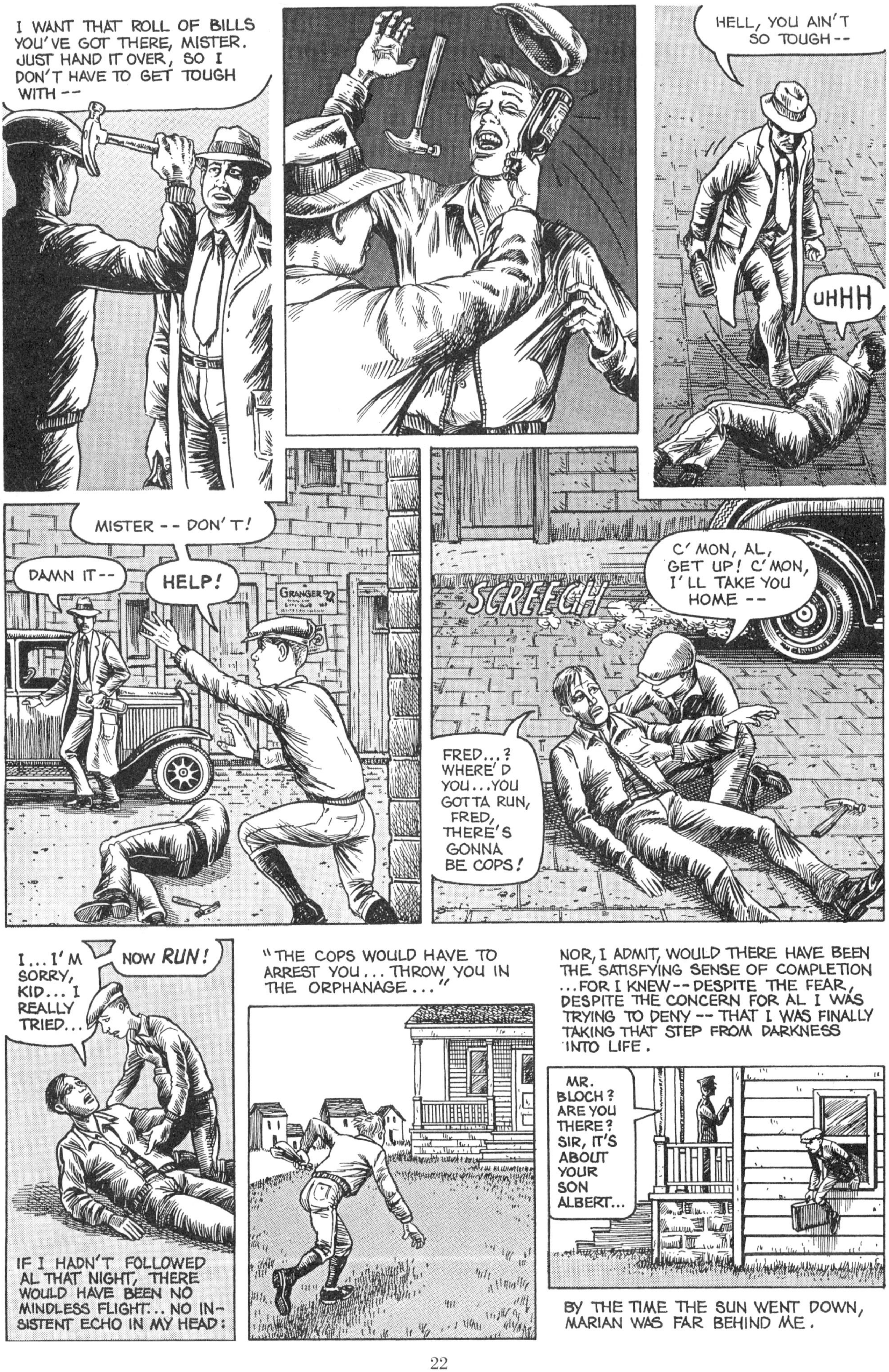

I WANT THAT ROLL OF BILLS YOU'VE GOT THERE, MISTER. JUST HAND IT OVER, SO I DON'T HAVE TO GET TOUGH WITH --
HELL, YOU AIN'T SO TOUGH --
UHHH
MISTER -- DON'T!
DAMN IT --
HELP!
SCREECH
C'MON, AL, GET UP! C'MON, I'LL TAKE YOU HOME --
FRED...? WHERE'D YOU...YOU GOTTA RUN, FRED, THERE'S GONNA BE COPS!
I...I'M SORRY, KID... I REALLY TRIED...
NOW RUN!
IF I HADN'T FOLLOWED AL THAT NIGHT, THERE WOULD HAVE BEEN NO MINDLESS FLIGHT... NO IN-SISTENT ECHO IN MY HEAD:
"THE COPS WOULD HAVE TO ARREST YOU... THROW YOU IN THE ORPHANAGE..."
NOR, I ADMIT, WOULD THERE HAVE BEEN THE SATISFYING SENSE OF COMPLETION ...FOR I KNEW--DESPITE THE FEAR, DESPITE THE CONCERN FOR AL I WAS TRYING TO DENY -- THAT I WAS FINALLY TAKING THAT STEP FROM DARKNESS INTO LIFE.
MR. BLOCH? ARE YOU THERE? SIR, IT'S ABOUT YOUR SON ALBERT...
BY THE TIME THE SUN WENT DOWN, MARIAN WAS FAR BEHIND ME.

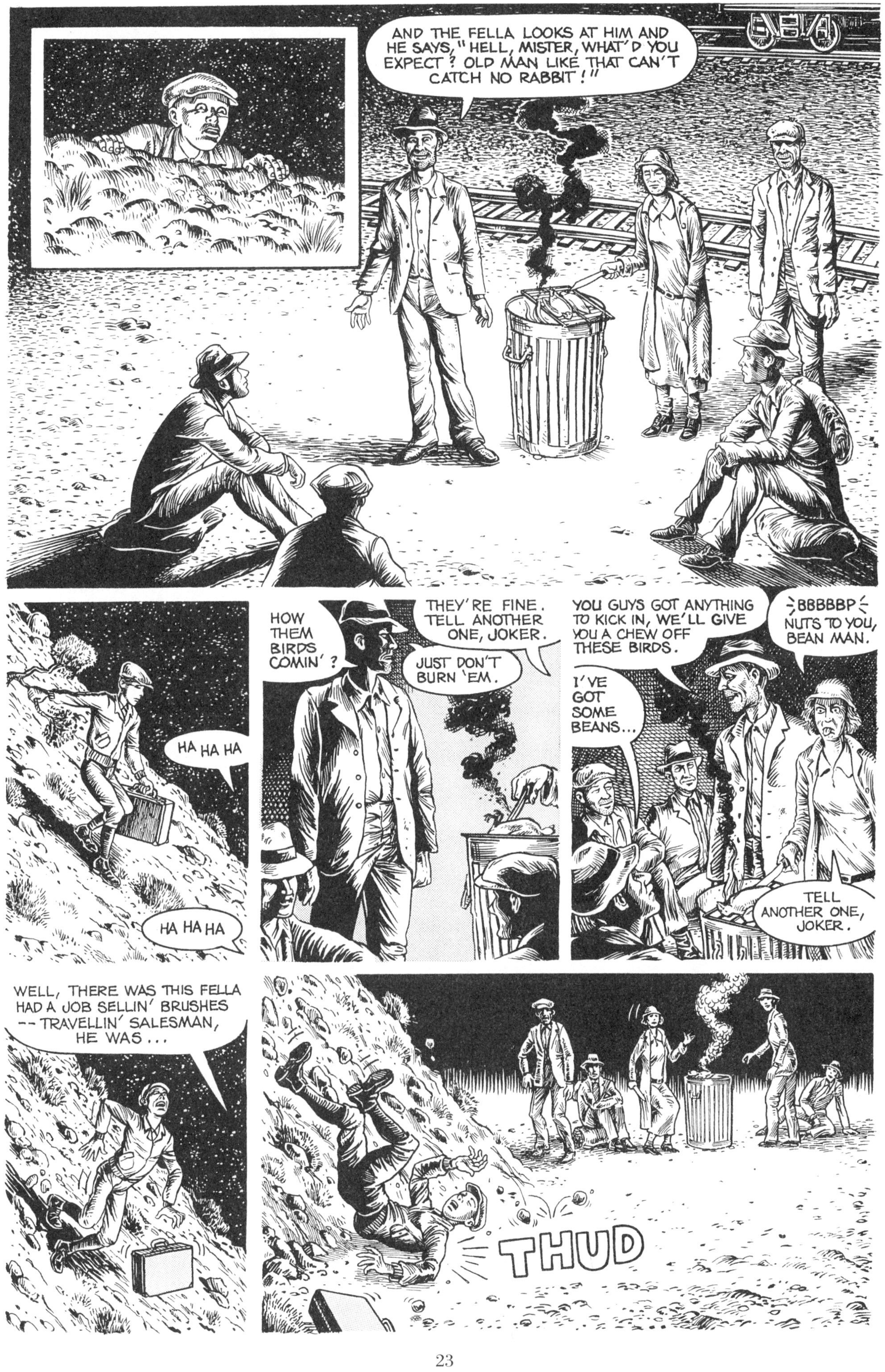
AND THE FELLA LOOKS AT HIM AND HE SAYS, "HELL, MISTER, WHAT'D YOU EXPECT? OLD MAN LIKE THAT CAN'T CATCH NO RABBIT!"
HA HA HA
HA HA HA
HOW THEM BIRDS COMIN'?
THEY'RE FINE. TELL ANOTHER ONE, JOKER.
JUST DON'T BURN 'EM.
YOU GUYS GOT ANYTHING TO KICK IN, WE'LL GIVE YOU A CHEW OFF THESE BIRDS.
I'VE GOT SOME BEANS...
BBBBBP
NUTS TO YOU, BEAN MAN.
TELL ANOTHER ONE, JOKER.
WELL, THERE WAS THIS FELLA HAD A JOB SELLIN' BRUSHES -- TRAVELLIN' SALESMAN, HE WAS...
THUD

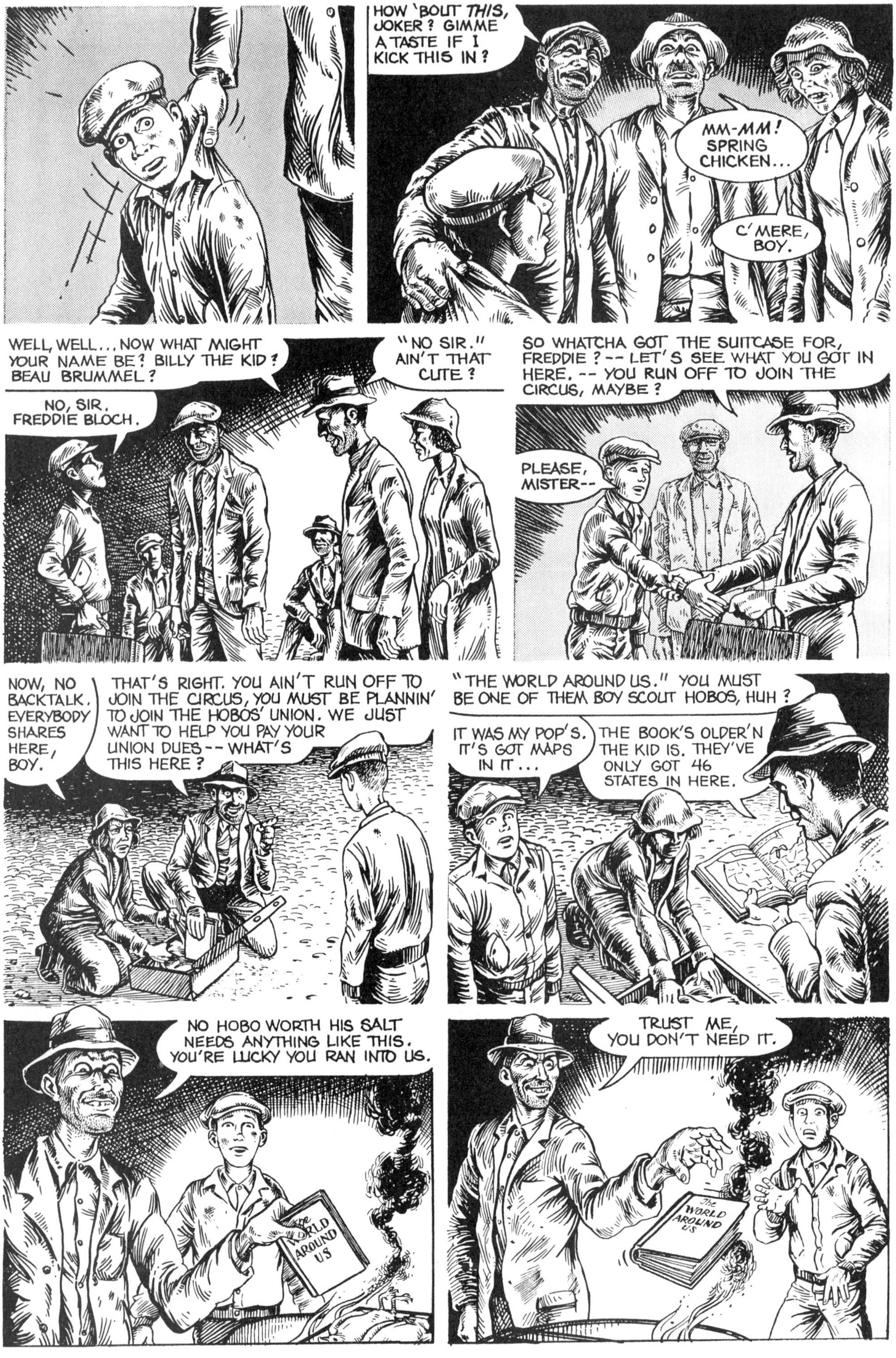
HOW 'BOUT THIS, JOKER? GIMME A TASTE IF I KICK THIS IN?
MM-MM! SPRING CHICKEN...
C'MERE, BOY.
WELL, WELL... NOW WHAT MIGHT YOUR NAME BE? BILLY THE KID? BEAU BRUMMEL?
NO, SIR. FREDDIE BLOCH.
"NO SIR." AIN'T THAT CUTE?
SO WHATCHA GOT THE SUITCASE FOR, FREDDIE? -- LET'S SEE WHAT YOU GOT IN HERE. -- YOU RUN OFF TO JOIN THE CIRCUS, MAYBE?
PLEASE, MISTER--
NOW, NO BACKTALK. EVERYBODY SHARES HERE, BOY.
THAT'S RIGHT. YOU AIN'T RUN OFF TO JOIN THE CIRCUS, YOU MUST BE PLANNIN' TO JOIN THE HOBOS' UNION. WE JUST WANT TO HELP YOU PAY YOUR UNION DUES -- WHAT'S THIS HERE?
"THE WORLD AROUND US." YOU MUST BE ONE OF THEM BOY SCOUT HOBOS, HUH?
IT WAS MY POP'S. IT'S GOT MAPS IN IT...
THE BOOK'S OLDER'N THE KID IS. THEY'VE ONLY GOT 46 STATES IN HERE.
NO HOBO WORTH HIS SALT NEEDS ANYTHING LIKE THIS. YOU'RE LUCKY YOU RAN INTO US.
The WORLD AROUND US
TRUST ME, YOU DON'T NEED IT.
The WORLD AROUND US

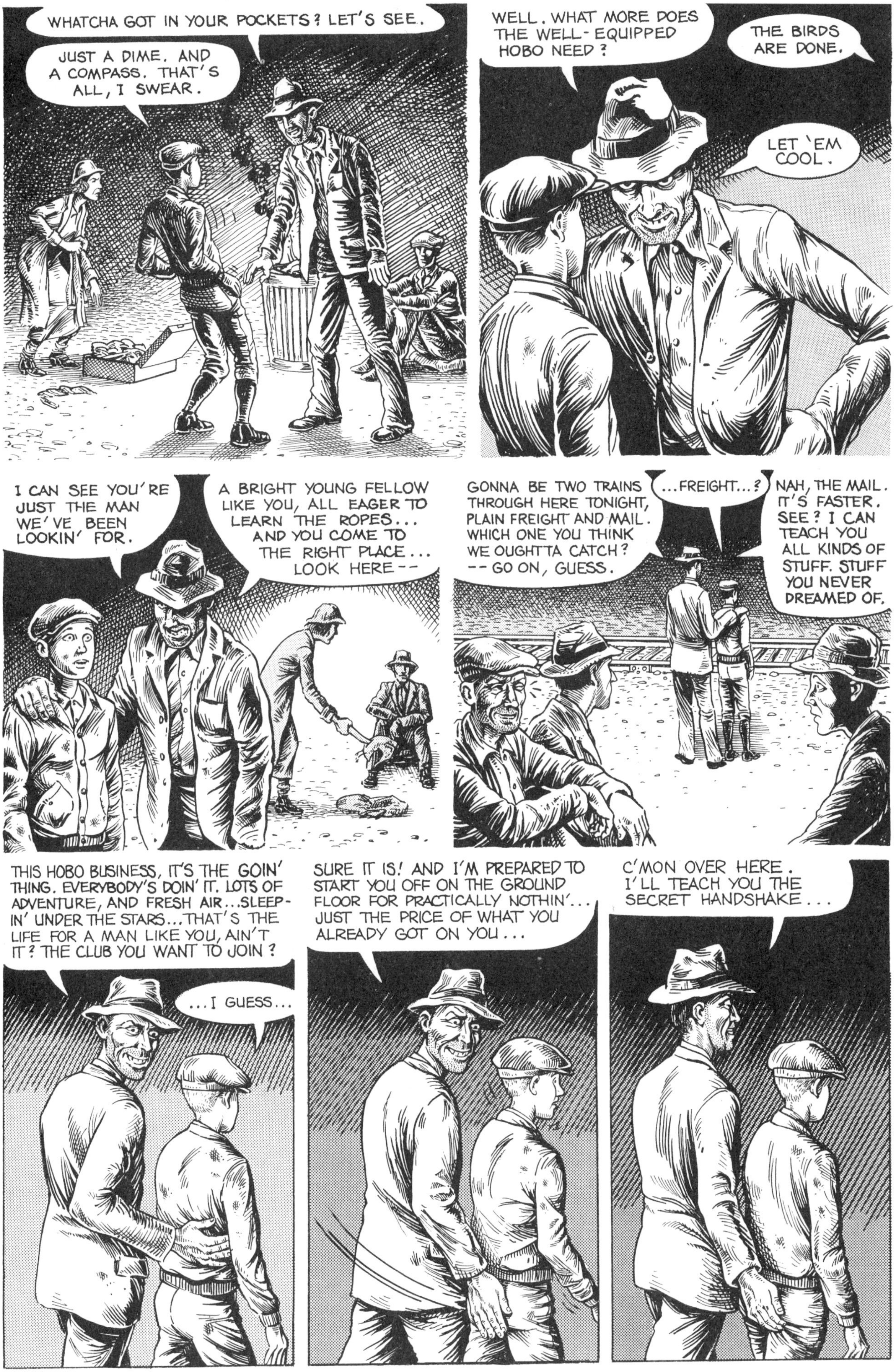
WHATCHA GOT IN YOUR POCKETS? LET'S SEE.
JUST A DIME. AND A COMPASS. THAT'S ALL, I SWEAR.
WELL. WHAT MORE DOES THE WELL-EQUIPPED HOBO NEED?
THE BIRDS ARE DONE.
LET 'EM COOL.
I CAN SEE YOU'RE JUST THE MAN WE'VE BEEN LOOKIN' FOR.
A BRIGHT YOUNG FELLOW LIKE YOU, ALL EAGER TO LEARN THE ROPES... AND YOU COME TO THE RIGHT PLACE... LOOK HERE--
GONNA BE TWO TRAINS THROUGH HERE TONIGHT, PLAIN FREIGHT AND MAIL. WHICH ONE YOU THINK WE OUGHTTA CATCH? -- GO ON, GUESS.
...FREIGHT...?
NAH, THE MAIL. IT'S FASTER. SEE? I CAN TEACH YOU ALL KINDS OF STUFF. STUFF YOU NEVER DREAMED OF.
THIS HOBO BUSINESS, IT'S THE GOIN' THING. EVERYBODY'S DOIN' IT. LOTS OF ADVENTURE, AND FRESH AIR...SLEEPIN' UNDER THE STARS...THAT'S THE LIFE FOR A MAN LIKE YOU, AIN'T IT? THE CLUB YOU WANT TO JOIN?
...I GUESS...
SURE IT IS! AND I'M PREPARED TO START YOU OFF ON THE GROUND FLOOR FOR PRACTICALLY NOTHIN'... JUST THE PRICE OF WHAT YOU ALREADY GOT ON YOU...
C'MON OVER HERE. I'LL TEACH YOU THE SECRET HANDSHAKE...

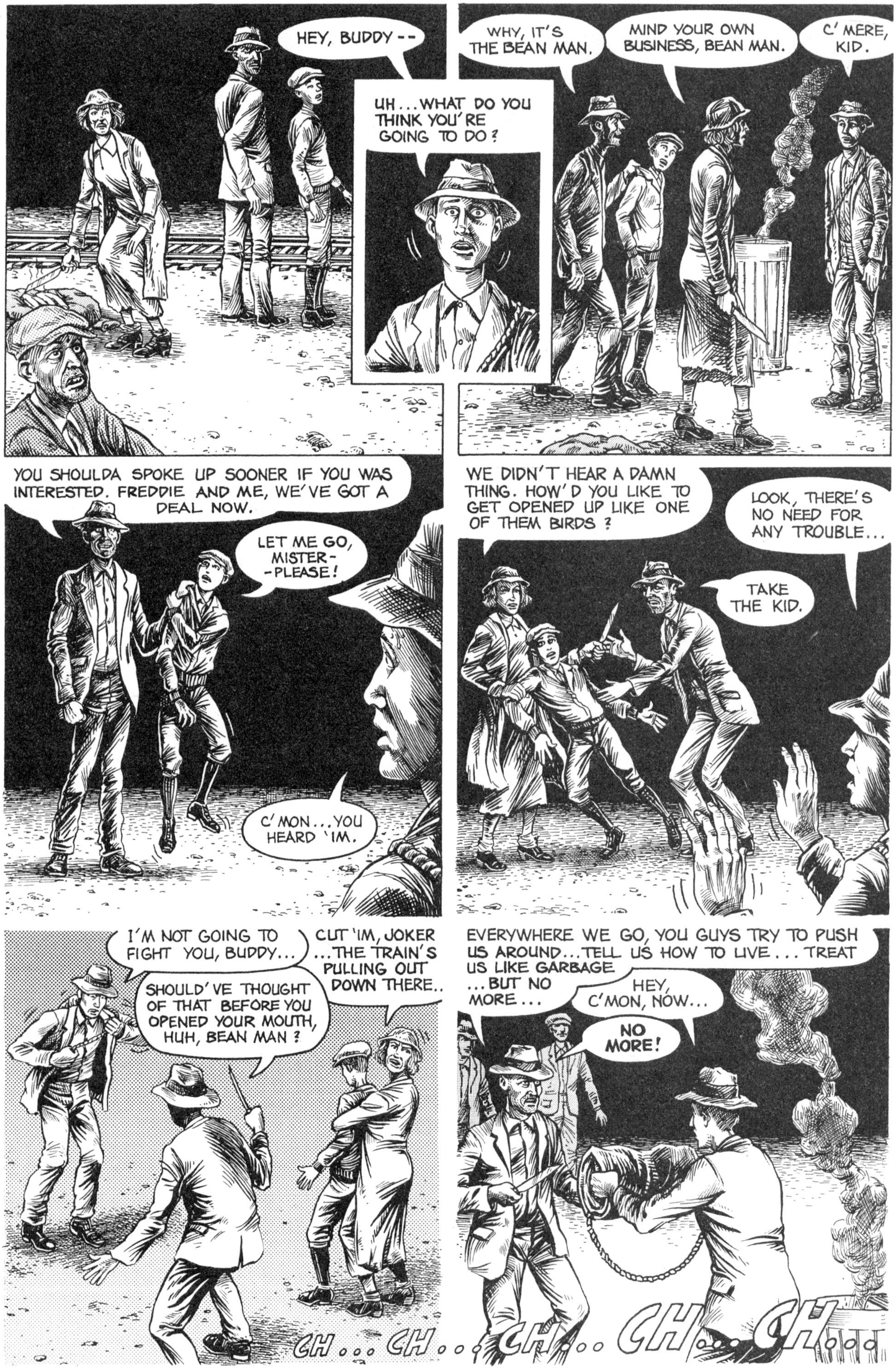
HEY, BUDDY --
UH...WHAT DO YOU THINK YOU'RE GOING TO DO?
WHY, IT'S THE BEAN MAN.
MIND YOUR OWN BUSINESS, BEAN MAN.
C'MERE, KID.
YOU SHOULDA SPOKE UP SOONER IF YOU WAS INTERESTED. FREDDIE AND ME, WE'VE GOT A DEAL NOW.
LET ME GO, MISTER--PLEASE!
C'MON...YOU HEARD 'IM.
WE DIDN'T HEAR A DAMN THING. HOW'D YOU LIKE TO GET OPENED UP LIKE ONE OF THEM BIRDS?
LOOK, THERE'S NO NEED FOR ANY TROUBLE...
TAKE THE KID.
I'M NOT GOING TO FIGHT YOU, BUDDY...
SHOULD'VE THOUGHT OF THAT BEFORE YOU OPENED YOUR MOUTH, HUH, BEAN MAN?
CUT 'IM, JOKER ...THE TRAIN'S PULLING OUT DOWN THERE..
EVERYWHERE WE GO, YOU GUYS TRY TO PUSH US AROUND...TELL US HOW TO LIVE... TREAT US LIKE GARBAGE ...BUT NO MORE...
HEY, C'MON, NOW...
NO MORE!
CH...CH...CH...CH...CH...

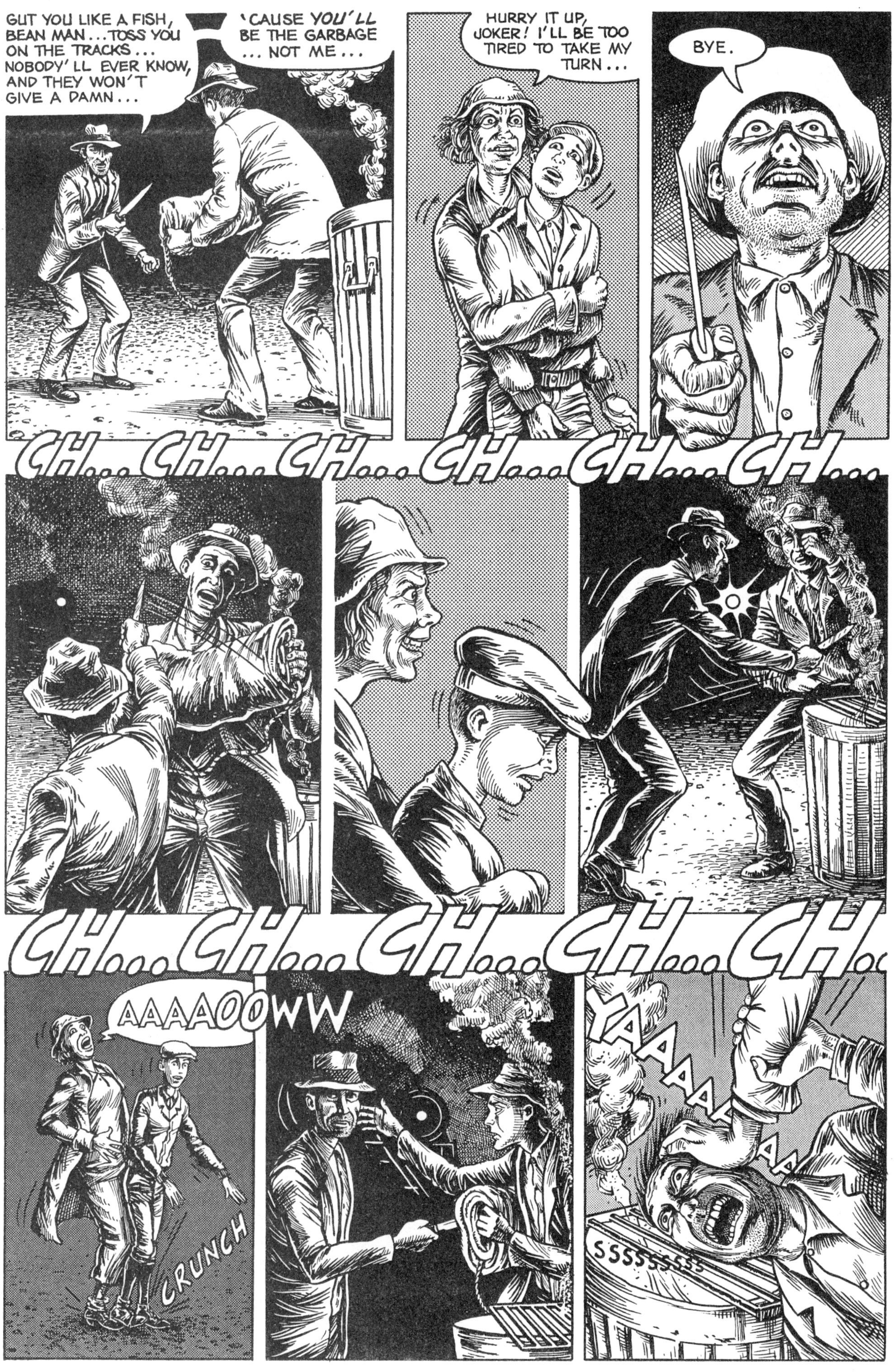
GUT YOU LIKE A FISH, BEAN MAN ... TOSS YOU ON THE TRACKS ... NOBODY'LL EVER KNOW, AND THEY WON'T GIVE A DAMN ...
'CAUSE YOU'LL BE THE GARBAGE ... NOT ME ...
HURRY IT UP, JOKER! I'LL BE TOO TIRED TO TAKE MY TURN ...
BYE.
CH... CH... CH... CH... CH... CH...
CH... CH... CH... CH... CH...
AAAAOOWW
CRUNCH
YAAAAAAA
SSSSSSSS

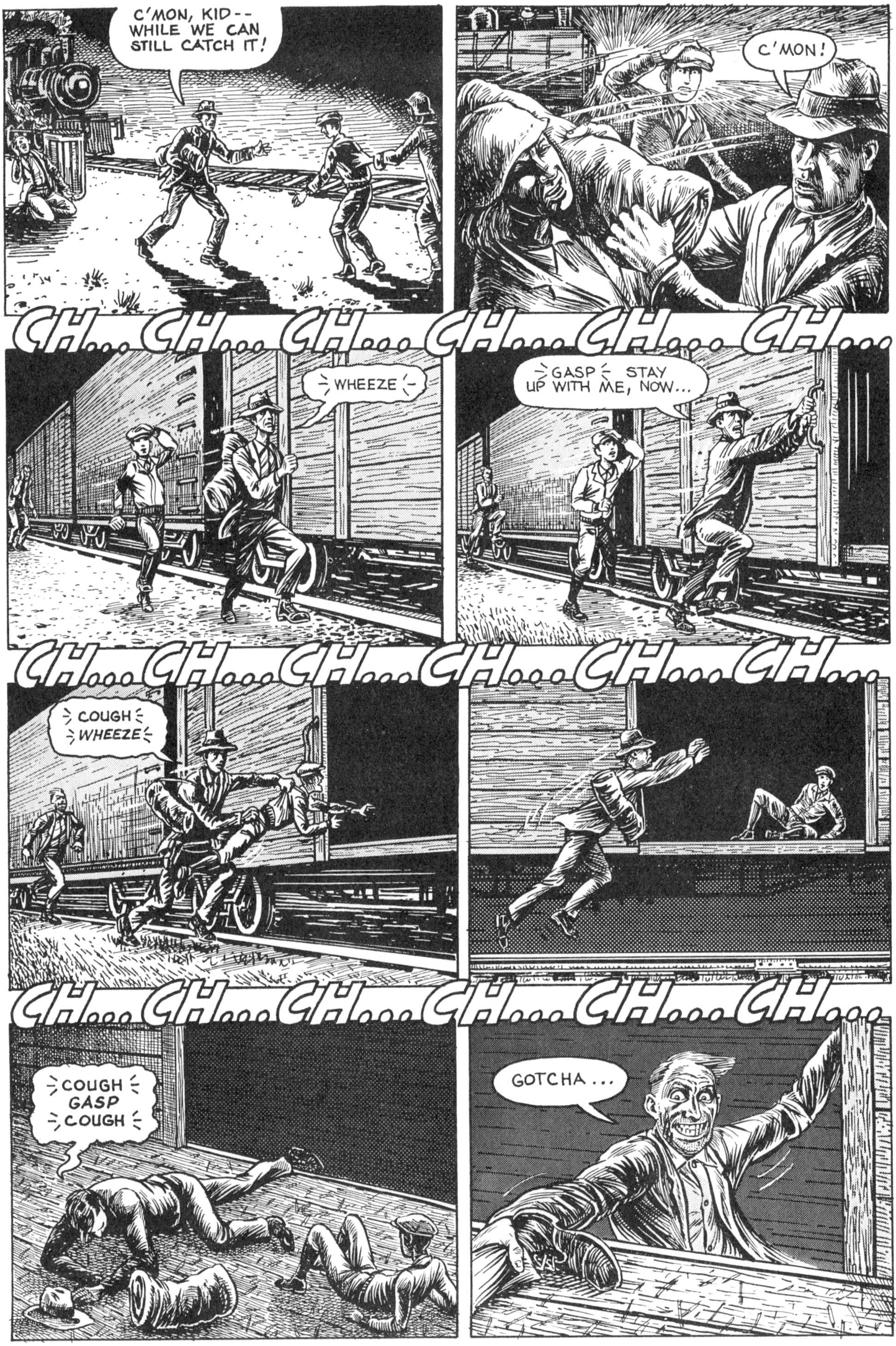
C'MON, KID-- WHILE WE CAN STILL CATCH IT!
C'MON!
CH... CH... CH... CH... CH... CH...
WHEEZE
GASP STAY UP WITH ME, NOW...
CH... CH... CH... CH... CH... CH...
COUGH WHEEZE
CH... CH... CH... CH... CH... CH...
COUGH GASP COUGH
GOTCHA ...

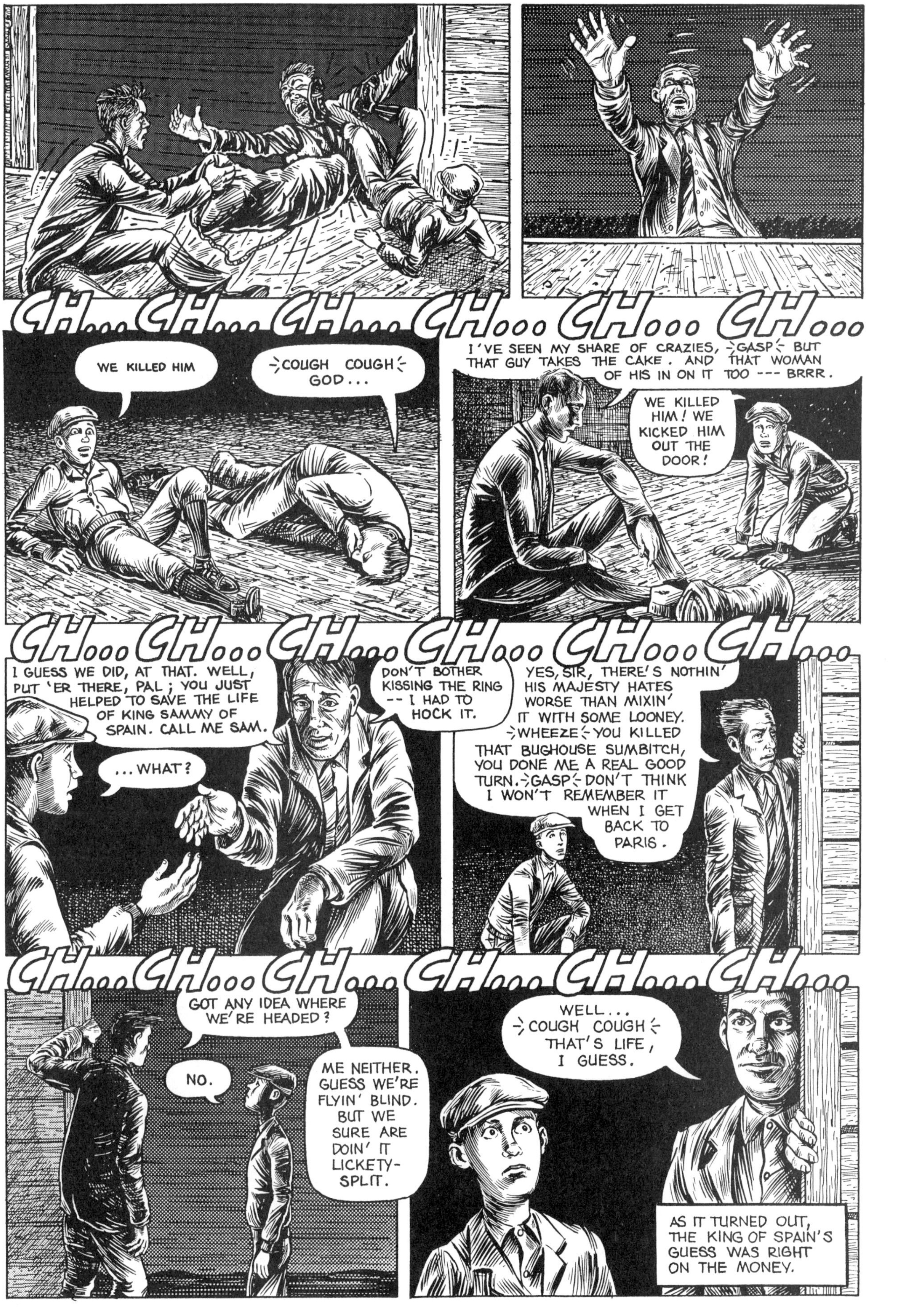
CH... CH... CH... CH... CH... CH...
WE KILLED HIM
COUGH COUGH GOD...
I'VE SEEN MY SHARE OF CRAZIES, GASP BUT THAT GUY TAKES THE CAKE. AND THAT WOMAN OF HIS IN ON IT TOO --- BRRR.
WE KILLED HIM! WE KICKED HIM OUT THE DOOR!
CH... CH... CH... CH... CH... CH...
I GUESS WE DID, AT THAT. WELL, PUT 'ER THERE, PAL; YOU JUST HELPED TO SAVE THE LIFE OF KING SAMMY OF SPAIN. CALL ME SAM.
... WHAT?
DON'T BOTHER KISSING THE RING -- I HAD TO HOCK IT.
YES, SIR, THERE'S NOTHIN' HIS MAJESTY HATES WORSE THAN MIXIN' IT WITH SOME LOONEY. WHEEZE YOU KILLED THAT BUGHOUSE SUMBITCH, YOU DONE ME A REAL GOOD TURN. GASP DON'T THINK I WON'T REMEMBER IT WHEN I GET BACK TO PARIS.
CH... CH... CH... CH... CH... CH...
GOT ANY IDEA WHERE WE'RE HEADED?
NO.
ME NEITHER. GUESS WE'RE FLYIN' BLIND. BUT WE SURE ARE DOIN' IT LICKETY-SPLIT.
WELL... COUGH COUGH THAT'S LIFE, I GUESS.
AS IT TURNED OUT, THE KING OF SPAIN'S GUESS WAS RIGHT ON THE MONEY.

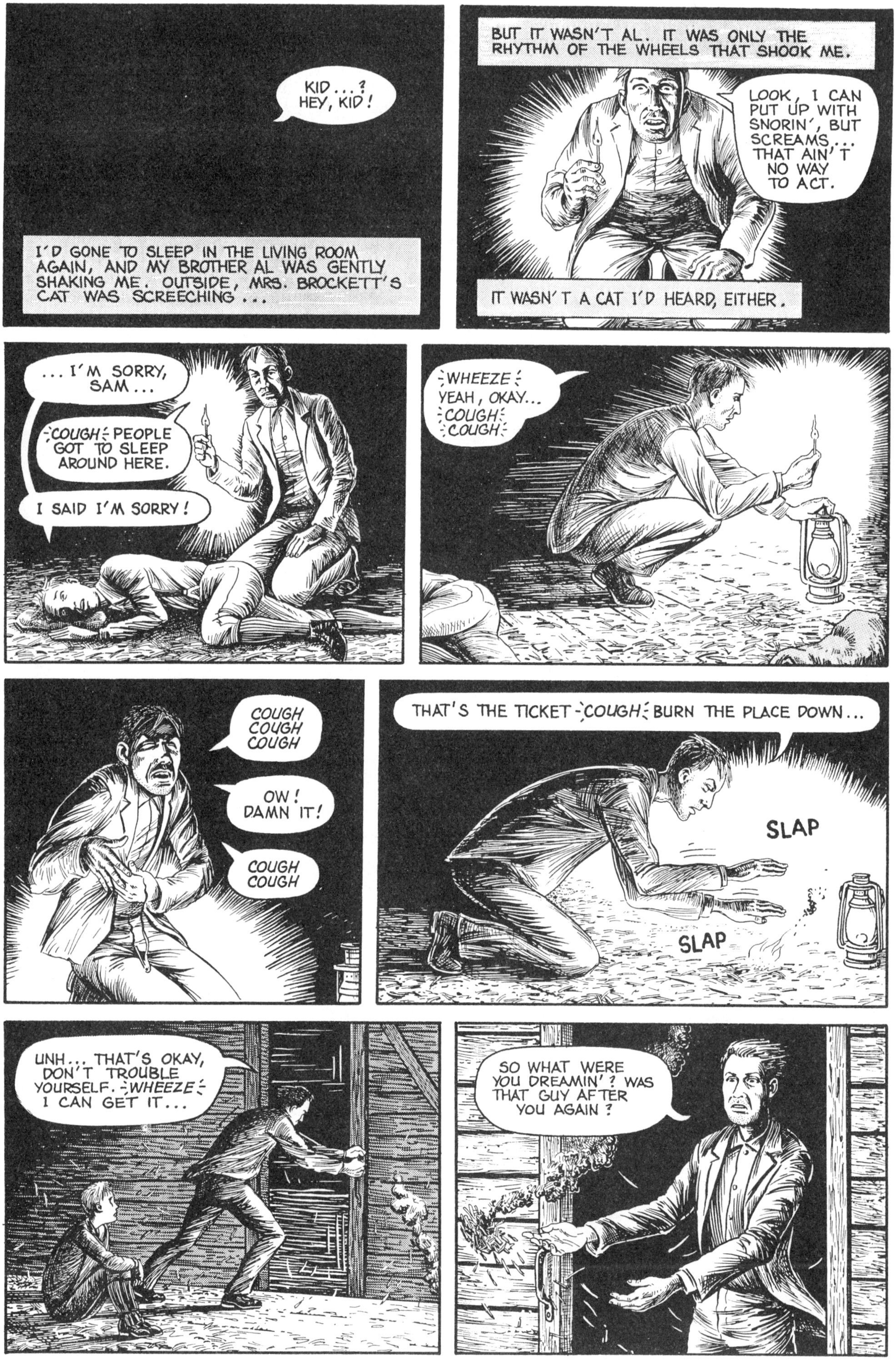
KID...? HEY, KID!
I'D GONE TO SLEEP IN THE LIVING ROOM AGAIN, AND MY BROTHER AL WAS GENTLY SHAKING ME. OUTSIDE, MRS. BROCKETT'S CAT WAS SCREECHING...
BUT IT WASN'T AL. IT WAS ONLY THE RHYTHM OF THE WHEELS THAT SHOOK ME.
LOOK, I CAN PUT UP WITH SNORIN', BUT SCREAMS... THAT AIN'T NO WAY TO ACT.
IT WASN'T A CAT I'D HEARD, EITHER.
...I'M SORRY, SAM...
-COUGH- PEOPLE GOT TO SLEEP AROUND HERE.
I SAID I'M SORRY!
-WHEEZE- YEAH, OKAY... -COUGH- -COUGH-
COUGH COUGH COUGH
OW! DAMN IT!
COUGH COUGH
THAT'S THE TICKET -COUGH- BURN THE PLACE DOWN...
SLAP
SLAP
UNH... THAT'S OKAY, DON'T TROUBLE YOURSELF. -WHEEZE- I CAN GET IT...
SO WHAT WERE YOU DREAMIN'? WAS THAT GUY AFTER YOU AGAIN?

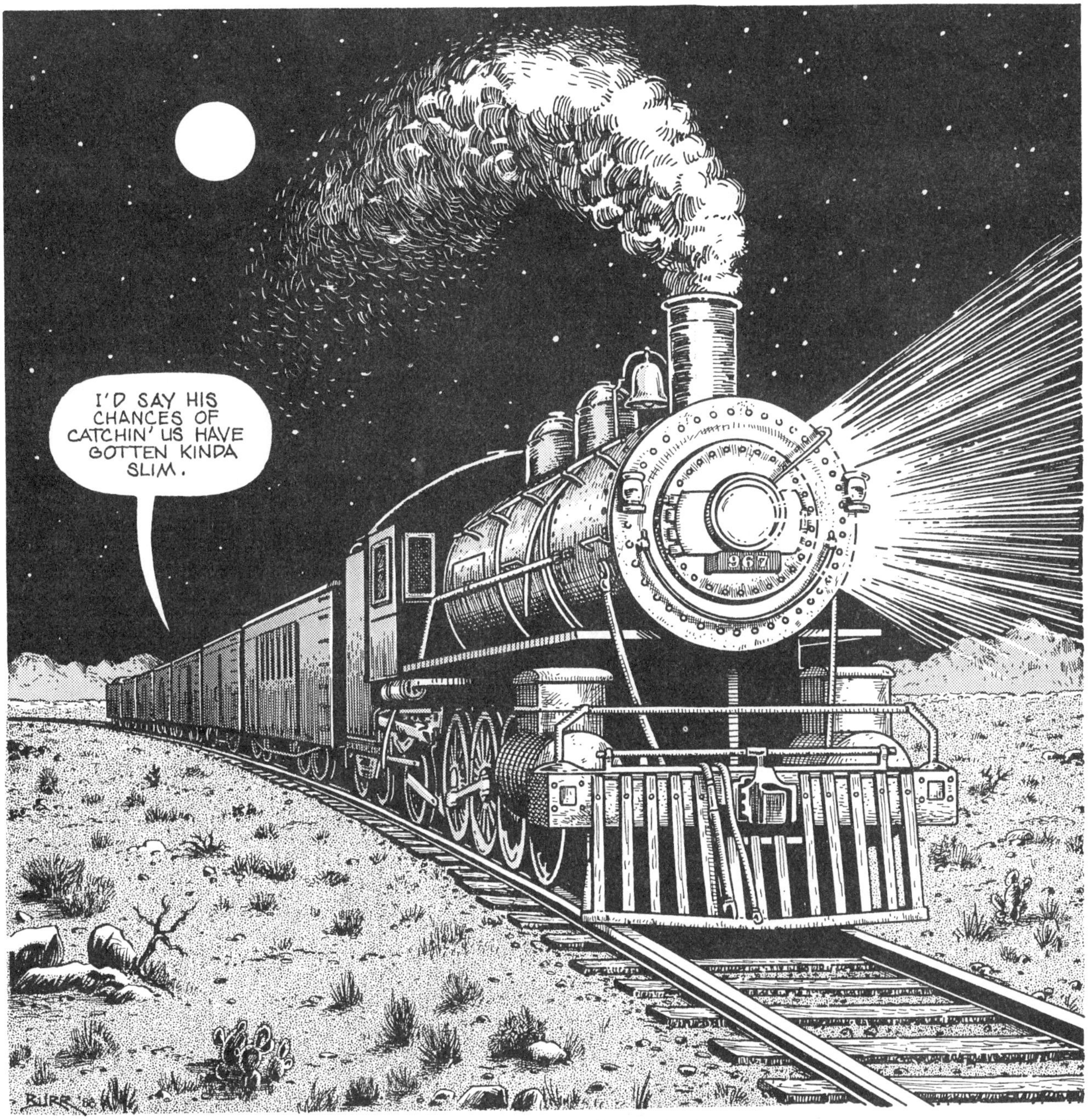
I'D SAY HIS CHANCES OF CATCHIN' US HAVE GOTTEN KINDA SLIM.
BURR '80

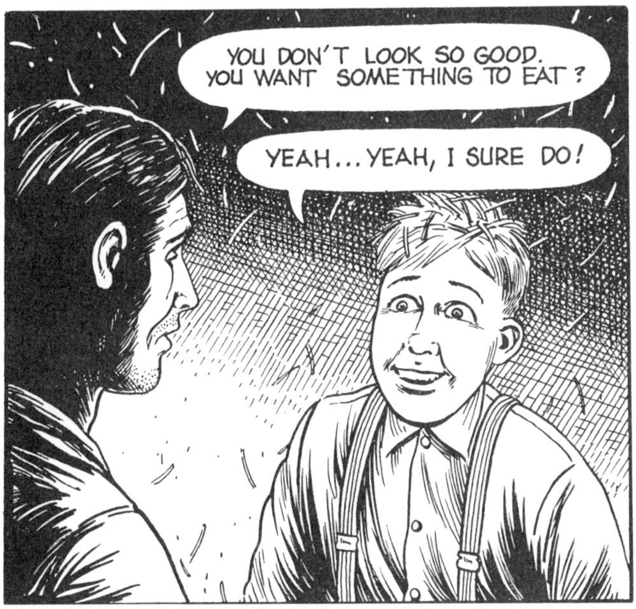
YOU DON'T LOOK SO GOOD. YOU WANT SOMETHING TO EAT?
YEAH... YEAH, I SURE DO!

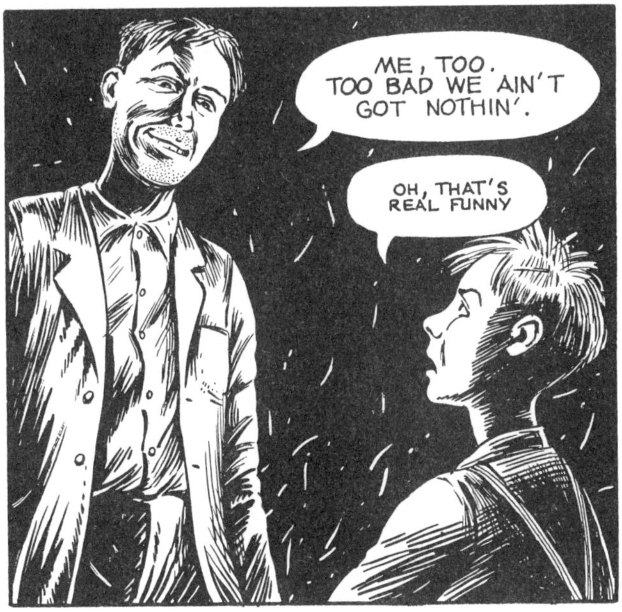
ME, TOO. TOO BAD WE AIN'T GOT NOTHIN'.
OH, THAT'S REAL FUNNY

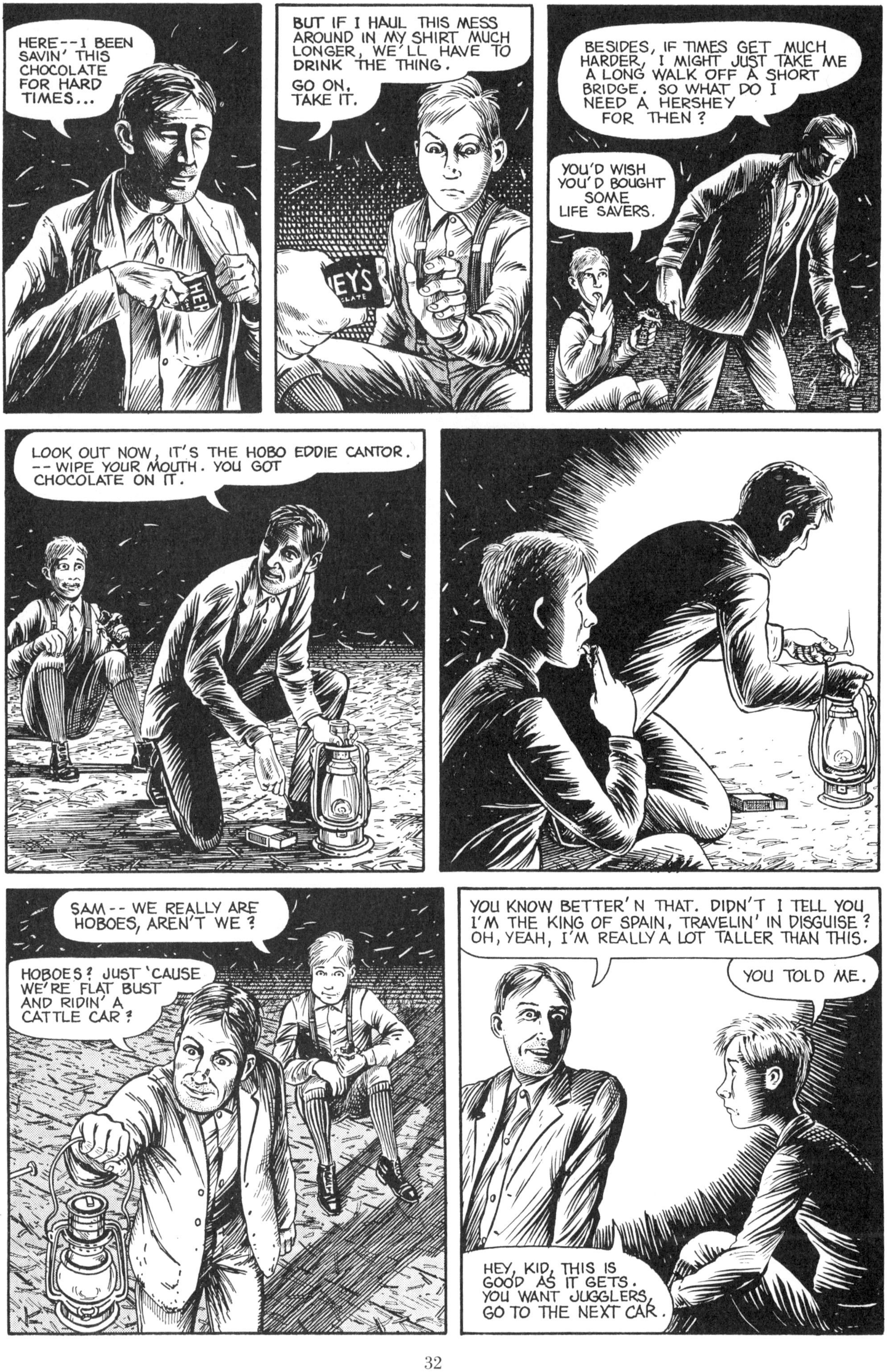
HERE--I BEEN SAVIN' THIS CHOCOLATE FOR HARD TIMES...
BUT IF I HAUL THIS MESS AROUND IN MY SHIRT MUCH LONGER, WE'LL HAVE TO DRINK THE THING.
GO ON, TAKE IT.
BESIDES, IF TIMES GET MUCH HARDER, I MIGHT JUST TAKE ME A LONG WALK OFF A SHORT BRIDGE. SO WHAT DO I NEED A HERSHEY FOR THEN?
YOU'D WISH YOU'D BOUGHT SOME LIFE SAVERS.
LOOK OUT NOW, IT'S THE HOBO EDDIE CANTOR. --WIPE YOUR MOUTH. YOU GOT CHOCOLATE ON IT.
SAM--WE REALLY ARE HOBOES, AREN'T WE?
HOBOES? JUST 'CAUSE WE'RE FLAT BUST AND RIDIN' A CATTLE CAR?
YOU KNOW BETTER'N THAT. DIDN'T I TELL YOU I'M THE KING OF SPAIN, TRAVELIN' IN DISGUISE? OH, YEAH, I'M REALLY A LOT TALLER THAN THIS.
YOU TOLD ME.
HEY, KID, THIS IS GOOD AS IT GETS. YOU WANT JUGGLERS, GO TO THE NEXT CAR.

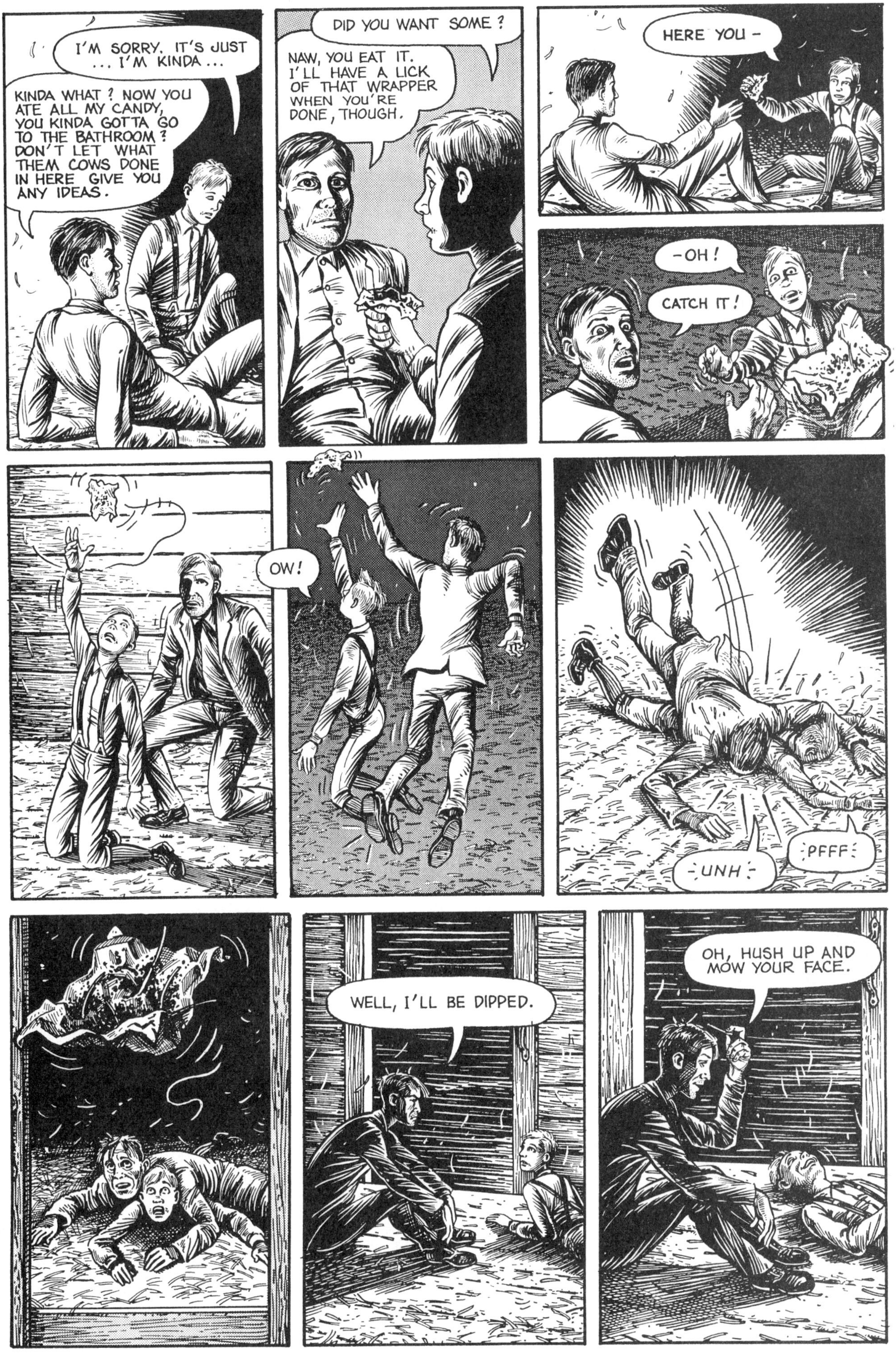
I'M SORRY. IT'S JUST ... I'M KINDA ...
KINDA WHAT? NOW YOU ATE ALL MY CANDY, YOU KINDA GOTTA GO TO THE BATHROOM? DON'T LET WHAT THEM COWS DONE IN HERE GIVE YOU ANY IDEAS.
DID YOU WANT SOME?
NAW, YOU EAT IT. I'LL HAVE A LICK OF THAT WRAPPER WHEN YOU'RE DONE, THOUGH.
HERE YOU -
-OH!
CATCH IT!
OW!
UNH
PFFF
WELL, I'LL BE DIPPED.
OH, HUSH UP AND MOW YOUR FACE.

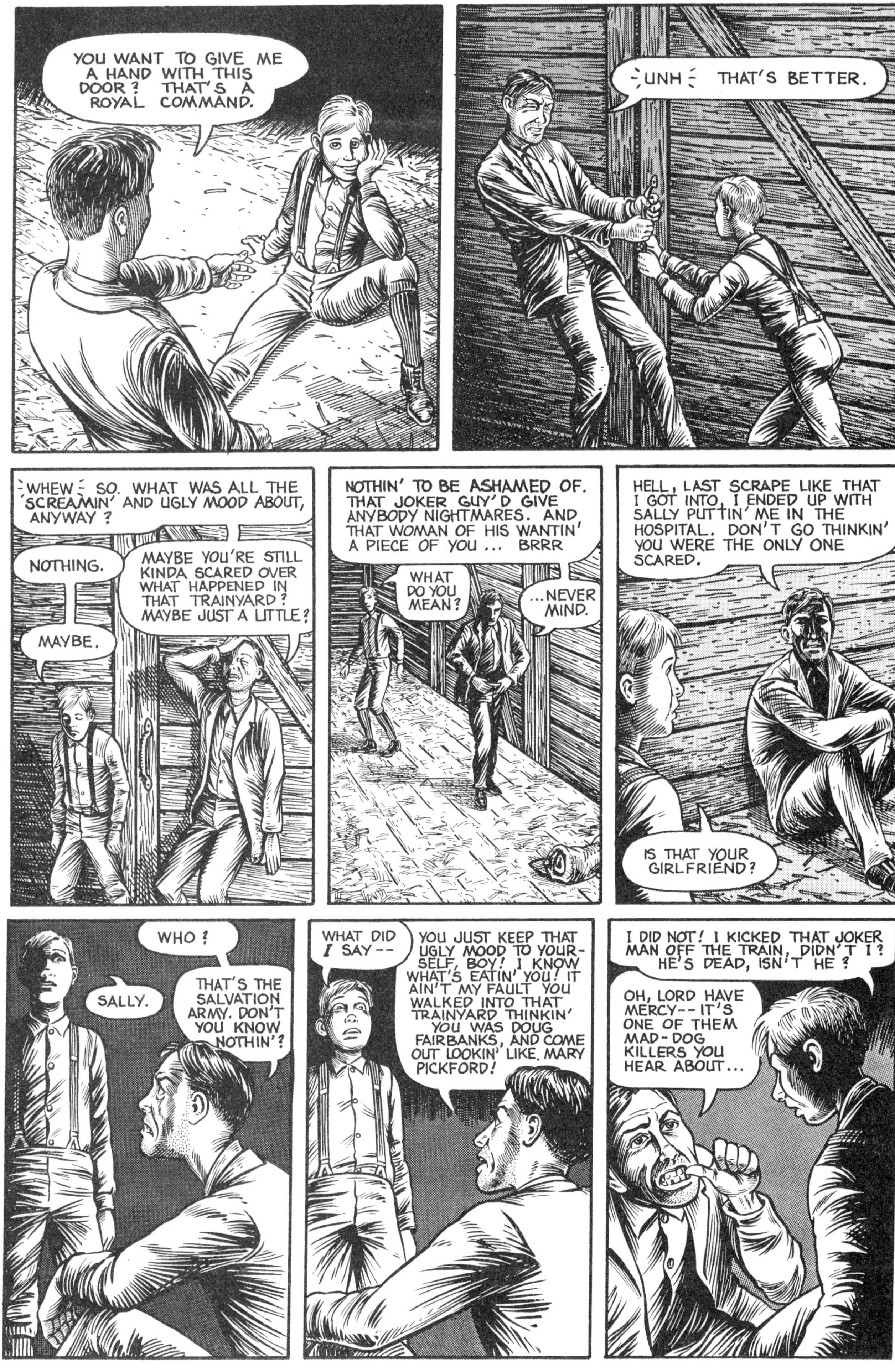
YOU WANT TO GIVE ME A HAND WITH THIS DOOR? THAT'S A ROYAL COMMAND.
UNH THAT'S BETTER.
WHEW SO. WHAT WAS ALL THE SCREAMIN' AND UGLY MOOD ABOUT, ANYWAY?
NOTHING.
MAYBE YOU'RE STILL KINDA SCARED OVER WHAT HAPPENED IN THAT TRAINYARD? MAYBE JUST A LITTLE?
MAYBE.
NOTHIN' TO BE ASHAMED OF. THAT JOKER GUY'D GIVE ANYBODY NIGHTMARES. AND THAT WOMAN OF HIS WANTIN' A PIECE OF YOU ... BRRR
WHAT DO YOU MEAN?
...NEVER MIND.
HELL, LAST SCRAPE LIKE THAT I GOT INTO, I ENDED UP WITH SALLY PUTTIN' ME IN THE HOSPITAL. DON'T GO THINKIN' YOU WERE THE ONLY ONE SCARED.
IS THAT YOUR GIRLFRIEND?
WHO?
SALLY.
THAT'S THE SALVATION ARMY. DON'T YOU KNOW NOTHIN'?
WHAT DID I SAY--
YOU JUST KEEP THAT UGLY MOOD TO YOURSELF, BOY! I KNOW WHAT'S EATIN' YOU! IT AIN'T MY FAULT YOU WALKED INTO THAT TRAINYARD THINKIN' YOU WAS DOUG FAIRBANKS, AND COME OUT LOOKIN' LIKE MARY PICKFORD!
I DID NOT! I KICKED THAT JOKER MAN OFF THE TRAIN, DIDN'T I? HE'S DEAD, ISN'T HE?
OH, LORD HAVE MERCY--IT'S ONE OF THEM MAD-DOG KILLERS YOU HEAR ABOUT...

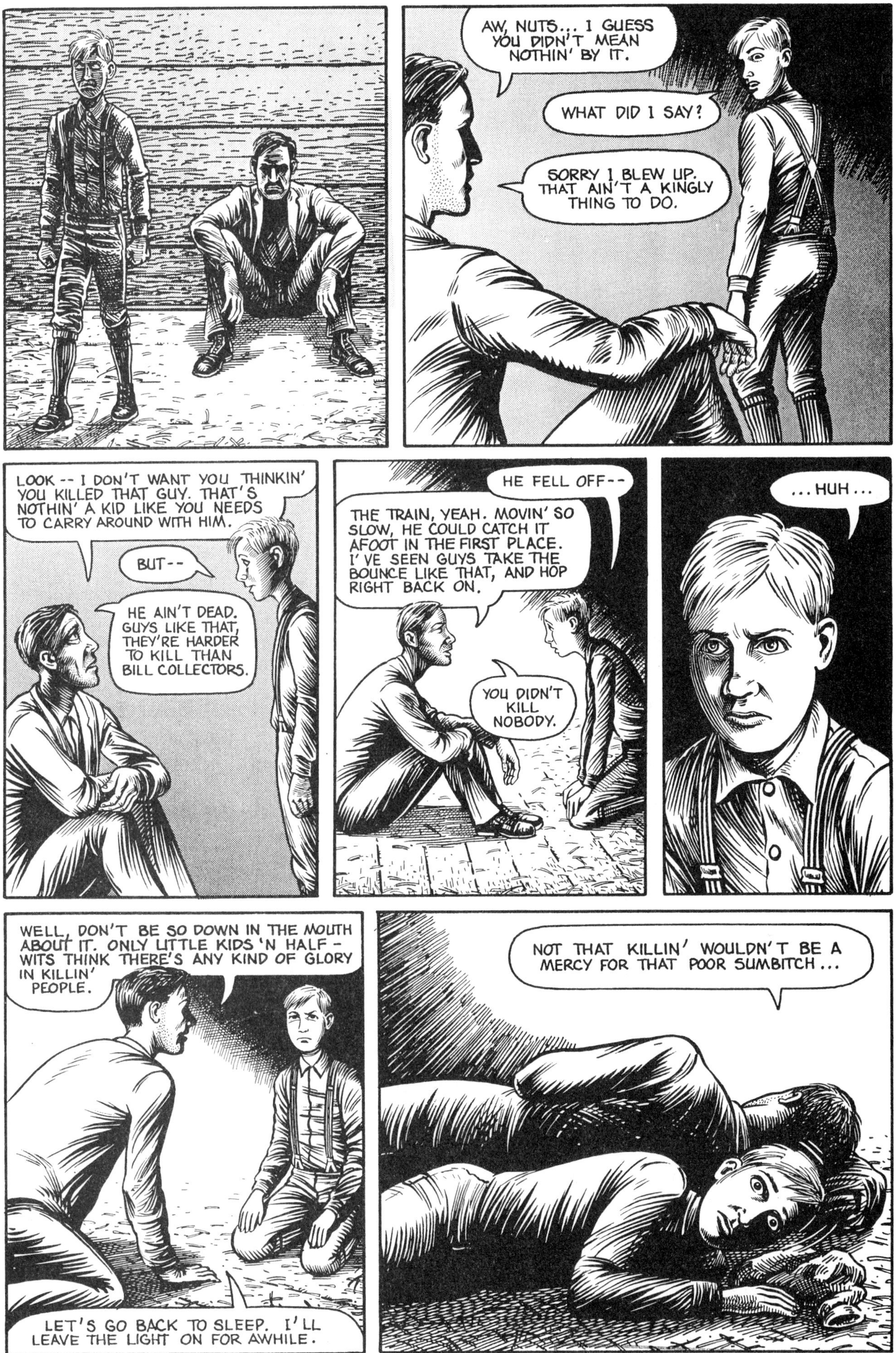
AW, NUTS... I GUESS YOU DIDN'T MEAN NOTHIN' BY IT.
WHAT DID I SAY?
SORRY I BLEW UP. THAT AIN'T A KINGLY THING TO DO.
LOOK -- I DON'T WANT YOU THINKIN' YOU KILLED THAT GUY. THAT'S NOTHIN' A KID LIKE YOU NEEDS TO CARRY AROUND WITH HIM.
BUT--
HE AIN'T DEAD. GUYS LIKE THAT, THEY'RE HARDER TO KILL THAN BILL COLLECTORS.
HE FELL OFF--
THE TRAIN, YEAH. MOVIN' SO SLOW, HE COULD CATCH IT AFOOT IN THE FIRST PLACE. I'VE SEEN GUYS TAKE THE BOUNCE LIKE THAT, AND HOP RIGHT BACK ON.
YOU DIDN'T KILL NOBODY.
...HUH...
WELL, DON'T BE SO DOWN IN THE MOUTH ABOUT IT. ONLY LITTLE KIDS 'N HALF-WITS THINK THERE'S ANY KIND OF GLORY IN KILLIN' PEOPLE.
LET'S GO BACK TO SLEEP. I'LL LEAVE THE LIGHT ON FOR AWHILE.
NOT THAT KILLIN' WOULDN'T BE A MERCY FOR THAT POOR SUMBITCH...

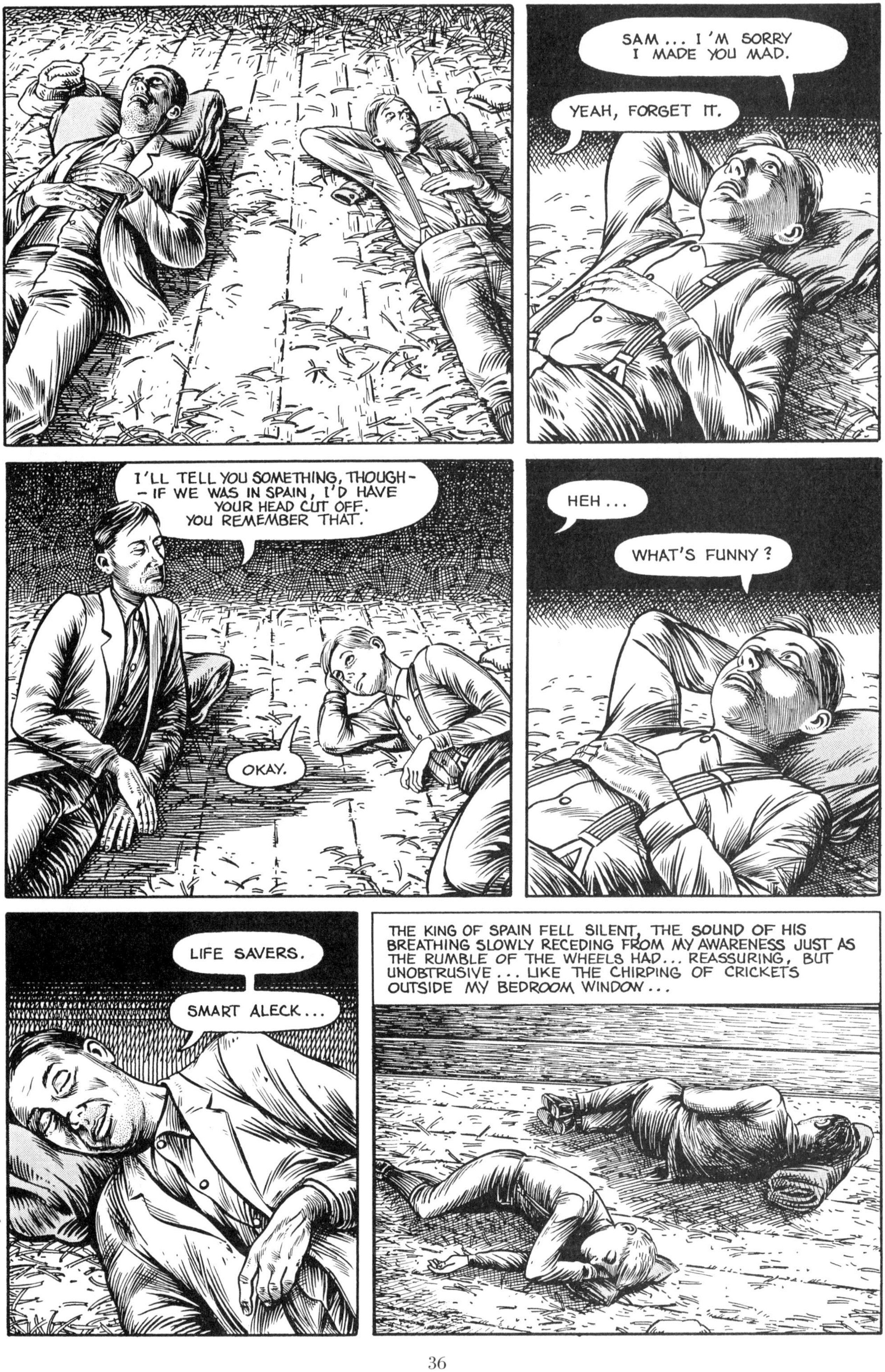
SAM ... I'M SORRY I MADE YOU MAD.
YEAH, FORGET IT.
I'LL TELL YOU SOMETHING, THOUGH- - IF WE WAS IN SPAIN, I'D HAVE YOUR HEAD CUT OFF. YOU REMEMBER THAT.
OKAY.
HEH ...
WHAT'S FUNNY?
LIFE SAVERS.
SMART ALECK ...
THE KING OF SPAIN FELL SILENT, THE SOUND OF HIS BREATHING SLOWLY RECEDING FROM MY AWARENESS JUST AS THE RUMBLE OF THE WHEELS HAD... REASSURING, BUT UNOBTRUSIVE ... LIKE THE CHIRPING OF CRICKETS OUTSIDE MY BEDROOM WINDOW ...

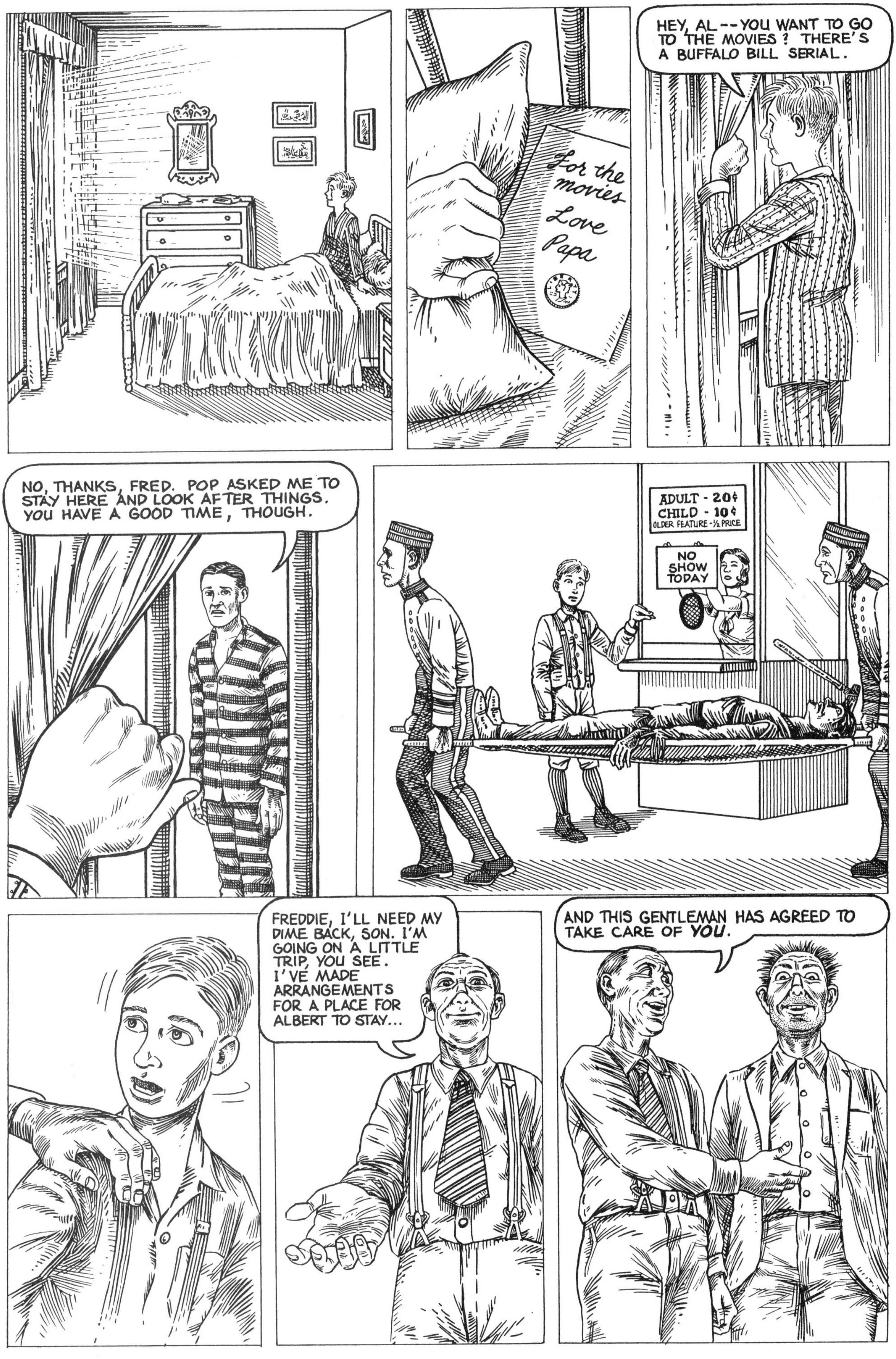
For the movies
Love Papa
HEY, AL -- YOU WANT TO GO TO THE MOVIES? THERE'S A BUFFALO BILL SERIAL.
NO, THANKS, FRED. POP ASKED ME TO STAY HERE AND LOOK AFTER THINGS. YOU HAVE A GOOD TIME, THOUGH.
ADULT - 20¢
CHILD - 10¢
OLDER FEATURE - ½ PRICE
NO SHOW TODAY
FREDDIE, I'LL NEED MY DIME BACK, SON. I'M GOING ON A LITTLE TRIP, YOU SEE. I'VE MADE ARRANGEMENTS FOR A PLACE FOR ALBERT TO STAY...
AND THIS GENTLEMAN HAS AGREED TO TAKE CARE OF *YOU*.

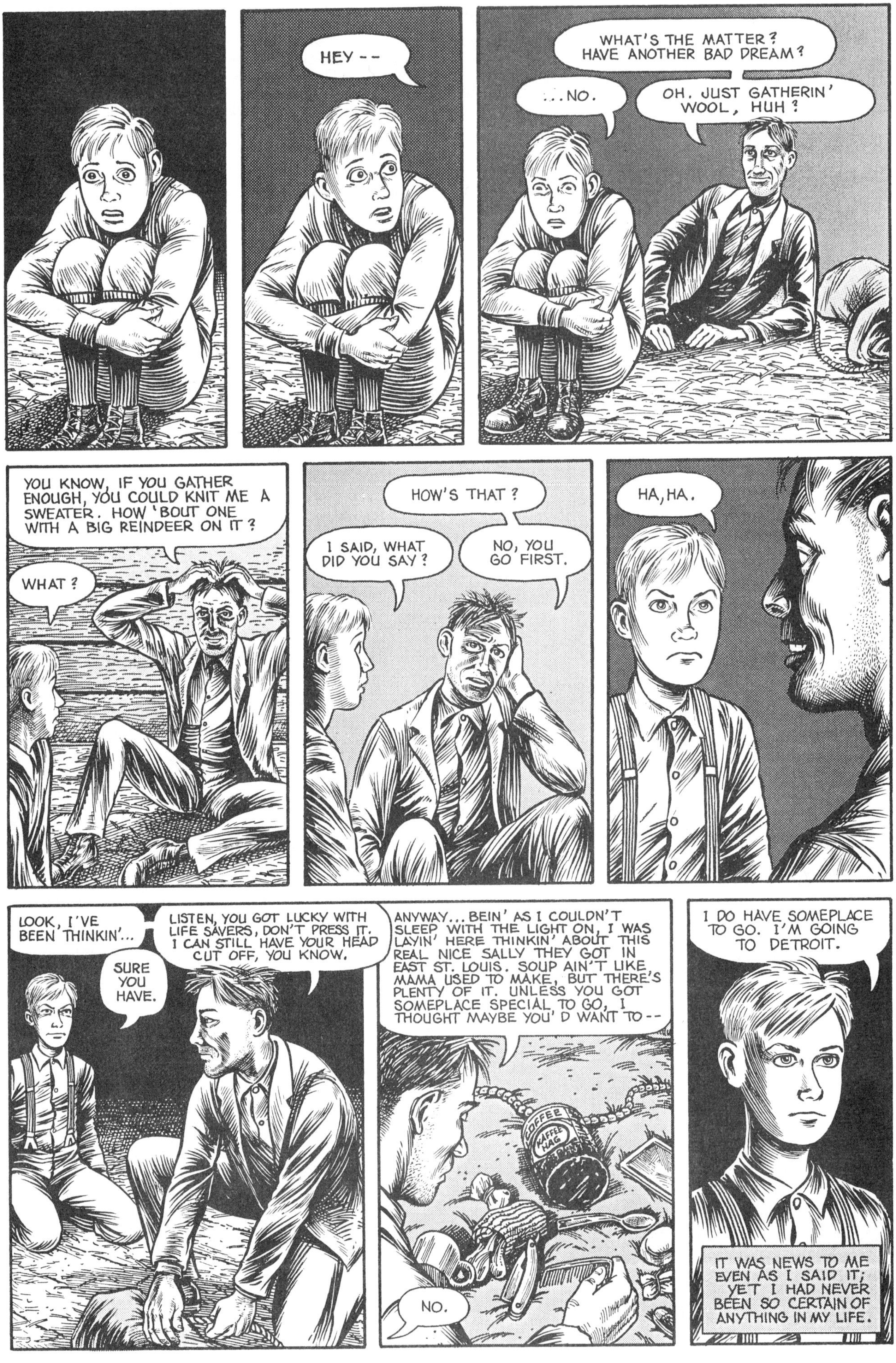
HEY --
WHAT'S THE MATTER? HAVE ANOTHER BAD DREAM?
...NO.
OH. JUST GATHERIN' WOOL, HUH?
YOU KNOW, IF YOU GATHER ENOUGH, YOU COULD KNIT ME A SWEATER. HOW 'BOUT ONE WITH A BIG REINDEER ON IT?
WHAT?
HOW'S THAT?
I SAID, WHAT DID YOU SAY?
NO, YOU GO FIRST.
HA, HA.
LOOK, I'VE BEEN THINKIN'...
LISTEN, YOU GOT LUCKY WITH LIFE SAVERS, DON'T PRESS IT. I CAN STILL HAVE YOUR HEAD CUT OFF, YOU KNOW.
SURE YOU HAVE.
ANYWAY... BEIN' AS I COULDN'T SLEEP WITH THE LIGHT ON, I WAS LAYIN' HERE THINKIN' ABOUT THIS REAL NICE SALLY THEY GOT IN EAST ST. LOUIS. SOUP AIN'T LIKE MAMA USED TO MAKE, BUT THERE'S PLENTY OF IT. UNLESS YOU GOT SOMEPLACE SPECIAL TO GO, I THOUGHT MAYBE YOU'D WANT TO --
COFFEE
KAFFEE HAG
NO.
I DO HAVE SOMEPLACE TO GO. I'M GOING TO DETROIT.
IT WAS NEWS TO ME EVEN AS I SAID IT; YET I HAD NEVER BEEN SO CERTAIN OF ANYTHING IN MY LIFE.

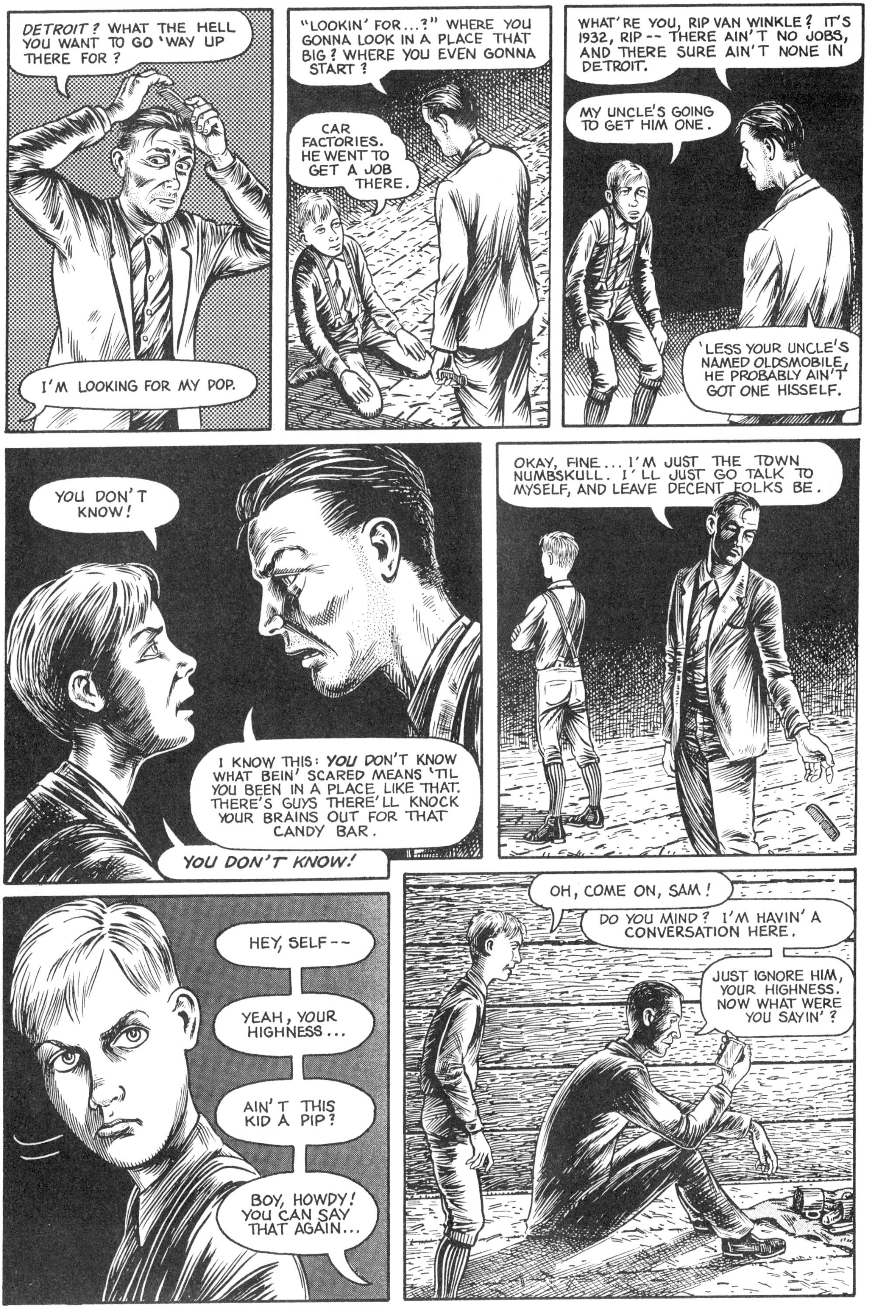
DETROIT? WHAT THE HELL YOU WANT TO GO 'WAY UP THERE FOR?
I'M LOOKING FOR MY POP.
"LOOKIN' FOR...?" WHERE YOU GONNA LOOK IN A PLACE THAT BIG? WHERE YOU EVEN GONNA START?
CAR FACTORIES. HE WENT TO GET A JOB THERE.
WHAT'RE YOU, RIP VAN WINKLE? IT'S 1932, RIP -- THERE AIN'T NO JOBS, AND THERE SURE AIN'T NONE IN DETROIT.
MY UNCLE'S GOING TO GET HIM ONE.
'LESS YOUR UNCLE'S NAMED OLDSMOBILE, HE PROBABLY AIN'T GOT ONE HISSELF.
YOU DON'T KNOW!
I KNOW THIS: YOU DON'T KNOW WHAT BEIN' SCARED MEANS 'TIL YOU BEEN IN A PLACE LIKE THAT. THERE'S GUYS THERE'LL KNOCK YOUR BRAINS OUT FOR THAT CANDY BAR.
YOU DON'T KNOW!
OKAY, FINE... I'M JUST THE TOWN NUMBSKULL. I'LL JUST GO TALK TO MYSELF, AND LEAVE DECENT FOLKS BE.
HEY, SELF--
YEAH, YOUR HIGHNESS...
AIN'T THIS KID A PIP?
BOY, HOWDY! YOU CAN SAY THAT AGAIN...
OH, COME ON, SAM!
DO YOU MIND? I'M HAVIN' A CONVERSATION HERE.
JUST IGNORE HIM, YOUR HIGHNESS. NOW WHAT WERE YOU SAYIN'?

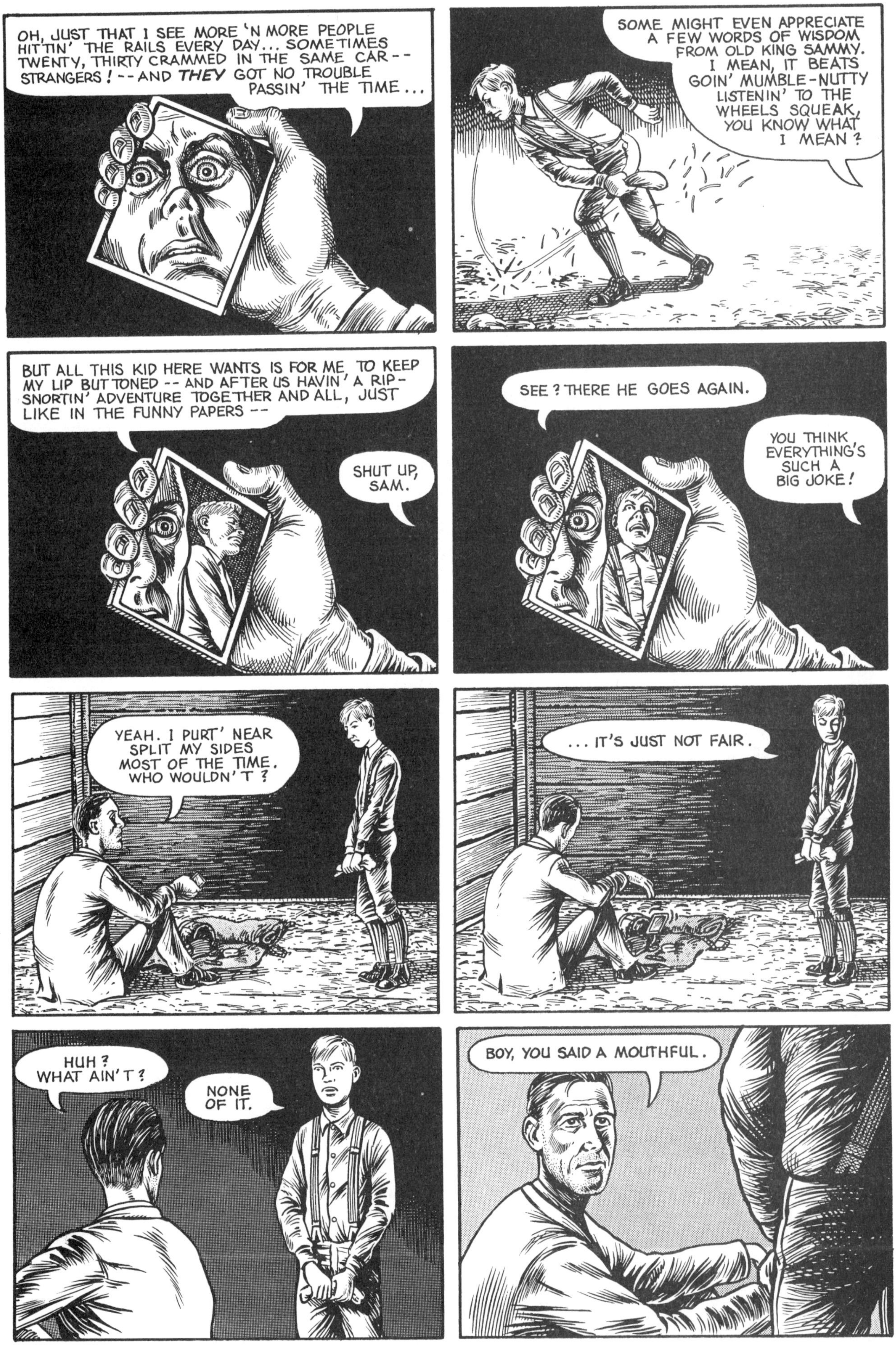
OH, JUST THAT I SEE MORE 'N MORE PEOPLE HIT'TIN' THE RAILS EVERY DAY... SOMETIMES TWENTY, THIRTY CRAMMED IN THE SAME CAR -- STRANGERS! -- AND THEY GOT NO TROUBLE PASSIN' THE TIME...
SOME MIGHT EVEN APPRECIATE A FEW WORDS OF WISDOM FROM OLD KING SAMMY. I MEAN, IT BEATS GOIN' MUMBLE-NUTTY LISTENIN' TO THE WHEELS SQUEAK, YOU KNOW WHAT I MEAN?
BUT ALL THIS KID HERE WANTS IS FOR ME TO KEEP MY LIP BUTTONED -- AND AFTER US HAVIN' A RIP-SNORTIN' ADVENTURE TOGETHER AND ALL, JUST LIKE IN THE FUNNY PAPERS --
SHUT UP, SAM.
SEE? THERE HE GOES AGAIN.
YOU THINK EVERYTHING'S SUCH A BIG JOKE!
YEAH. I PURT' NEAR SPLIT MY SIDES MOST OF THE TIME. WHO WOULDN'T?
... IT'S JUST NOT FAIR.
HUH? WHAT AIN'T?
NONE OF IT.
BOY, YOU SAID A MOUTHFUL.

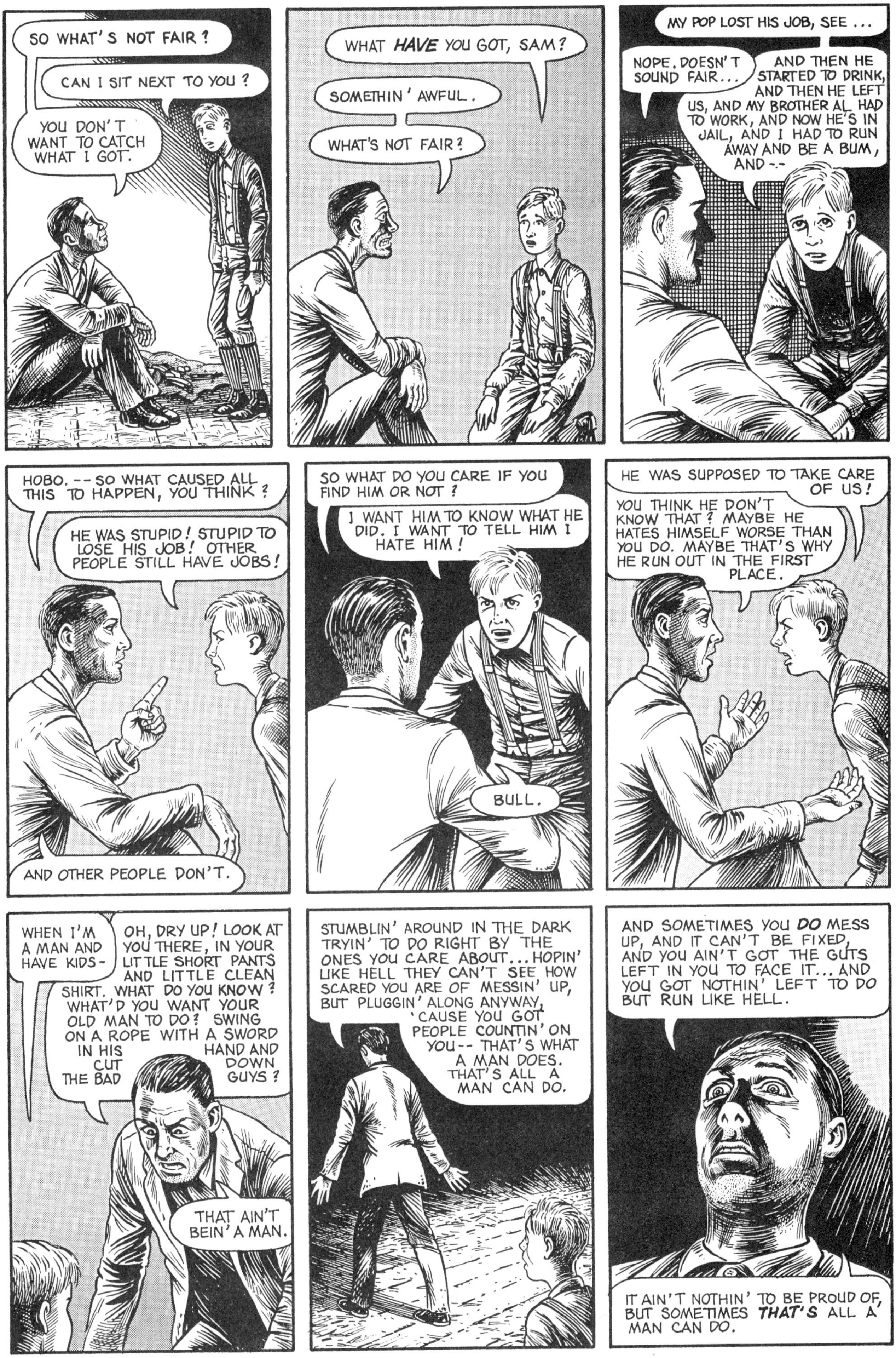
SO WHAT'S NOT FAIR?
CAN I SIT NEXT TO YOU?
YOU DON'T WANT TO CATCH WHAT I GOT.
WHAT HAVE YOU GOT, SAM?
SOMETHIN' AWFUL.
WHAT'S NOT FAIR?
MY POP LOST HIS JOB, SEE ...
NOPE. DOESN'T SOUND FAIR...
AND THEN HE STARTED TO DRINK, AND THEN HE LEFT US, AND MY BROTHER AL HAD TO WORK, AND NOW HE'S IN JAIL, AND I HAD TO RUN AWAY AND BE A BUM, AND--
HOBO. --SO WHAT CAUSED ALL THIS TO HAPPEN, YOU THINK?
HE WAS STUPID! STUPID TO LOSE HIS JOB! OTHER PEOPLE STILL HAVE JOBS!
AND OTHER PEOPLE DON'T.
SO WHAT DO YOU CARE IF YOU FIND HIM OR NOT?
I WANT HIM TO KNOW WHAT HE DID. I WANT TO TELL HIM I HATE HIM!
BULL.
HE WAS SUPPOSED TO TAKE CARE OF US!
YOU THINK HE DON'T KNOW THAT? MAYBE HE HATES HIMSELF WORSE THAN YOU DO. MAYBE THAT'S WHY HE RUN OUT IN THE FIRST PLACE.
WHEN I'M A MAN AND HAVE KIDS-
OH, DRY UP! LOOK AT YOU THERE, IN YOUR LITTLE SHORT PANTS AND LITTLE CLEAN SHIRT. WHAT DO YOU KNOW? WHAT'D YOU WANT YOUR OLD MAN TO DO? SWING ON A ROPE WITH A SWORD IN HIS HAND AND CUT DOWN THE BAD GUYS?
THAT AIN'T BEIN' A MAN.
STUMBLIN' AROUND IN THE DARK TRYIN' TO DO RIGHT BY THE ONES YOU CARE ABOUT... HOPIN' LIKE HELL THEY CAN'T SEE HOW SCARED YOU ARE OF MESSIN' UP, BUT PLUGGIN' ALONG ANYWAY, 'CAUSE YOU GOT PEOPLE COUNTIN' ON YOU-- THAT'S WHAT A MAN DOES. THAT'S ALL A MAN CAN DO.
AND SOMETIMES YOU DO MESS UP, AND IT CAN'T BE FIXED, AND YOU AIN'T GOT THE GUTS LEFT IN YOU TO FACE IT... AND YOU GOT NOTHIN' LEFT TO DO BUT RUN LIKE HELL.
IT AIN'T NOTHIN' TO BE PROUD OF, BUT SOMETIMES THAT'S ALL A MAN CAN DO.

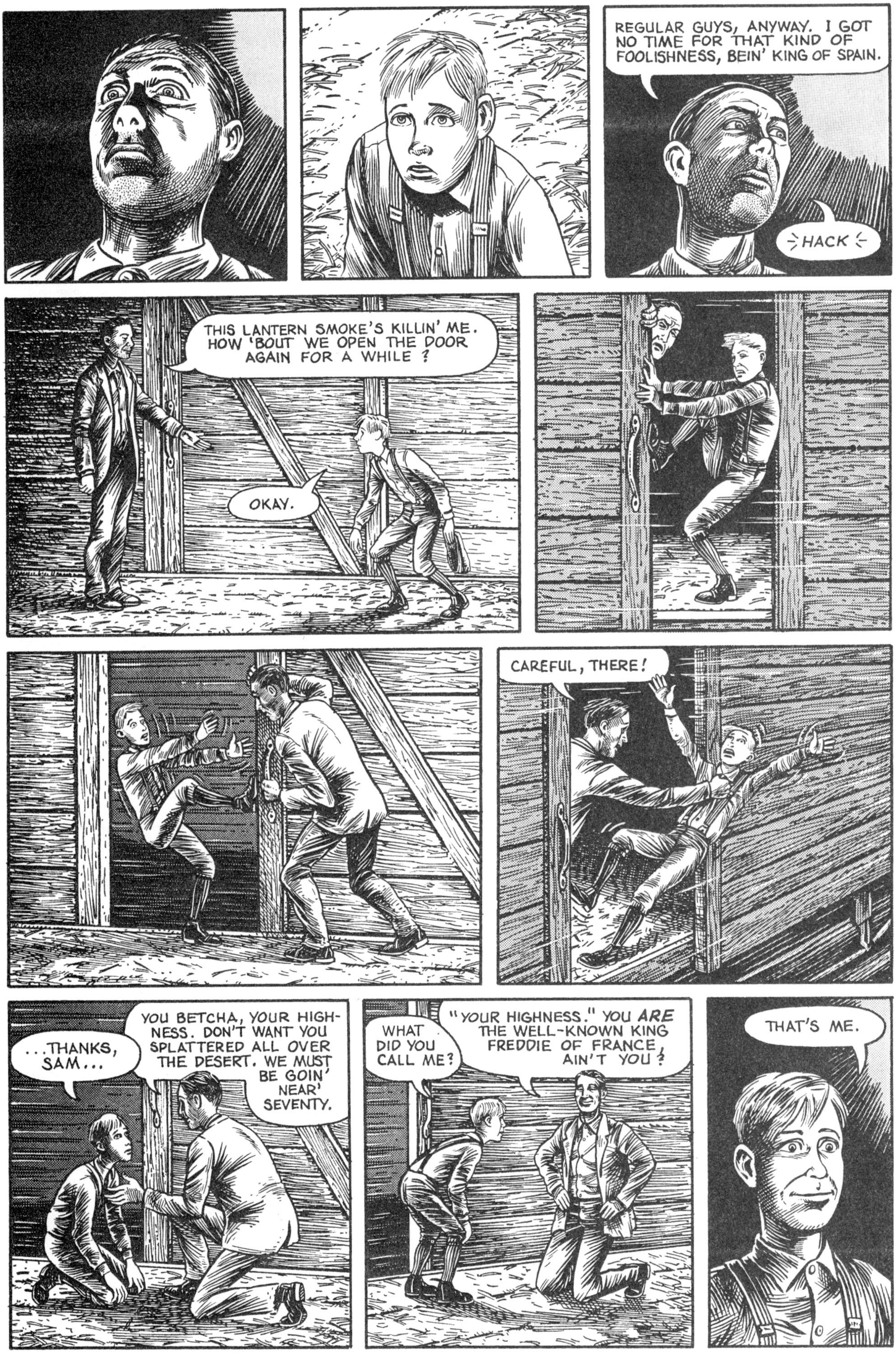
REGULAR GUYS, ANYWAY. I GOT NO TIME FOR THAT KIND OF FOOLISHNESS, BEIN' KING OF SPAIN.
HACK
THIS LANTERN SMOKE'S KILLIN' ME. HOW 'BOUT WE OPEN THE DOOR AGAIN FOR A WHILE ?
OKAY.
CAREFUL, THERE!
...THANKS, SAM...
YOU BETCHA, YOUR HIGHNESS. DON'T WANT YOU SPLATTERED ALL OVER THE DESERT. WE MUST BE GOIN' NEAR' SEVENTY.
WHAT DID YOU CALL ME?
"YOUR HIGHNESS." YOU ARE THE WELL-KNOWN KING FREDDIE OF FRANCE, AIN'T YOU ?
THAT'S ME.

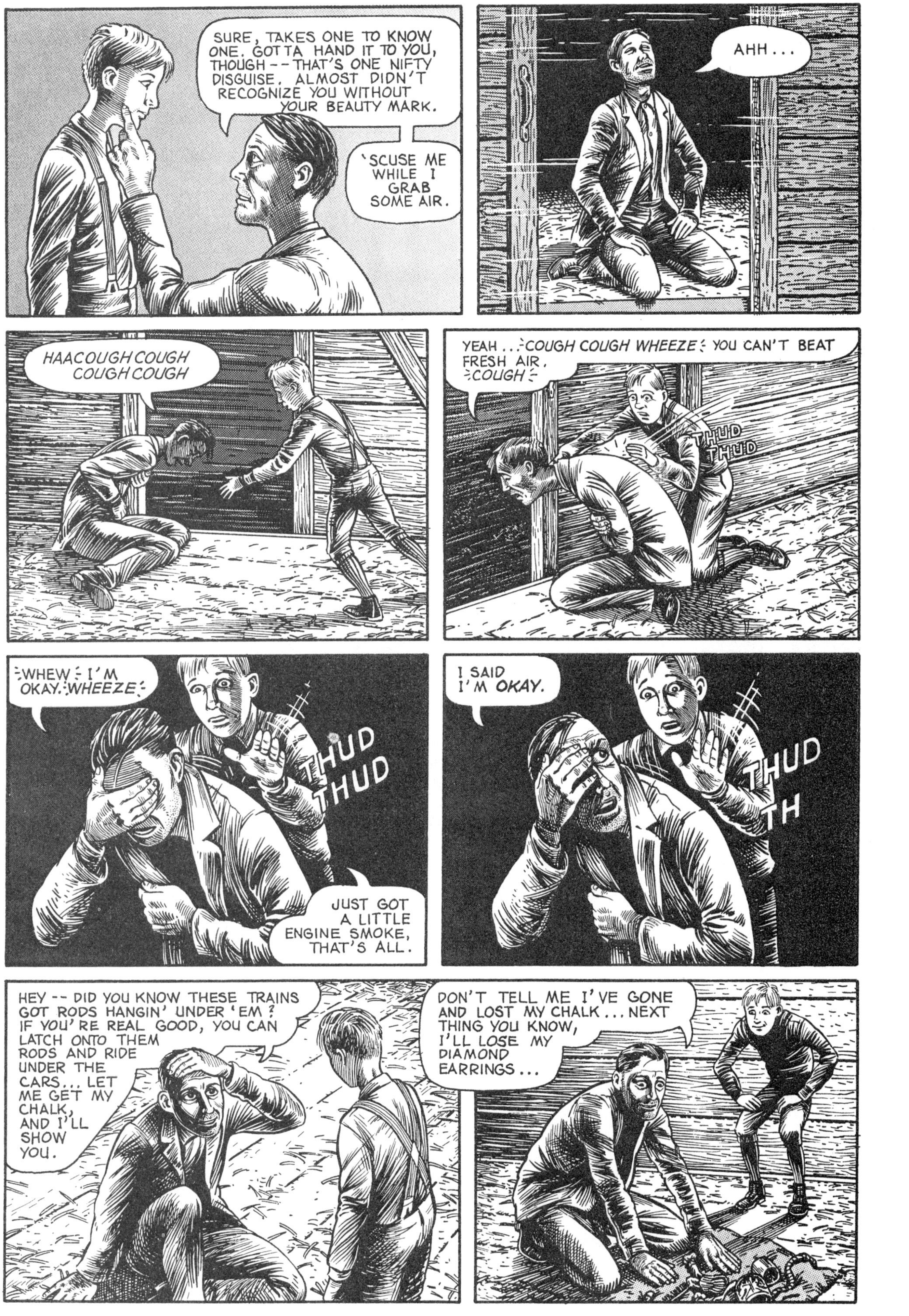
SURE, TAKES ONE TO KNOW ONE. GOTTA HAND IT TO YOU, THOUGH -- THAT'S ONE NIFTY DISGUISE. ALMOST DIDN'T RECOGNIZE YOU WITHOUT YOUR BEAUTY MARK.
'SCUSE ME WHILE I GRAB SOME AIR.
AHH...
HAACOUGH COUGH COUGH COUGH
YEAH... COUGH COUGH WHEEZE YOU CAN'T BEAT FRESH AIR. COUGH
THUD THUD
WHEW I'M OKAY. WHEEZE
THUD THUD
JUST GOT A LITTLE ENGINE SMOKE, THAT'S ALL.
I SAID I'M OKAY.
THUD TH
HEY -- DID YOU KNOW THESE TRAINS GOT RODS HANGIN' UNDER 'EM? IF YOU'RE REAL GOOD, YOU CAN LATCH ONTO THEM RODS AND RIDE UNDER THE CARS... LET ME GET MY CHALK, AND I'LL SHOW YOU.
DON'T TELL ME I'VE GONE AND LOST MY CHALK... NEXT THING YOU KNOW, I'LL LOSE MY DIAMOND EARRINGS...

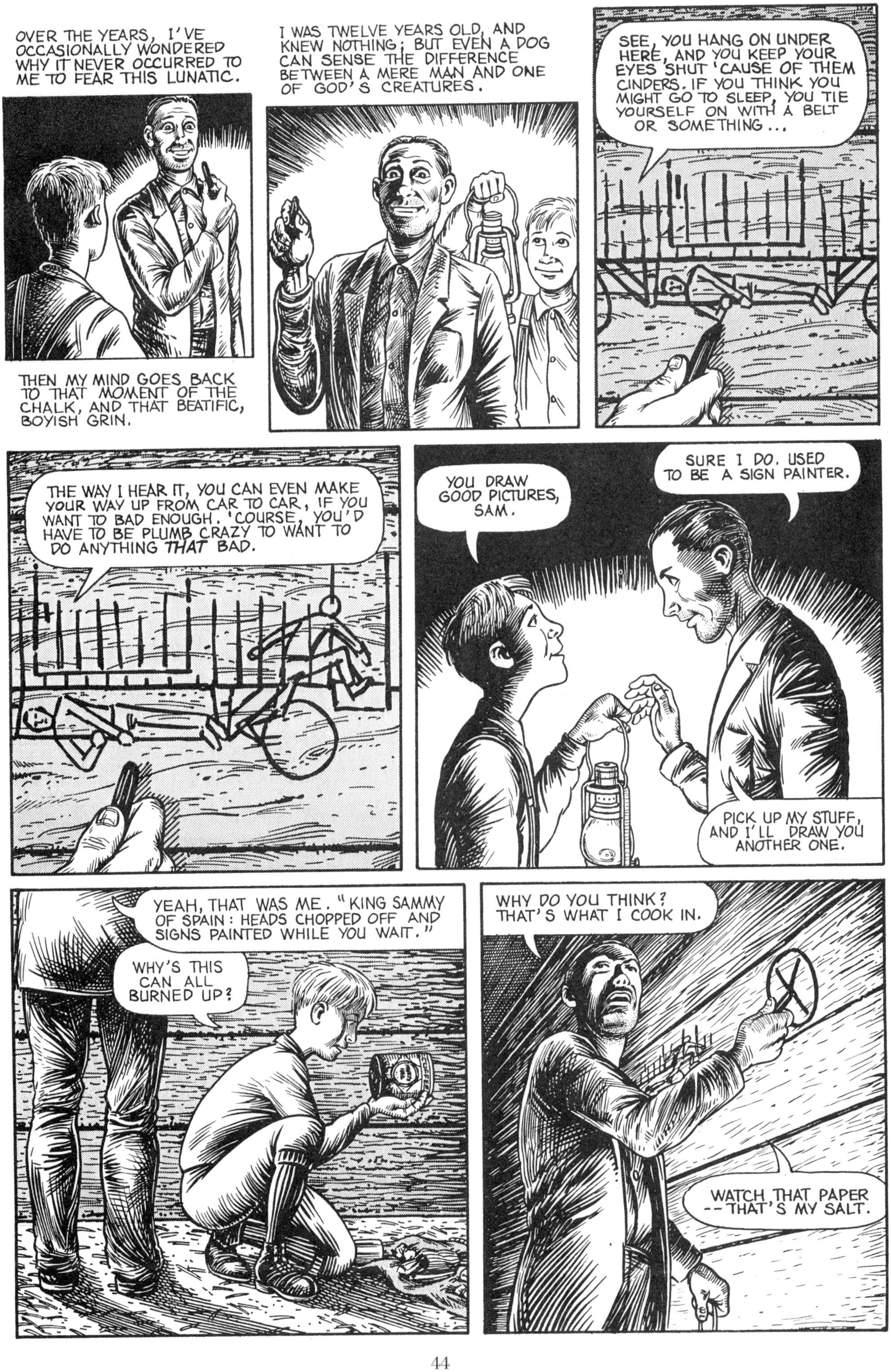
OVER THE YEARS, I'VE OCCASIONALLY WONDERED WHY IT NEVER OCCURRED TO ME TO FEAR THIS LUNATIC.
THEN MY MIND GOES BACK TO THAT MOMENT OF THE CHALK, AND THAT BEATIFIC, BOYISH GRIN.
I WAS TWELVE YEARS OLD, AND KNEW NOTHING; BUT EVEN A DOG CAN SENSE THE DIFFERENCE BETWEEN A MERE MAN AND ONE OF GOD'S CREATURES.
SEE, YOU HANG ON UNDER HERE, AND YOU KEEP YOUR EYES SHUT 'CAUSE OF THEM CINDERS. IF YOU THINK YOU MIGHT GO TO SLEEP, YOU TIE YOURSELF ON WITH A BELT OR SOMETHING...
THE WAY I HEAR IT, YOU CAN EVEN MAKE YOUR WAY UP FROM CAR TO CAR, IF YOU WANT TO BAD ENOUGH. 'COURSE, YOU'D HAVE TO BE PLUMB CRAZY TO WANT TO DO ANYTHING *THAT* BAD.
YOU DRAW GOOD PICTURES, SAM.
SURE I DO. USED TO BE A SIGN PAINTER.
PICK UP MY STUFF, AND I'LL DRAW YOU ANOTHER ONE.
YEAH, THAT WAS ME. "KING SAMMY OF SPAIN: HEADS CHOPPED OFF AND SIGNS PAINTED WHILE YOU WAIT."
WHY'S THIS CAN ALL BURNED UP?
WHY DO YOU THINK? THAT'S WHAT I COOK IN.
WATCH THAT PAPER -- THAT'S MY SALT.

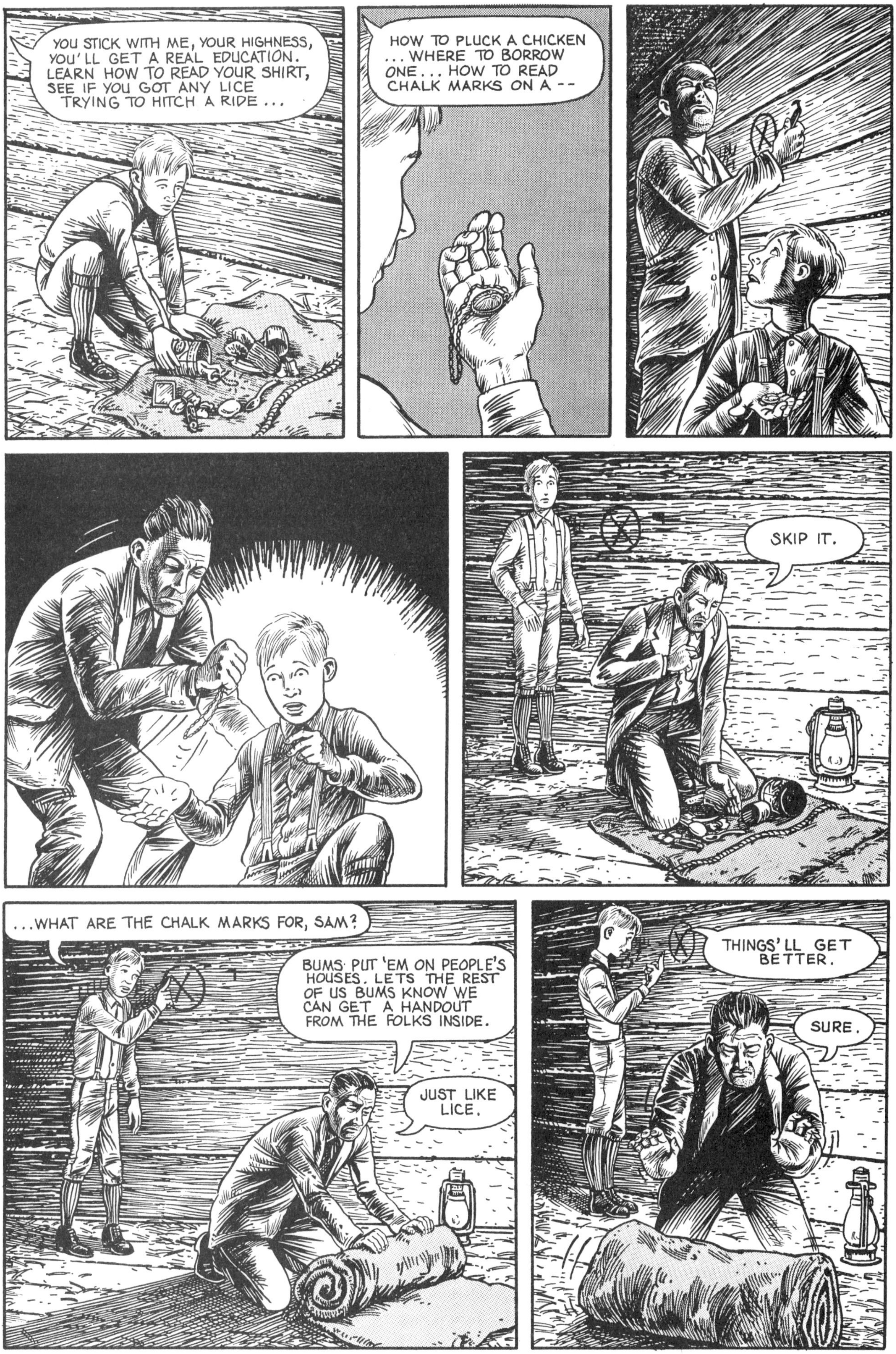
YOU STICK WITH ME, YOUR HIGHNESS, YOU'LL GET A REAL EDUCATION. LEARN HOW TO READ YOUR SHIRT, SEE IF YOU GOT ANY LICE TRYING TO HITCH A RIDE ...
HOW TO PLUCK A CHICKEN ... WHERE TO BORROW ONE ... HOW TO READ CHALK MARKS ON A --
SKIP IT.
...WHAT ARE THE CHALK MARKS FOR, SAM?
BUMS PUT 'EM ON PEOPLE'S HOUSES. LETS THE REST OF US BUMS KNOW WE CAN GET A HANDOUT FROM THE FOLKS INSIDE.
JUST LIKE LICE.
THINGS'LL GET BETTER.
SURE.

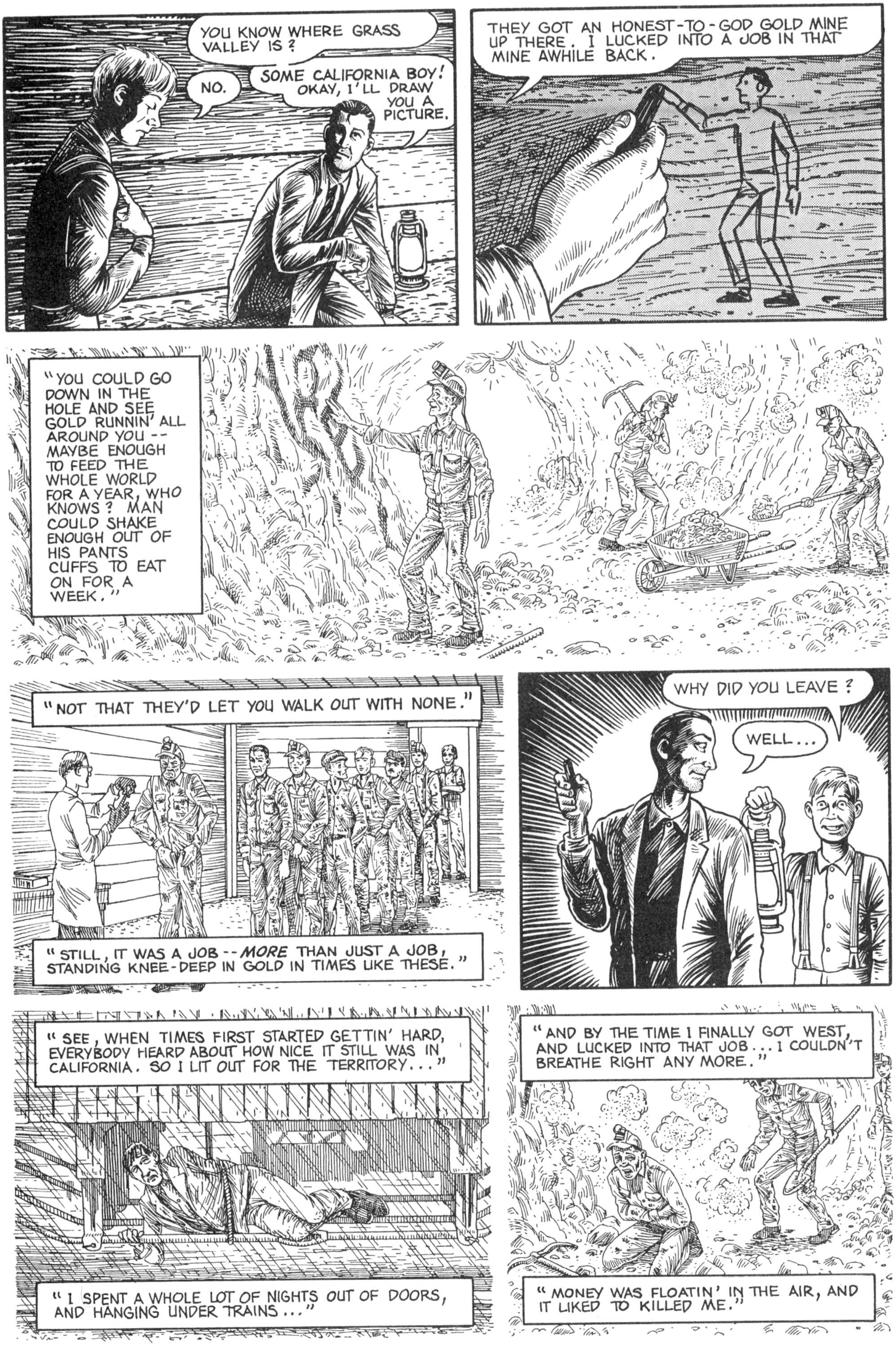

YOU KNOW WHERE GRASS VALLEY IS?
NO.
SOME CALIFORNIA BOY! OKAY, I'LL DRAW YOU A PICTURE.
THEY GOT AN HONEST-TO-GOD GOLD MINE UP THERE. I LUCKED INTO A JOB IN THAT MINE AWHILE BACK.
"YOU COULD GO DOWN IN THE HOLE AND SEE GOLD RUNNIN' ALL AROUND YOU -- MAYBE ENOUGH TO FEED THE WHOLE WORLD FOR A YEAR, WHO KNOWS? MAN COULD SHAKE ENOUGH OUT OF HIS PANTS CUFFS TO EAT ON FOR A WEEK."
"NOT THAT THEY'D LET YOU WALK OUT WITH NONE."
"STILL, IT WAS A JOB -- MORE THAN JUST A JOB, STANDING KNEE-DEEP IN GOLD IN TIMES LIKE THESE."
WHY DID YOU LEAVE?
WELL...
"SEE, WHEN TIMES FIRST STARTED GETTIN' HARD, EVERYBODY HEARD ABOUT HOW NICE IT STILL WAS IN CALIFORNIA. SO I LIT OUT FOR THE TERRITORY..."
"I SPENT A WHOLE LOT OF NIGHTS OUT OF DOORS, AND HANGING UNDER TRAINS..."
"AND BY THE TIME I FINALLY GOT WEST, AND LUCKED INTO THAT JOB... I COULDN'T BREATHE RIGHT ANY MORE."
"MONEY WAS FLOATIN' IN THE AIR, AND IT LIKED TO KILLED ME."

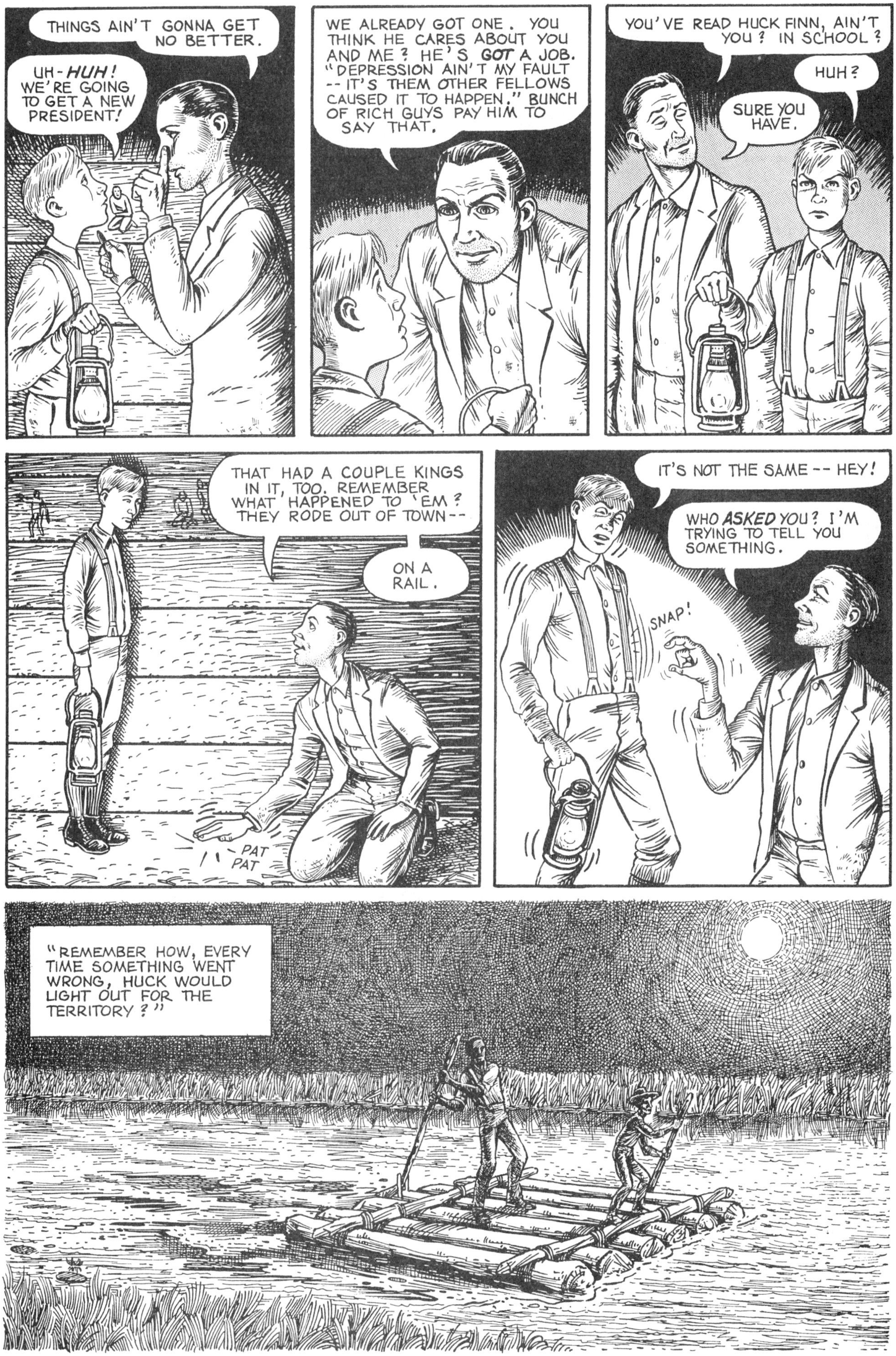
THINGS AIN'T GONNA GET NO BETTER.
UH-HUH! WE'RE GOING TO GET A NEW PRESIDENT!
WE ALREADY GOT ONE. YOU THINK HE CARES ABOUT YOU AND ME? HE'S GOT A JOB. "DEPRESSION AIN'T MY FAULT -- IT'S THEM OTHER FELLOWS CAUSED IT TO HAPPEN." BUNCH OF RICH GUYS PAY HIM TO SAY THAT.
YOU'VE READ HUCK FINN, AIN'T YOU? IN SCHOOL?
HUH?
SURE YOU HAVE.
THAT HAD A COUPLE KINGS IN IT, TOO. REMEMBER WHAT HAPPENED TO 'EM? THEY RODE OUT OF TOWN--
ON A RAIL.
PAT PAT
IT'S NOT THE SAME -- HEY!
WHO ASKED YOU? I'M TRYING TO TELL YOU SOMETHING.
SNAP!
"REMEMBER HOW, EVERY TIME SOMETHING WENT WRONG, HUCK WOULD LIGHT OUT FOR THE TERRITORY?"

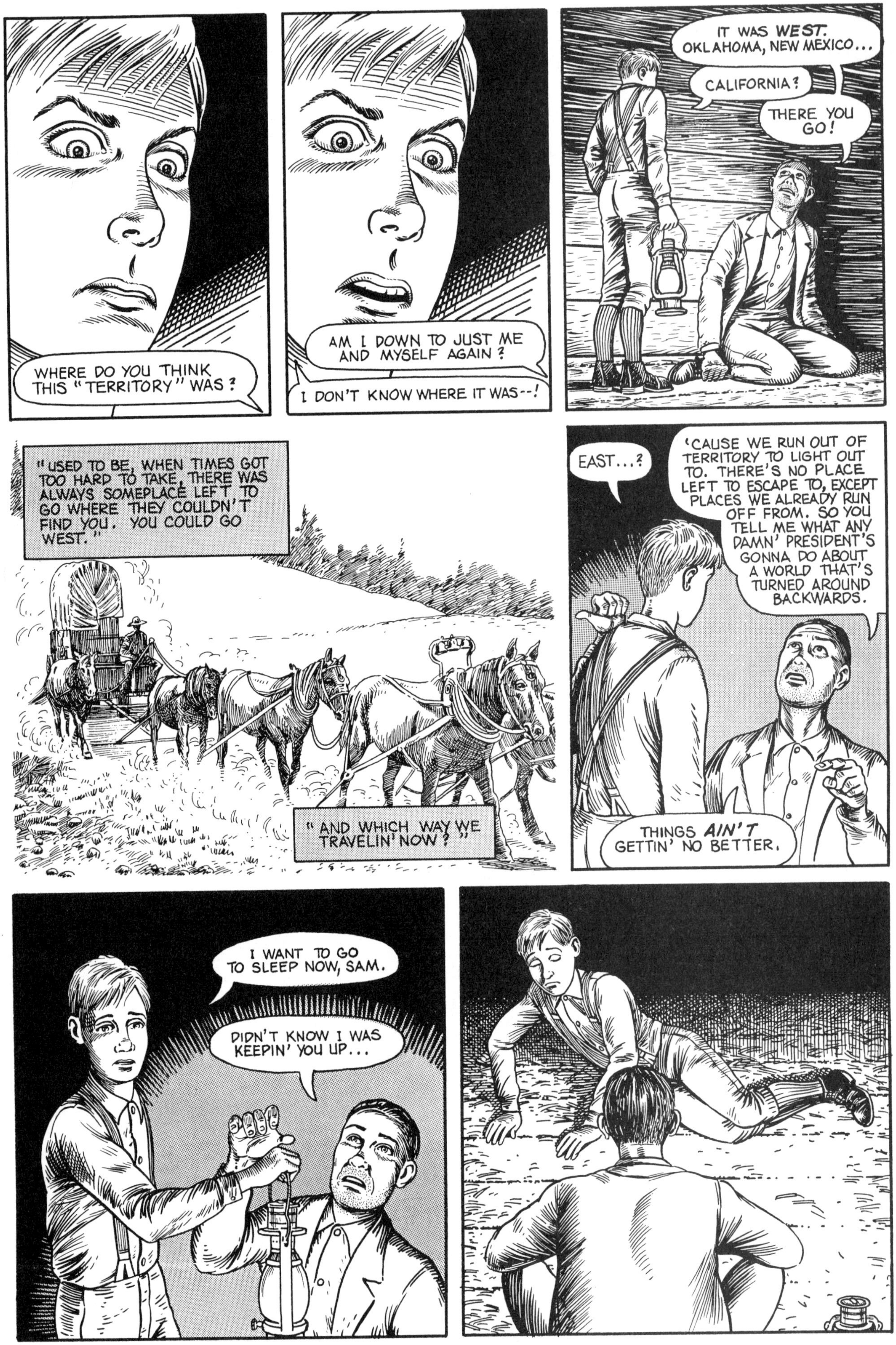
WHERE DO YOU THINK THIS "TERRITORY" WAS?
AM I DOWN TO JUST ME AND MYSELF AGAIN?
I DON'T KNOW WHERE IT WAS--!
IT WAS WEST. OKLAHOMA, NEW MEXICO...
CALIFORNIA?
THERE YOU GO!
"USED TO BE, WHEN TIMES GOT TOO HARD TO TAKE, THERE WAS ALWAYS SOMEPLACE LEFT TO GO WHERE THEY COULDN'T FIND YOU. YOU COULD GO WEST."
"AND WHICH WAY WE TRAVELIN' NOW?"
EAST...?
'CAUSE WE RUN OUT OF TERRITORY TO LIGHT OUT TO. THERE'S NO PLACE LEFT TO ESCAPE TO, EXCEPT PLACES WE ALREADY RUN OFF FROM. SO YOU TELL ME WHAT ANY DAMN' PRESIDENT'S GONNA DO ABOUT A WORLD THAT'S TURNED AROUND BACKWARDS.
THINGS AIN'T GETTIN' NO BETTER.
I WANT TO GO TO SLEEP NOW, SAM.
DIDN'T KNOW I WAS KEEPIN' YOU UP...

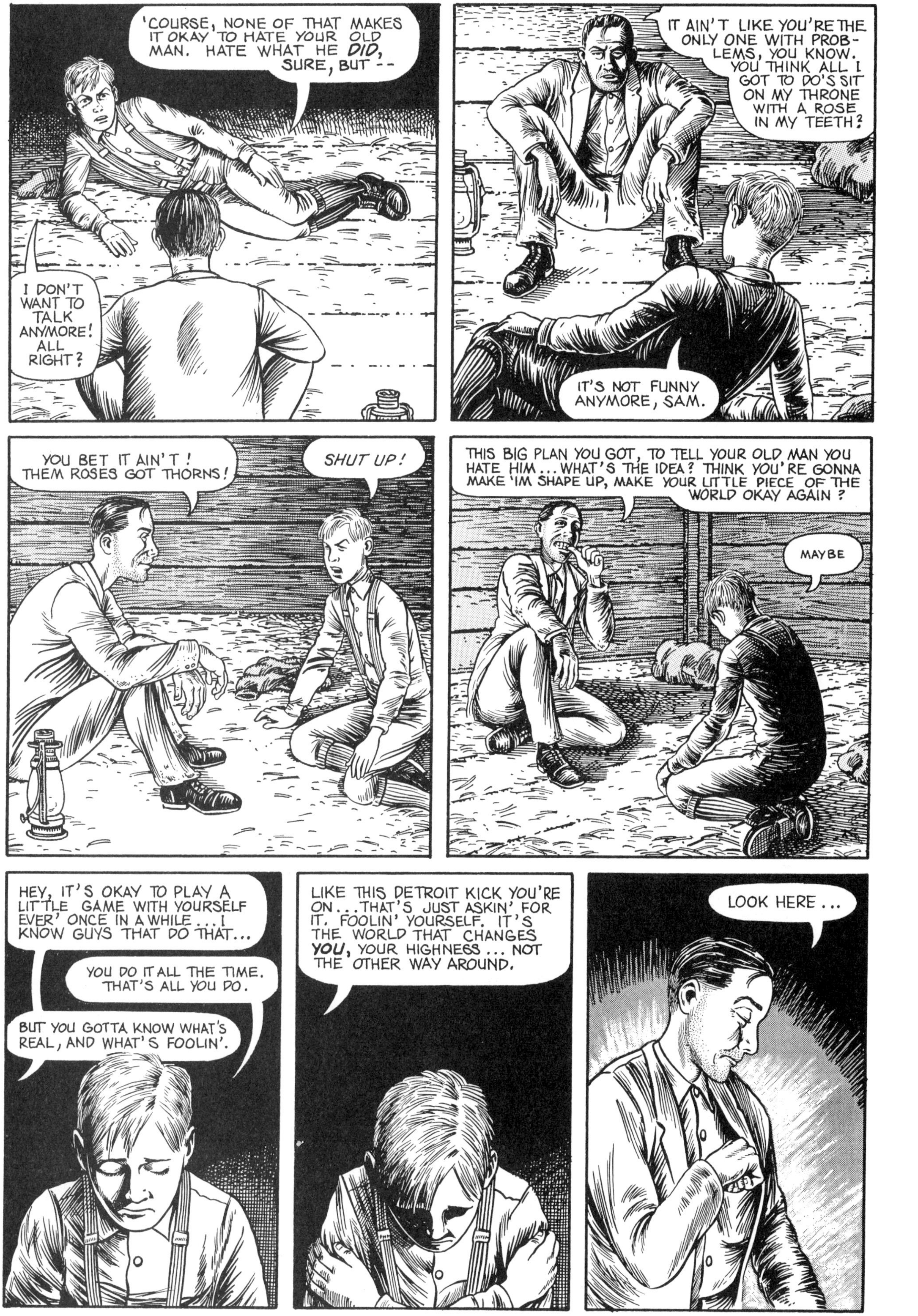
'COURSE, NONE OF THAT MAKES IT OKAY TO HATE YOUR OLD MAN. HATE WHAT HE *DID*, SURE, BUT --
I DON'T WANT TO TALK ANYMORE! ALL RIGHT?
IT AIN'T LIKE *YOU'RE* THE ONLY ONE WITH PROB-LEMS, YOU KNOW. YOU THINK ALL I GOT TO DO'S SIT ON MY THRONE WITH A ROSE IN MY TEETH?
IT'S NOT FUNNY ANYMORE, SAM.
YOU BET IT AIN'T! THEM ROSES GOT THORNS!
SHUT UP!
THIS BIG PLAN *YOU* GOT, TO TELL *YOUR* OLD MAN YOU HATE HIM... WHAT'S THE IDEA? THINK *YOU'RE* GONNA MAKE 'IM SHAPE UP, MAKE YOUR LITTLE PIECE OF THE WORLD OKAY AGAIN?
MAYBE
HEY, IT'S OKAY TO PLAY A LITTLE GAME WITH YOURSELF EVER' ONCE IN A WHILE... I KNOW GUYS THAT DO THAT...
YOU DO IT ALL THE TIME. THAT'S ALL YOU DO.
BUT YOU GOTTA KNOW WHAT'S REAL, AND WHAT'S FOOLIN'.
LIKE THIS DETROIT KICK YOU'RE ON... THAT'S JUST ASKIN' FOR IT. FOOLIN' YOURSELF. IT'S THE WORLD THAT CHANGES **YOU**, YOUR HIGHNESS... NOT THE OTHER WAY AROUND.
LOOK HERE...

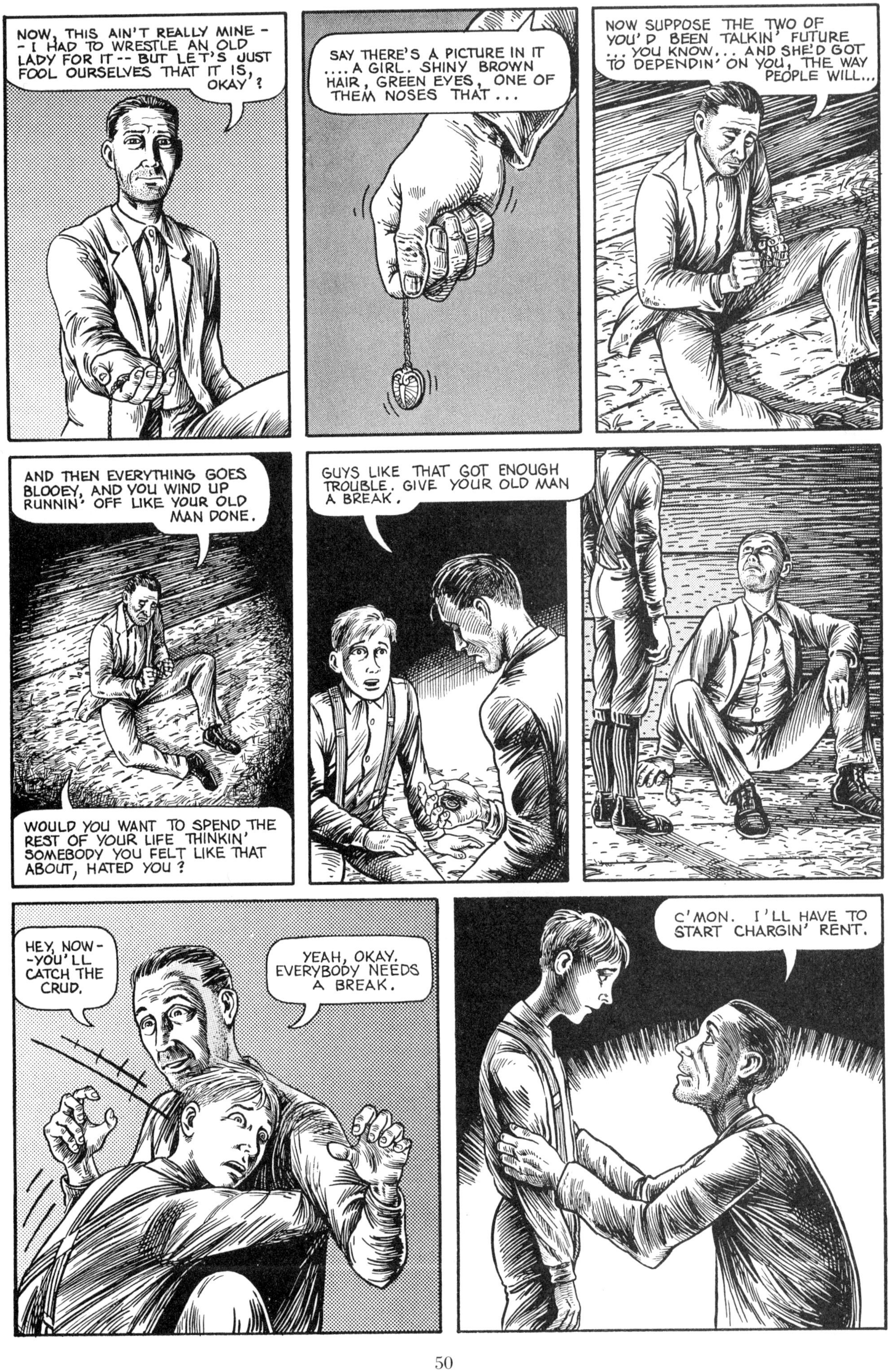
NOW, THIS AIN'T REALLY MINE - - I HAD TO WRESTLE AN OLD LADY FOR IT -- BUT LET'S JUST FOOL OURSELVES THAT IT IS, OKAY'?
SAY THERE'S A PICTURE IN IT ....A GIRL. SHINY BROWN HAIR, GREEN EYES, ONE OF THEM NOSES THAT ...
NOW SUPPOSE THE TWO OF YOU'D BEEN TALKIN' FUTURE ... YOU KNOW... AND SHE'D GOT TO DEPENDIN' ON YOU, THE WAY PEOPLE WILL...
AND THEN EVERYTHING GOES BLOOEY, AND YOU WIND UP RUNNIN' OFF LIKE YOUR OLD MAN DONE.
WOULD YOU WANT TO SPEND THE REST OF YOUR LIFE THINKIN' SOMEBODY YOU FELT LIKE THAT ABOUT, HATED YOU?
GUYS LIKE THAT GOT ENOUGH TROUBLE. GIVE YOUR OLD MAN A BREAK.
HEY, NOW- -YOU'LL CATCH THE CRUD.
YEAH, OKAY. EVERYBODY NEEDS A BREAK.
C'MON. I'LL HAVE TO START CHARGIN' RENT.

...WHAT DO YOU DO, SAM? WHERE DO YOU GO?

AIN'T REALLY THOUGHT ABOUT IT. MAYBE THAT SALLY IN EAST ST. LOUIS--THEY'LL PUT YOU UP A NIGHT OR TWO. CLEAN SHEETS. NO BUGS. YEAH, THAT'S FOR ME.

THEN WHAT?

WELL... MIGHT HEAD ON EAST. MIGHT TURN AROUND, HEAD BACK TO CALIFORNIA. DEPENDS ON HOW I FEEL. THAT'S THE NICE PART OF BEIN' KING OF SPAIN.

YOU JUST RIDE BACK AND FORTH LIKE THIS? FOREVER?

I WON'T DO NOTHIN' FOREVER.

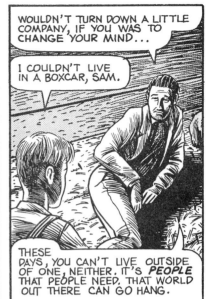

WOULDN'T TURN DOWN A LITTLE COMPANY, IF YOU WAS TO CHANGE YOUR MIND...

I COULDN'T LIVE IN A BOXCAR, SAM.

THESE DAYS, YOU CAN'T LIVE OUTSIDE OF ONE, NEITHER. IT'S *PEOPLE* THAT PEOPLE NEED. THAT WORLD OUT THERE CAN GO HANG.

BUT YOU'RE THE ORIGINAL LONE WOLF HISSELF, RIGHT? DON'T NEED NOBODY. DETROIT OR BUST.

WELL, IT'S BEEN NICE KNOWIN' YOU, YOUR HIGHNESS. -- LET'S CALL IT A NIGHT.

WOULDN'T BE NO BARGAIN HOOKIN' UP WITH ME, ANYWAY. I BEEN STARTIN' TO GET THE SWEATS. ANY DAY NOW MIGHT BE ALL SHE WROTE. YOU'RE BETTER OFF.

=WHEEZE=

I DIDN'T SURRENDER, I ESCAPED INTO SLEEP, PREFERRING THE DISQUIET OF MY DREAMS TO THE CERTAINTY OF WAKING. THERE WERE NO DREAMS, THOUGH, ONLY THE AWARENESS OF SOMETHING...

SOMETHING OR SOMEONE...

SOMEONE WALKING IN MY SLEEP.

MM...?

M--!

KKH-

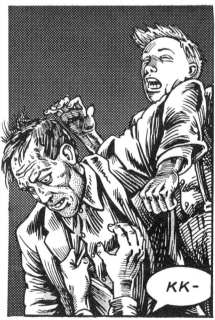

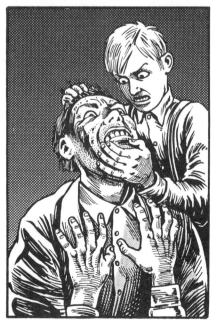

KK-

K-

52

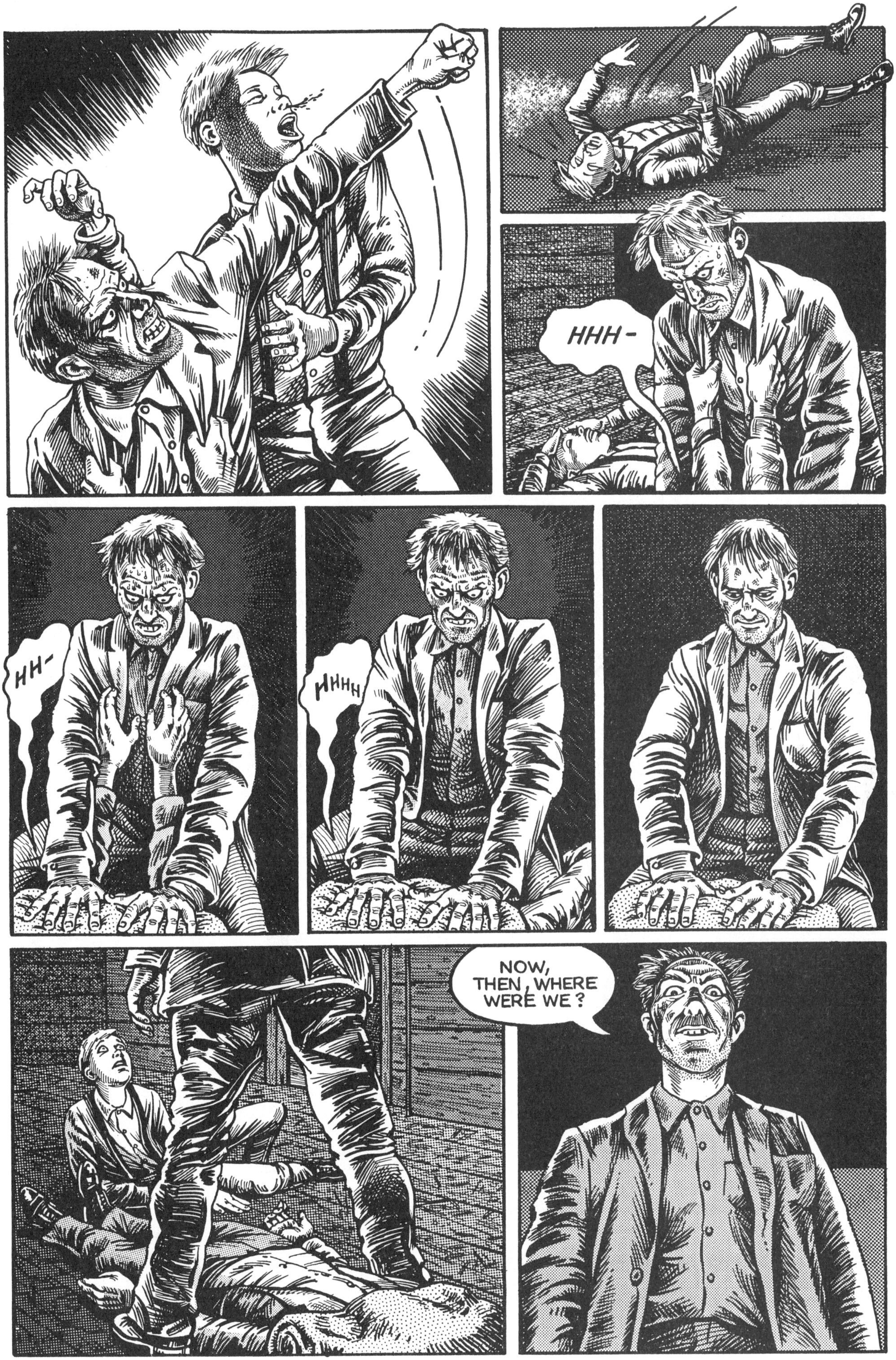
HHH-
HH-
HHHH
NOW, THEN, WHERE WERE WE?

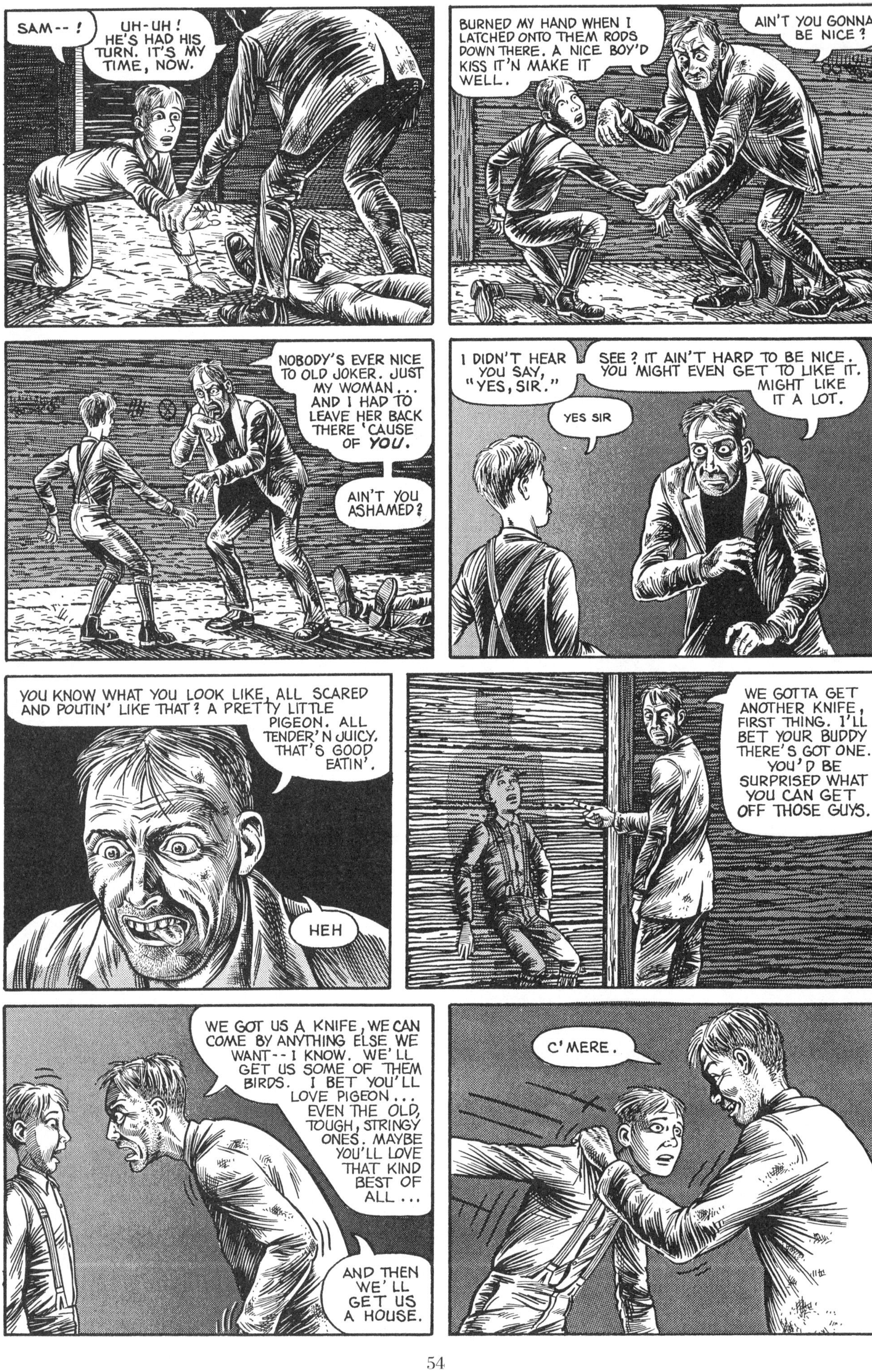
SAM-- !
UH-UH! HE'S HAD HIS TURN. IT'S MY TIME, NOW.
BURNED MY HAND WHEN I LATCHED ONTO THEM RODS DOWN THERE. A NICE BOY'D KISS IT'N MAKE IT WELL.
AIN'T YOU GONNA BE NICE?
NOBODY'S EVER NICE TO OLD JOKER. JUST MY WOMAN... AND I HAD TO LEAVE HER BACK THERE 'CAUSE OF YOU.
AIN'T YOU ASHAMED?
I DIDN'T HEAR YOU SAY, "YES, SIR."
YES SIR
SEE? IT AIN'T HARD TO BE NICE. YOU MIGHT EVEN GET TO LIKE IT. MIGHT LIKE IT A LOT.
YOU KNOW WHAT YOU LOOK LIKE, ALL SCARED AND POUTIN' LIKE THAT? A PRETTY LITTLE PIGEON. ALL TENDER'N JUICY. THAT'S GOOD EATIN'.
HEH
WE GOTTA GET ANOTHER KNIFE, FIRST THING. I'LL BET YOUR BUDDY THERE'S GOT ONE. YOU'D BE SURPRISED WHAT YOU CAN GET OFF THOSE GUYS.
WE GOT US A KNIFE, WE CAN COME BY ANYTHING ELSE WE WANT-- I KNOW. WE'LL GET US SOME OF THEM BIRDS. I BET YOU'LL LOVE PIGEON... EVEN THE OLD, TOUGH, STRINGY ONES. MAYBE YOU'LL LOVE THAT KIND BEST OF ALL...
AND THEN WE'LL GET US A HOUSE.
C'MERE.

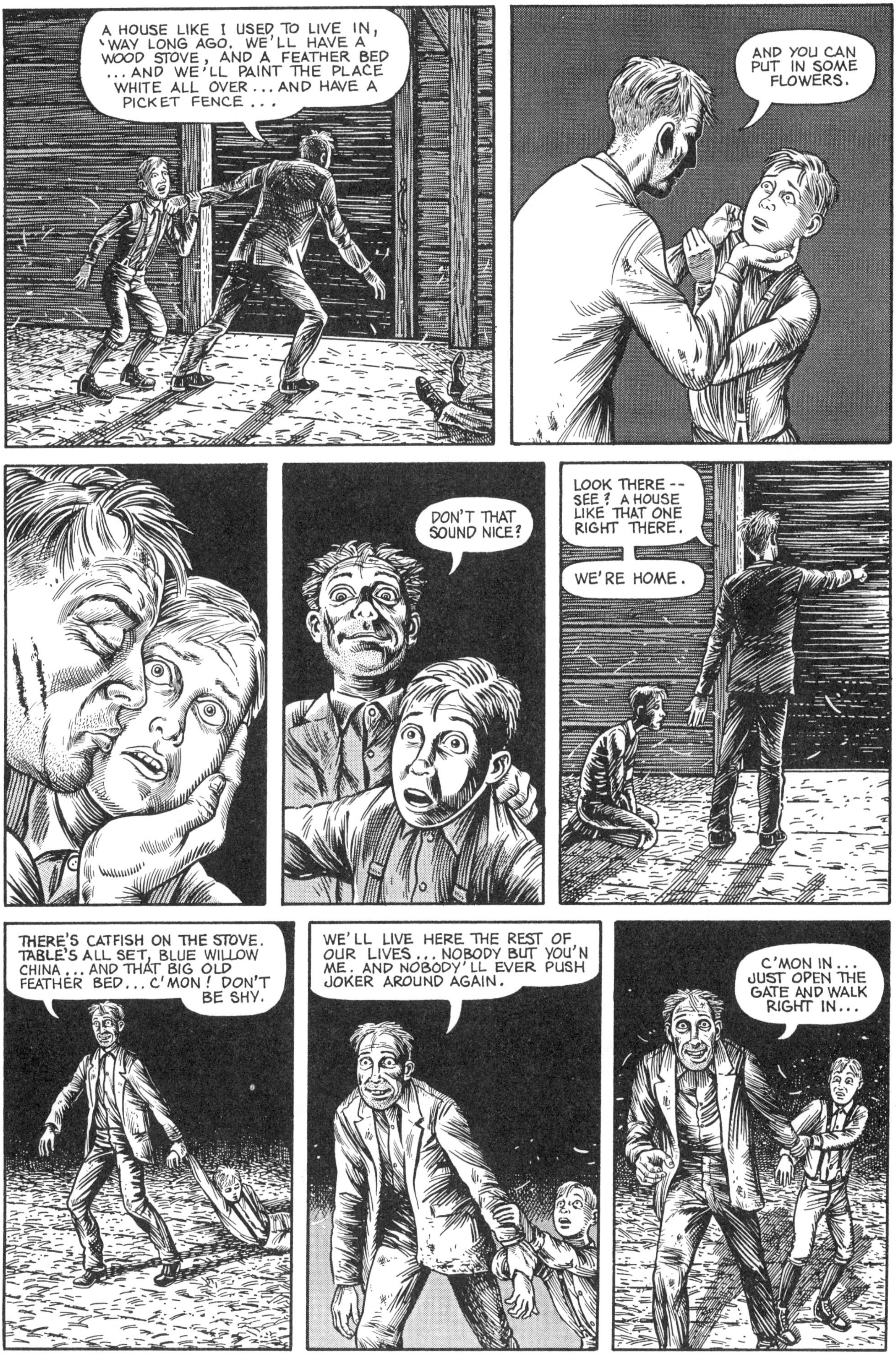
A HOUSE LIKE I USED TO LIVE IN, 'WAY LONG AGO. WE'LL HAVE A WOOD STOVE, AND A FEATHER BED ... AND WE'LL PAINT THE PLACE WHITE ALL OVER ... AND HAVE A PICKET FENCE ...
AND YOU CAN PUT IN SOME FLOWERS.
DON'T THAT SOUND NICE?
LOOK THERE -- SEE? A HOUSE LIKE THAT ONE RIGHT THERE.
WE'RE HOME.
THERE'S CATFISH ON THE STOVE. TABLE'S ALL SET, BLUE WILLOW CHINA ... AND THAT BIG OLD FEATHER BED ... C'MON! DON'T BE SHY.
WE'LL LIVE HERE THE REST OF OUR LIVES ... NOBODY BUT YOU'N ME. AND NOBODY'LL EVER PUSH JOKER AROUND AGAIN.
C'MON IN ... JUST OPEN THE GATE AND WALK RIGHT IN ...

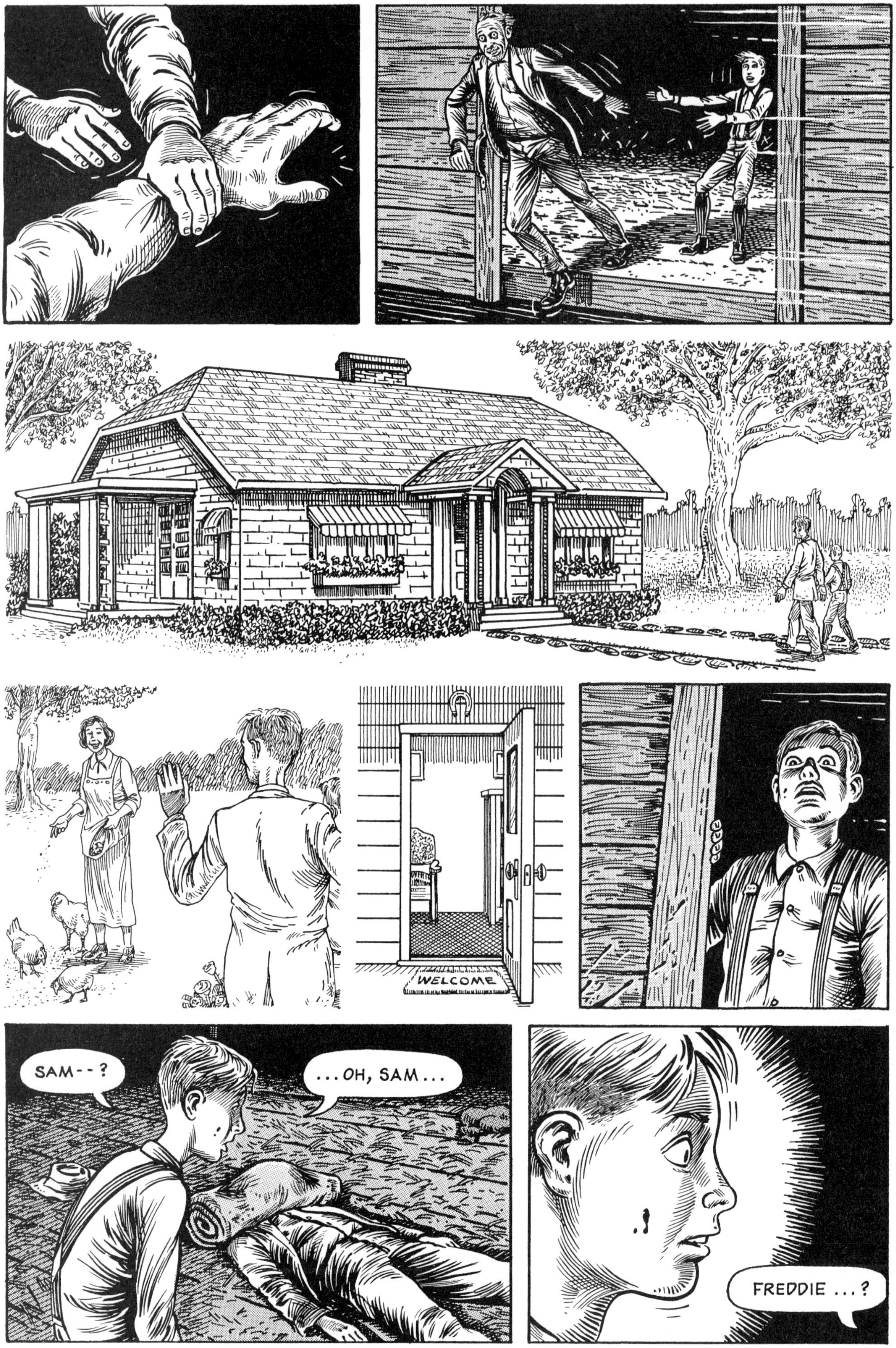
WELCOME
SAM--?
...OH, SAM...
FREDDIE ...?

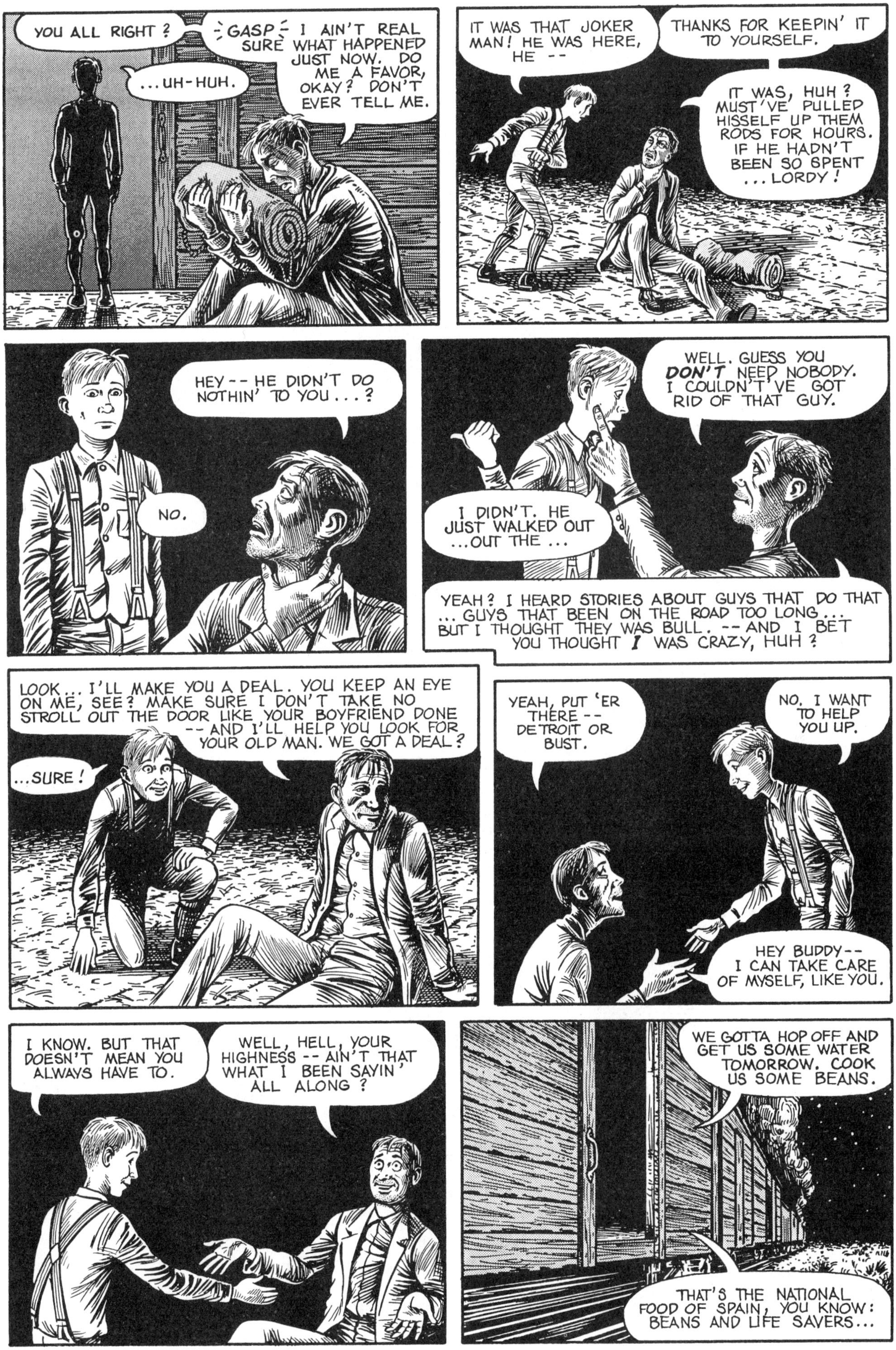
YOU ALL RIGHT ?
GASP I AIN'T REAL SURE WHAT HAPPENED JUST NOW. DO ME A FAVOR, OKAY? DON'T EVER TELL ME.
...UH-HUH.
IT WAS THAT JOKER MAN! HE WAS HERE, HE --
THANKS FOR KEEPIN' IT TO YOURSELF.
IT WAS, HUH ? MUST'VE PULLED HISSELF UP THEM RODS FOR HOURS. IF HE HADN'T BEEN SO SPENT ...LORDY !
HEY -- HE DIDN'T DO NOTHIN' TO YOU . . . ?
NO.
WELL. GUESS YOU DON'T NEED NOBODY. I COULDN'T'VE GOT RID OF THAT GUY.
I DIDN'T. HE JUST WALKED OUT ...OUT THE ...
YEAH ? I HEARD STORIES ABOUT GUYS THAT DO THAT ... GUYS THAT BEEN ON THE ROAD TOO LONG ... BUT I THOUGHT THEY WAS BULL. -- AND I BET YOU THOUGHT I WAS CRAZY, HUH ?
LOOK... I'LL MAKE YOU A DEAL. YOU KEEP AN EYE ON ME, SEE? MAKE SURE I DON'T TAKE NO STROLL OUT THE DOOR LIKE YOUR BOYFRIEND DONE -- AND I'LL HELP YOU LOOK FOR YOUR OLD MAN. WE GOT A DEAL ?
...SURE !
YEAH, PUT 'ER THERE -- DETROIT OR BUST.
NO. I WANT TO HELP YOU UP.
HEY BUDDY-- I CAN TAKE CARE OF MYSELF, LIKE YOU.
I KNOW. BUT THAT DOESN'T MEAN YOU ALWAYS HAVE TO.
WELL, HELL, YOUR HIGHNESS -- AIN'T THAT WHAT I BEEN SAYIN' ALL ALONG ?
WE GOTTA HOP OFF AND GET US SOME WATER TOMORROW. COOK US SOME BEANS.
THAT'S THE NATIONAL FOOD OF SPAIN, YOU KNOW: BEANS AND LIFE SAVERS...

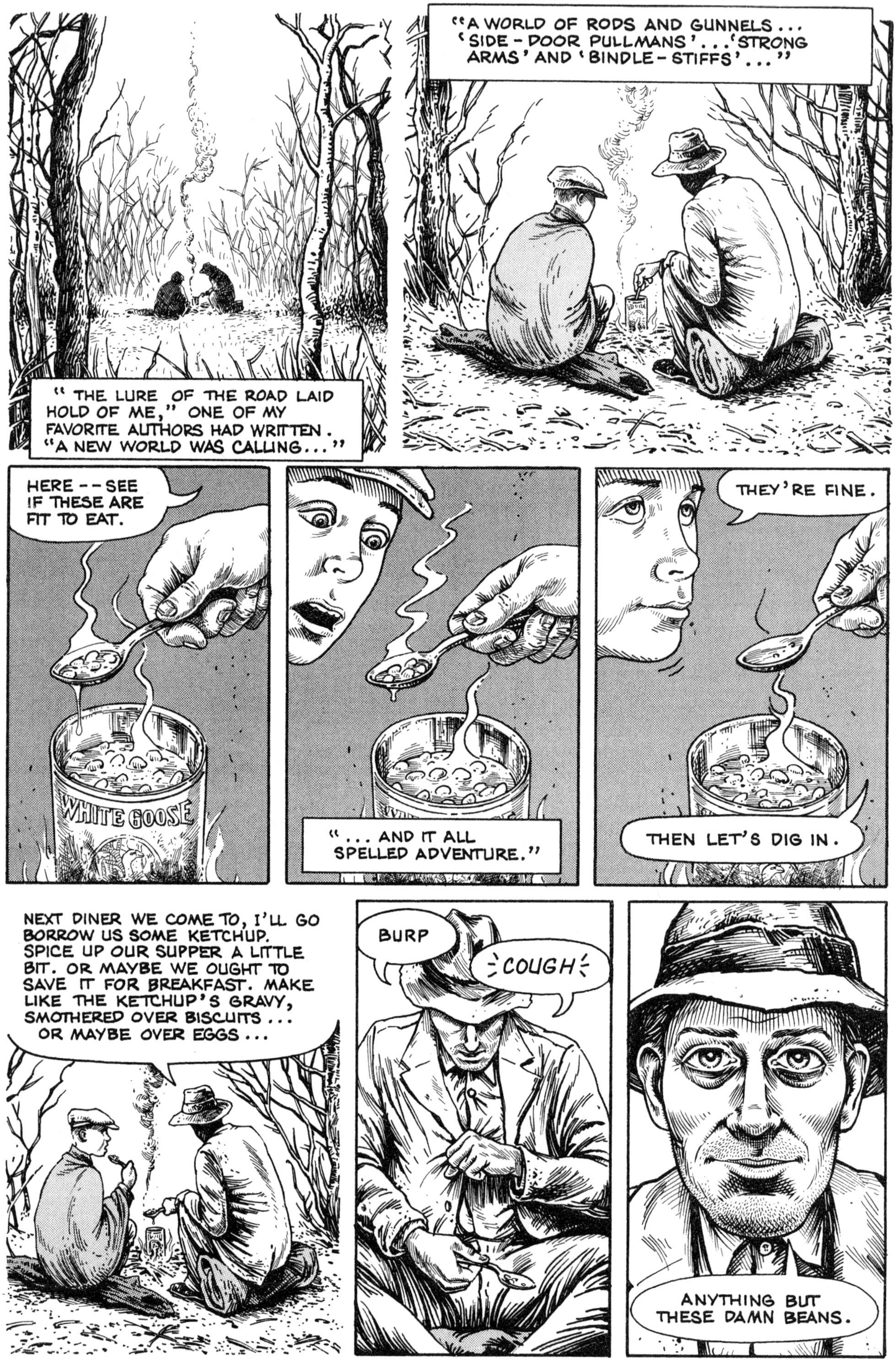
" THE LURE OF THE ROAD LAID HOLD OF ME," ONE OF MY FAVORITE AUTHORS HAD WRITTEN. "A NEW WORLD WAS CALLING..."
"A WORLD OF RODS AND GUNNELS... 'SIDE-DOOR PULLMANS'...'STRONG ARMS' AND 'BINDLE-STIFFS'..."
HERE--SEE IF THESE ARE FIT TO EAT.
WHITE GOOSE
"... AND IT ALL SPELLED ADVENTURE."
THEY'RE FINE.
THEN LET'S DIG IN.
NEXT DINER WE COME TO, I'LL GO BORROW US SOME KETCHUP. SPICE UP OUR SUPPER A LITTLE BIT. OR MAYBE WE OUGHT TO SAVE IT FOR BREAKFAST. MAKE LIKE THE KETCHUP'S GRAVY, SMOTHERED OVER BISCUITS... OR MAYBE OVER EGGS...
BURP
COUGH
ANYTHING BUT THESE DAMN BEANS.

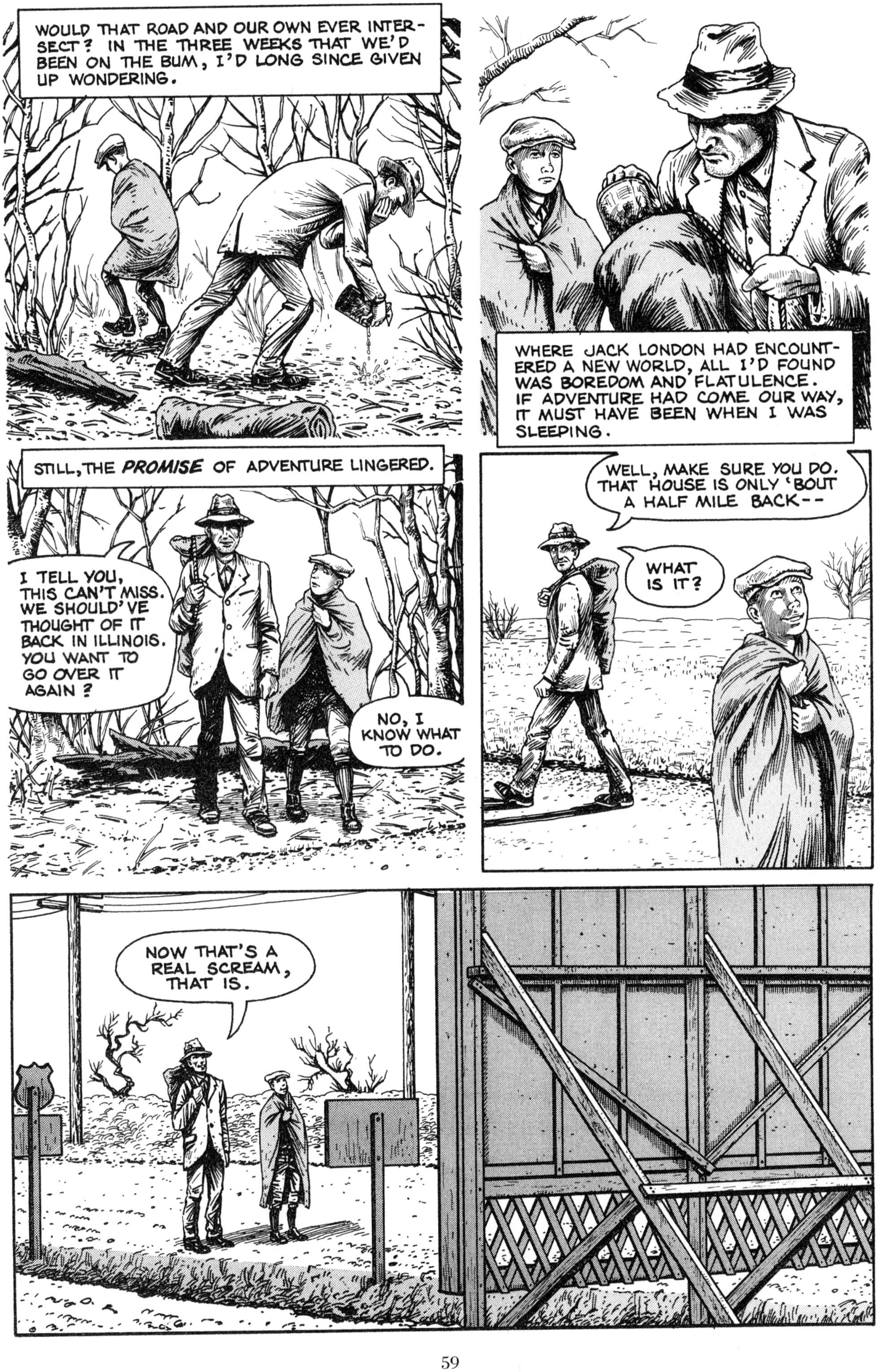
WOULD THAT ROAD AND OUR OWN EVER INTER-SECT? IN THE THREE WEEKS THAT WE'D BEEN ON THE BUM, I'D LONG SINCE GIVEN UP WONDERING.
WHERE JACK LONDON HAD ENCOUNT-ERED A NEW WORLD, ALL I'D FOUND WAS BOREDOM AND FLATULENCE. IF ADVENTURE HAD COME OUR WAY, IT MUST HAVE BEEN WHEN I WAS SLEEPING.
STILL, THE *PROMISE* OF ADVENTURE LINGERED.
I TELL YOU, THIS CAN'T MISS. WE SHOULD'VE THOUGHT OF IT BACK IN ILLINOIS. YOU WANT TO GO OVER IT AGAIN?
NO, I KNOW WHAT TO DO.
WELL, MAKE SURE YOU DO. THAT HOUSE IS ONLY 'BOUT A HALF MILE BACK--
WHAT IS IT?
NOW THAT'S A REAL SCREAM, THAT IS.

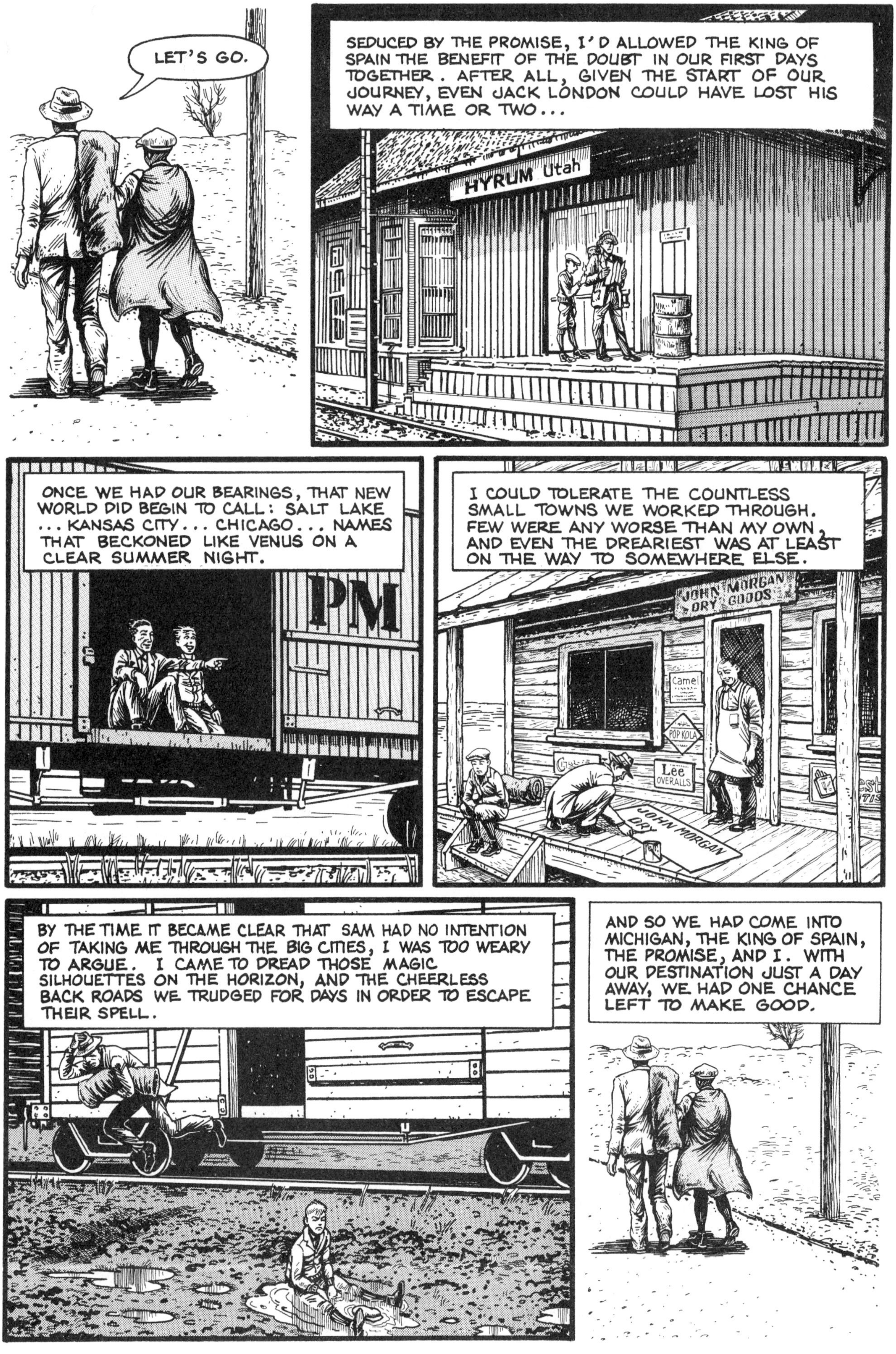
LET'S GO.
SEDUCED BY THE PROMISE, I'D ALLOWED THE KING OF SPAIN THE BENEFIT OF THE DOUBT IN OUR FIRST DAYS TOGETHER. AFTER ALL, GIVEN THE START OF OUR JOURNEY, EVEN JACK LONDON COULD HAVE LOST HIS WAY A TIME OR TWO...
HYRUM Utah
ONCE WE HAD OUR BEARINGS, THAT NEW WORLD DID BEGIN TO CALL: SALT LAKE ... KANSAS CITY... CHICAGO... NAMES THAT BECKONED LIKE VENUS ON A CLEAR SUMMER NIGHT.
PM
I COULD TOLERATE THE COUNTLESS SMALL TOWNS WE WORKED THROUGH. FEW WERE ANY WORSE THAN MY OWN, AND EVEN THE DREARIEST WAS AT LEAST ON THE WAY TO SOMEWHERE ELSE.
JOHN MORGAN DRY GOODS
Camel
POP KOLA
Lee OVERALLS
JOHN MORGAN DRY
BY THE TIME IT BECAME CLEAR THAT SAM HAD NO INTENTION OF TAKING ME THROUGH THE BIG CITIES, I WAS TOO WEARY TO ARGUE. I CAME TO DREAD THOSE MAGIC SILHOUETTES ON THE HORIZON, AND THE CHEERLESS BACK ROADS WE TRUDGED FOR DAYS IN ORDER TO ESCAPE THEIR SPELL.
AND SO WE HAD COME INTO MICHIGAN, THE KING OF SPAIN, THE PROMISE, AND I. WITH OUR DESTINATION JUST A DAY AWAY, WE HAD ONE CHANCE LEFT TO MAKE GOOD.

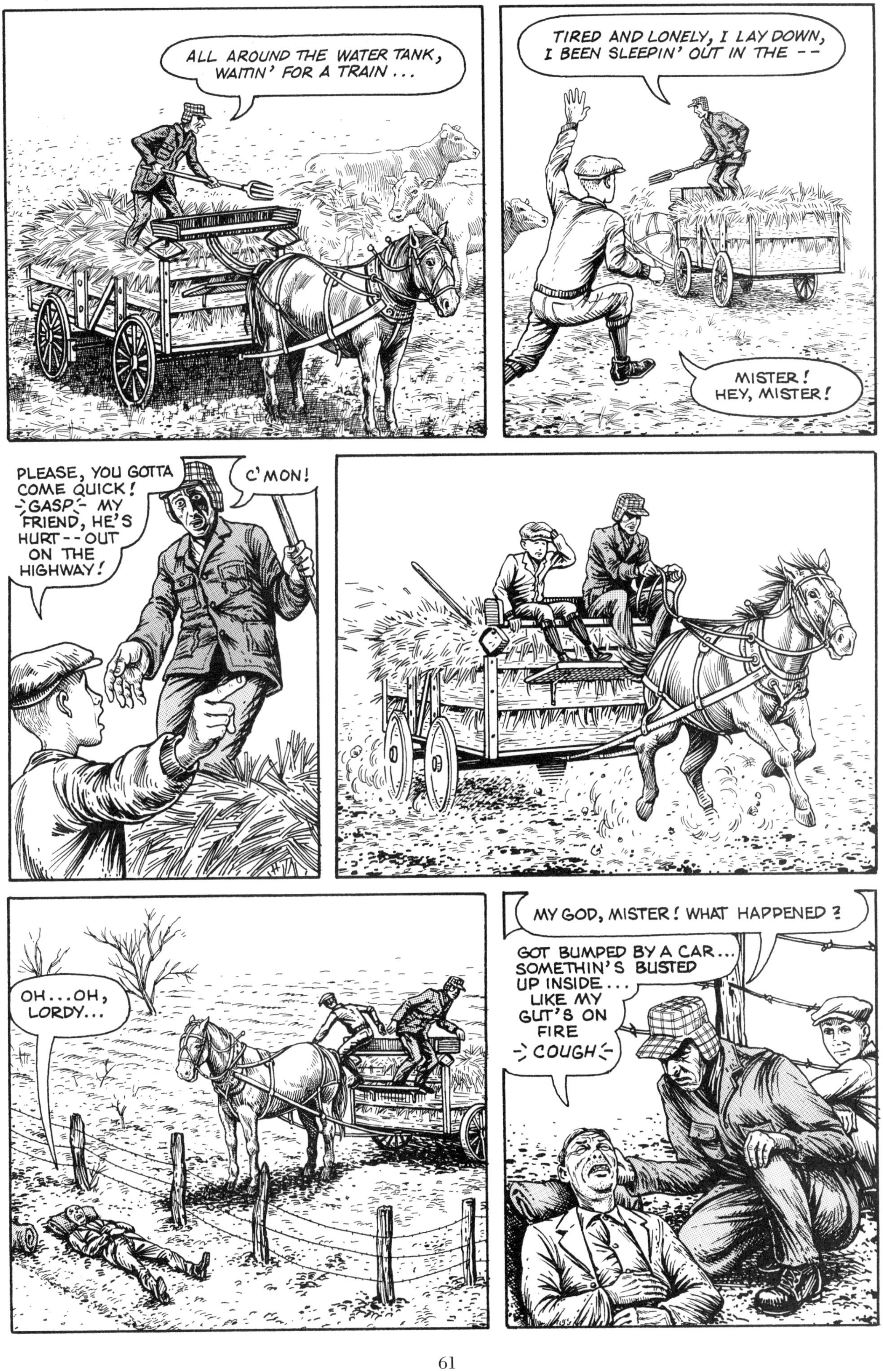
ALL AROUND THE WATER TANK, WAITIN' FOR A TRAIN...
TIRED AND LONELY, I LAY DOWN, I BEEN SLEEPIN' OUT IN THE --
MISTER! HEY, MISTER!
PLEASE, YOU GOTTA COME QUICK! -GASP- MY FRIEND, HE'S HURT--OUT ON THE HIGHWAY!
C'MON!
OH...OH, LORDY...
MY GOD, MISTER! WHAT HAPPENED?
GOT BUMPED BY A CAR... SOMETHIN'S BUSTED UP INSIDE... LIKE MY GUT'S ON FIRE -COUGH-

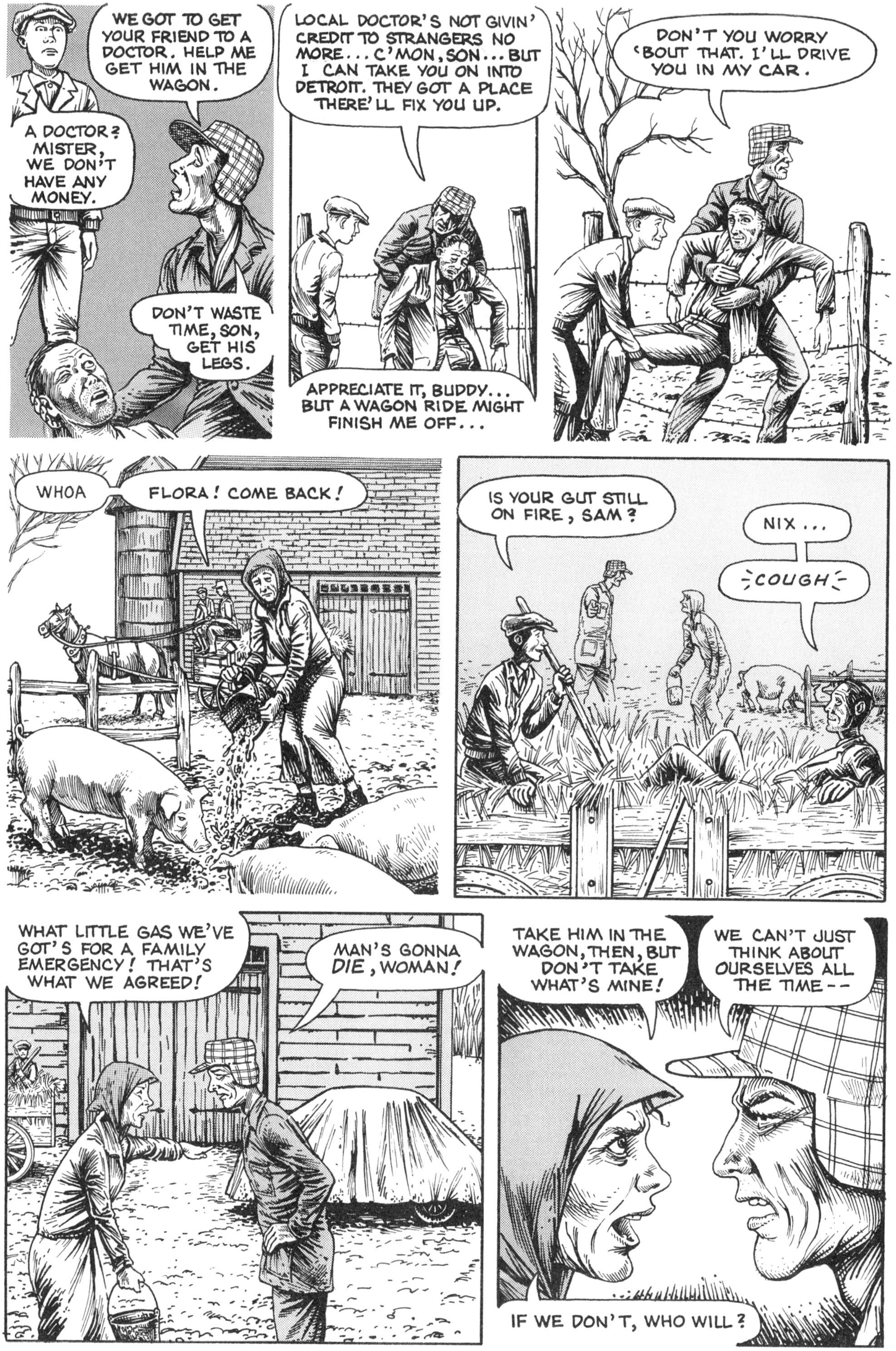
WE GOT TO GET YOUR FRIEND TO A DOCTOR. HELP ME GET HIM IN THE WAGON.
A DOCTOR? MISTER, WE DON'T HAVE ANY MONEY.
DON'T WASTE TIME, SON, GET HIS LEGS.
LOCAL DOCTOR'S NOT GIVIN' CREDIT TO STRANGERS NO MORE... C'MON, SON... BUT I CAN TAKE YOU ON INTO DETROIT. THEY GOT A PLACE THERE'LL FIX YOU UP.
APPRECIATE IT, BUDDY... BUT A WAGON RIDE MIGHT FINISH ME OFF...
DON'T YOU WORRY 'BOUT THAT. I'LL DRIVE YOU IN MY CAR.
WHOA
FLORA! COME BACK!
IS YOUR GUT STILL ON FIRE, SAM?
NIX...
COUGH
WHAT LITTLE GAS WE'VE GOT'S FOR A FAMILY EMERGENCY! THAT'S WHAT WE AGREED!
MAN'S GONNA DIE, WOMAN!
TAKE HIM IN THE WAGON, THEN, BUT DON'T TAKE WHAT'S MINE!
WE CAN'T JUST THINK ABOUT OURSELVES ALL THE TIME--
IF WE DON'T, WHO WILL?

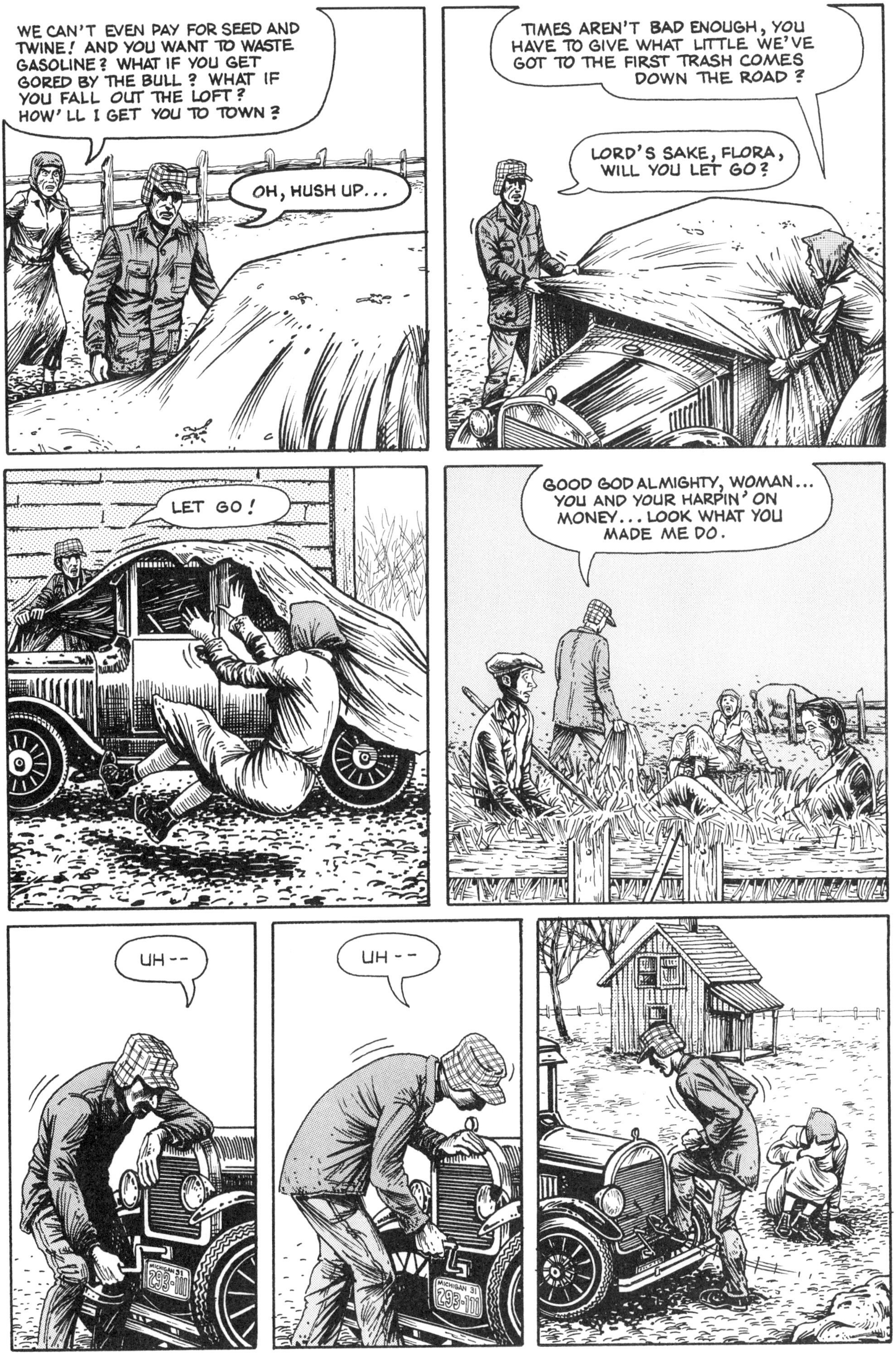

WE CAN'T EVEN PAY FOR SEED AND TWINE! AND YOU WANT TO WASTE GASOLINE? WHAT IF YOU GET GORED BY THE BULL? WHAT IF YOU FALL OUT THE LOFT? HOW'LL I GET YOU TO TOWN?
OH, HUSH UP...
TIMES AREN'T BAD ENOUGH, YOU HAVE TO GIVE WHAT LITTLE WE'VE GOT TO THE FIRST TRASH COMES DOWN THE ROAD?
LORD'S SAKE, FLORA, WILL YOU LET GO?
LET GO!
GOOD GOD ALMIGHTY, WOMAN... YOU AND YOUR HARPIN' ON MONEY... LOOK WHAT YOU MADE ME DO.
UH --
UH --

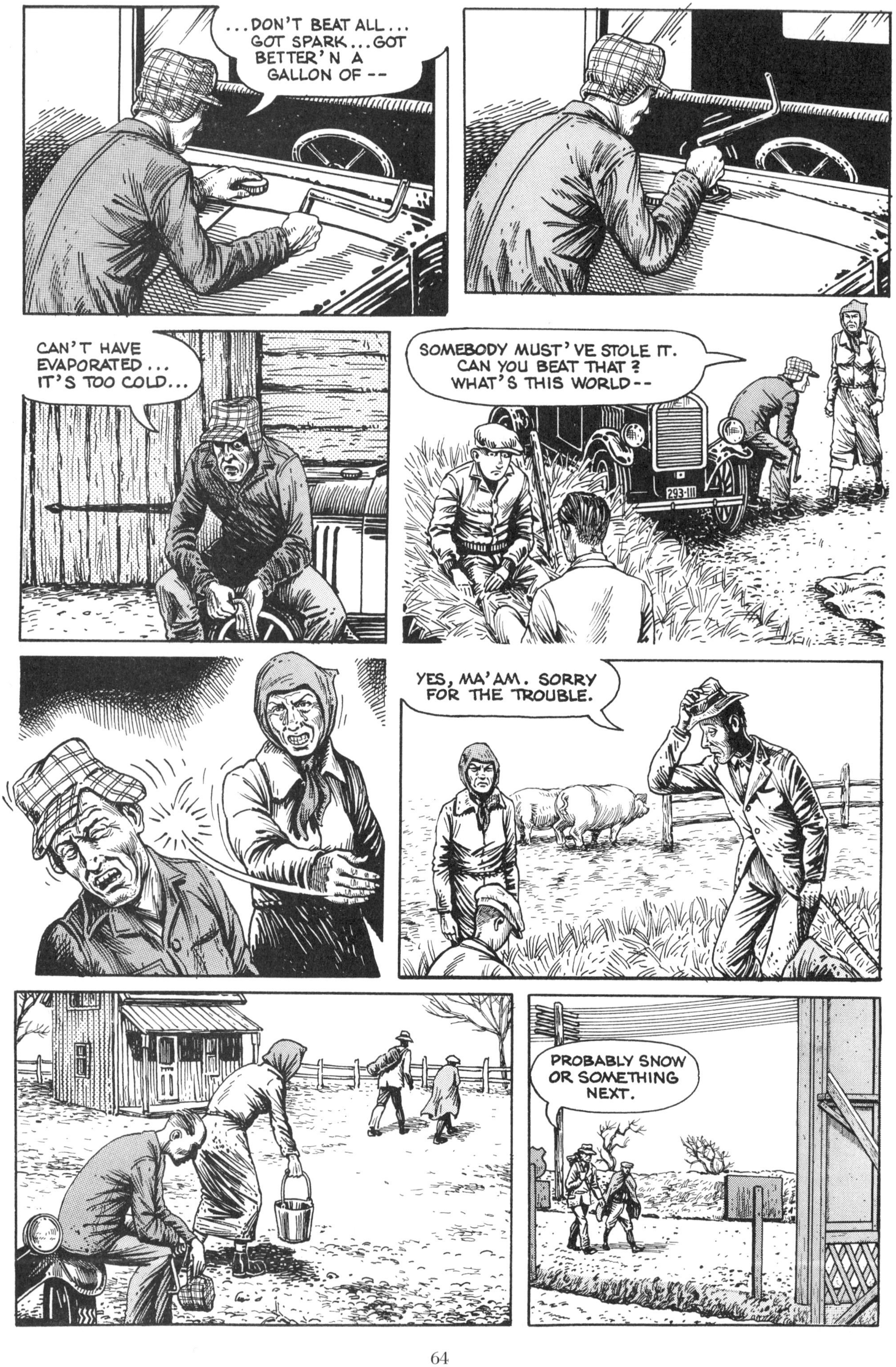
...DON'T BEAT ALL... GOT SPARK...GOT BETTER'N A GALLON OF --
CAN'T HAVE EVAPORATED... IT'S TOO COLD...
SOMEBODY MUST'VE STOLE IT. CAN YOU BEAT THAT? WHAT'S THIS WORLD--
YES, MA'AM. SORRY FOR THE TROUBLE.
PROBABLY SNOW OR SOMETHING NEXT.

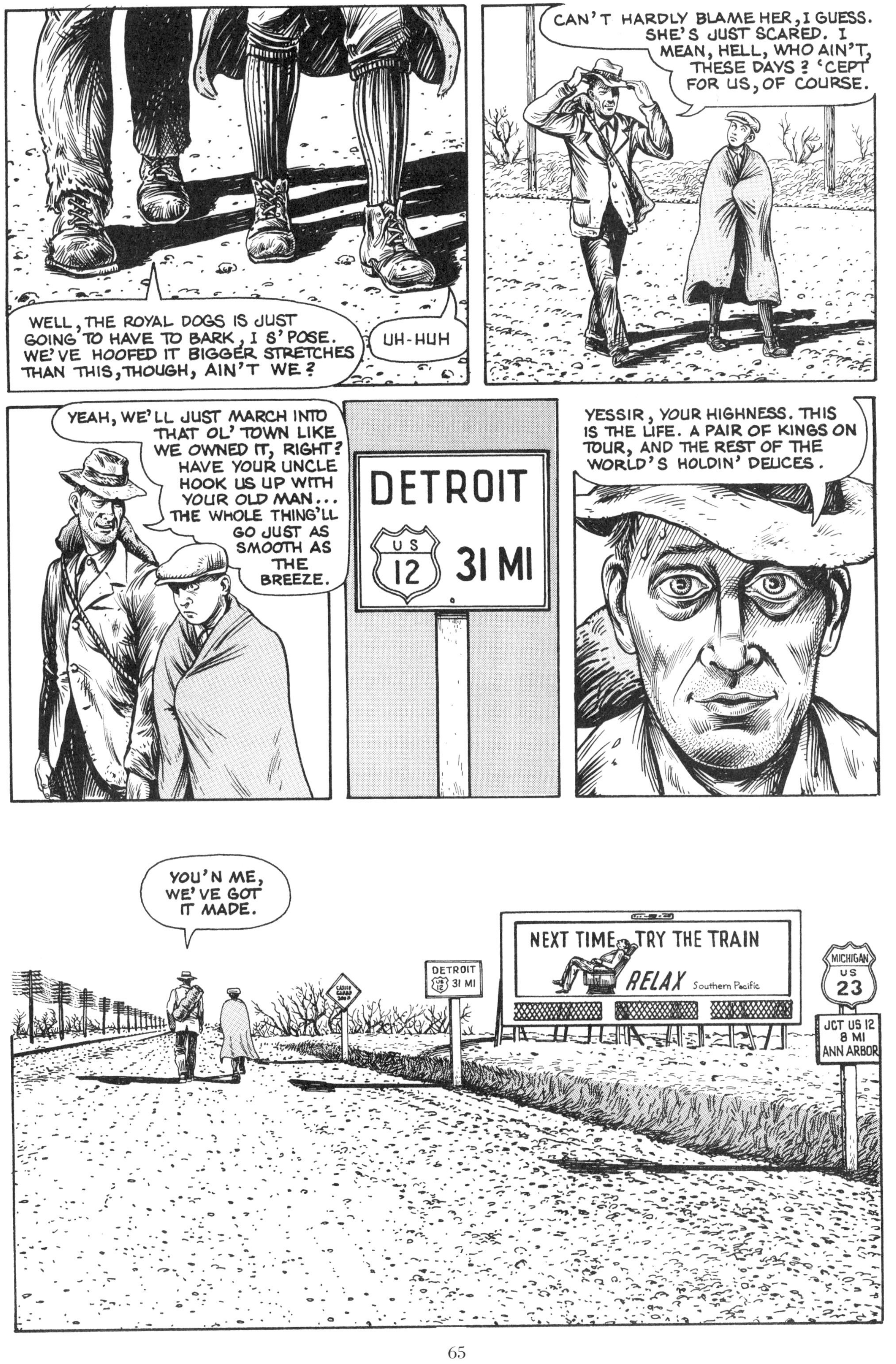
WELL, THE ROYAL DOGS IS JUST GOING TO HAVE TO BARK, I S'POSE. WE'VE HOOFED IT BIGGER STRETCHES THAN THIS, THOUGH, AIN'T WE?
UH-HUH
CAN'T HARDLY BLAME HER, I GUESS. SHE'S JUST SCARED. I MEAN, HELL, WHO AIN'T, THESE DAYS? 'CEPT FOR US, OF COURSE.
YEAH, WE'LL JUST MARCH INTO THAT OL' TOWN LIKE WE OWNED IT, RIGHT? HAVE YOUR UNCLE HOOK US UP WITH YOUR OLD MAN... THE WHOLE THING'LL GO JUST AS SMOOTH AS THE BREEZE.
DETROIT
US 12
31 MI
YESSIR, YOUR HIGHNESS. THIS IS THE LIFE. A PAIR OF KINGS ON TOUR, AND THE REST OF THE WORLD'S HOLDIN' DEUCES.
YOU'N ME, WE'VE GOT IT MADE.
DETROIT
US 12 31 MI
NEXT TIME TRY THE TRAIN
RELAX
Southern Pacific
MICHIGAN
US
23
JCT US 12
8 MI
ANN ARBOR

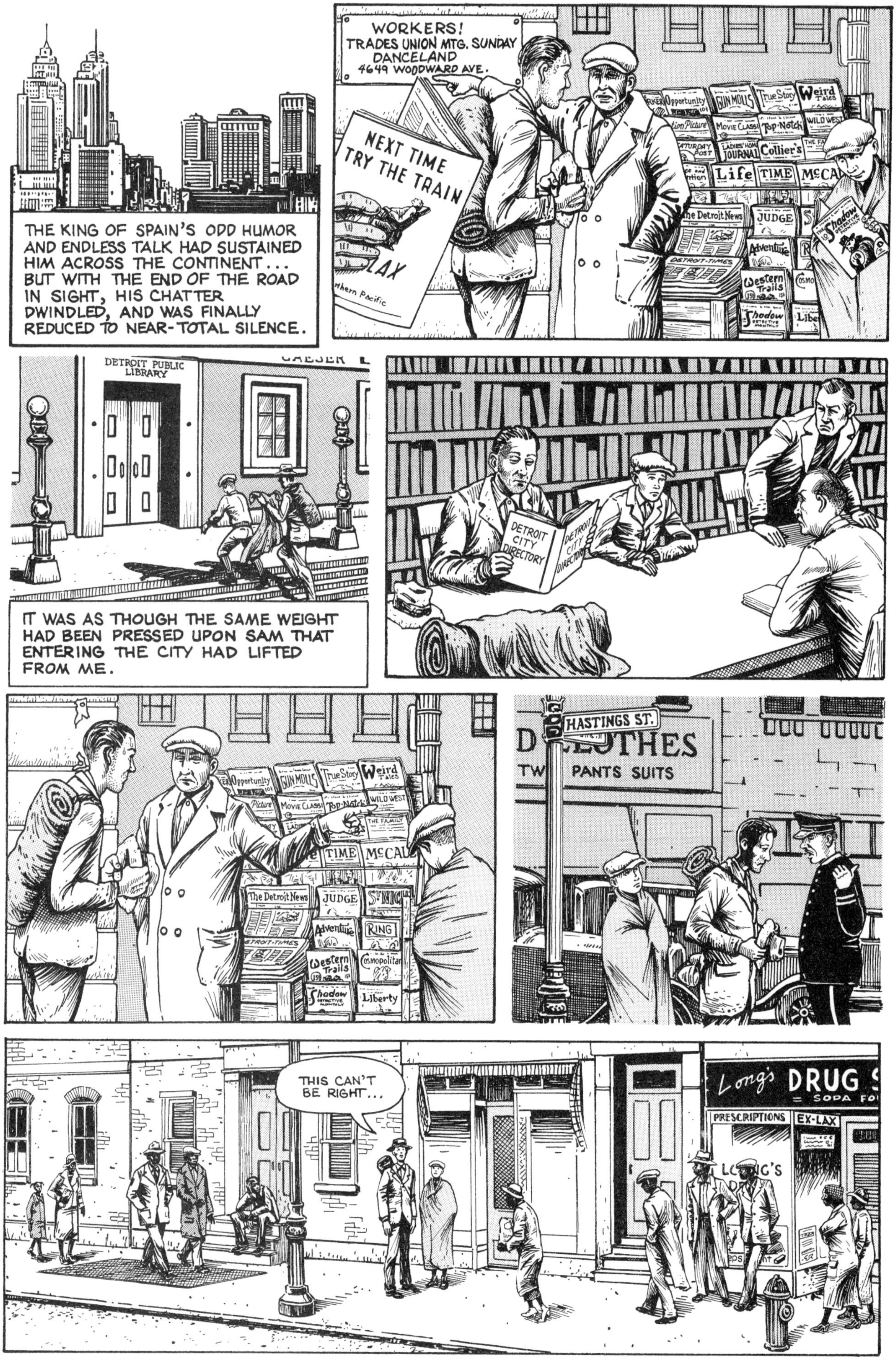
THE KING OF SPAIN'S ODD HUMOR AND ENDLESS TALK HAD SUSTAINED HIM ACROSS THE CONTINENT . . . BUT WITH THE END OF THE ROAD IN SIGHT, HIS CHATTER DWINDLED, AND WAS FINALLY REDUCED TO NEAR-TOTAL SILENCE.
WORKERS! TRADES UNION MTG. SUNDAY DANCELAND 4649 WOODWARD AVE.
NEXT TIME TRY THE TRAIN
The Detroit News
DETROIT PUBLIC LIBRARY
IT WAS AS THOUGH THE SAME WEIGHT HAD BEEN PRESSED UPON SAM THAT ENTERING THE CITY HAD LIFTED FROM ME.
DETROIT CITY DIRECTORY
DETROIT CITY DIRECTORY
HASTINGS ST.
PANTS SUITS
THIS CAN'T BE RIGHT . . .
PRESCRIPTIONS
EX-LAX

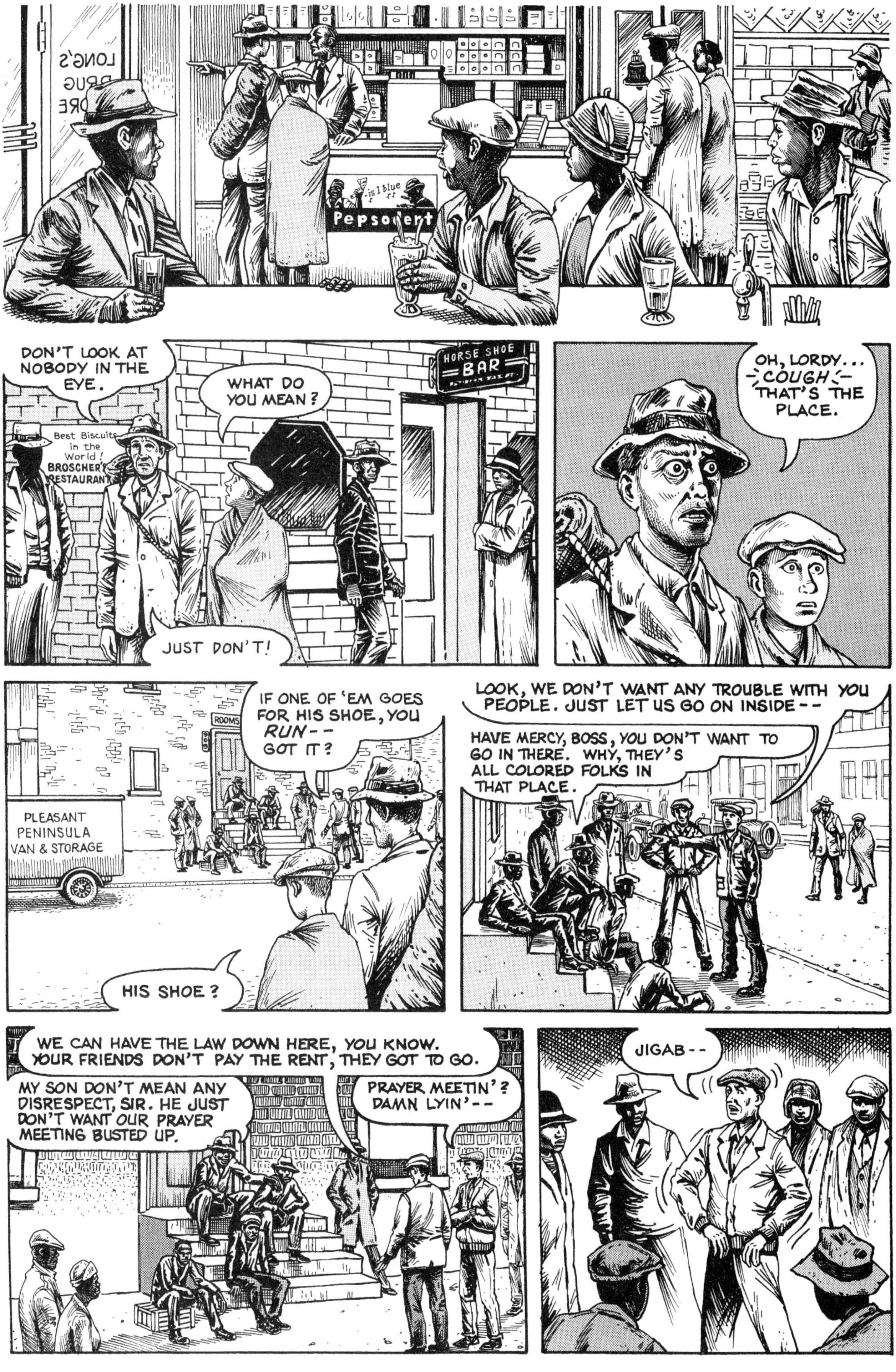
LONG'S DRUG STORE
is I blue
Pepsodent
DON'T LOOK AT NOBODY IN THE EYE.
WHAT DO YOU MEAN?
HORSE SHOE BAR
Best Biscuits in the World! BROSCHER'S RESTAURANT
JUST DON'T!
OH, LORDY... COUGH THAT'S THE PLACE.
IF ONE OF 'EM GOES FOR HIS SHOE, YOU RUN-- GOT IT?
ROOMS
PLEASANT PENINSULA VAN & STORAGE
HIS SHOE?
LOOK, WE DON'T WANT ANY TROUBLE WITH YOU PEOPLE. JUST LET US GO ON INSIDE--
HAVE MERCY, BOSS, YOU DON'T WANT TO GO IN THERE. WHY, THEY'S ALL COLORED FOLKS IN THAT PLACE.
WE CAN HAVE THE LAW DOWN HERE, YOU KNOW. YOUR FRIENDS DON'T PAY THE RENT, THEY GOT TO GO.
MY SON DON'T MEAN ANY DISRESPECT, SIR. HE JUST DON'T WANT OUR PRAYER MEETING BUSTED UP.
PRAYER MEETIN'? DAMN LYIN'--
JIGAB--

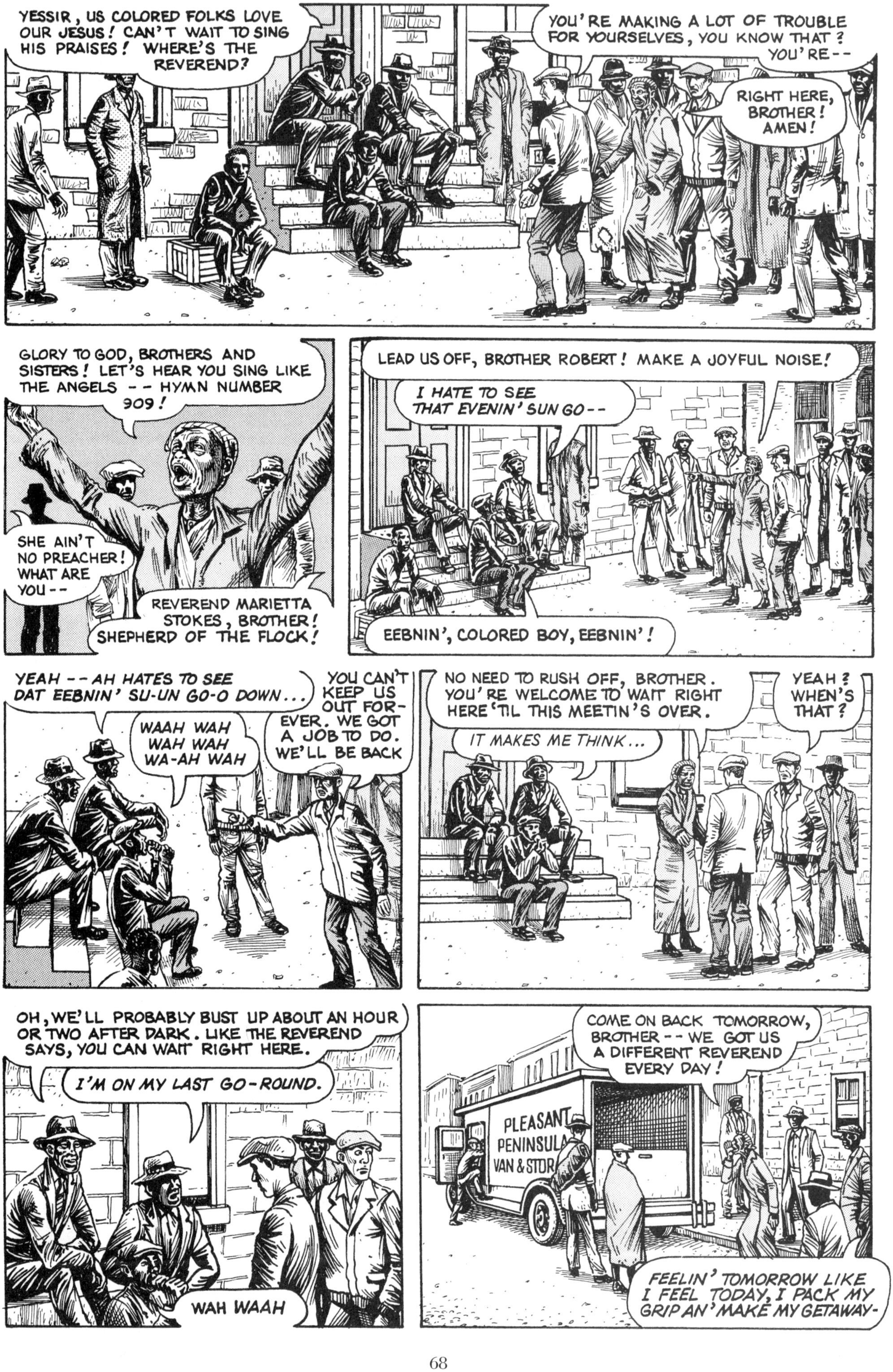
YESSIR, US COLORED FOLKS LOVE OUR JESUS! CAN'T WAIT TO SING HIS PRAISES! WHERE'S THE REVEREND?
YOU'RE MAKING A LOT OF TROUBLE FOR YOURSELVES, YOU KNOW THAT? YOU'RE--
RIGHT HERE, BROTHER! AMEN!
GLORY TO GOD, BROTHERS AND SISTERS! LET'S HEAR YOU SING LIKE THE ANGELS -- HYMN NUMBER 909!
SHE AIN'T NO PREACHER! WHAT ARE YOU--
REVEREND MARIETTA STOKES, BROTHER! SHEPHERD OF THE FLOCK!
LEAD US OFF, BROTHER ROBERT! MAKE A JOYFUL NOISE!
I HATE TO SEE THAT EVENIN' SUN GO--
EEBNIN', COLORED BOY, EEBNIN'!
YEAH -- AH HATES TO SEE DAT EEBNIN' SU-UN GO-O DOWN...
WAAH WAH WAH WAH WA-AH WAH
YOU CAN'T KEEP US OUT FOR-EVER. WE GOT A JOB TO DO. WE'LL BE BACK
NO NEED TO RUSH OFF, BROTHER. YOU'RE WELCOME TO WAIT RIGHT HERE 'TIL THIS MEETIN'S OVER.
YEAH? WHEN'S THAT?
IT MAKES ME THINK...
OH, WE'LL PROBABLY BUST UP ABOUT AN HOUR OR TWO AFTER DARK. LIKE THE REVEREND SAYS, YOU CAN WAIT RIGHT HERE.
I'M ON MY LAST GO-ROUND.
WAH WAAH
COME ON BACK TOMORROW, BROTHER -- WE GOT US A DIFFERENT REVEREND EVERY DAY!
PLEASANT PENINSULA VAN & STOR
FEELIN' TOMORROW LIKE I FEEL TODAY, I PACK MY GRIP AN' MAKE MY GETAWAY-

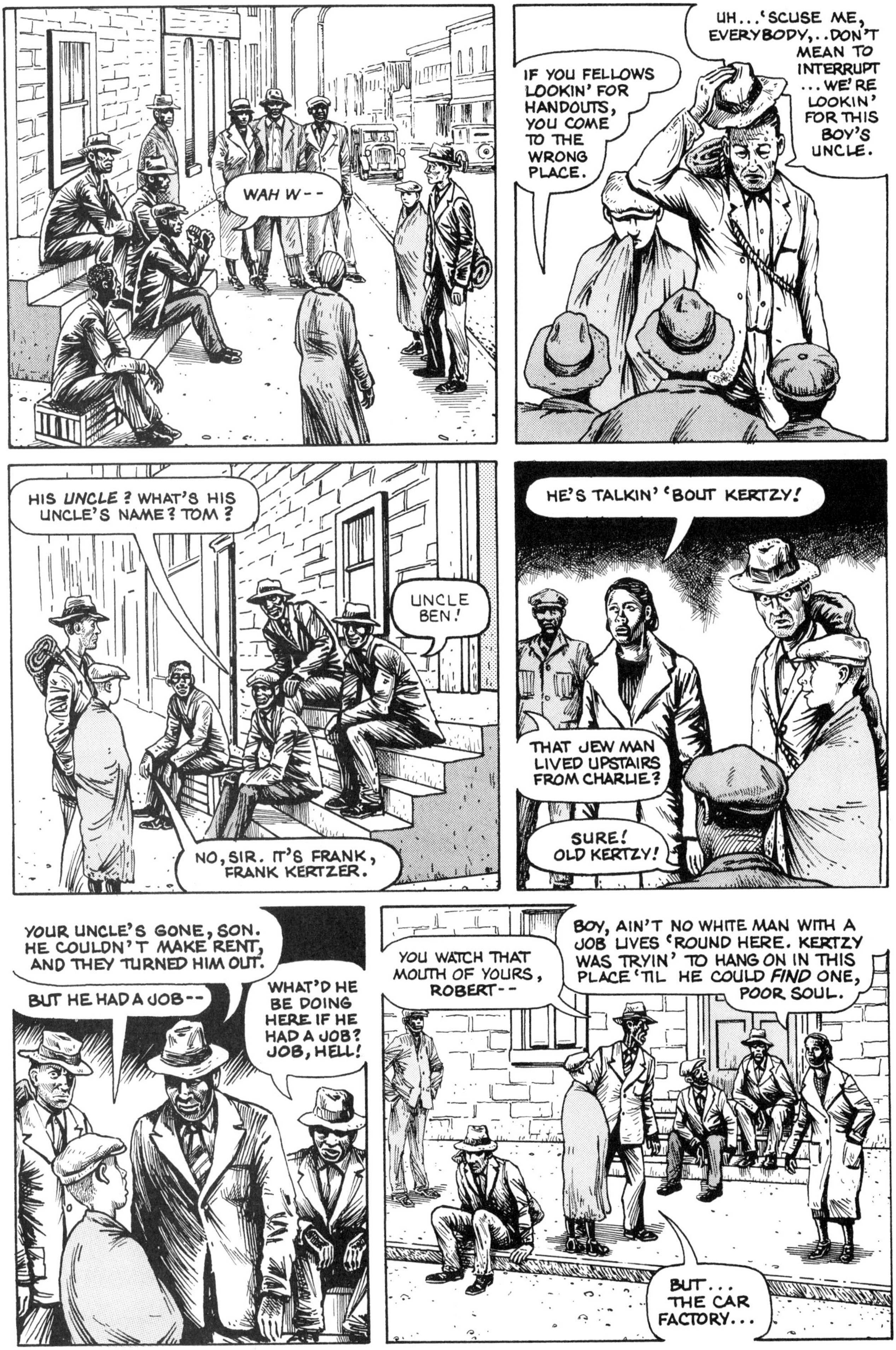
WAH W--
IF YOU FELLOWS LOOKIN' FOR HANDOUTS, YOU COME TO THE WRONG PLACE.
UH...'SCUSE ME, EVERYBODY,..DON'T MEAN TO INTERRUPT ...WE'RE LOOKIN' FOR THIS BOY'S UNCLE.
HIS *UNCLE*? WHAT'S HIS UNCLE'S NAME? TOM?
UNCLE BEN!
NO, SIR. IT'S FRANK, FRANK KERTZER.
HE'S TALKIN' 'BOUT KERTZY!
THAT JEW MAN LIVED UPSTAIRS FROM CHARLIE?
SURE! OLD KERTZY!
YOUR UNCLE'S GONE, SON. HE COULDN'T MAKE RENT, AND THEY TURNED HIM OUT.
BUT HE HAD A JOB--
WHAT'D HE BE DOING HERE IF HE HAD A JOB? JOB, HELL!
YOU WATCH THAT MOUTH OF YOURS, ROBERT--
BOY, AIN'T NO WHITE MAN WITH A JOB LIVES 'ROUND HERE. KERTZY WAS TRYIN' TO HANG ON IN THIS PLACE 'TIL HE COULD *FIND* ONE, POOR SOUL.
BUT... THE CAR FACTORY...

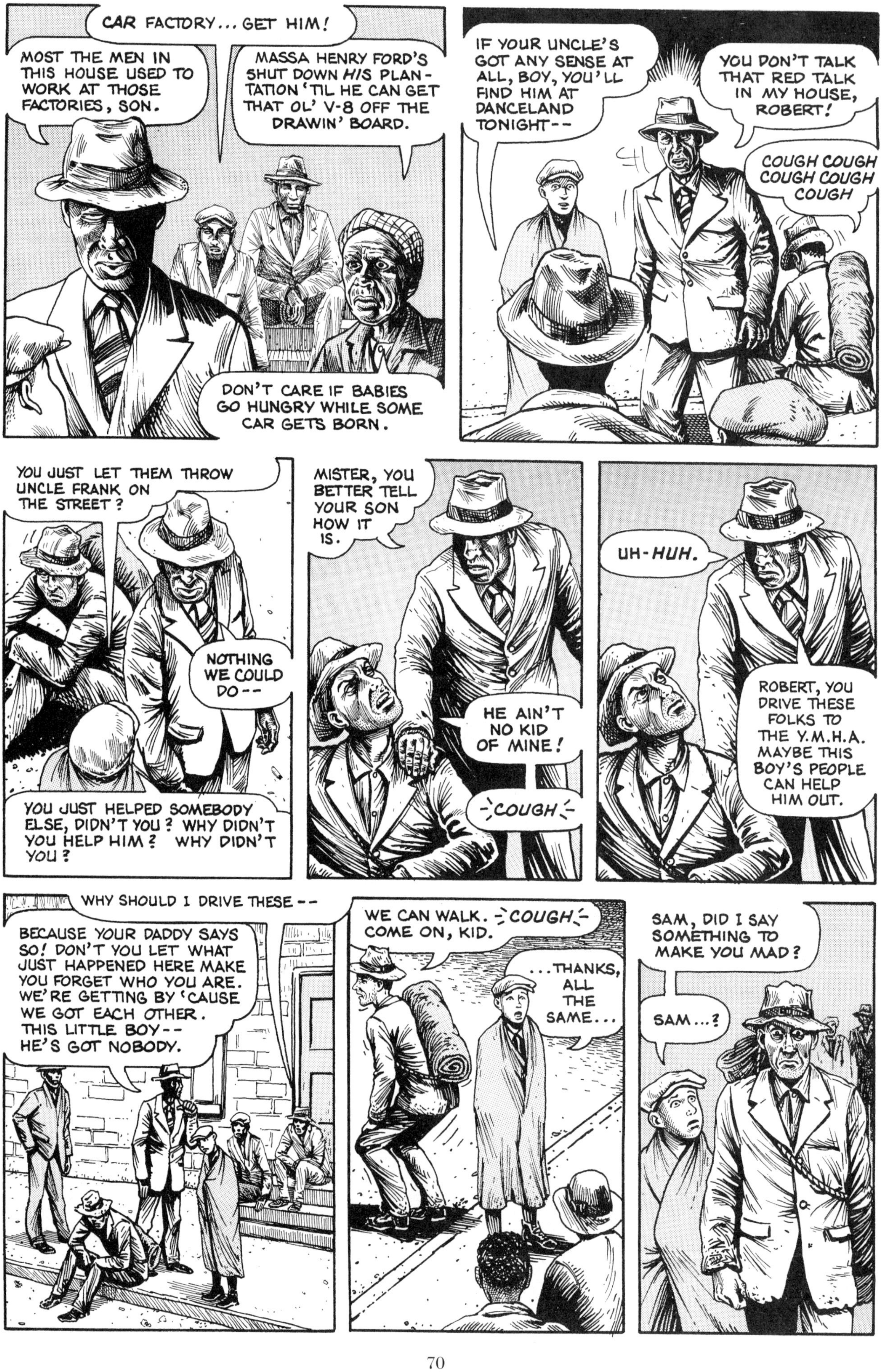
CAR FACTORY... GET HIM!
MOST THE MEN IN THIS HOUSE USED TO WORK AT THOSE FACTORIES, SON.
MASSA HENRY FORD'S SHUT DOWN HIS PLANTATION 'TIL HE CAN GET THAT OL' V-8 OFF THE DRAWIN' BOARD.
DON'T CARE IF BABIES GO HUNGRY WHILE SOME CAR GETS BORN.
IF YOUR UNCLE'S GOT ANY SENSE AT ALL, BOY, YOU'LL FIND HIM AT DANCELAND TONIGHT--
YOU DON'T TALK THAT RED TALK IN MY HOUSE, ROBERT!
COUGH COUGH COUGH COUGH COUGH
YOU JUST LET THEM THROW UNCLE FRANK ON THE STREET?
NOTHING WE COULD DO--
YOU JUST HELPED SOMEBODY ELSE, DIDN'T YOU? WHY DIDN'T YOU HELP HIM? WHY DIDN'T YOU?
MISTER, YOU BETTER TELL YOUR SON HOW IT IS.
HE AIN'T NO KID OF MINE!
COUGH
UH-HUH.
ROBERT, YOU DRIVE THESE FOLKS TO THE Y.M.H.A. MAYBE THIS BOY'S PEOPLE CAN HELP HIM OUT.
WHY SHOULD I DRIVE THESE--
BECAUSE YOUR DADDY SAYS SO! DON'T YOU LET WHAT JUST HAPPENED HERE MAKE YOU FORGET WHO YOU ARE. WE'RE GETTING BY 'CAUSE WE GOT EACH OTHER. THIS LITTLE BOY-- HE'S GOT NOBODY.
WE CAN WALK. COUGH COME ON, KID.
...THANKS, ALL THE SAME...
SAM, DID I SAY SOMETHING TO MAKE YOU MAD?
SAM...?

ARE WE GOING TO THAT PLACE, SAM? THE YMCA?

NO! AND IT AIN'T THE YMCA...

POOL ROOM

WORK IS WHAT I WANT — NOT CHARITY

S. H. GARLICK

SO YOUR UNCLE BLEW TOWN. ~COUGH~ THAT'S JUST DANDY. ~WHEEZE~ AND ME WITH MY LUNGS BURNIN'... TOO DAMN FROSTY FOR THE JUNGLE... BUT I BETCHA WE CAN FIND A PLACE. AND I BETCHA FOR SURE YOUR UNCLE AIN'T THERE.

Drink MOXIE

AYS IN GOOD TASTE
esterfield

AND THE LORD TOOK THOSE MEAGER FISH AND THOSE FEW LOAVES OF BREAD, AND HE SAID, "GO, AND FEED THE MULTITUDE"...

NEW TESTAMENT SALVATION MISSION

ROOMS

FREE SOUP & BREAD

AND THE DISCIPLES SAID, "LORD, THERE AIN'T ENOUGH HERE TO GO AROUND," BUT THE LORD JUST SENT 'EM ON THEIR WAY...

YOU GETTIN' ANYTHING OUT OF THIS?

SHH

AND, LO, THERE WAS ENOUGH TO FEED THAT MULTITUDE... FOR THAT IS EVER THE WAY OF THE LORD. JUST AS THERE'S ENOUGH FOR YOU TODAY, BROTHERS AND SISTERS. YOU WHO TRULY BELIEVE, FOLLOW ME INTO OUR DINING HALL AND PARTAKE OF A CUP OF MY WIFE'S GOOD SOUP... AND REMEMBER THE BOUNTY OF THE LORD. AMEN!

JESUS SAVES

PLACES LIKE THIS GOT COTS UPSTAIRS. YOU FOLLOW MY LEAD, SEE, AND WE GOT US A BUNK FOR THE NIGHT.

I DON'T WANT TO STAY HERE. I WANT TO FIND MY--

SHUT UP!

WE'RE STAYIN' HERE, AND THAT'S IT. AND WHATEVER YOU DO, DON'T LET ON TO ANYBODY THAT YOU'RE A--

AW, SKIP IT.

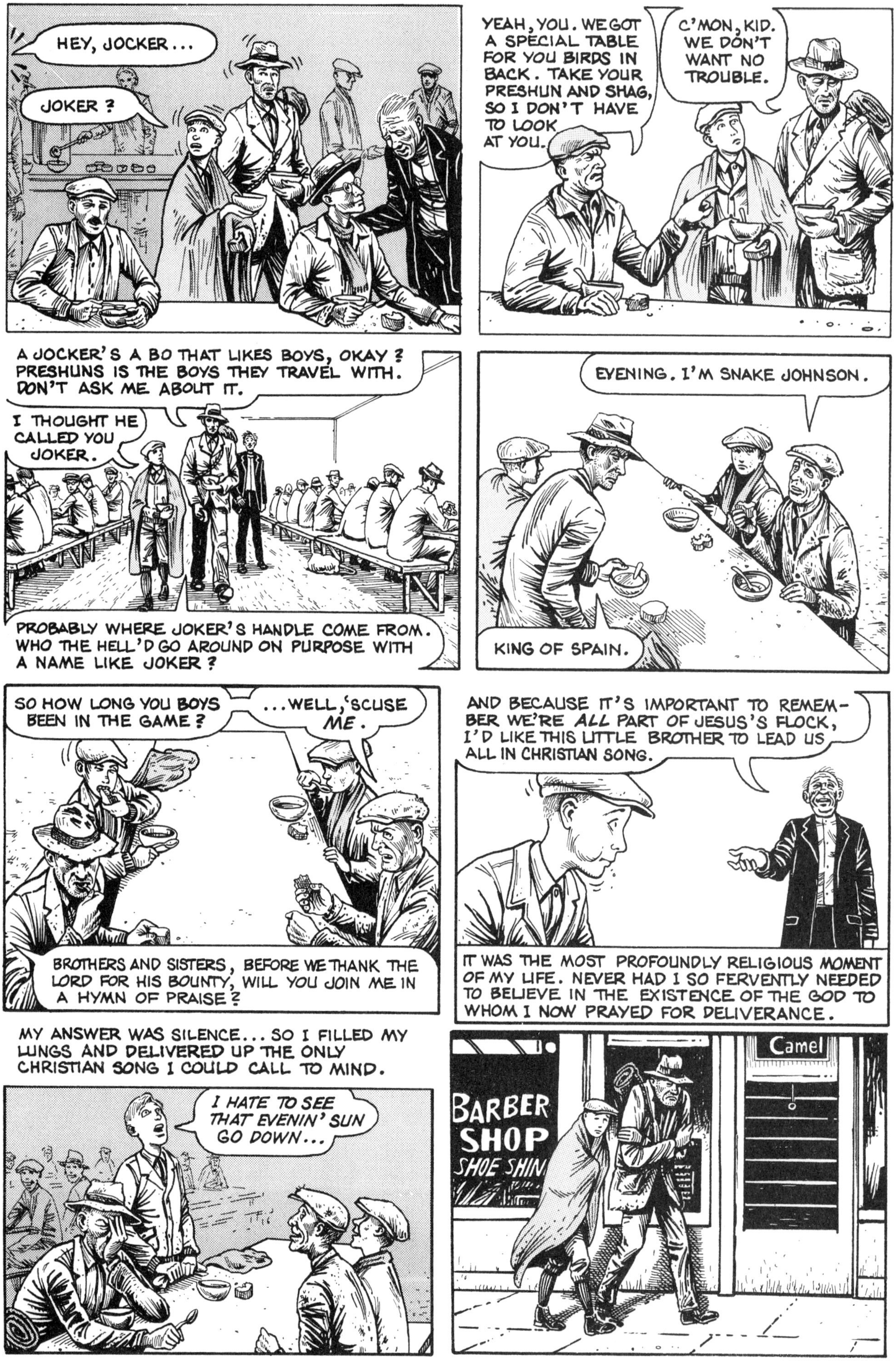
HEY, JOCKER...
JOKER?
YEAH, YOU. WE GOT A SPECIAL TABLE FOR YOU BIRDS IN BACK. TAKE YOUR PRESHUN AND SHAG, SO I DON'T HAVE TO LOOK AT YOU.
C'MON, KID. WE DON'T WANT NO TROUBLE.
A JOCKER'S A BO THAT LIKES BOYS, OKAY? PRESHUNS IS THE BOYS THEY TRAVEL WITH. DON'T ASK ME ABOUT IT.
I THOUGHT HE CALLED YOU JOKER.
PROBABLY WHERE JOKER'S HANDLE COME FROM. WHO THE HELL'D GO AROUND ON PURPOSE WITH A NAME LIKE JOKER?
EVENING. I'M SNAKE JOHNSON.
KING OF SPAIN.
SO HOW LONG YOU BOYS BEEN IN THE GAME?
...WELL, 'SCUSE ME.
BROTHERS AND SISTERS, BEFORE WE THANK THE LORD FOR HIS BOUNTY, WILL YOU JOIN ME IN A HYMN OF PRAISE?
AND BECAUSE IT'S IMPORTANT TO REMEMBER WE'RE ALL PART OF JESUS'S FLOCK, I'D LIKE THIS LITTLE BROTHER TO LEAD US ALL IN CHRISTIAN SONG.
IT WAS THE MOST PROFOUNDLY RELIGIOUS MOMENT OF MY LIFE. NEVER HAD I SO FERVENTLY NEEDED TO BELIEVE IN THE EXISTENCE OF THE GOD TO WHOM I NOW PRAYED FOR DELIVERANCE.
MY ANSWER WAS SILENCE... SO I FILLED MY LUNGS AND DELIVERED UP THE ONLY CHRISTIAN SONG I COULD CALL TO MIND.
I HATE TO SEE THAT EVENIN' SUN GO DOWN...
Camel
BARBER SHOP
SHOE SHIN

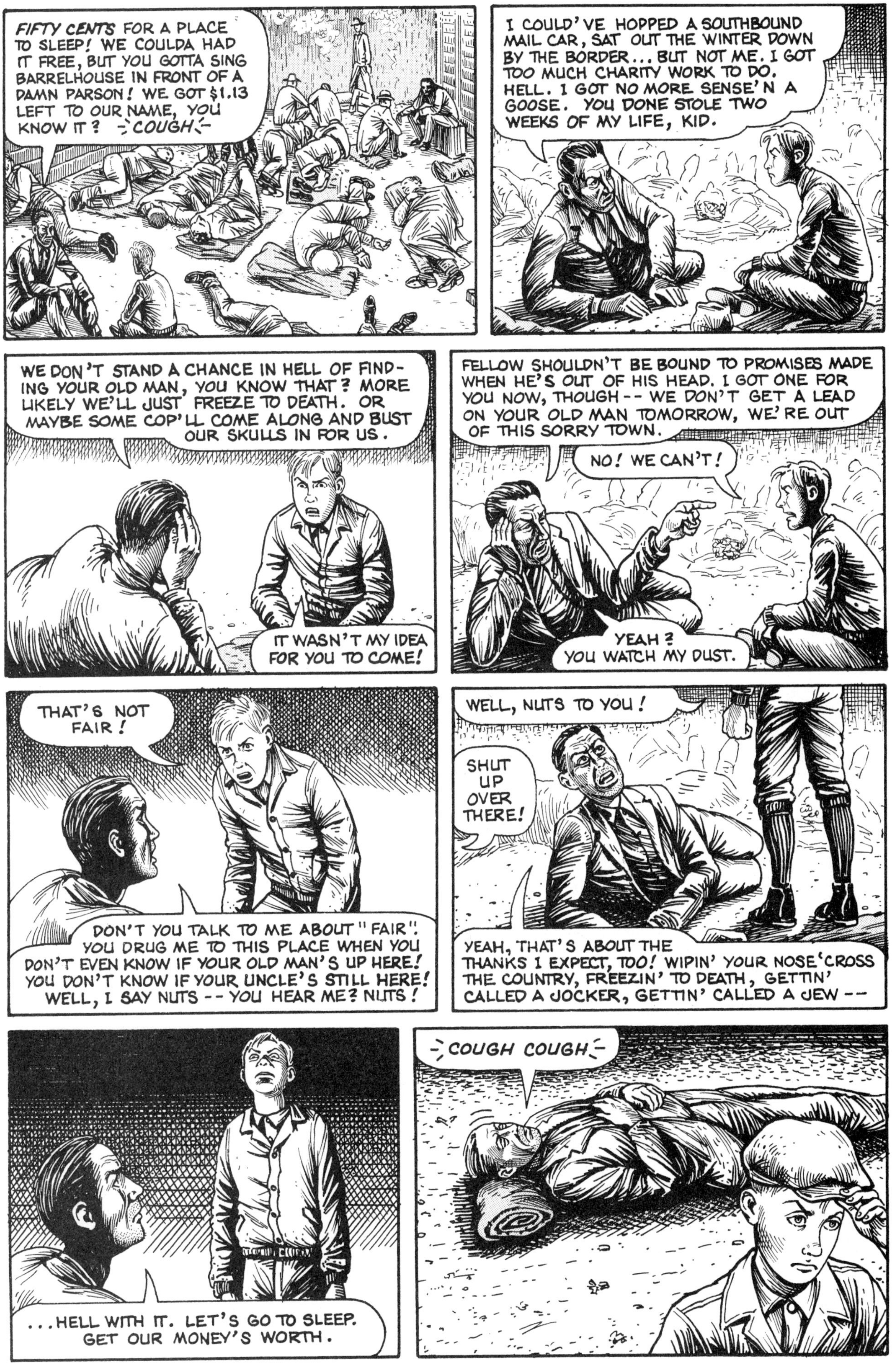
FIFTY CENTS FOR A PLACE TO SLEEP! WE COULDA HAD IT FREE, BUT YOU GOTTA SING BARRELHOUSE IN FRONT OF A DAMN PARSON! WE GOT $1.13 LEFT TO OUR NAME, YOU KNOW IT? -COUGH-
I COULD'VE HOPPED A SOUTHBOUND MAIL CAR, SAT OUT THE WINTER DOWN BY THE BORDER... BUT NOT ME. I GOT TOO MUCH CHARITY WORK TO DO. HELL. I GOT NO MORE SENSE'N A GOOSE. YOU DONE STOLE TWO WEEKS OF MY LIFE, KID.
WE DON'T STAND A CHANCE IN HELL OF FINDING YOUR OLD MAN, YOU KNOW THAT? MORE LIKELY WE'LL JUST FREEZE TO DEATH. OR MAYBE SOME COP'LL COME ALONG AND BUST OUR SKULLS IN FOR US.
IT WASN'T MY IDEA FOR YOU TO COME!
FELLOW SHOULDN'T BE BOUND TO PROMISES MADE WHEN HE'S OUT OF HIS HEAD. I GOT ONE FOR YOU NOW, THOUGH -- WE DON'T GET A LEAD ON YOUR OLD MAN TOMORROW, WE'RE OUT OF THIS SORRY TOWN.
NO! WE CAN'T!
YEAH? YOU WATCH MY DUST.
THAT'S NOT FAIR!
DON'T YOU TALK TO ME ABOUT "FAIR". YOU DRUG ME TO THIS PLACE WHEN YOU DON'T EVEN KNOW IF YOUR OLD MAN'S UP HERE! YOU DON'T KNOW IF YOUR UNCLE'S STILL HERE! WELL, I SAY NUTS -- YOU HEAR ME? NUTS!
WELL, NUTS TO YOU!
SHUT UP OVER THERE!
YEAH, THAT'S ABOUT THE THANKS I EXPECT, TOO! WIPIN' YOUR NOSE 'CROSS THE COUNTRY, FREEZIN' TO DEATH, GETTIN' CALLED A JOCKER, GETTIN' CALLED A JEW --
...HELL WITH IT. LET'S GO TO SLEEP. GET OUR MONEY'S WORTH.
-COUGH COUGH-

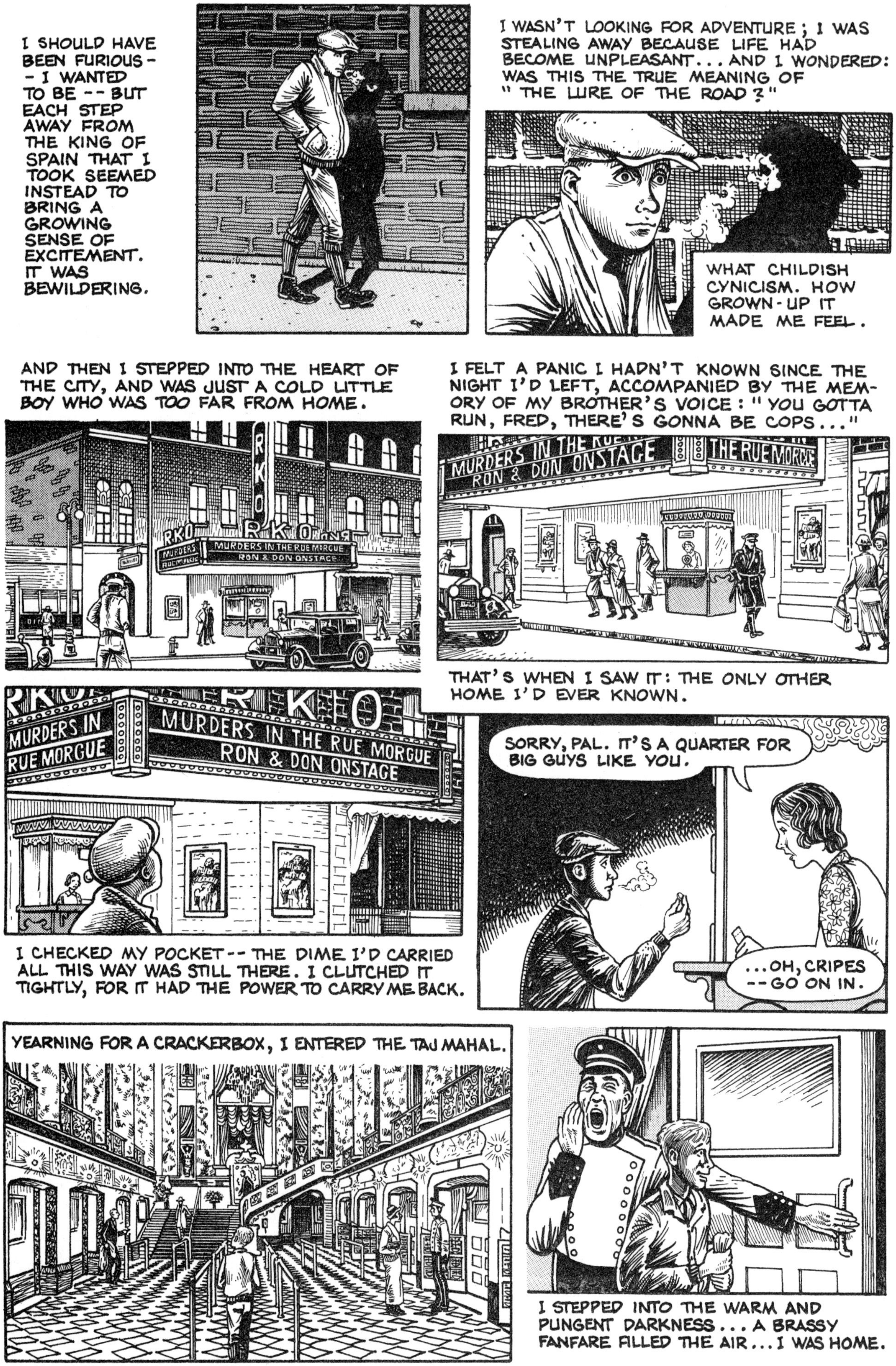

I SHOULD HAVE BEEN FURIOUS--I WANTED TO BE -- BUT EACH STEP AWAY FROM THE KING OF SPAIN THAT I TOOK SEEMED INSTEAD TO BRING A GROWING SENSE OF EXCITEMENT. IT WAS BEWILDERING.
I WASN'T LOOKING FOR ADVENTURE; I WAS STEALING AWAY BECAUSE LIFE HAD BECOME UNPLEASANT... AND I WONDERED: WAS THIS THE TRUE MEANING OF "THE LURE OF THE ROAD?"
WHAT CHILDISH CYNICISM. HOW GROWN-UP IT MADE ME FEEL.
AND THEN I STEPPED INTO THE HEART OF THE CITY, AND WAS JUST A COLD LITTLE BOY WHO WAS TOO FAR FROM HOME.
RKO
MURDERS IN THE RUE MORGUE
RON & DON ONSTAGE
I FELT A PANIC I HADN'T KNOWN SINCE THE NIGHT I'D LEFT, ACCOMPANIED BY THE MEMORY OF MY BROTHER'S VOICE: "YOU GOTTA RUN, FRED, THERE'S GONNA BE COPS..."
MURDERS IN THE RUE MORGUE
RON & DON ONSTAGE
THAT'S WHEN I SAW IT: THE ONLY OTHER HOME I'D EVER KNOWN.
RKO
MURDERS IN RUE MORGUE
MURDERS IN THE RUE MORGUE
RON & DON ONSTAGE
I CHECKED MY POCKET -- THE DIME I'D CARRIED ALL THIS WAY WAS STILL THERE. I CLUTCHED IT TIGHTLY, FOR IT HAD THE POWER TO CARRY ME BACK.
SORRY, PAL. IT'S A QUARTER FOR BIG GUYS LIKE YOU.
...OH, CRIPES --GO ON IN.
YEARNING FOR A CRACKERBOX, I ENTERED THE TAJ MAHAL.
I STEPPED INTO THE WARM AND PUNGENT DARKNESS... A BRASSY FANFARE FILLED THE AIR... I WAS HOME.

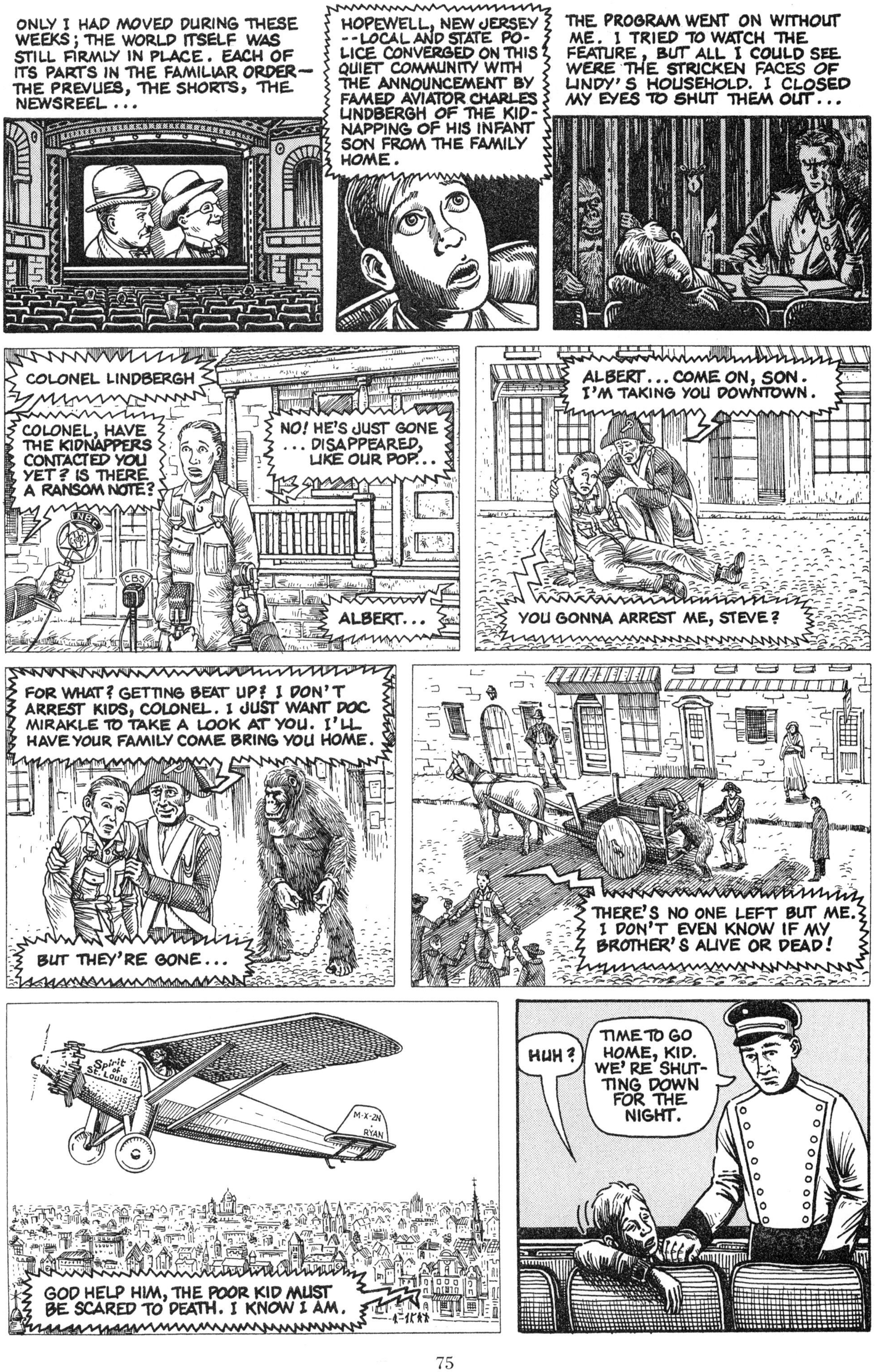
ONLY I HAD MOVED DURING THESE WEEKS; THE WORLD ITSELF WAS STILL FIRMLY IN PLACE. EACH OF ITS PARTS IN THE FAMILIAR ORDER— THE PREVUES, THE SHORTS, THE NEWSREEL...
HOPEWELL, NEW JERSEY --LOCAL AND STATE POLICE CONVERGED ON THIS QUIET COMMUNITY WITH THE ANNOUNCEMENT BY FAMED AVIATOR CHARLES LINDBERGH OF THE KIDNAPPING OF HIS INFANT SON FROM THE FAMILY HOME.
THE PROGRAM WENT ON WITHOUT ME. I TRIED TO WATCH THE FEATURE, BUT ALL I COULD SEE WERE THE STRICKEN FACES OF LINDY'S HOUSEHOLD. I CLOSED MY EYES TO SHUT THEM OUT...
COLONEL LINDBERGH
COLONEL, HAVE THE KIDNAPPERS CONTACTED YOU YET? IS THERE A RANSOM NOTE?
NBC
CBS
NO! HE'S JUST GONE ... DISAPPEARED, LIKE OUR POP...
ALBERT...
ALBERT... COME ON, SON. I'M TAKING YOU DOWNTOWN.
YOU GONNA ARREST ME, STEVE?
FOR WHAT? GETTING BEAT UP? I DON'T ARREST KIDS, COLONEL. I JUST WANT DOC MIRAKLE TO TAKE A LOOK AT YOU. I'LL HAVE YOUR FAMILY COME BRING YOU HOME.
BUT THEY'RE GONE...
THERE'S NO ONE LEFT BUT ME. I DON'T EVEN KNOW IF MY BROTHER'S ALIVE OR DEAD!
Spirit of St. Louis
M-X-2N
RYAN
GOD HELP HIM, THE POOR KID MUST BE SCARED TO DEATH. I KNOW I AM.
HUH?
TIME TO GO HOME, KID. WE'RE SHUTTING DOWN FOR THE NIGHT.

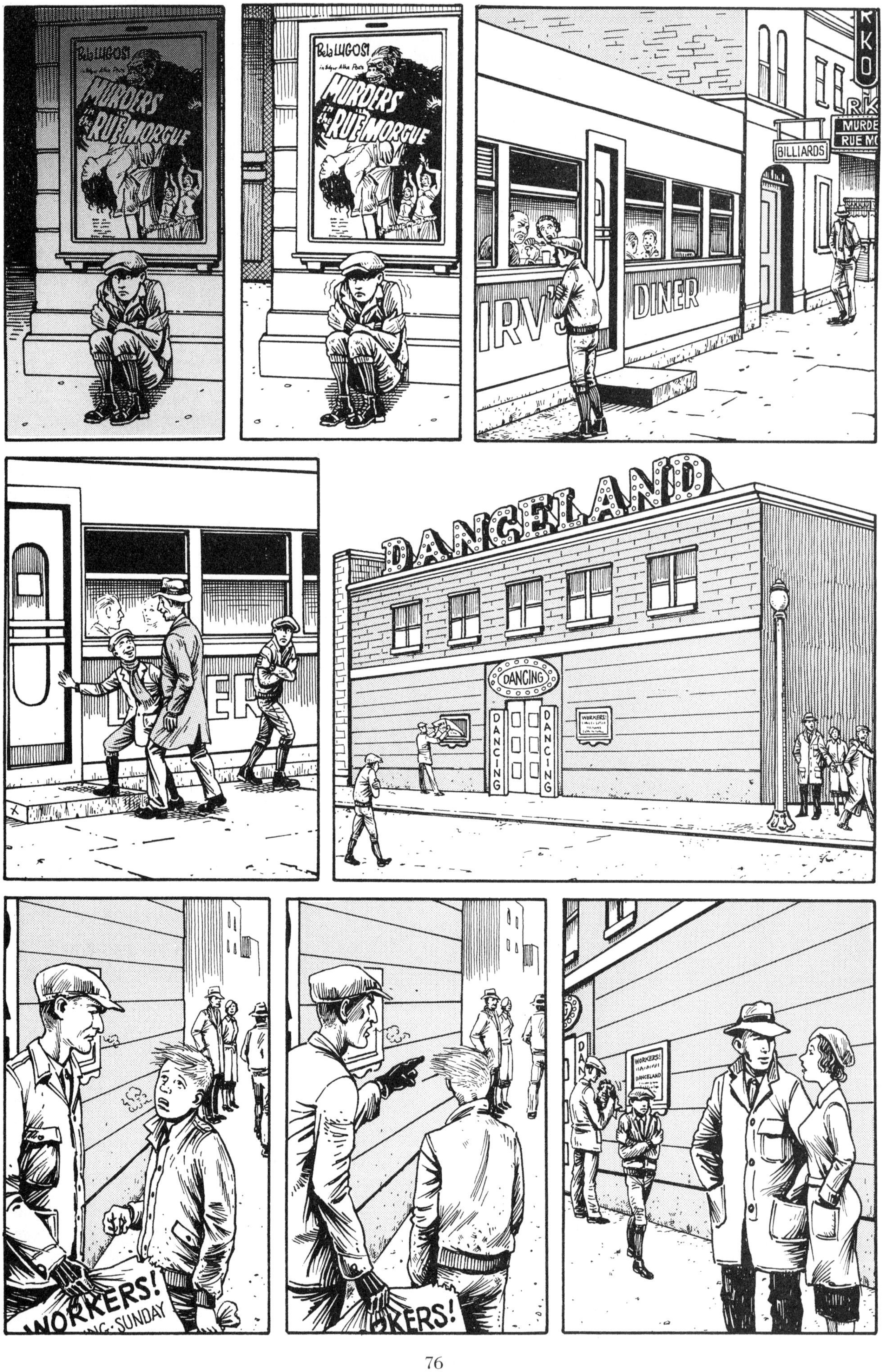
Bela LUGOSI
MURDERS in the RUE MORGUE
Bela LUGOSI
in Edgar Allan Poe's
MURDERS in the RUE MORGUE
IRV'S DINER
BILLIARDS
RKO
MURDE
RUE MO
DANCELAND
DANCING
DANCING
DANCING
WORKERS!
WORKERS!
ING · SUNDAY
RKERS!
WORKERS!
DANCELAND

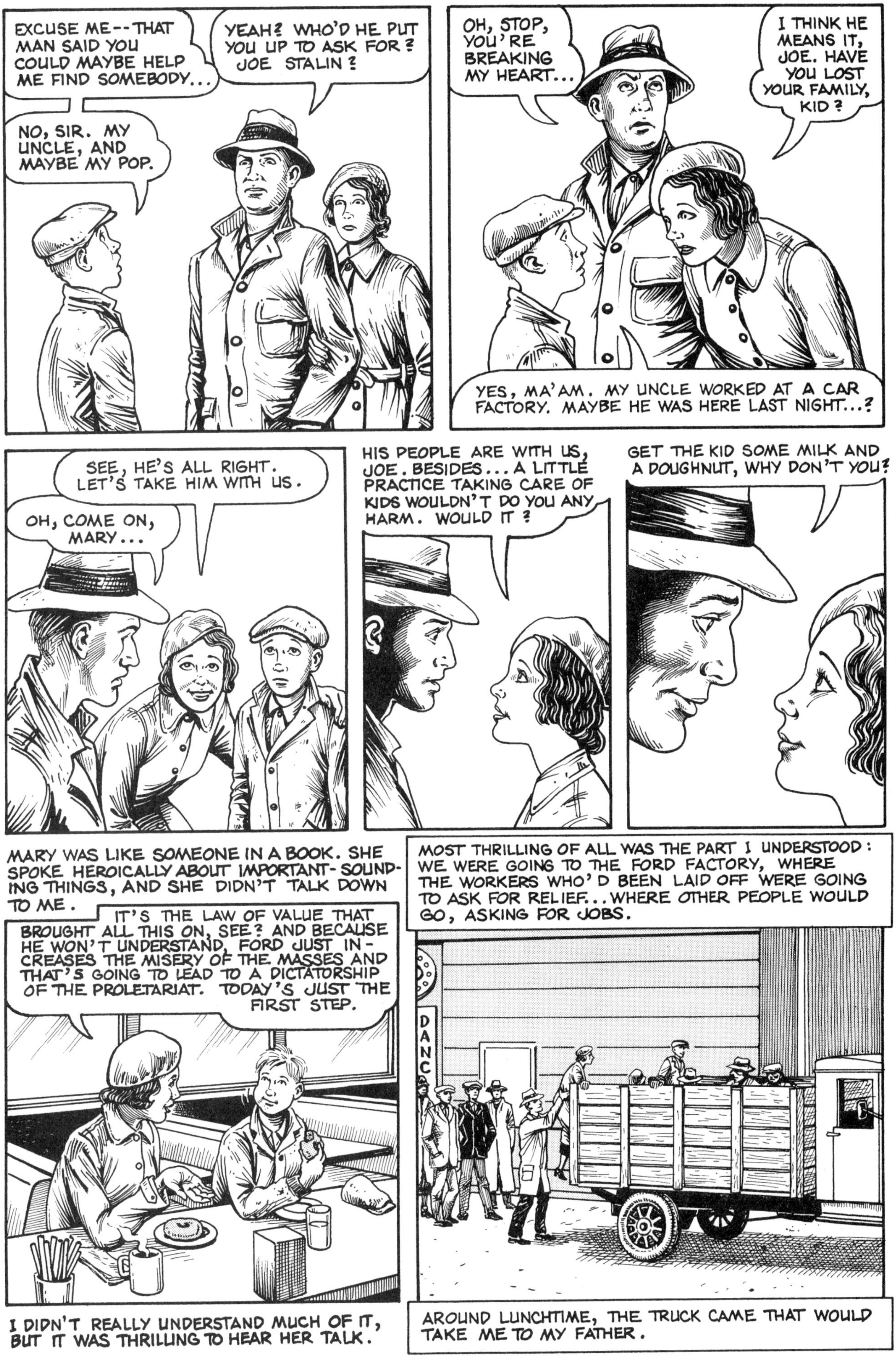
EXCUSE ME--THAT MAN SAID YOU COULD MAYBE HELP ME FIND SOMEBODY...
YEAH? WHO'D HE PUT YOU UP TO ASK FOR? JOE STALIN?
NO, SIR. MY UNCLE, AND MAYBE MY POP.
OH, STOP, YOU'RE BREAKING MY HEART...
I THINK HE MEANS IT, JOE. HAVE YOU LOST YOUR FAMILY, KID?
YES, MA'AM. MY UNCLE WORKED AT A CAR FACTORY. MAYBE HE WAS HERE LAST NIGHT...?
SEE, HE'S ALL RIGHT. LET'S TAKE HIM WITH US.
OH, COME ON, MARY...
HIS PEOPLE ARE WITH US, JOE. BESIDES... A LITTLE PRACTICE TAKING CARE OF KIDS WOULDN'T DO YOU ANY HARM. WOULD IT?
GET THE KID SOME MILK AND A DOUGHNUT, WHY DON'T YOU?
MARY WAS LIKE SOMEONE IN A BOOK. SHE SPOKE HEROICALLY ABOUT IMPORTANT-SOUNDING THINGS, AND SHE DIDN'T TALK DOWN TO ME.
IT'S THE LAW OF VALUE THAT BROUGHT ALL THIS ON, SEE? AND BECAUSE HE WON'T UNDERSTAND, FORD JUST IN-CREASES THE MISERY OF THE MASSES AND THAT'S GOING TO LEAD TO A DICTATORSHIP OF THE PROLETARIAT. TODAY'S JUST THE FIRST STEP.
I DIDN'T REALLY UNDERSTAND MUCH OF IT, BUT IT WAS THRILLING TO HEAR HER TALK.
MOST THRILLING OF ALL WAS THE PART I UNDERSTOOD: WE WERE GOING TO THE FORD FACTORY, WHERE THE WORKERS WHO'D BEEN LAID OFF WERE GOING TO ASK FOR RELIEF... WHERE OTHER PEOPLE WOULD GO, ASKING FOR JOBS.
DANC
AROUND LUNCHTIME, THE TRUCK CAME THAT WOULD TAKE ME TO MY FATHER.

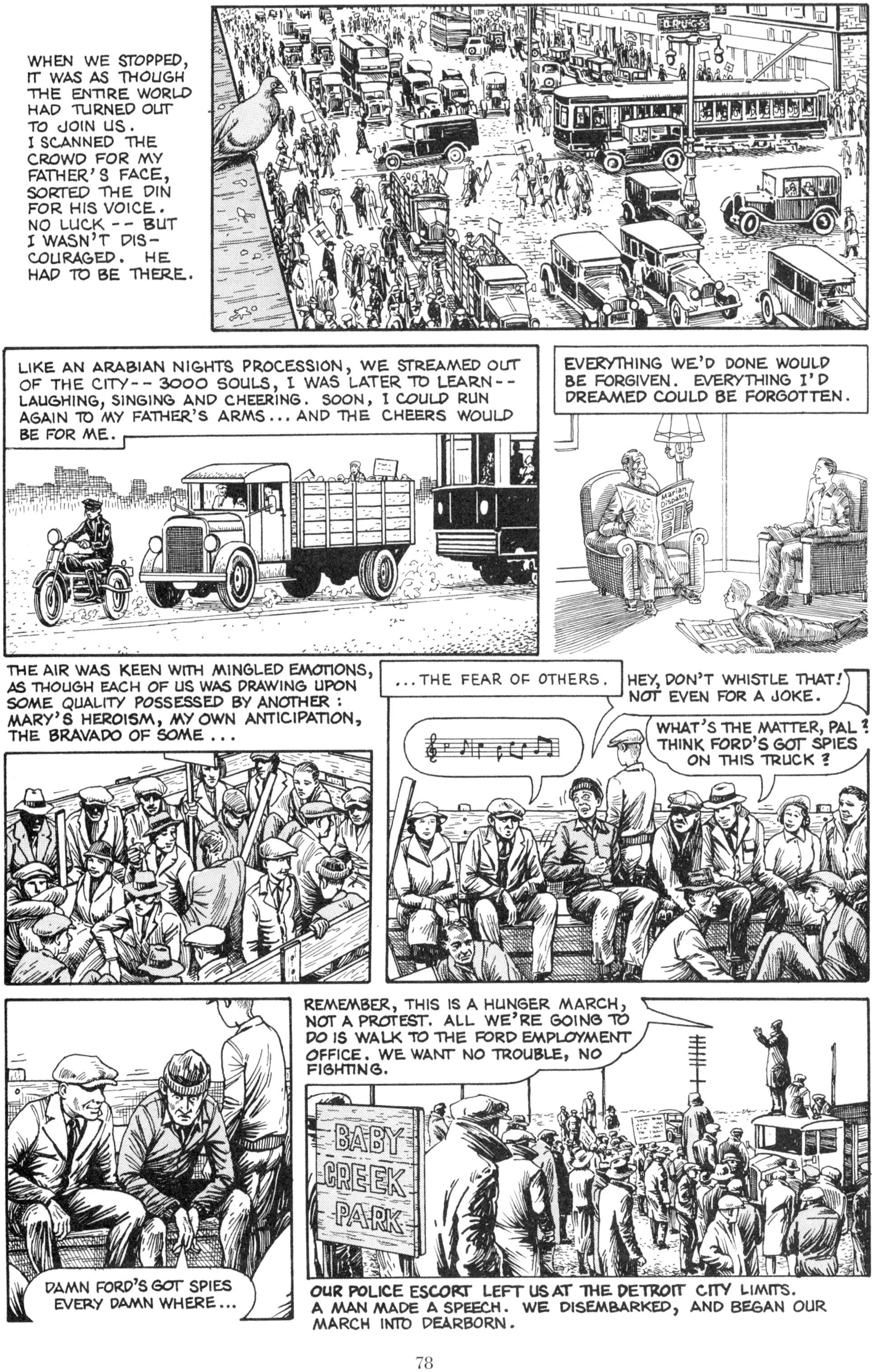
WHEN WE STOPPED, IT WAS AS THOUGH THE ENTIRE WORLD HAD TURNED OUT TO JOIN US. I SCANNED THE CROWD FOR MY FATHER'S FACE, SORTED THE DIN FOR HIS VOICE. NO LUCK -- BUT I WASN'T DIS-COURAGED. HE HAD TO BE THERE.
DRUGS
LIKE AN ARABIAN NIGHTS PROCESSION, WE STREAMED OUT OF THE CITY -- 3000 SOULS, I WAS LATER TO LEARN -- LAUGHING, SINGING AND CHEERING. SOON, I COULD RUN AGAIN TO MY FATHER'S ARMS... AND THE CHEERS WOULD BE FOR ME.
EVERYTHING WE'D DONE WOULD BE FORGIVEN. EVERYTHING I'D DREAMED COULD BE FORGOTTEN.
Marian Dispatch
THE AIR WAS KEEN WITH MINGLED EMOTIONS, AS THOUGH EACH OF US WAS DRAWING UPON SOME QUALITY POSSESSED BY ANOTHER: MARY'S HEROISM, MY OWN ANTICIPATION, THE BRAVADO OF SOME...
...THE FEAR OF OTHERS.
HEY, DON'T WHISTLE THAT! NOT EVEN FOR A JOKE.
WHAT'S THE MATTER, PAL? THINK FORD'S GOT SPIES ON THIS TRUCK?
DAMN FORD'S GOT SPIES EVERY DAMN WHERE...
REMEMBER, THIS IS A HUNGER MARCH, NOT A PROTEST. ALL WE'RE GOING TO DO IS WALK TO THE FORD EMPLOYMENT OFFICE. WE WANT NO TROUBLE, NO FIGHTING.
BABY CREEK PARK
OUR POLICE ESCORT LEFT US AT THE DETROIT CITY LIMITS. A MAN MADE A SPEECH. WE DISEMBARKED, AND BEGAN OUR MARCH INTO DEARBORN.

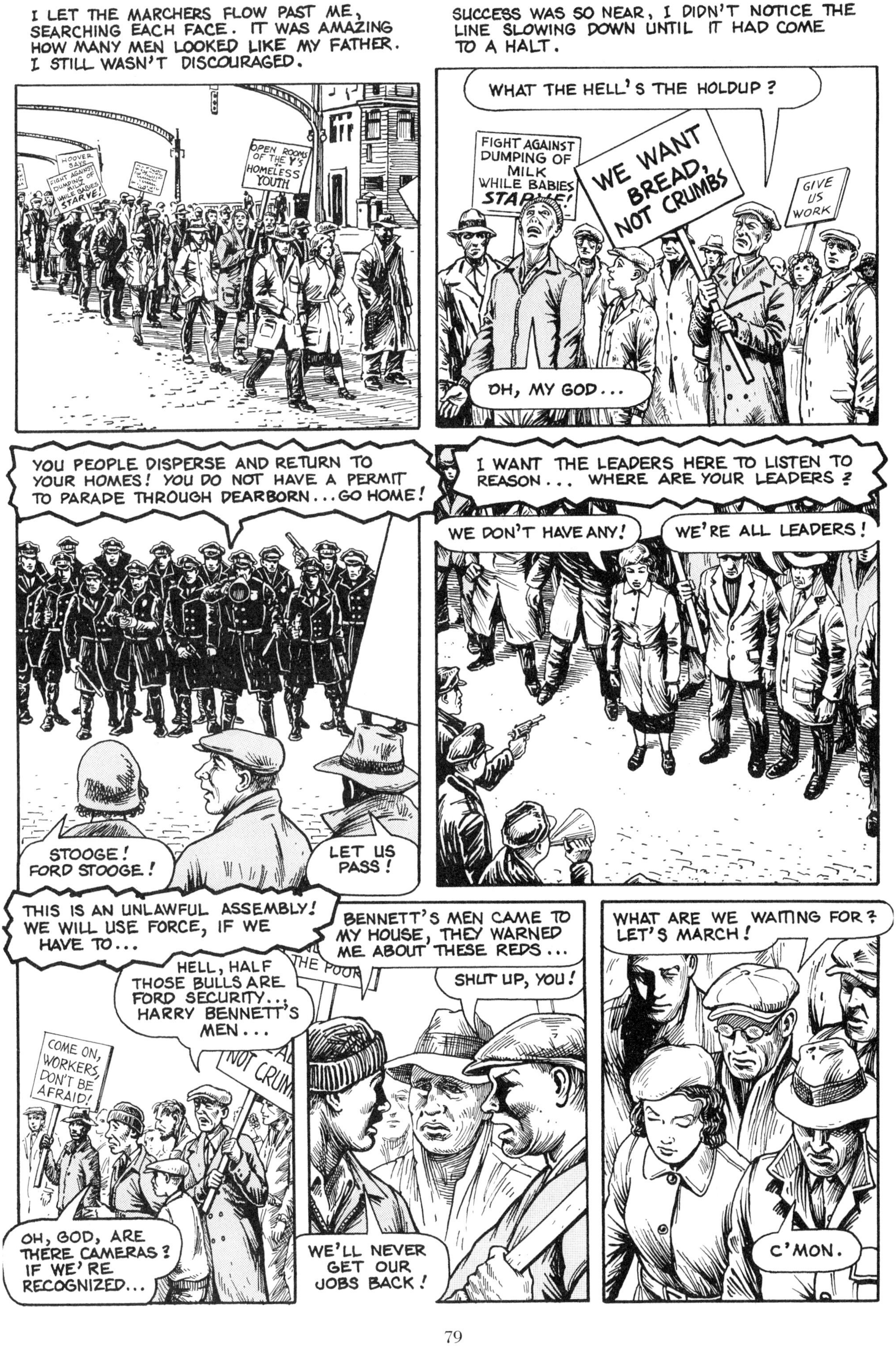
I LET THE MARCHERS FLOW PAST ME, SEARCHING EACH FACE. IT WAS AMAZING HOW MANY MEN LOOKED LIKE MY FATHER. I STILL WASN'T DISCOURAGED.
HOOVER SAYS
FIGHT AGAINST DUMPING OF MILK WHILE BABIES STARVE!
OPEN ROOMS OF THE Y'S TO HOMELESS YOUTH
SUCCESS WAS SO NEAR, I DIDN'T NOTICE THE LINE SLOWING DOWN UNTIL IT HAD COME TO A HALT.
WHAT THE HELL'S THE HOLDUP?
FIGHT AGAINST DUMPING OF MILK WHILE BABIES STARVE!
WE WANT BREAD, NOT CRUMBS
GIVE US WORK
OH, MY GOD...
YOU PEOPLE DISPERSE AND RETURN TO YOUR HOMES! YOU DO NOT HAVE A PERMIT TO PARADE THROUGH DEARBORN... GO HOME!
STOOGE! FORD STOOGE!
LET US PASS!
I WANT THE LEADERS HERE TO LISTEN TO REASON... WHERE ARE YOUR LEADERS?
WE DON'T HAVE ANY!
WE'RE ALL LEADERS!
THIS IS AN UNLAWFUL ASSEMBLY! WE WILL USE FORCE, IF WE HAVE TO...
HELL, HALF THOSE BULLS ARE FORD SECURITY... HARRY BENNETT'S MEN...
COME ON, WORKERS, DON'T BE AFRAID!
OH, GOD, ARE THERE CAMERAS? IF WE'RE RECOGNIZED...
BENNETT'S MEN CAME TO MY HOUSE, THEY WARNED ME ABOUT THESE REDS...
SHUT UP, YOU!
WE'LL NEVER GET OUR JOBS BACK!
WHAT ARE WE WAITING FOR? LET'S MARCH!
C'MON.

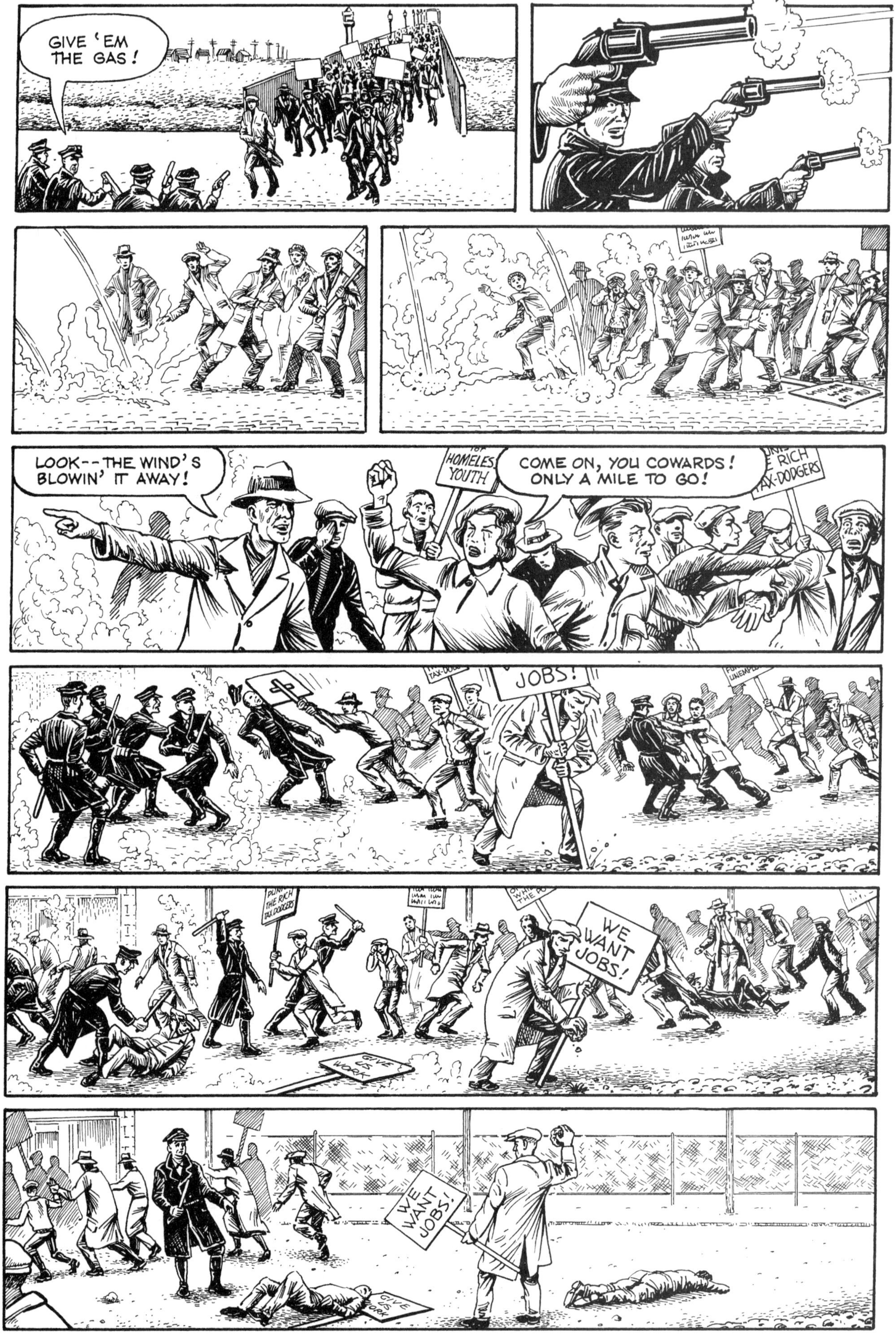

GIVE 'EM THE GAS!
LOOK--THE WIND'S BLOWIN' IT AWAY!
HOMELES YOUTH
COME ON, YOU COWARDS! ONLY A MILE TO GO!
RICH TAX-DODGERS
JOBS!
WE WANT JOBS!
GIVE US WORK
WE WANT JOBS!
GIVE US WORK

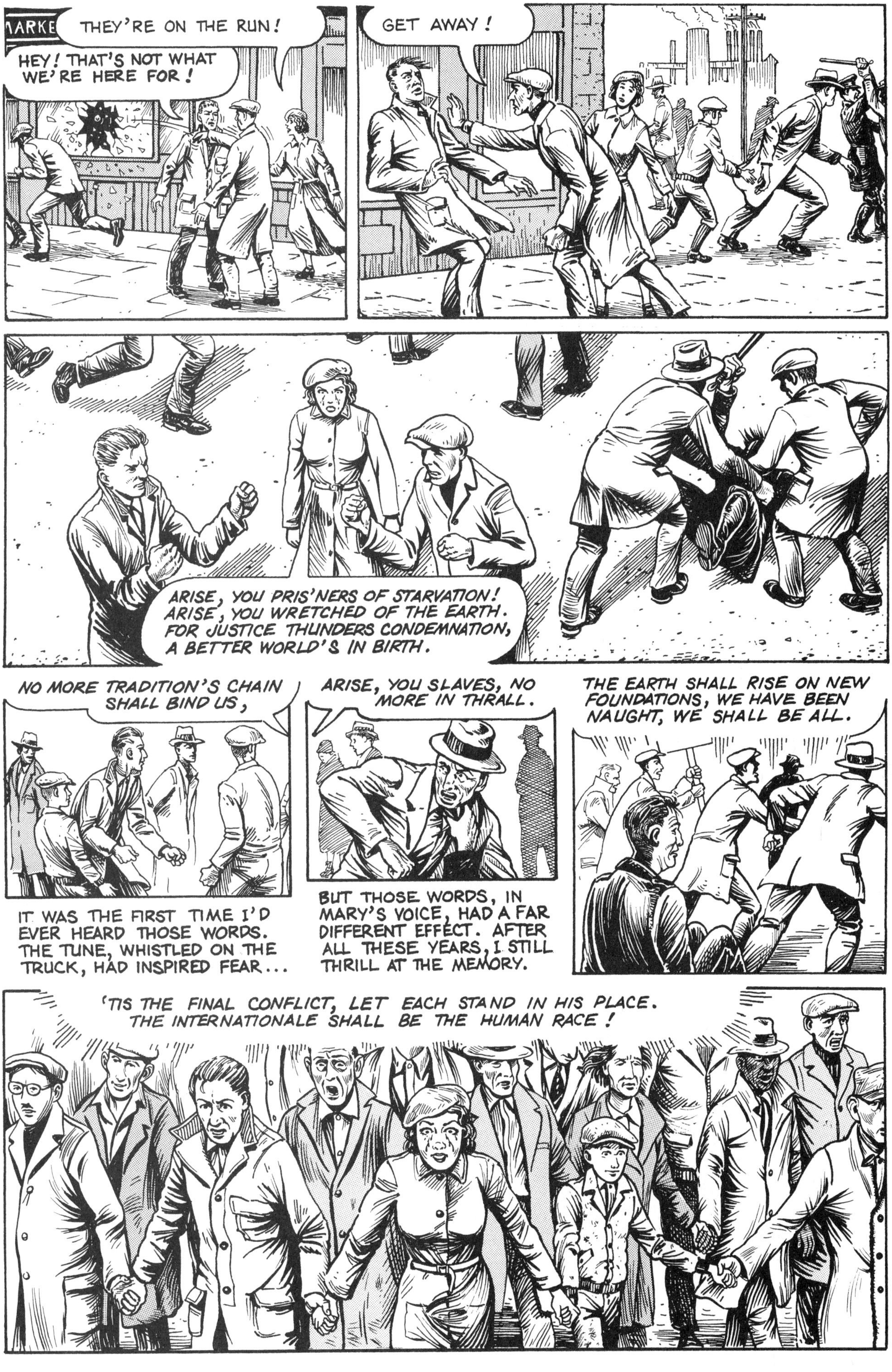
THEY'RE ON THE RUN!
HEY! THAT'S NOT WHAT WE'RE HERE FOR!
GET AWAY!
ARISE, YOU PRIS'NERS OF STARVATION! ARISE, YOU WRETCHED OF THE EARTH. FOR JUSTICE THUNDERS CONDEMNATION, A BETTER WORLD'S IN BIRTH.
NO MORE TRADITION'S CHAIN SHALL BIND US,
IT WAS THE FIRST TIME I'D EVER HEARD THOSE WORDS. THE TUNE, WHISTLED ON THE TRUCK, HAD INSPIRED FEAR...
ARISE, YOU SLAVES, NO MORE IN THRALL.
BUT THOSE WORDS, IN MARY'S VOICE, HAD A FAR DIFFERENT EFFECT. AFTER ALL THESE YEARS, I STILL THRILL AT THE MEMORY.
THE EARTH SHALL RISE ON NEW FOUNDATIONS, WE HAVE BEEN NAUGHT, WE SHALL BE ALL.
'TIS THE FINAL CONFLICT, LET EACH STAND IN HIS PLACE. THE INTERNATIONALE SHALL BE THE HUMAN RACE!

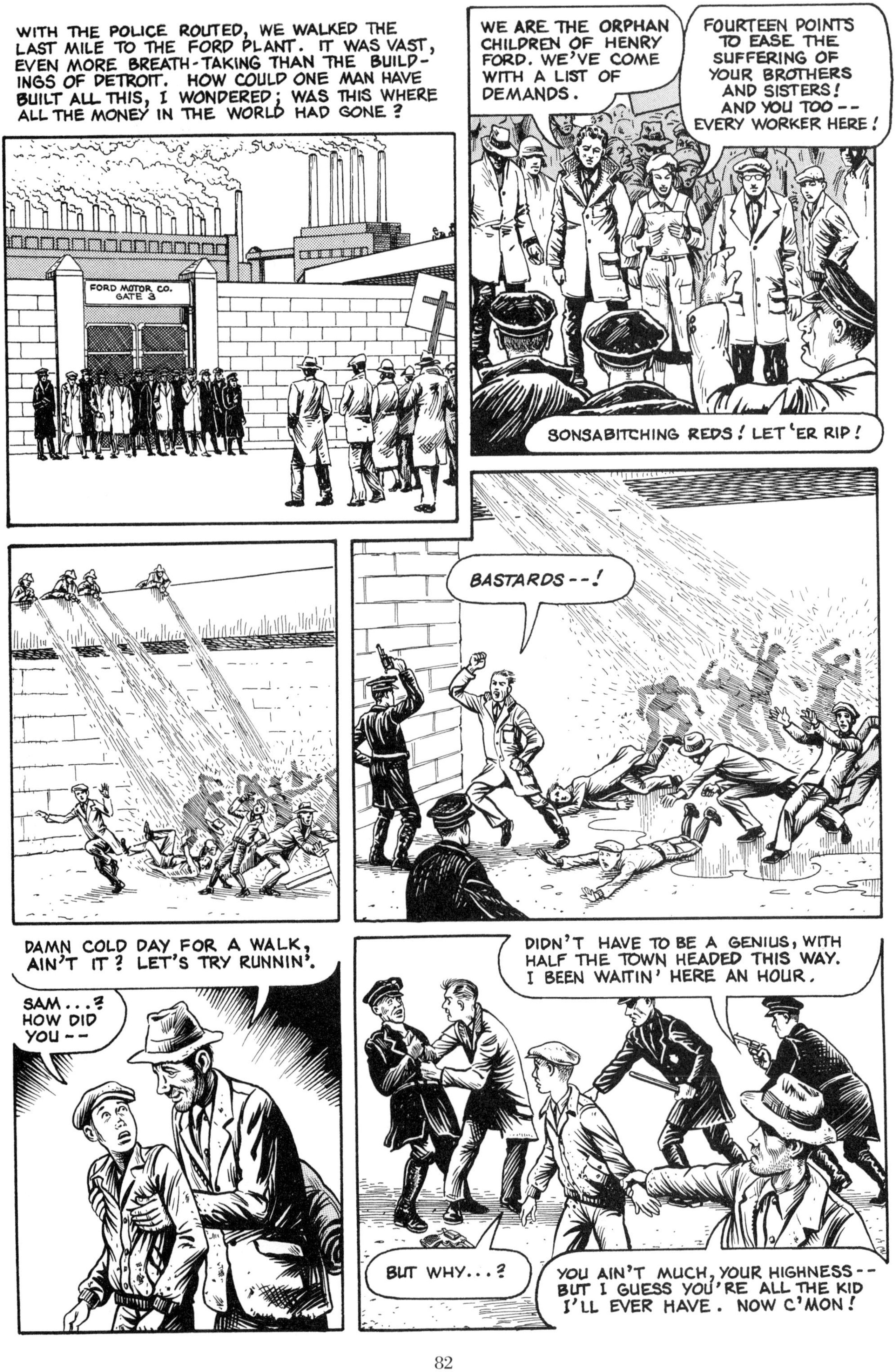
WITH THE POLICE ROUTED, WE WALKED THE LAST MILE TO THE FORD PLANT. IT WAS VAST, EVEN MORE BREATH-TAKING THAN THE BUILDINGS OF DETROIT. HOW COULD ONE MAN HAVE BUILT ALL THIS, I WONDERED; WAS THIS WHERE ALL THE MONEY IN THE WORLD HAD GONE?
FORD MOTOR CO. GATE 3
WE ARE THE ORPHAN CHILDREN OF HENRY FORD. WE'VE COME WITH A LIST OF DEMANDS.
FOURTEEN POINTS TO EASE THE SUFFERING OF YOUR BROTHERS AND SISTERS! AND YOU TOO -- EVERY WORKER HERE!
SONSABITCHING REDS! LET 'ER RIP!
BASTARDS --!
DAMN COLD DAY FOR A WALK, AIN'T IT? LET'S TRY RUNNIN'.
SAM...? HOW DID YOU --
DIDN'T HAVE TO BE A GENIUS, WITH HALF THE TOWN HEADED THIS WAY. I BEEN WAITIN' HERE AN HOUR.
BUT WHY...?
YOU AIN'T MUCH, YOUR HIGHNESS -- BUT I GUESS YOU'RE ALL THE KID I'LL EVER HAVE. NOW C'MON!

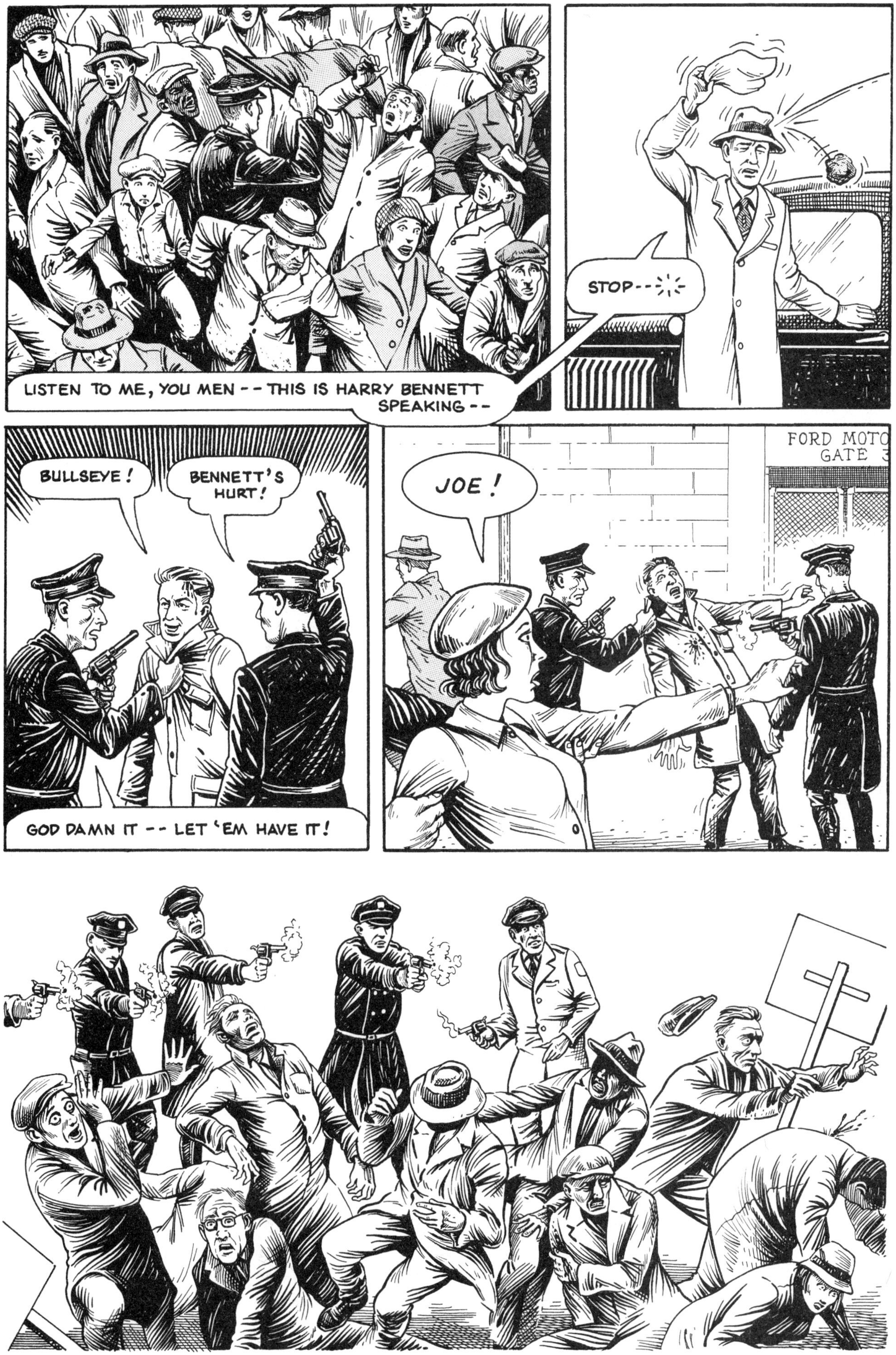
LISTEN TO ME, YOU MEN -- THIS IS HARRY BENNETT SPEAKING --
STOP--
BULLSEYE!
BENNETT'S HURT!
GOD DAMN IT -- LET 'EM HAVE IT!
JOE!
FORD MOTO
GATE 3

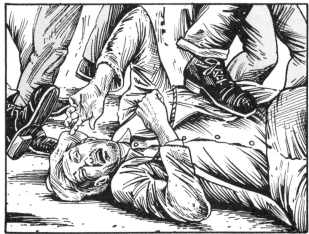

OH, MY GOD...
ALL THAT TIME IN
FRANCE AND NEVER
GOT HIT...

HOLD YOUR
FIRE!

AND THEN I GET HIT
LOOKIN' FOR A JOB...

STOP ME IF YOU HEARD
THIS ONE BEFORE...
-; COUGH ;-

OHH...

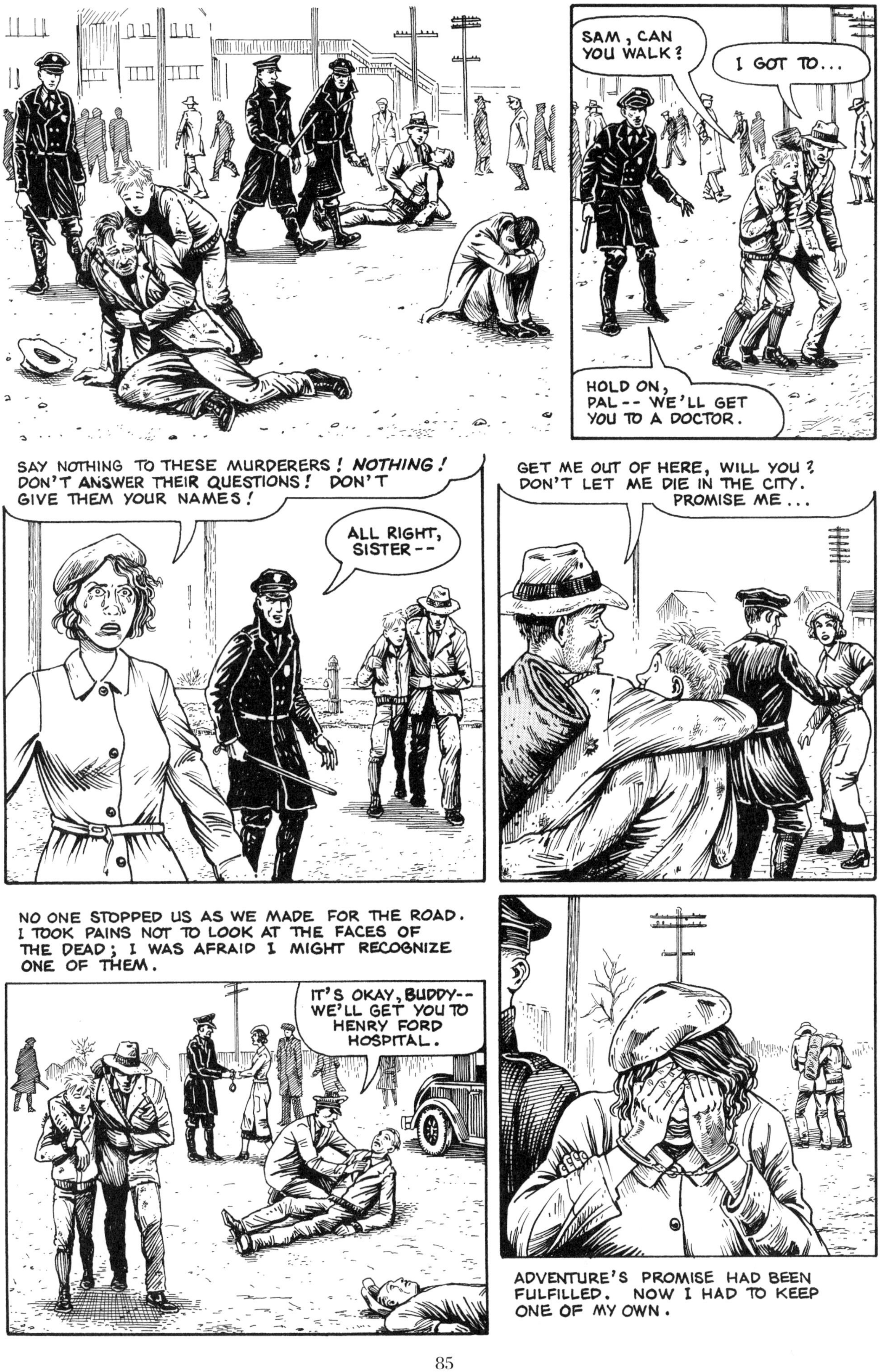
SAM, CAN YOU WALK?
I GOT TO...
HOLD ON, PAL -- WE'LL GET YOU TO A DOCTOR.
SAY NOTHING TO THESE MURDERERS! *NOTHING!* DON'T ANSWER THEIR QUESTIONS! DON'T GIVE THEM YOUR NAMES!
ALL RIGHT, SISTER --
GET ME OUT OF HERE, WILL YOU? DON'T LET ME DIE IN THE CITY. PROMISE ME...
NO ONE STOPPED US AS WE MADE FOR THE ROAD. I TOOK PAINS NOT TO LOOK AT THE FACES OF THE DEAD; I WAS AFRAID I MIGHT RECOGNIZE ONE OF THEM.
IT'S OKAY, BUDDY -- WE'LL GET YOU TO HENRY FORD HOSPITAL.
ADVENTURE'S PROMISE HAD BEEN FULFILLED. NOW I HAD TO KEEP ONE OF MY OWN.

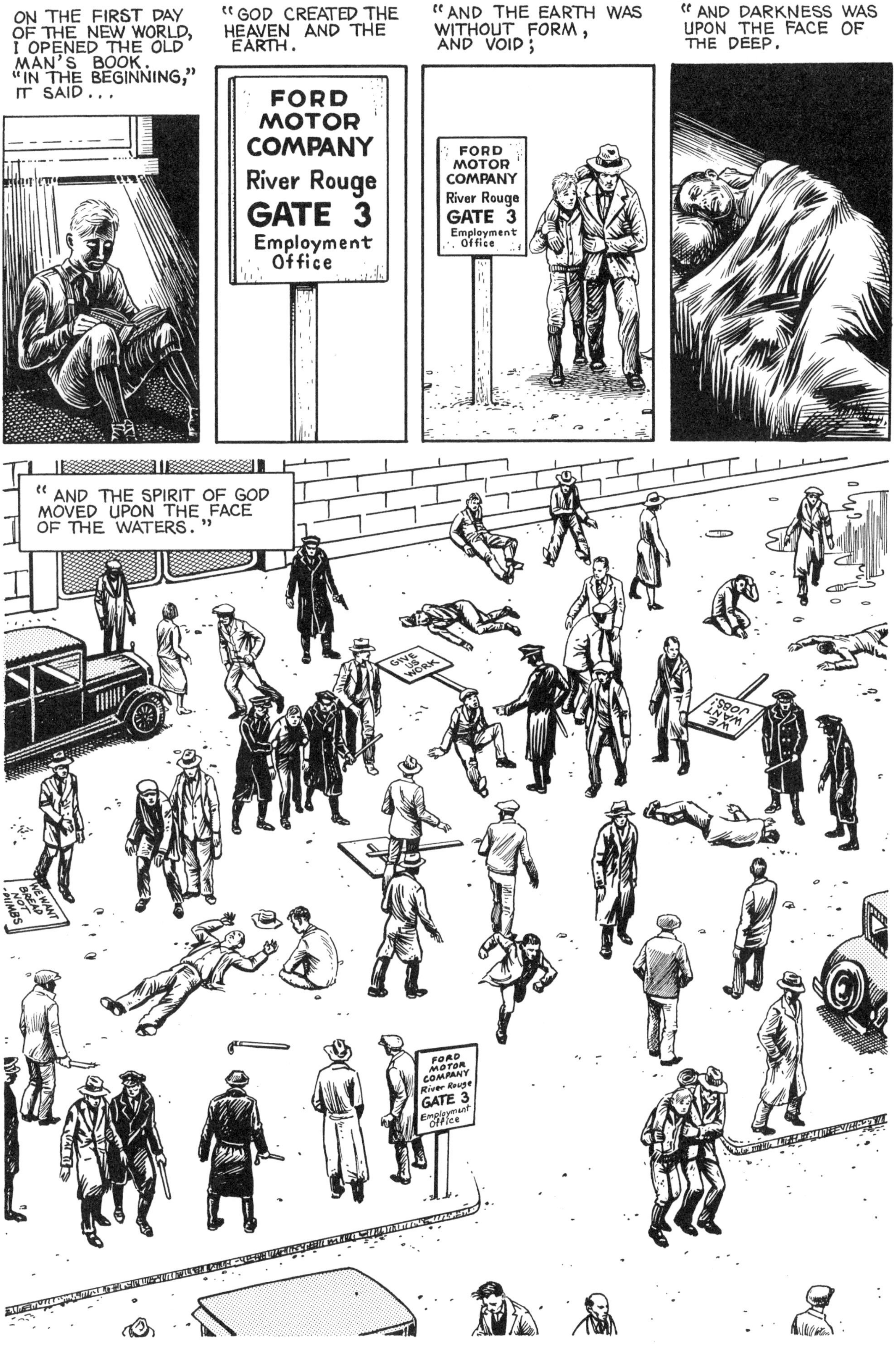
ON THE FIRST DAY OF THE NEW WORLD, I OPENED THE OLD MAN'S BOOK. "IN THE BEGINNING," IT SAID...
FORD MOTOR COMPANY River Rouge GATE 3 Employment Office
"GOD CREATED THE HEAVEN AND THE EARTH.
"AND THE EARTH WAS WITHOUT FORM, AND VOID;
FORD MOTOR COMPANY River Rouge GATE 3 Employment Office
"AND DARKNESS WAS UPON THE FACE OF THE DEEP.
"AND THE SPIRIT OF GOD MOVED UPON THE FACE OF THE WATERS."
GIVE US WORK
WE WANT JOBS!
FORD MOTOR COMPANY River Rouge GATE 3 Employment Office

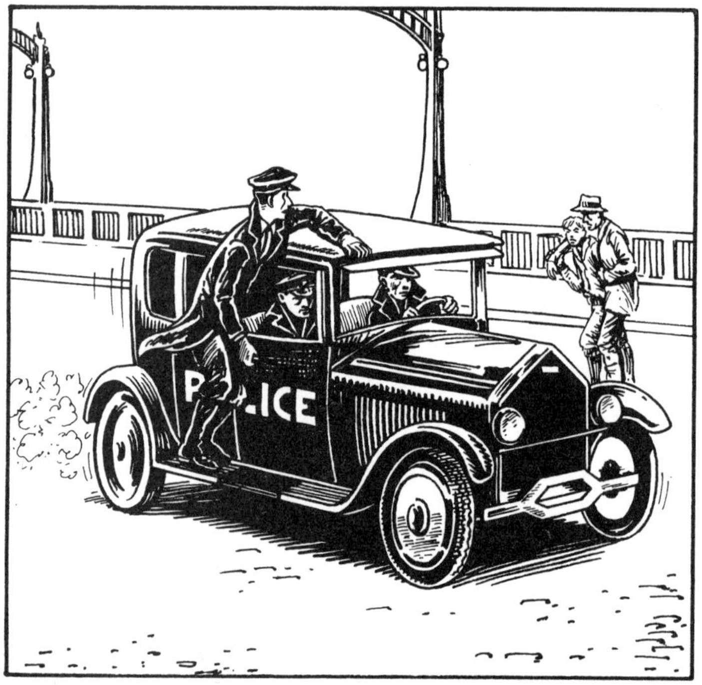
P LICE

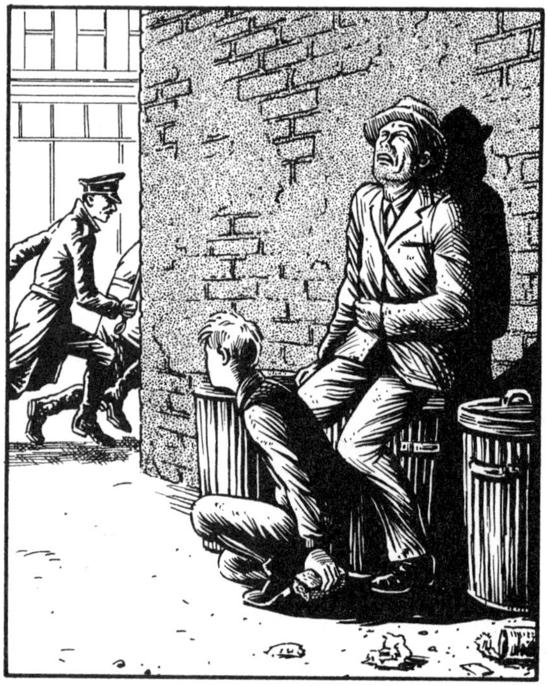

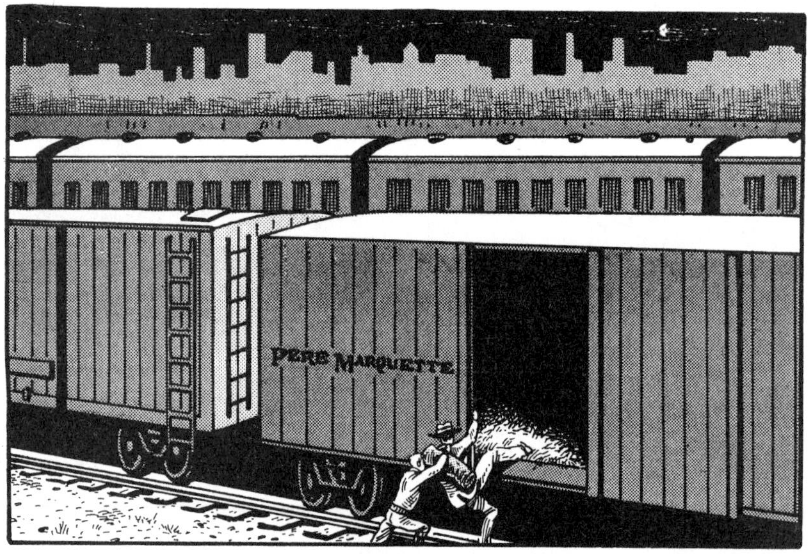
PERE MARQUETTE

"AND GOD SAID, LET THERE BE LIGHT: AND THERE WAS LIGHT.

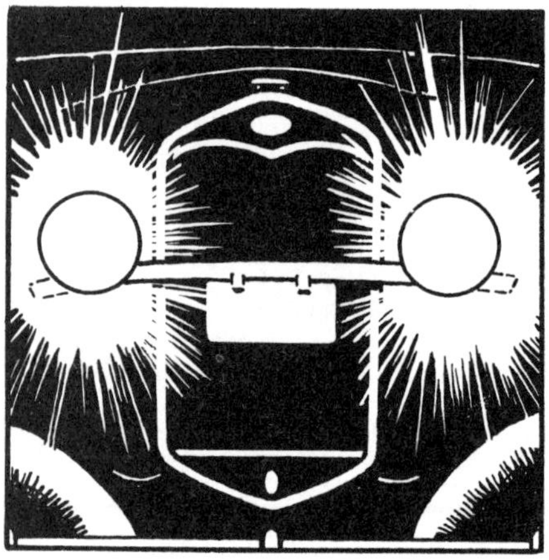

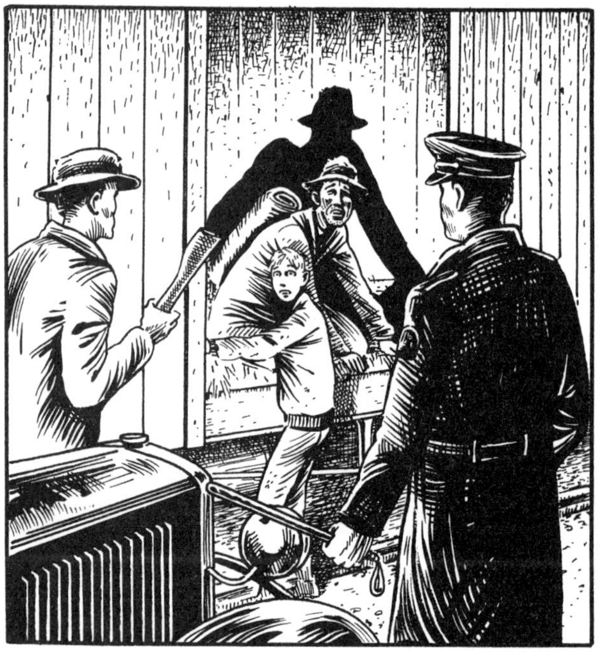

"AND GOD SAW THE LIGHT, THAT IT WAS GOOD: AND GOD DIVIDED THE LIGHT FROM THE DARKNESS."

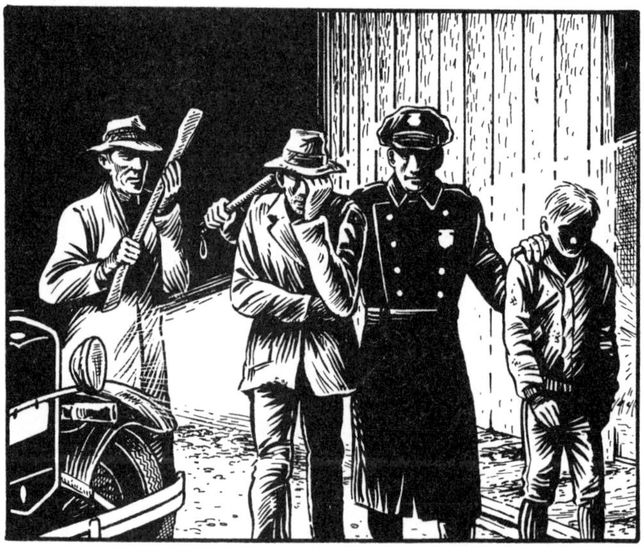

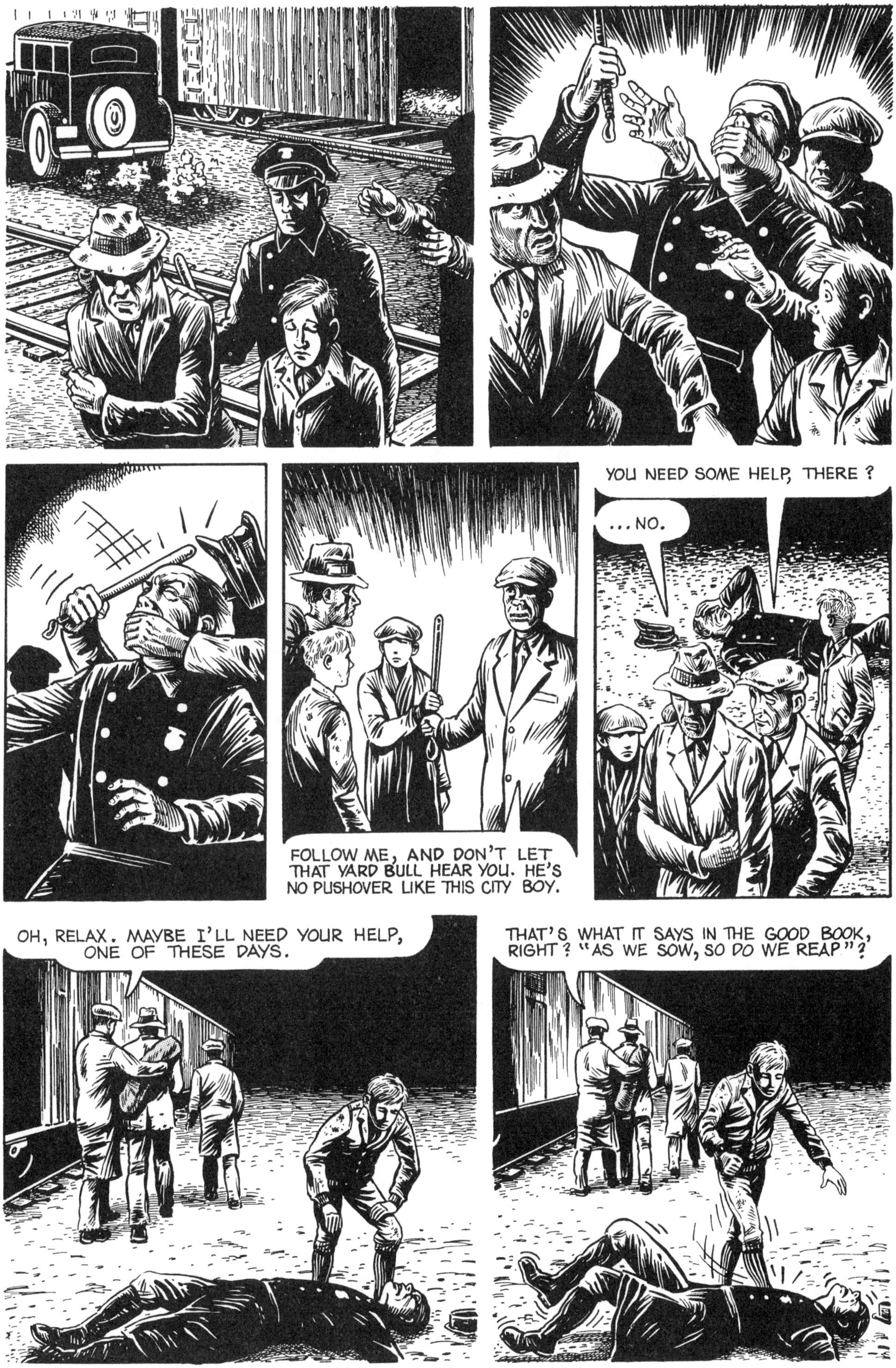
YOU NEED SOME HELP, THERE ?
...NO.
FOLLOW ME, AND DON'T LET THAT YARD BULL HEAR YOU. HE'S NO PUSHOVER LIKE THIS CITY BOY.
OH, RELAX. MAYBE I'LL NEED YOUR HELP, ONE OF THESE DAYS.
THAT'S WHAT IT SAYS IN THE GOOD BOOK, RIGHT ? "AS WE SOW, SO DO WE REAP" ?

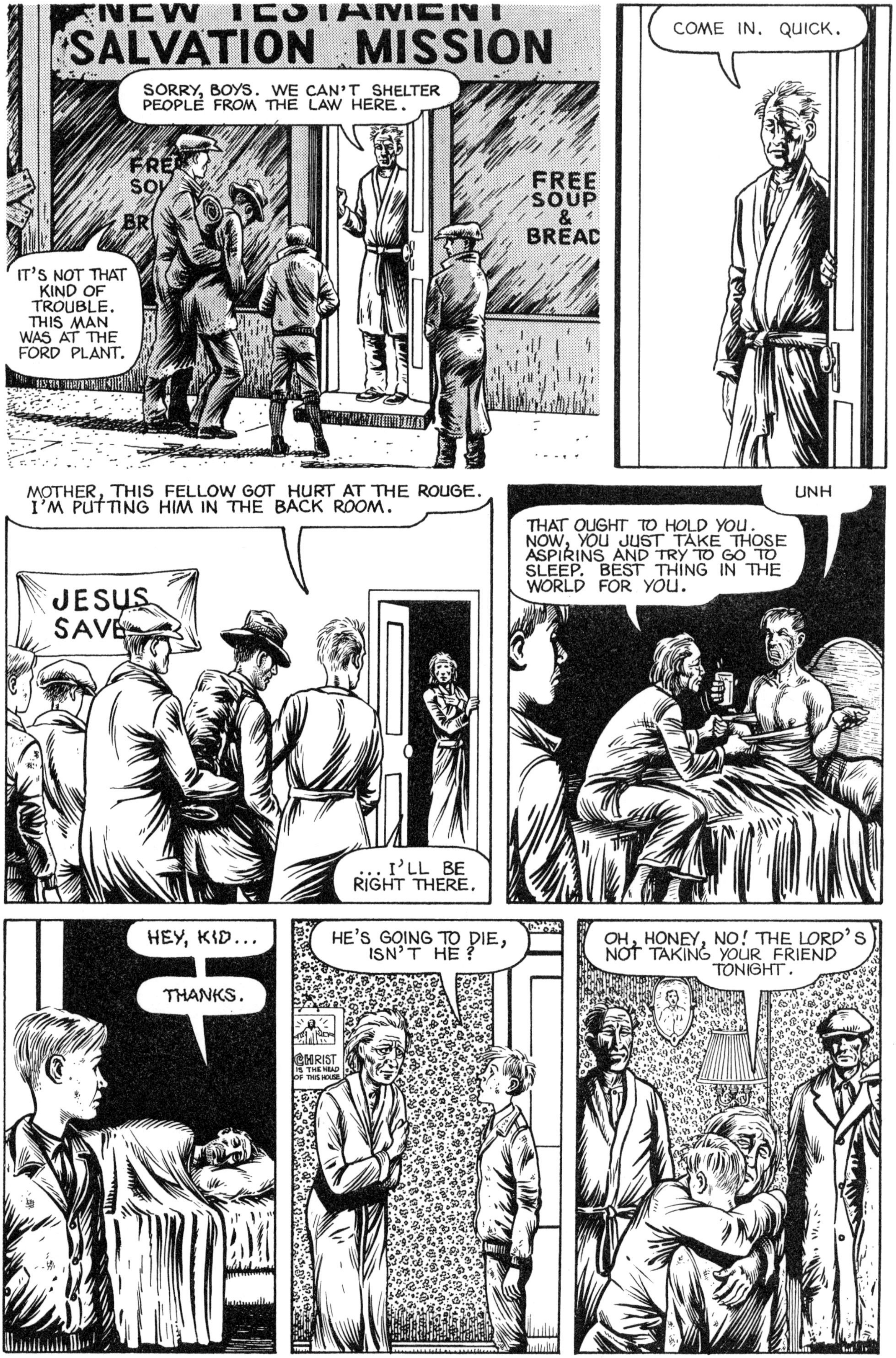
NEW TESTAMENT
SALVATION MISSION
SORRY, BOYS. WE CAN'T SHELTER PEOPLE FROM THE LAW HERE.
FREE SOUP & BREAD
IT'S NOT THAT KIND OF TROUBLE. THIS MAN WAS AT THE FORD PLANT.
COME IN. QUICK.
MOTHER, THIS FELLOW GOT HURT AT THE ROUGE. I'M PUTTING HIM IN THE BACK ROOM.
JESUS SAVE
... I'LL BE RIGHT THERE.
UNH
THAT OUGHT TO HOLD YOU. NOW, YOU JUST TAKE THOSE ASPIRINS AND TRY TO GO TO SLEEP. BEST THING IN THE WORLD FOR YOU.
HEY, KID...
THANKS.
HE'S GOING TO DIE, ISN'T HE?
CHRIST IS THE HEAD OF THIS HOUSE
OH, HONEY, NO! THE LORD'S NOT TAKING YOUR FRIEND TONIGHT.

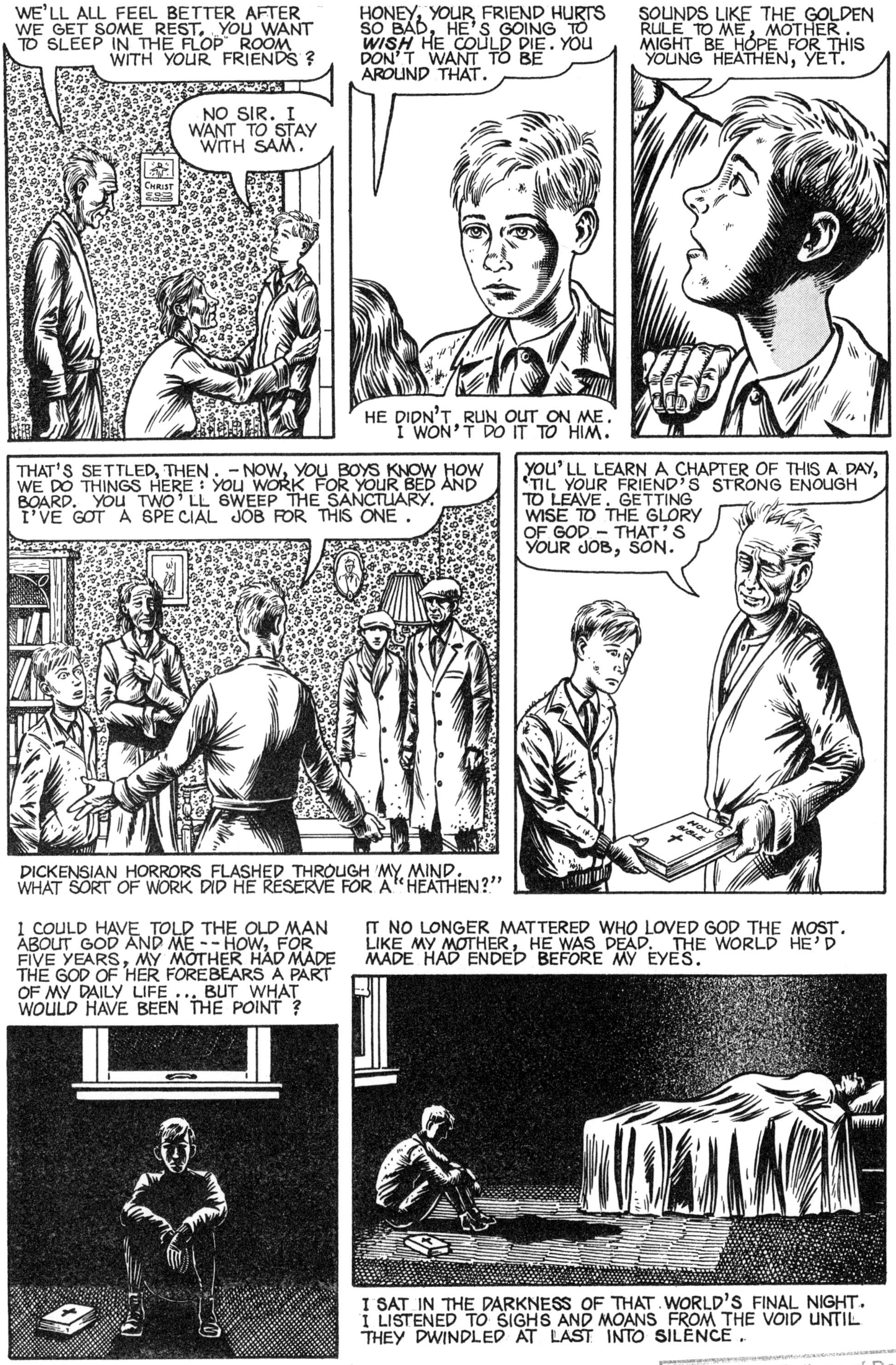
WE'LL ALL FEEL BETTER AFTER WE GET SOME REST. YOU WANT TO SLEEP IN THE FLOP ROOM WITH YOUR FRIENDS?
NO SIR. I WANT TO STAY WITH SAM.
CHRIST
HONEY, YOUR FRIEND HURTS SO BAD, HE'S GOING TO *WISH* HE COULD DIE. YOU DON'T WANT TO BE AROUND THAT.
HE DIDN'T RUN OUT ON ME. I WON'T DO IT TO HIM.
SOUNDS LIKE THE GOLDEN RULE TO ME, MOTHER. MIGHT BE HOPE FOR THIS YOUNG HEATHEN, YET.
THAT'S SETTLED, THEN. - NOW, YOU BOYS KNOW HOW WE DO THINGS HERE: YOU WORK FOR YOUR BED AND BOARD. YOU TWO'LL SWEEP THE SANCTUARY. I'VE GOT A SPECIAL JOB FOR THIS ONE.
DICKENSIAN HORRORS FLASHED THROUGH MY MIND. WHAT SORT OF WORK DID HE RESERVE FOR A "HEATHEN?"
YOU'LL LEARN A CHAPTER OF THIS A DAY, 'TIL YOUR FRIEND'S STRONG ENOUGH TO LEAVE. GETTING WISE TO THE GLORY OF GOD - THAT'S YOUR JOB, SON.
HOLY BIBLE
I COULD HAVE TOLD THE OLD MAN ABOUT GOD AND ME -- HOW, FOR FIVE YEARS, MY MOTHER HAD MADE THE GOD OF HER FOREBEARS A PART OF MY DAILY LIFE ... BUT WHAT WOULD HAVE BEEN THE POINT?
IT NO LONGER MATTERED WHO LOVED GOD THE MOST. LIKE MY MOTHER, HE WAS DEAD. THE WORLD HE'D MADE HAD ENDED BEFORE MY EYES.
I SAT IN THE DARKNESS OF THAT WORLD'S FINAL NIGHT. I LISTENED TO SIGHS AND MOANS FROM THE VOID UNTIL THEY DWINDLED AT LAST INTO SILENCE.

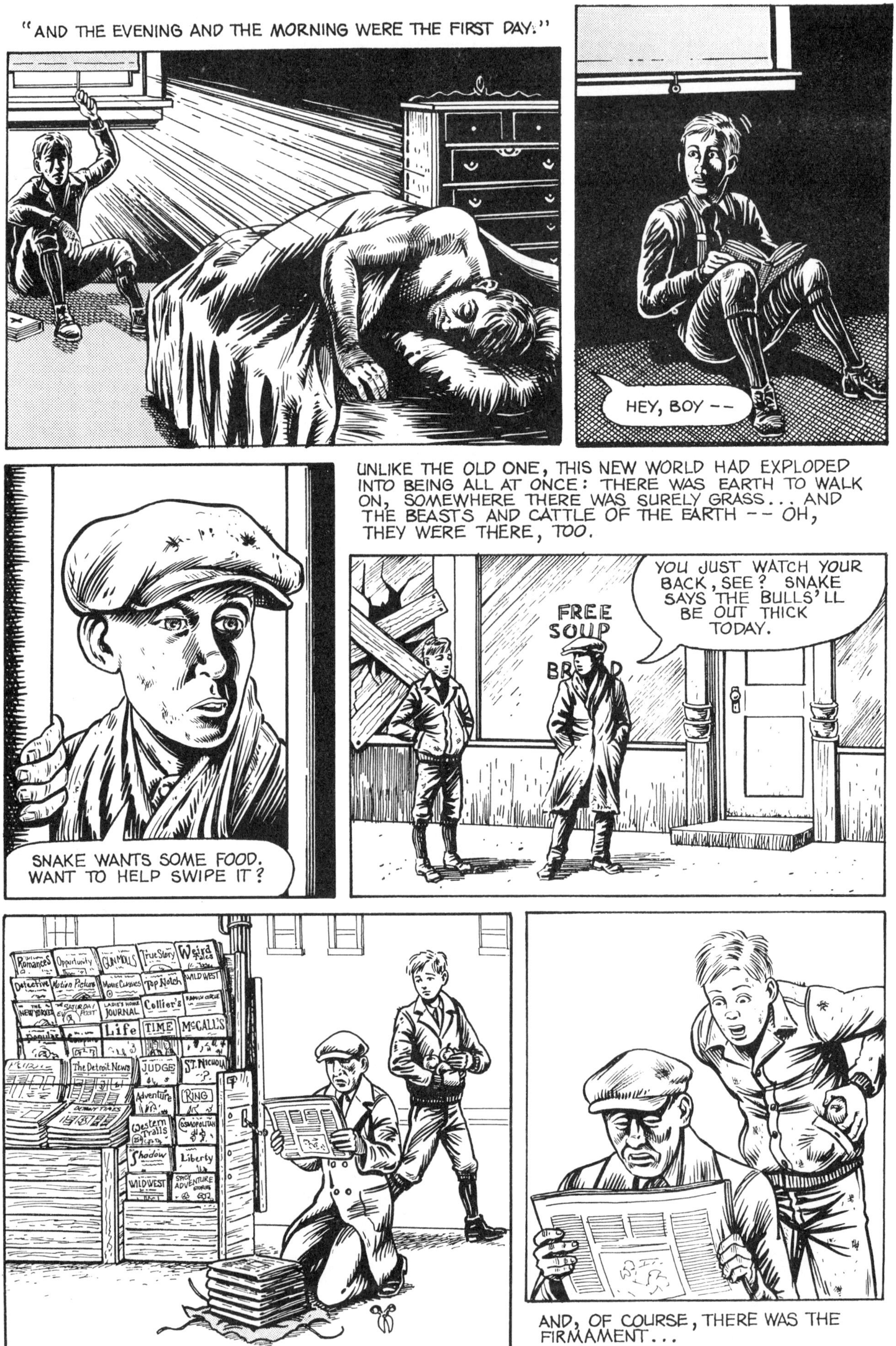
"AND THE EVENING AND THE MORNING WERE THE FIRST DAY."
HEY, BOY --
UNLIKE THE OLD ONE, THIS NEW WORLD HAD EXPLODED INTO BEING ALL AT ONCE: THERE WAS EARTH TO WALK ON, SOMEWHERE THERE WAS SURELY GRASS... AND THE BEASTS AND CATTLE OF THE EARTH -- OH, THEY WERE THERE, TOO.
SNAKE WANTS SOME FOOD. WANT TO HELP SWIPE IT?
FREE SOUP
YOU JUST WATCH YOUR BACK, SEE? SNAKE SAYS THE BULLS'LL BE OUT THICK TODAY.
AND, OF COURSE, THERE WAS THE FIRMAMENT...

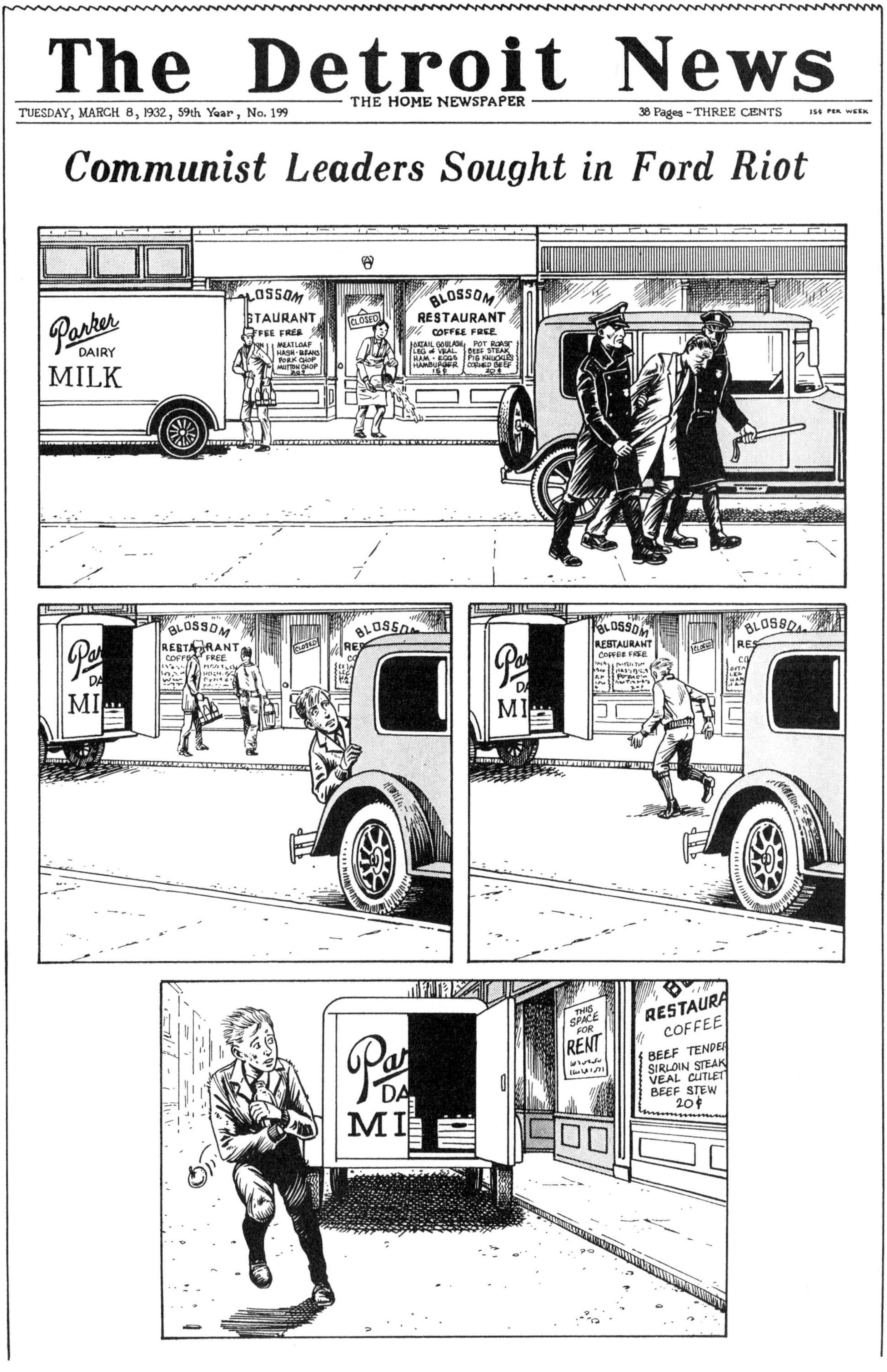

The Detroit News
THE HOME NEWSPAPER
TUESDAY, MARCH 8, 1932, 59th Year, No. 199
38 Pages - THREE CENTS
15¢ PER WEEK
Communist Leaders Sought in Ford Riot
Parker DAIRY MILK
BLOSSOM RESTAURANT COFFEE FREE
CLOSED
MEATLOAF HASH-BEANS PORK CHOP MUTTON CHOP
OXTAIL GOULASH LEG of VEAL HAM - EGGS HAMBURGER 15¢
POT ROAST BEEF STEAK PIG KNUCKLES CORNED BEEF 20¢
THIS SPACE FOR RENT
RESTAURA
COFFEE
BEEF TENDER
SIRLOIN STEAK
VEAL CUTLET
BEEF STEW
20¢

THE "FIRMAMENT" IS THE MOST MYSTICAL PART OF THE STORY OF CREATION: SOME HOLD IT TO BE THE ARCH OF HEAVEN, THE FRAMEWORK OF THE UNIVERSE -- OTHERS SAY IT MEANS THE RAW STUFF OF CREATION ITSELF, FROM WHICH ALL THAT EXISTS WAS FORMED.

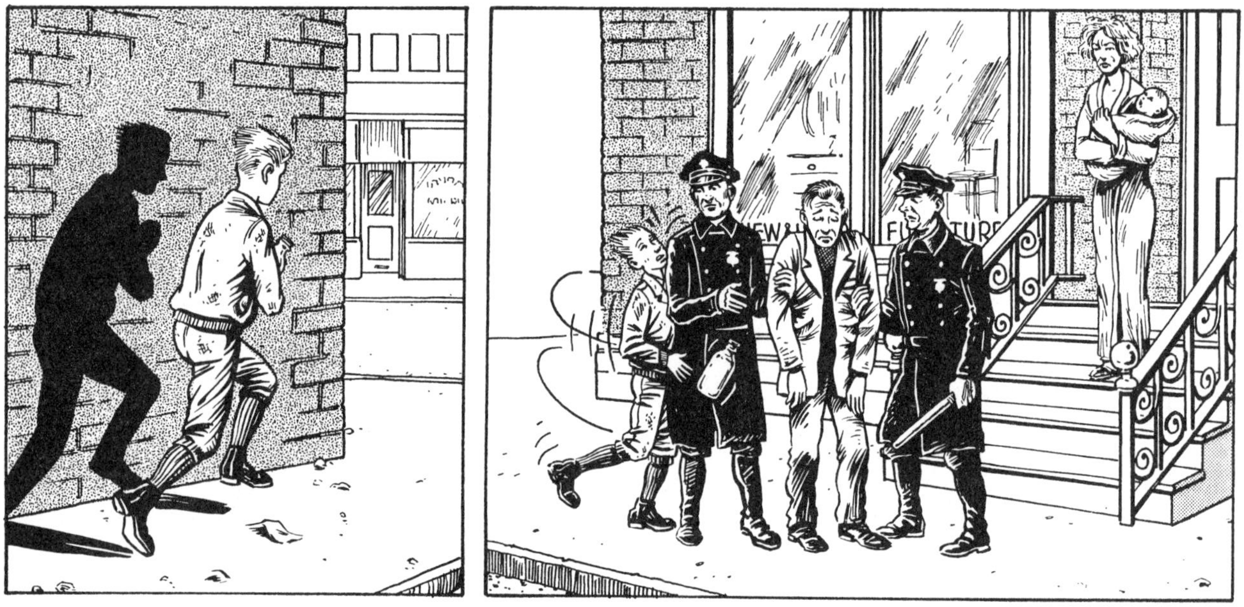

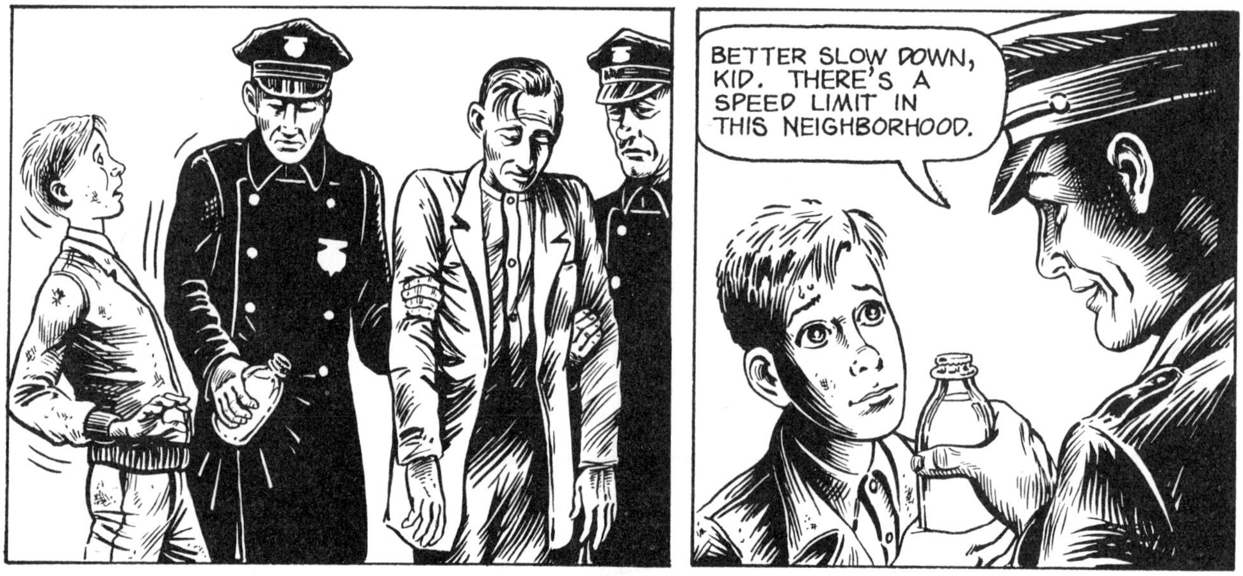
BETTER SLOW DOWN, KID. THERE'S A SPEED LIMIT IN THIS NEIGHBORHOOD.

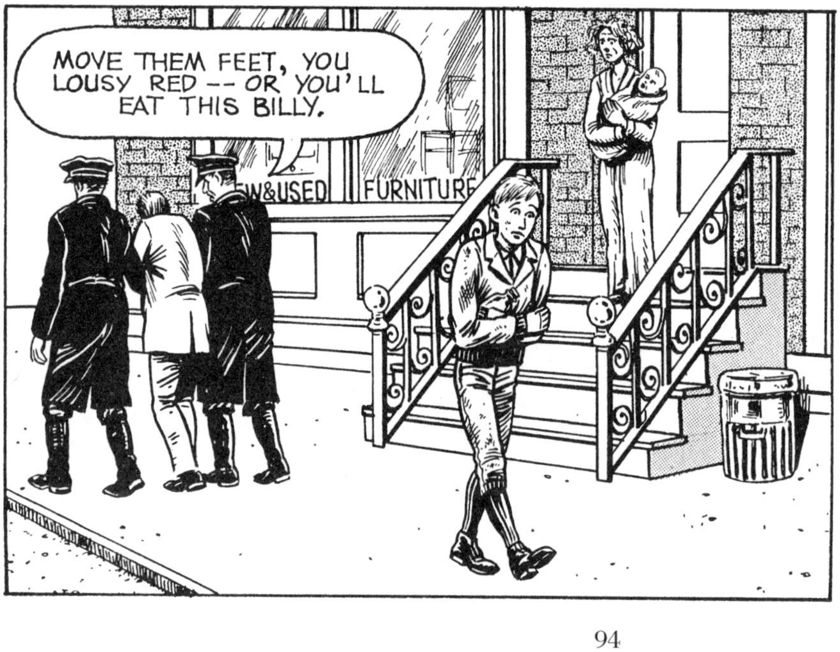
MOVE THEM FEET, YOU LOUSY RED -- OR YOU'LL EAT THIS BILLY.
FURNITURE

LIKE HIS PREDECESSOR, THE NEW LORD OF CREATION HAD SAID, "LET THERE BE A FIRMAMENT," AND IT WAS SO. "THUS THE HEAVENS AND THE EARTH WERE FINISHED, AND ALL THE HOST OF THEM" -- AND MY PLACE IN THE NEW ORDER WAS SET.

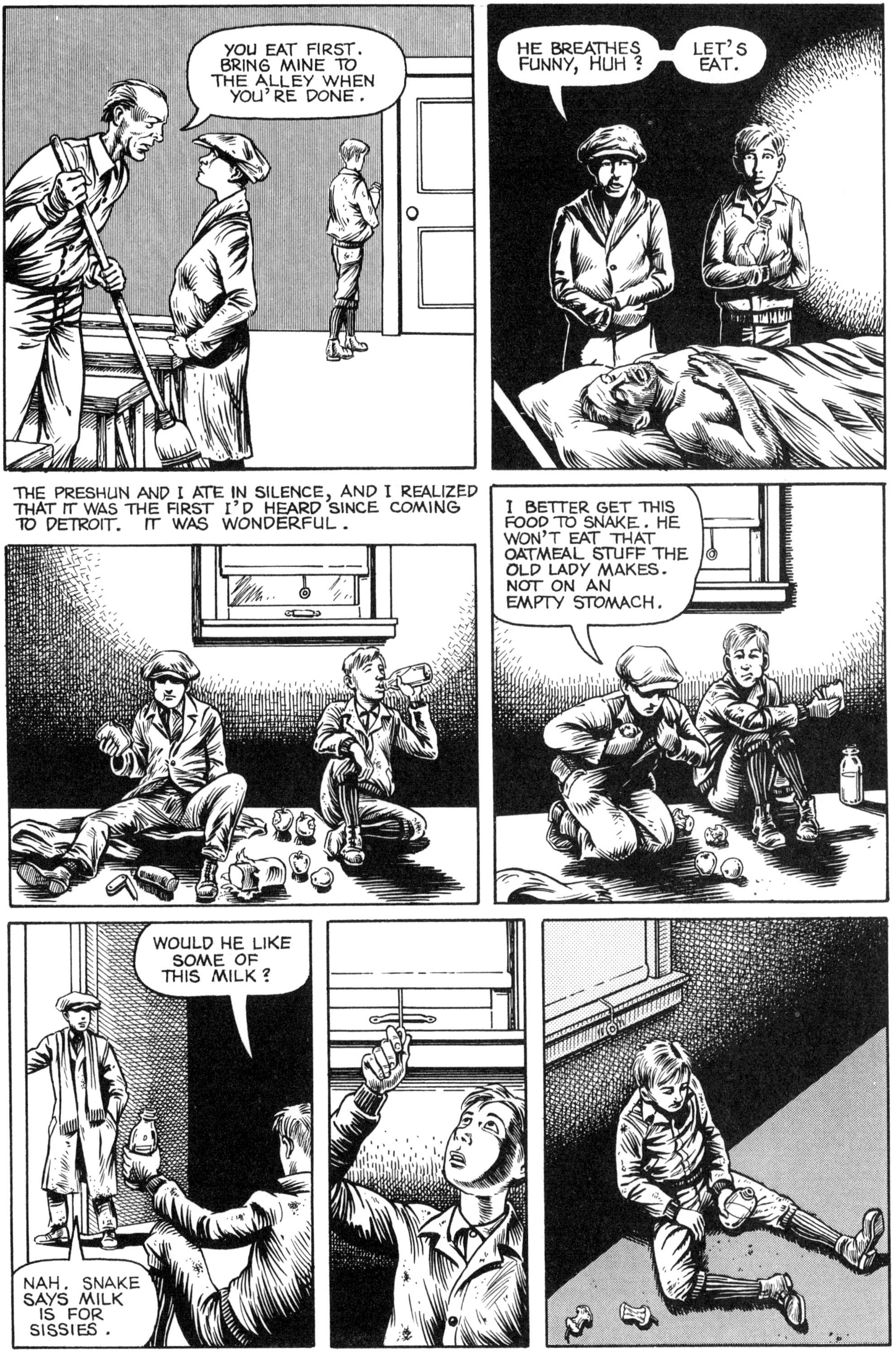
YOU EAT FIRST. BRING MINE TO THE ALLEY WHEN YOU'RE DONE.
HE BREATHES FUNNY, HUH ?
LET'S EAT.
THE PRESHUN AND I ATE IN SILENCE, AND I REALIZED THAT IT WAS THE FIRST I'D HEARD SINCE COMING TO DETROIT. IT WAS WONDERFUL.
I BETTER GET THIS FOOD TO SNAKE. HE WON'T EAT THAT OATMEAL STUFF THE OLD LADY MAKES. NOT ON AN EMPTY STOMACH.
WOULD HE LIKE SOME OF THIS MILK ?
NAH. SNAKE SAYS MILK IS FOR SISSIES.

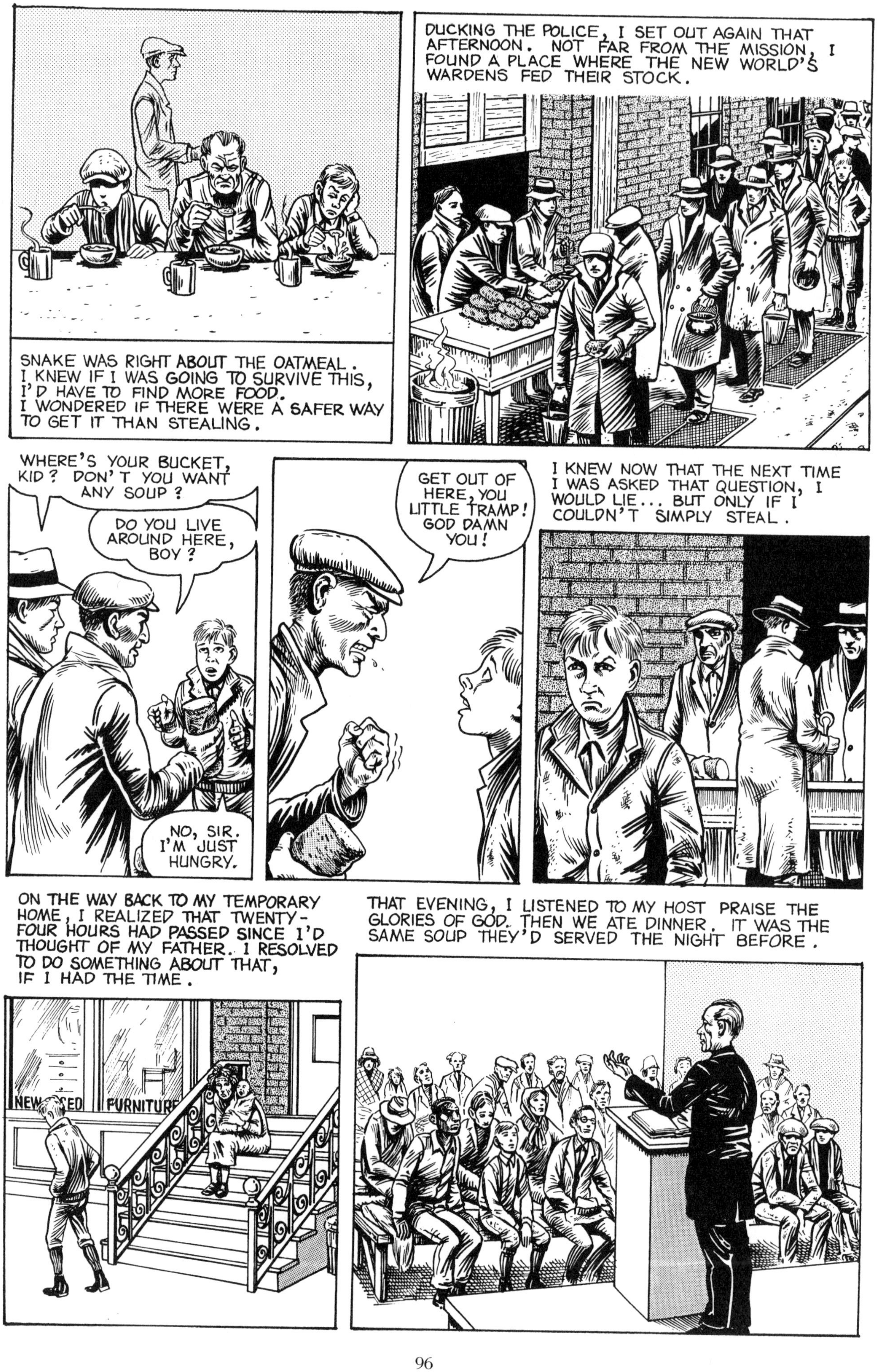
SNAKE WAS RIGHT ABOUT THE OATMEAL. I KNEW IF I WAS GOING TO SURVIVE THIS, I'D HAVE TO FIND MORE FOOD. I WONDERED IF THERE WERE A SAFER WAY TO GET IT THAN STEALING.
DUCKING THE POLICE, I SET OUT AGAIN THAT AFTERNOON. NOT FAR FROM THE MISSION, I FOUND A PLACE WHERE THE NEW WORLD'S WARDENS FED THEIR STOCK.
WHERE'S YOUR BUCKET, KID? DON'T YOU WANT ANY SOUP?
DO YOU LIVE AROUND HERE, BOY?
NO, SIR. I'M JUST HUNGRY.
GET OUT OF HERE, YOU LITTLE TRAMP! GOD DAMN YOU!
I KNEW NOW THAT THE NEXT TIME I WAS ASKED THAT QUESTION, I WOULD LIE... BUT ONLY IF I COULDN'T SIMPLY STEAL.
ON THE WAY BACK TO MY TEMPORARY HOME, I REALIZED THAT TWENTY-FOUR HOURS HAD PASSED SINCE I'D THOUGHT OF MY FATHER. I RESOLVED TO DO SOMETHING ABOUT THAT, IF I HAD THE TIME.
THAT EVENING, I LISTENED TO MY HOST PRAISE THE GLORIES OF GOD. THEN WE ATE DINNER. IT WAS THE SAME SOUP THEY'D SERVED THE NIGHT BEFORE.

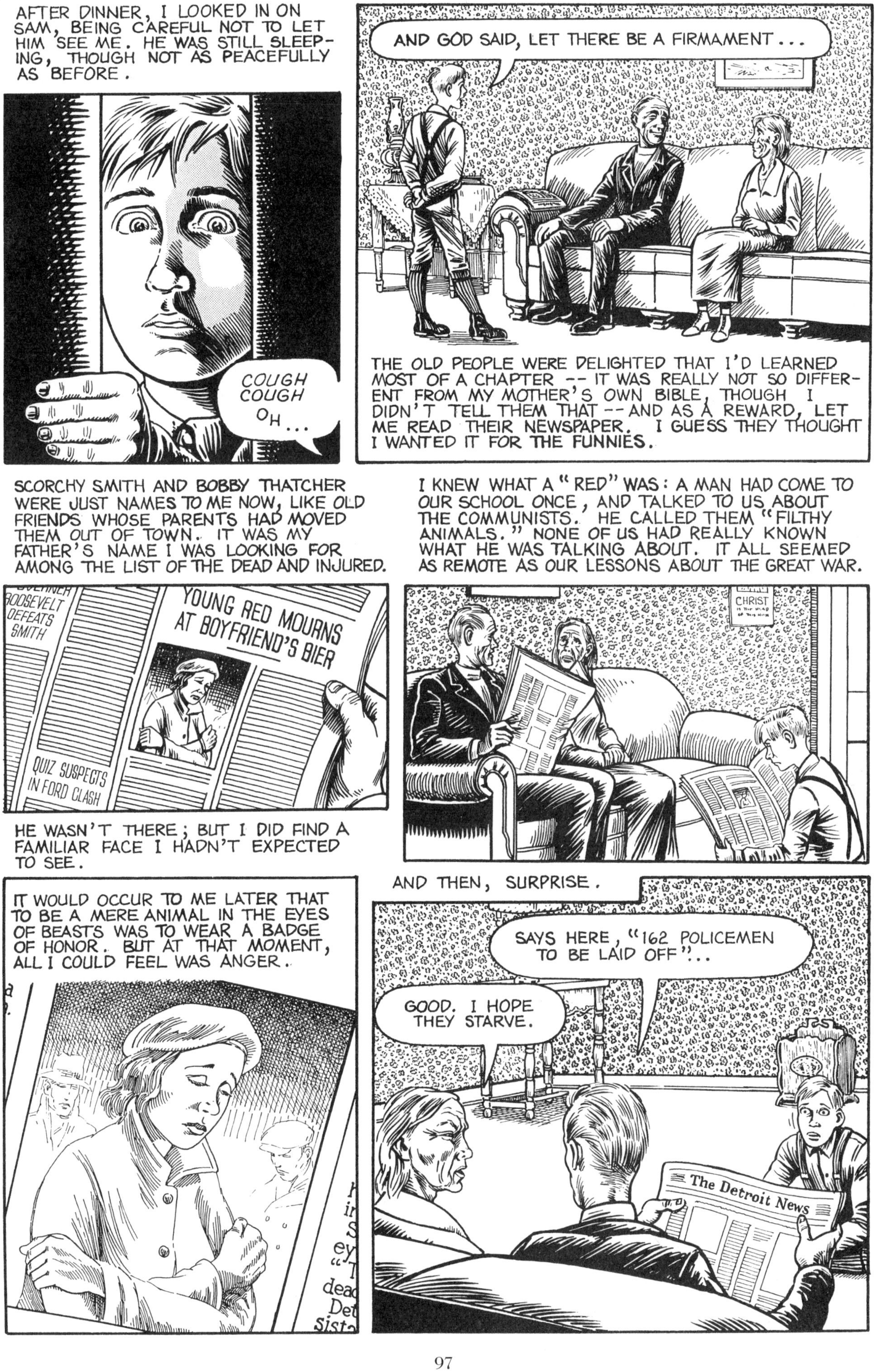
AFTER DINNER, I LOOKED IN ON SAM, BEING CAREFUL NOT TO LET HIM SEE ME. HE WAS STILL SLEEPING, THOUGH NOT AS PEACEFULLY AS BEFORE.
COUGH COUGH OH...
AND GOD SAID, LET THERE BE A FIRMAMENT...
THE OLD PEOPLE WERE DELIGHTED THAT I'D LEARNED MOST OF A CHAPTER -- IT WAS REALLY NOT SO DIFFERENT FROM MY MOTHER'S OWN BIBLE, THOUGH I DIDN'T TELL THEM THAT -- AND AS A REWARD, LET ME READ THEIR NEWSPAPER. I GUESS THEY THOUGHT I WANTED IT FOR THE FUNNIES.
SCORCHY SMITH AND BOBBY THATCHER WERE JUST NAMES TO ME NOW, LIKE OLD FRIENDS WHOSE PARENTS HAD MOVED THEM OUT OF TOWN. IT WAS MY FATHER'S NAME I WAS LOOKING FOR AMONG THE LIST OF THE DEAD AND INJURED.
ROOSEVELT DEFEATS SMITH
YOUNG RED MOURNS AT BOYFRIEND'S BIER
QUIZ SUSPECTS IN FORD CLASH
HE WASN'T THERE; BUT I DID FIND A FAMILIAR FACE I HADN'T EXPECTED TO SEE.
I KNEW WHAT A "RED" WAS: A MAN HAD COME TO OUR SCHOOL ONCE, AND TALKED TO US ABOUT THE COMMUNISTS. HE CALLED THEM "FILTHY ANIMALS." NONE OF US HAD REALLY KNOWN WHAT HE WAS TALKING ABOUT. IT ALL SEEMED AS REMOTE AS OUR LESSONS ABOUT THE GREAT WAR.
CHRIST
IT WOULD OCCUR TO ME LATER THAT TO BE A MERE ANIMAL IN THE EYES OF BEASTS WAS TO WEAR A BADGE OF HONOR. BUT AT THAT MOMENT, ALL I COULD FEEL WAS ANGER.
AND THEN, SURPRISE.
SAYS HERE, "162 POLICEMEN TO BE LAID OFF"...
GOOD. I HOPE THEY STARVE.
The Detroit News

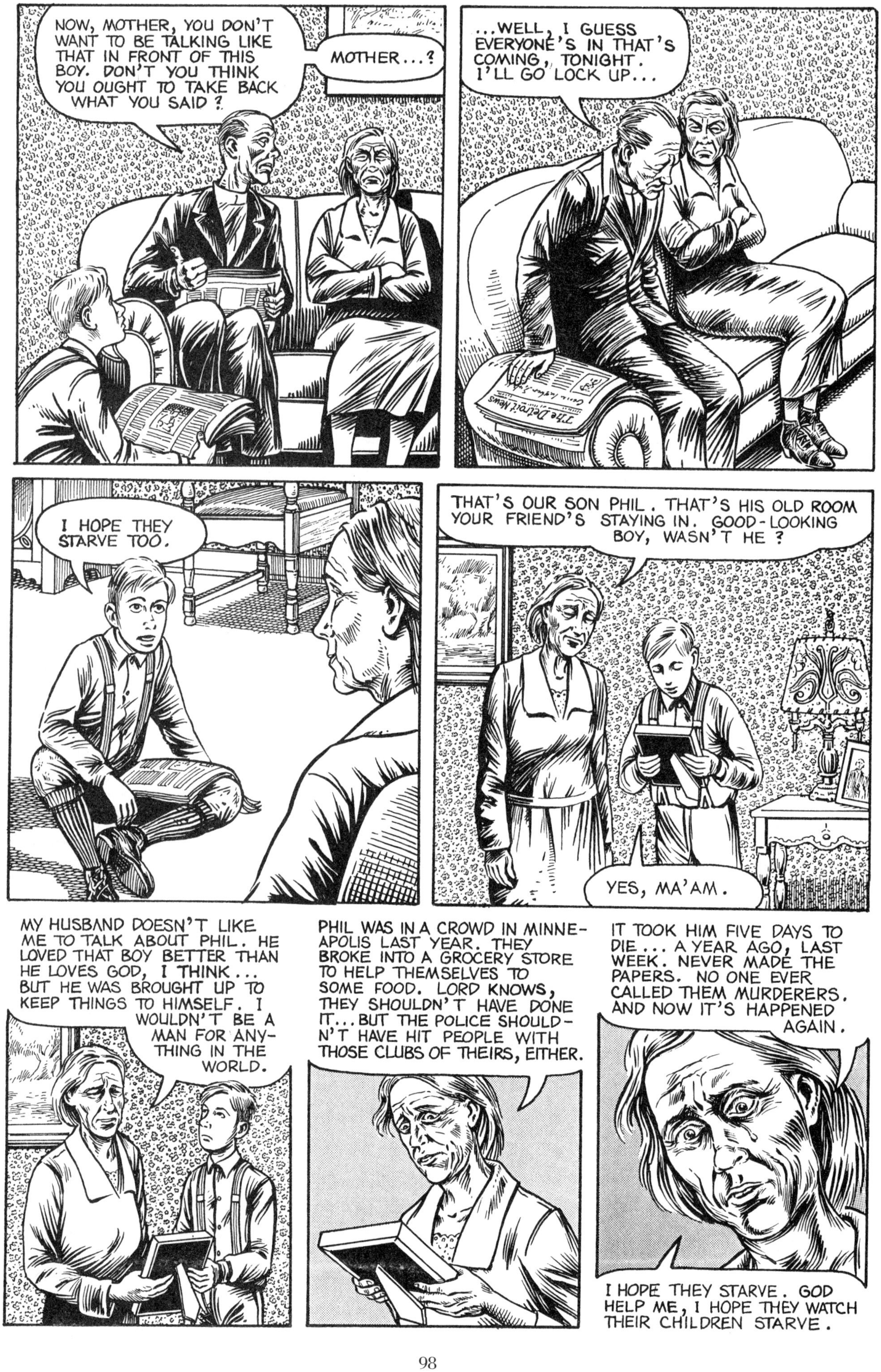
NOW, MOTHER, YOU DON'T WANT TO BE TALKING LIKE THAT IN FRONT OF THIS BOY. DON'T YOU THINK YOU OUGHT TO TAKE BACK WHAT YOU SAID?
MOTHER...?
...WELL, I GUESS EVERYONE'S IN THAT'S COMING, TONIGHT. I'LL GO LOCK UP...
I HOPE THEY STARVE TOO.
THAT'S OUR SON PHIL. THAT'S HIS OLD ROOM YOUR FRIEND'S STAYING IN. GOOD-LOOKING BOY, WASN'T HE?
YES, MA'AM.
MY HUSBAND DOESN'T LIKE ME TO TALK ABOUT PHIL. HE LOVED THAT BOY BETTER THAN HE LOVES GOD, I THINK... BUT HE WAS BROUGHT UP TO KEEP THINGS TO HIMSELF. I WOULDN'T BE A MAN FOR ANYTHING IN THE WORLD.
PHIL WAS IN A CROWD IN MINNEAPOLIS LAST YEAR. THEY BROKE INTO A GROCERY STORE TO HELP THEMSELVES TO SOME FOOD. LORD KNOWS, THEY SHOULDN'T HAVE DONE IT... BUT THE POLICE SHOULDN'T HAVE HIT PEOPLE WITH THOSE CLUBS OF THEIRS, EITHER.
IT TOOK HIM FIVE DAYS TO DIE... A YEAR AGO, LAST WEEK. NEVER MADE THE PAPERS. NO ONE EVER CALLED THEM MURDERERS. AND NOW IT'S HAPPENED AGAIN.
I HOPE THEY STARVE. GOD HELP ME, I HOPE THEY WATCH THEIR CHILDREN STARVE.

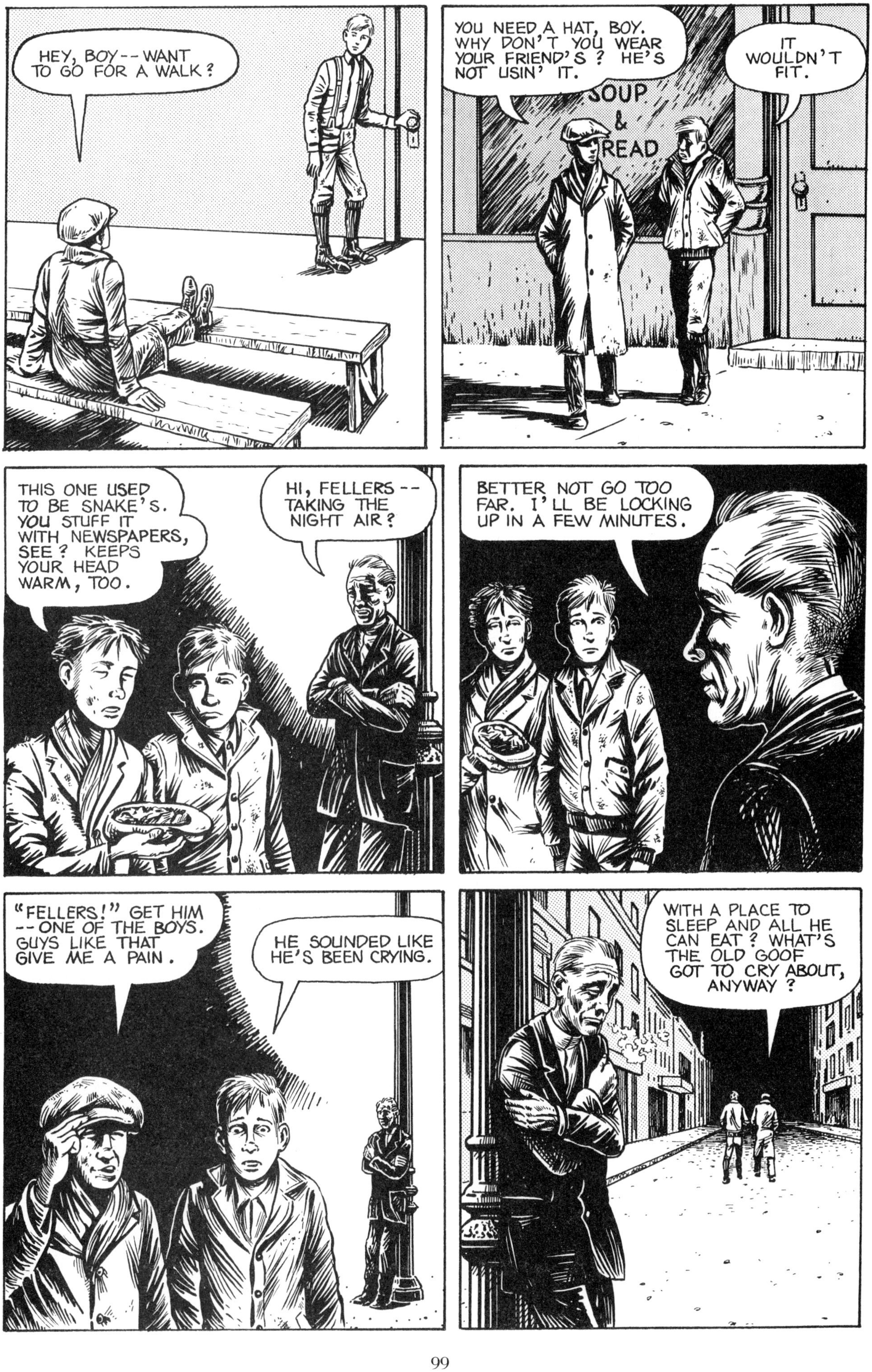
HEY, BOY--WANT TO GO FOR A WALK?
YOU NEED A HAT, BOY. WHY DON'T YOU WEAR YOUR FRIEND'S? HE'S NOT USIN' IT.
IT WOULDN'T FIT.
SOUP & READ
THIS ONE USED TO BE SNAKE'S. YOU STUFF IT WITH NEWSPAPERS, SEE? KEEPS YOUR HEAD WARM, TOO.
HI, FELLERS--TAKING THE NIGHT AIR?
BETTER NOT GO TOO FAR. I'LL BE LOCKING UP IN A FEW MINUTES.
"FELLERS!" GET HIM --ONE OF THE BOYS. GUYS LIKE THAT GIVE ME A PAIN.
HE SOUNDED LIKE HE'S BEEN CRYING.
WITH A PLACE TO SLEEP AND ALL HE CAN EAT? WHAT'S THE OLD GOOF GOT TO CRY ABOUT, ANYWAY?

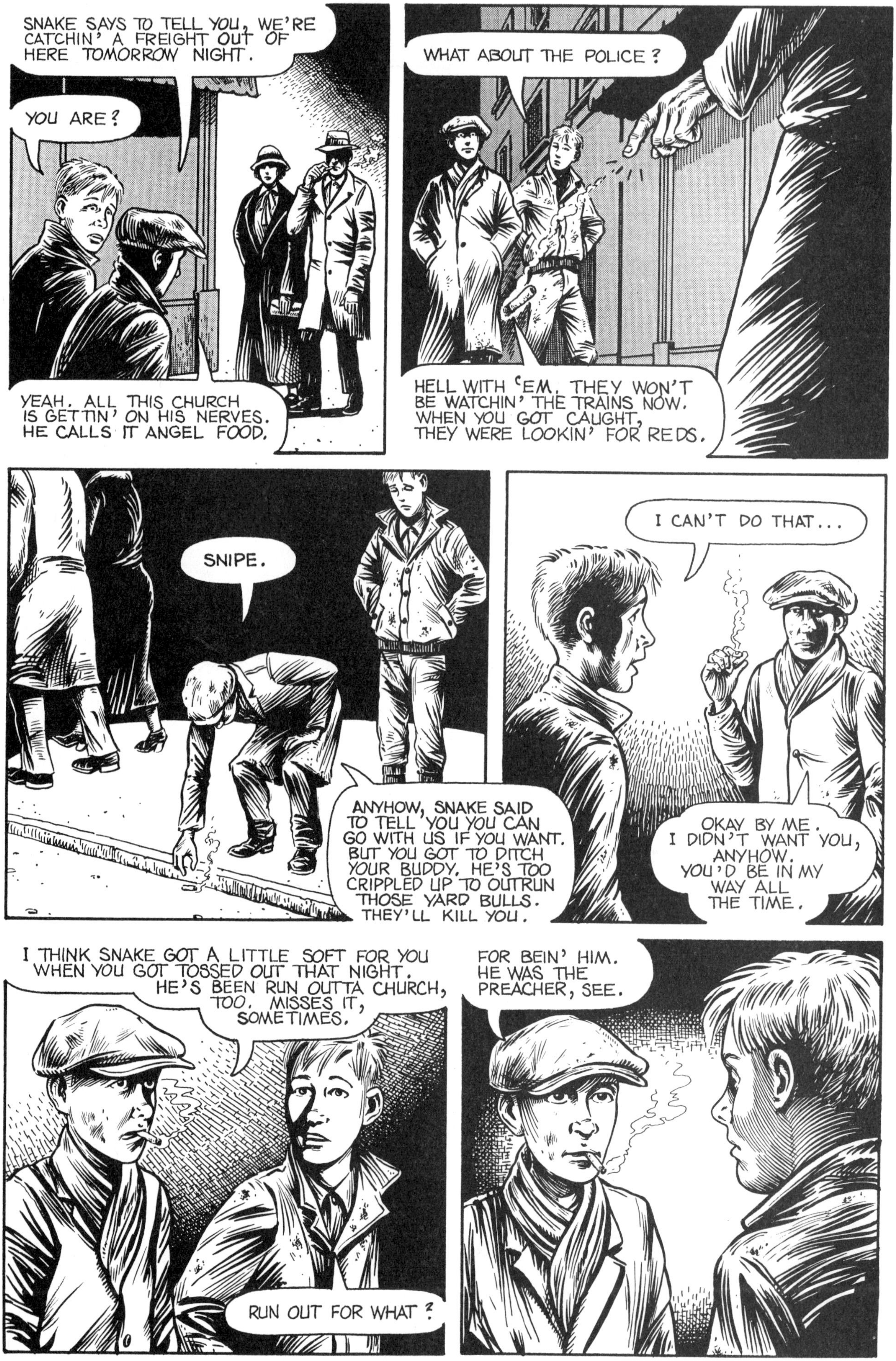
SNAKE SAYS TO TELL YOU, WE'RE CATCHIN' A FREIGHT OUT OF HERE TOMORROW NIGHT.
YOU ARE?
YEAH. ALL THIS CHURCH IS GETTIN' ON HIS NERVES. HE CALLS IT ANGEL FOOD.
WHAT ABOUT THE POLICE?
HELL WITH 'EM. THEY WON'T BE WATCHIN' THE TRAINS NOW. WHEN YOU GOT CAUGHT, THEY WERE LOOKIN' FOR REDS.
SNIPE.
ANYHOW, SNAKE SAID TO TELL YOU YOU CAN GO WITH US IF YOU WANT. BUT YOU GOT TO DITCH YOUR BUDDY. HE'S TOO CRIPPLED UP TO OUTRUN THOSE YARD BULLS. THEY'LL KILL YOU.
I CAN'T DO THAT...
OKAY BY ME. I DIDN'T WANT YOU, ANYHOW. YOU'D BE IN MY WAY ALL THE TIME.
I THINK SNAKE GOT A LITTLE SOFT FOR YOU WHEN YOU GOT TOSSED OUT THAT NIGHT. HE'S BEEN RUN OUTTA CHURCH, TOO. MISSES IT, SOMETIMES.
RUN OUT FOR WHAT?
FOR BEIN' HIM. HE WAS THE PREACHER, SEE.

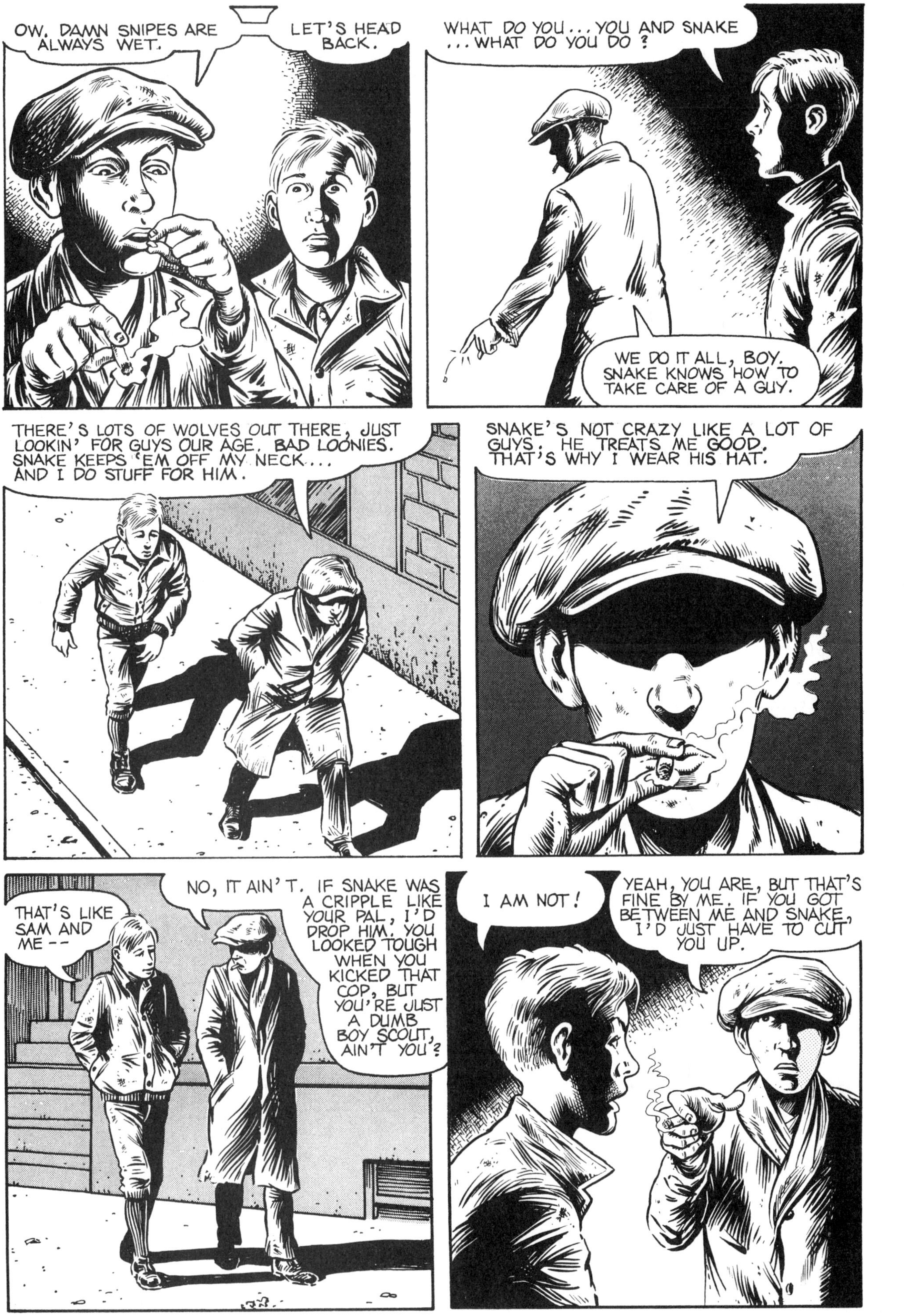
OW. DAMN SNIPES ARE ALWAYS WET.
LET'S HEAD BACK.
WHAT DO YOU... YOU AND SNAKE ...WHAT DO YOU DO?
WE DO IT ALL, BOY. SNAKE KNOWS HOW TO TAKE CARE OF A GUY.
THERE'S LOTS OF WOLVES OUT THERE, JUST LOOKIN' FOR GUYS OUR AGE. BAD LOONIES. SNAKE KEEPS 'EM OFF MY NECK... AND I DO STUFF FOR HIM.
SNAKE'S NOT CRAZY LIKE A LOT OF GUYS. HE TREATS ME GOOD. THAT'S WHY I WEAR HIS HAT.
THAT'S LIKE SAM AND ME --
NO, IT AIN'T. IF SNAKE WAS A CRIPPLE LIKE YOUR PAL, I'D DROP HIM. YOU LOOKED TOUGH WHEN YOU KICKED THAT COP, BUT YOU'RE JUST A DUMB BOY SCOUT, AIN'T YOU?
I AM NOT!
YEAH, YOU ARE, BUT THAT'S FINE BY ME. IF YOU GOT BETWEEN ME AND SNAKE, I'D JUST HAVE TO CUT YOU UP.

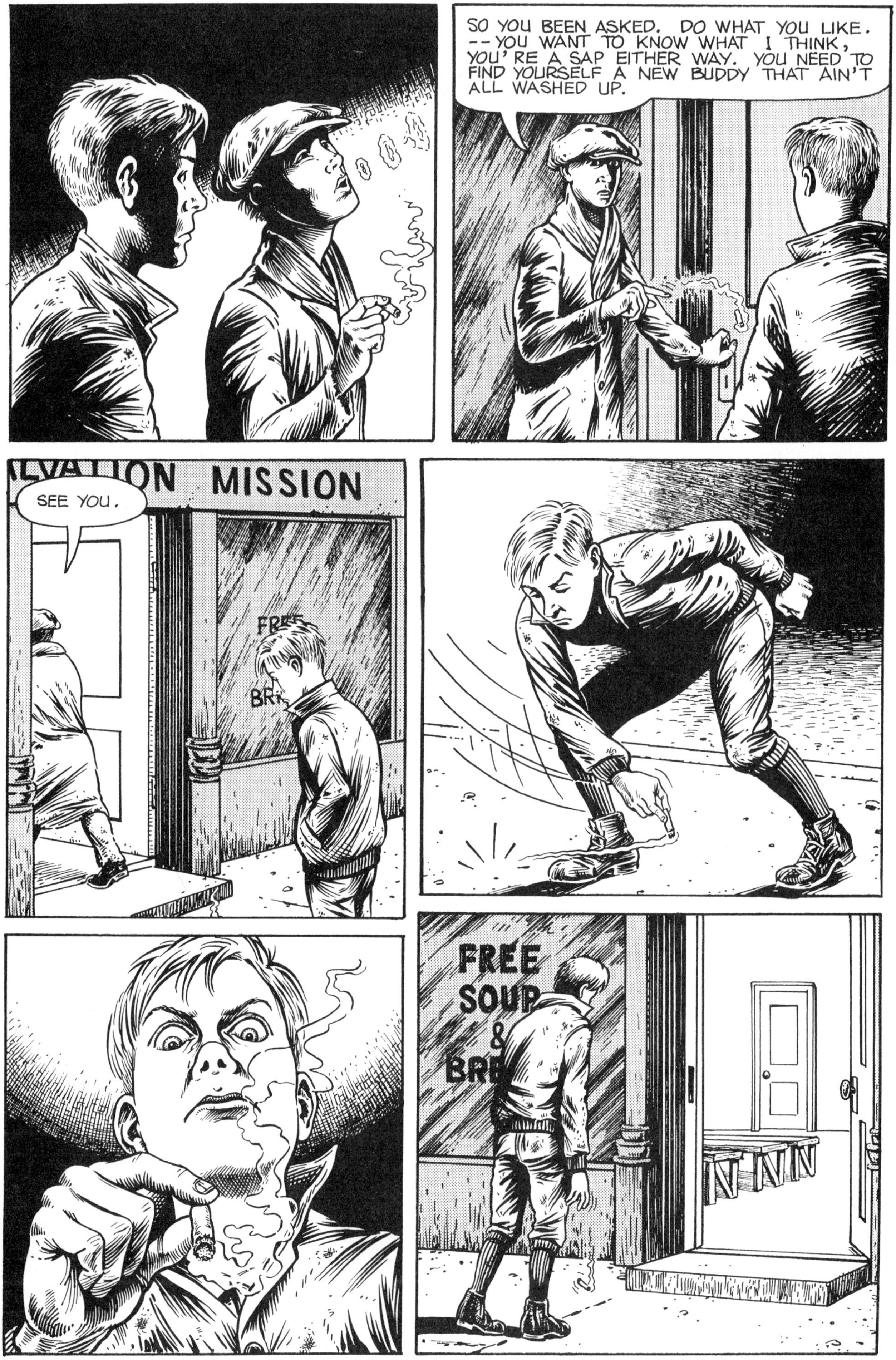
SO YOU BEEN ASKED. DO WHAT YOU LIKE. --YOU WANT TO KNOW WHAT I THINK, YOU'RE A SAP EITHER WAY. YOU NEED TO FIND YOURSELF A NEW BUDDY THAT AIN'T ALL WASHED UP.
ALVATION MISSION
SEE YOU.
FREE SOUP &
BRE

THE DREAM I HAD THAT NIGHT WAS THE FIRST
I'D HAD SINCE DEARBORN.

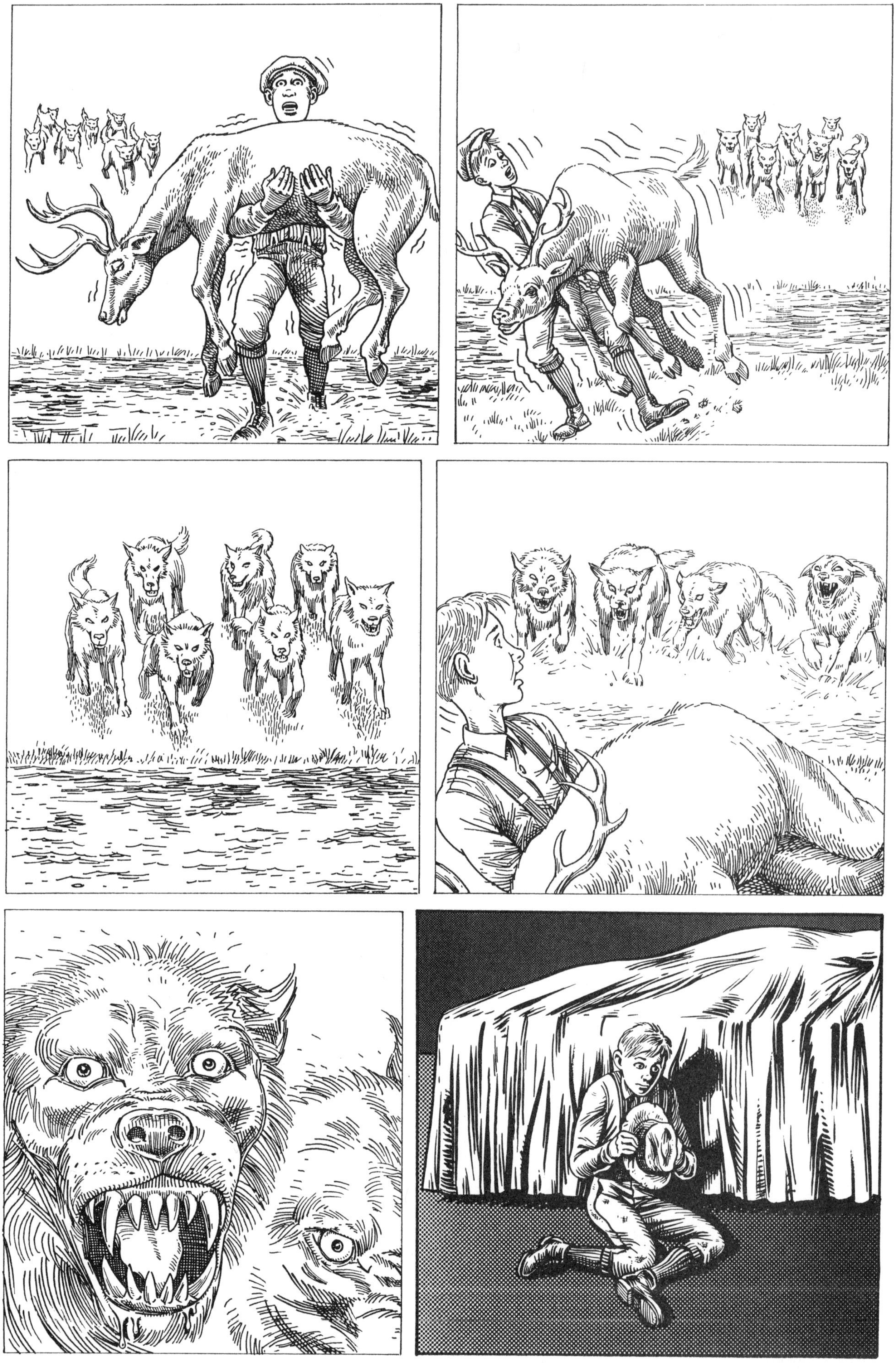

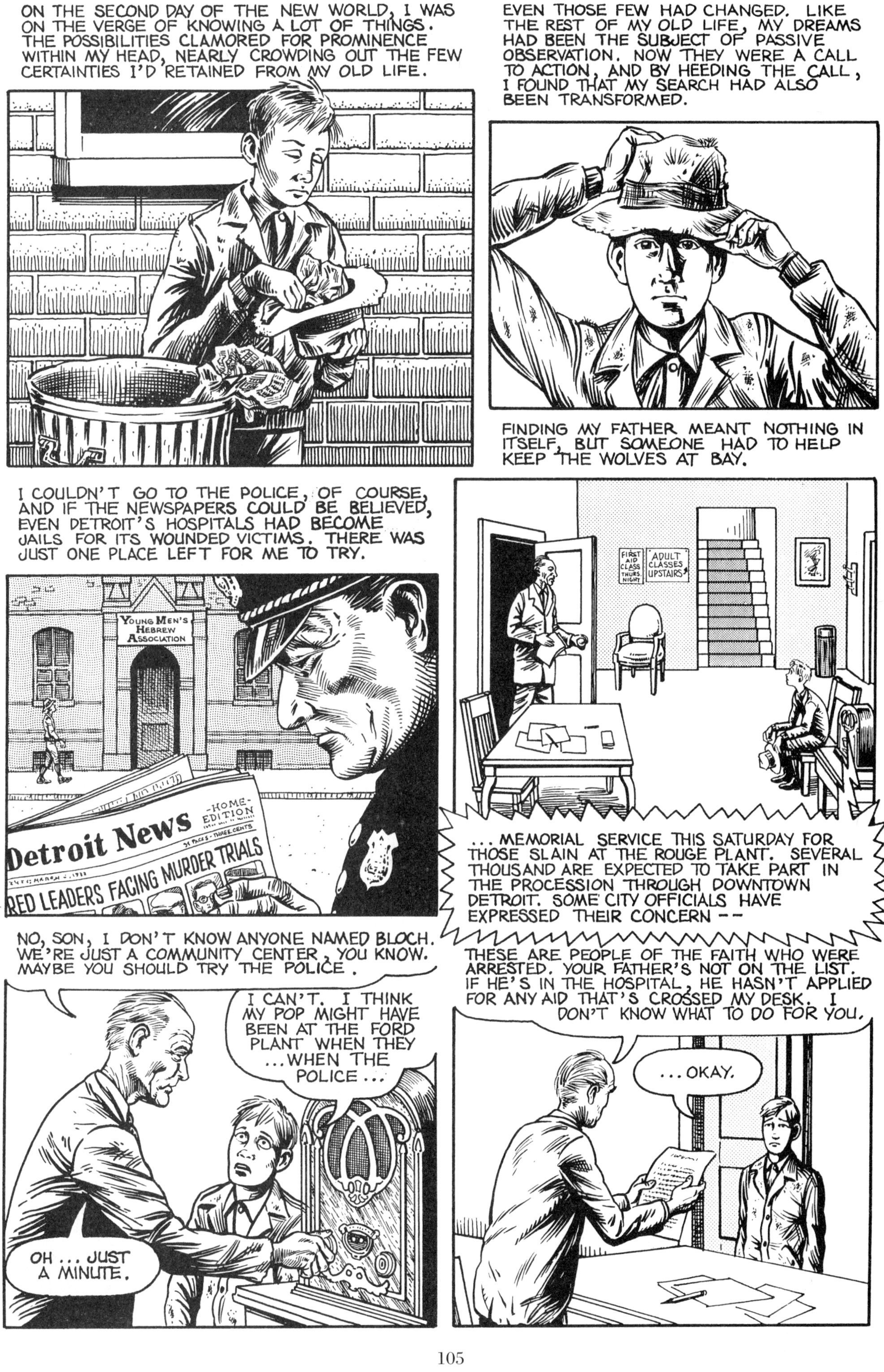
ON THE SECOND DAY OF THE NEW WORLD, I WAS ON THE VERGE OF KNOWING A LOT OF THINGS. THE POSSIBILITIES CLAMORED FOR PROMINENCE WITHIN MY HEAD, NEARLY CROWDING OUT THE FEW CERTAINTIES I'D RETAINED FROM MY OLD LIFE.
EVEN THOSE FEW HAD CHANGED. LIKE THE REST OF MY OLD LIFE, MY DREAMS HAD BEEN THE SUBJECT OF PASSIVE OBSERVATION. NOW THEY WERE A CALL TO ACTION, AND BY HEEDING THE CALL, I FOUND THAT MY SEARCH HAD ALSO BEEN TRANSFORMED.
FINDING MY FATHER MEANT NOTHING IN ITSELF, BUT SOMEONE HAD TO HELP KEEP THE WOLVES AT BAY.
I COULDN'T GO TO THE POLICE, OF COURSE, AND IF THE NEWSPAPERS COULD BE BELIEVED, EVEN DETROIT'S HOSPITALS HAD BECOME JAILS FOR ITS WOUNDED VICTIMS. THERE WAS JUST ONE PLACE LEFT FOR ME TO TRY.
YOUNG MEN'S HEBREW ASSOCIATION
Detroit News
-HOME- EDITION
RED LEADERS FACING MURDER TRIALS
FIRST AID CLASS THURS. NIGHT
ADULT CLASSES UPSTAIRS
NO, SON, I DON'T KNOW ANYONE NAMED BLOCH. WE'RE JUST A COMMUNITY CENTER, YOU KNOW. MAYBE YOU SHOULD TRY THE POLICE.
I CAN'T. I THINK MY POP MIGHT HAVE BEEN AT THE FORD PLANT WHEN THEY ...WHEN THE POLICE...
OH ... JUST A MINUTE.
... MEMORIAL SERVICE THIS SATURDAY FOR THOSE SLAIN AT THE ROUGE PLANT. SEVERAL THOUSAND ARE EXPECTED TO TAKE PART IN THE PROCESSION THROUGH DOWNTOWN DETROIT. SOME CITY OFFICIALS HAVE EXPRESSED THEIR CONCERN --
THESE ARE PEOPLE OF THE FAITH WHO WERE ARRESTED. YOUR FATHER'S NOT ON THE LIST. IF HE'S IN THE HOSPITAL, HE HASN'T APPLIED FOR ANY AID THAT'S CROSSED MY DESK. I DON'T KNOW WHAT TO DO FOR YOU.
... OKAY.

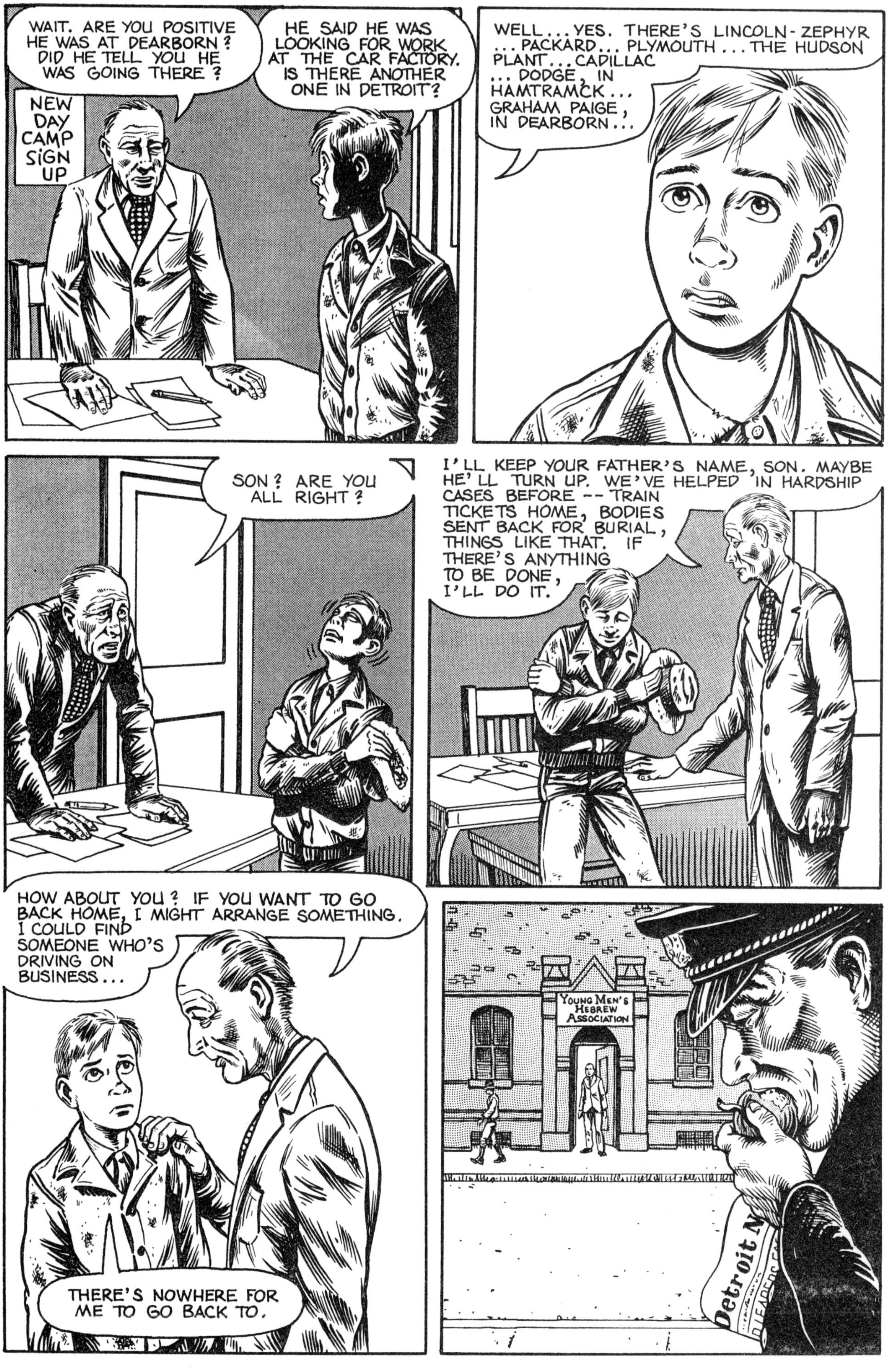
WAIT. ARE YOU POSITIVE HE WAS AT DEARBORN? DID HE TELL YOU HE WAS GOING THERE?
NEW DAY CAMP SIGN UP
HE SAID HE WAS LOOKING FOR WORK AT THE CAR FACTORY. IS THERE ANOTHER ONE IN DETROIT?
WELL... YES. THERE'S LINCOLN-ZEPHYR ... PACKARD... PLYMOUTH ... THE HUDSON PLANT... CADILLAC ... DODGE, IN HAMTRAMCK... GRAHAM PAIGE, IN DEARBORN...
SON? ARE YOU ALL RIGHT?
I'LL KEEP YOUR FATHER'S NAME, SON. MAYBE HE'LL TURN UP. WE'VE HELPED IN HARDSHIP CASES BEFORE -- TRAIN TICKETS HOME, BODIES SENT BACK FOR BURIAL, THINGS LIKE THAT. IF THERE'S ANYTHING TO BE DONE, I'LL DO IT.
HOW ABOUT YOU? IF YOU WANT TO GO BACK HOME, I MIGHT ARRANGE SOMETHING. I COULD FIND SOMEONE WHO'S DRIVING ON BUSINESS...
THERE'S NOWHERE FOR ME TO GO BACK TO.
YOUNG MEN'S HEBREW ASSOCIATION
Detroit N

LOOK OUT, MYRTLE, WE GOT US A PROWLER. WHERE'S MY TOMMYGUN?

SAM...HOW DO YOU FEEL?

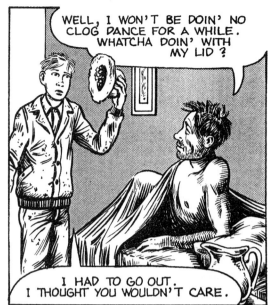

WELL, I WON'T BE DOIN' NO CLOG DANCE FOR A WHILE. WHATCHA DOIN' WITH MY LID?

I HAD TO GO OUT. I THOUGHT YOU WOULDN'T CARE.

CARE?...UNH...TELL YOU WHAT, YOUR HIGH-NESS -- FOR A WHILE THERE, I FIGURED I'D EITHER WAKE UP IN THE POKEY OR THE BONE-YARD. SURE DIDN'T FIGURE YOU'D HAUL ME TO NO FEATHER MATTRESS.
FAR AS I'M CONCERNED, YOU CAN BORROW MY SOCKS AND UNDERWEAR, TOO.

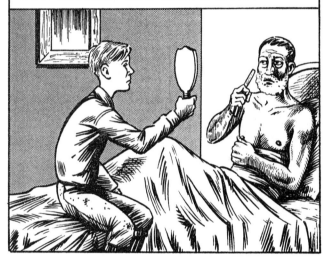

FOR THE NEXT HOUR, SAM ALTERNATELY PRAISED AND THANKED ME FOR "RESCUING" HIM, UNTIL I THOUGHT I WOULD SCREAM. IT WAS A RELIEF WHEN HE FINALLY WENT BACK TO SLEEP.

THE PREACHER WAS SICK, WE WERE TOLD, SO THERE WERE NO SERVICES THAT DAY, AND NO BIBLE RECITATION THAT NIGHT. I HAD SOMETHING ELSE TO DO, ANYWAY.

FREE SOUP & BRE

NICE HAT, KID. DOES THAT MEAN YOU'RE NOT COMING WITH US?

YES, SIR. I'M STAYING WITH SAM.

WELL, THAT'S FINE. THE WORLD COULD DO WITH A LOT MORE OF THAT.

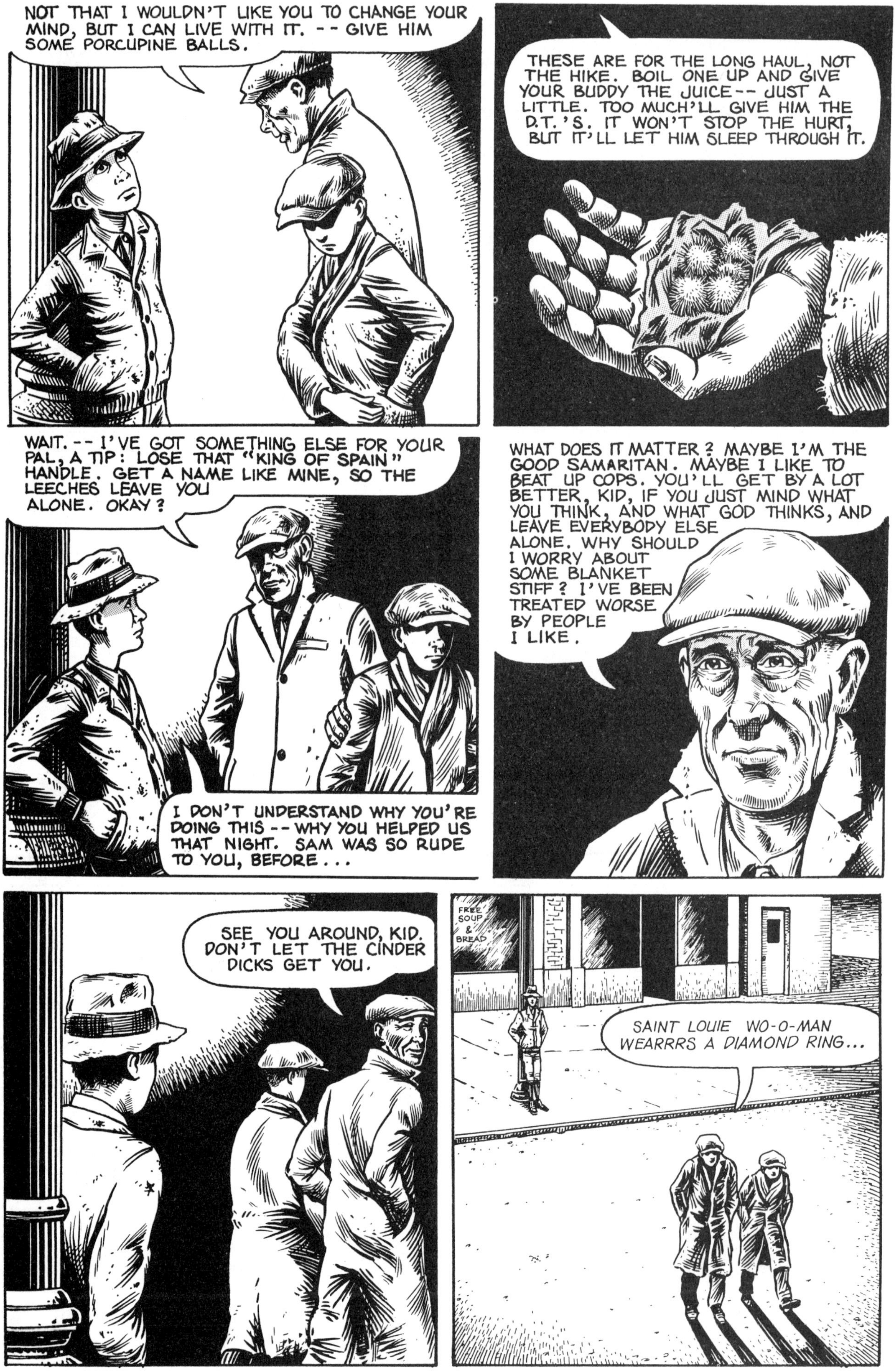
NOT THAT I WOULDN'T LIKE YOU TO CHANGE YOUR MIND, BUT I CAN LIVE WITH IT. -- GIVE HIM SOME PORCUPINE BALLS.
THESE ARE FOR THE LONG HAUL, NOT THE HIKE. BOIL ONE UP AND GIVE YOUR BUDDY THE JUICE -- JUST A LITTLE. TOO MUCH'LL GIVE HIM THE D.T.'S. IT WON'T STOP THE HURT, BUT IT'LL LET HIM SLEEP THROUGH IT.
WAIT. -- I'VE GOT SOMETHING ELSE FOR YOUR PAL, A TIP: LOSE THAT "KING OF SPAIN" HANDLE. GET A NAME LIKE MINE, SO THE LEECHES LEAVE YOU ALONE. OKAY?
I DON'T UNDERSTAND WHY YOU'RE DOING THIS -- WHY YOU HELPED US THAT NIGHT. SAM WAS SO RUDE TO YOU, BEFORE...
WHAT DOES IT MATTER? MAYBE I'M THE GOOD SAMARITAN. MAYBE I LIKE TO BEAT UP COPS. YOU'LL GET BY A LOT BETTER, KID, IF YOU JUST MIND WHAT YOU THINK, AND WHAT GOD THINKS, AND LEAVE EVERYBODY ELSE ALONE. WHY SHOULD I WORRY ABOUT SOME BLANKET STIFF? I'VE BEEN TREATED WORSE BY PEOPLE I LIKE.
SEE YOU AROUND, KID. DON'T LET THE CINDER DICKS GET YOU.
FREE SOUP & BREAD
SAINT LOUIE WO-O-MAN WEARRRS A DIAMOND RING...

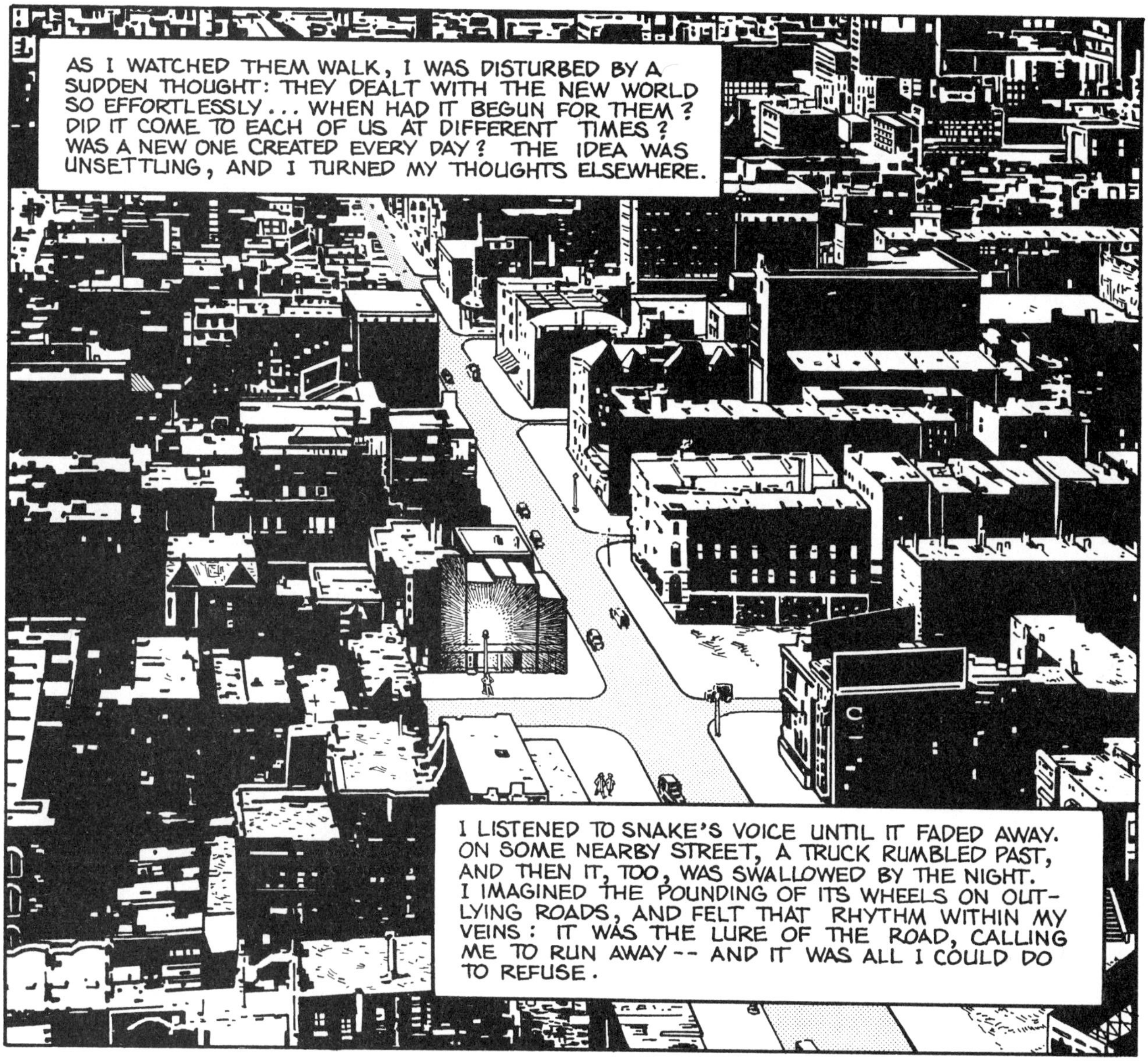
AS I WATCHED THEM WALK, I WAS DISTURBED BY A SUDDEN THOUGHT: THEY DEALT WITH THE NEW WORLD SO EFFORTLESSLY... WHEN HAD IT BEGUN FOR THEM? DID IT COME TO EACH OF US AT DIFFERENT TIMES? WAS A NEW ONE CREATED EVERY DAY? THE IDEA WAS UNSETTLING, AND I TURNED MY THOUGHTS ELSEWHERE.
I LISTENED TO SNAKE'S VOICE UNTIL IT FADED AWAY. ON SOME NEARBY STREET, A TRUCK RUMBLED PAST, AND THEN IT, TOO, WAS SWALLOWED BY THE NIGHT. I IMAGINED THE POUNDING OF ITS WHEELS ON OUTLYING ROADS, AND FELT THAT RHYTHM WITHIN MY VEINS: IT WAS THE LURE OF THE ROAD, CALLING ME TO RUN AWAY -- AND IT WAS ALL I COULD DO TO REFUSE.

IT CONTINUED TO WHISPER SOFTLY OVER THE NEXT TWO DAYS, AND I PUSHED SAM HARD TO GET BACK ON HIS FEET. HE REFUSED TO STEP OUTSIDE, BUT AT LEAST HE WAS MOVING, AND MY AGITATION COULD BE CONTAINED.

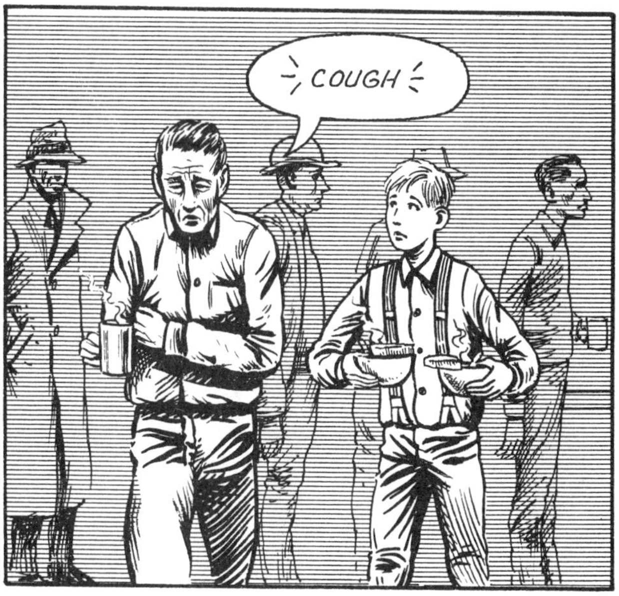
COUGH

ON EACH OF THOSE DAYS, WE'D ASSEMBLED DUTIFULLY FOR SERVICES THAT NEVER TOOK PLACE, HEARING ONLY THAT THE PREACHER WAS STILL SICK. SAM HAD JOKED THAT AT LEAST WE COULDN'T BE CALLED "MISSION STIFFS," WITH SO LITTLE CHURCH TAKING PLACE. ON FRIDAY NIGHT, THE JOKES ENDED.

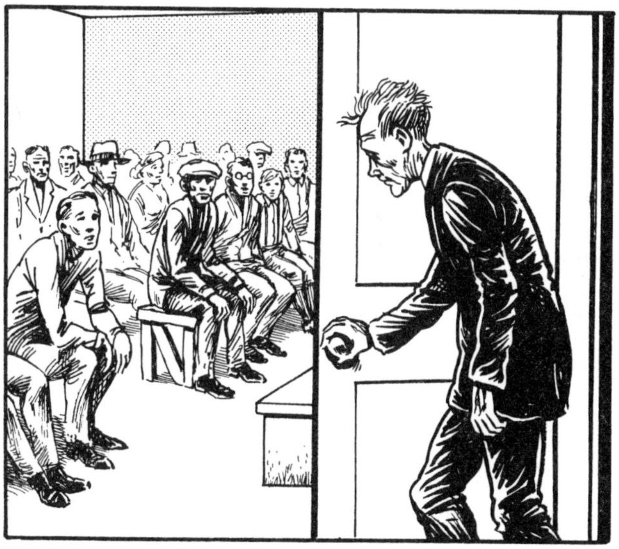

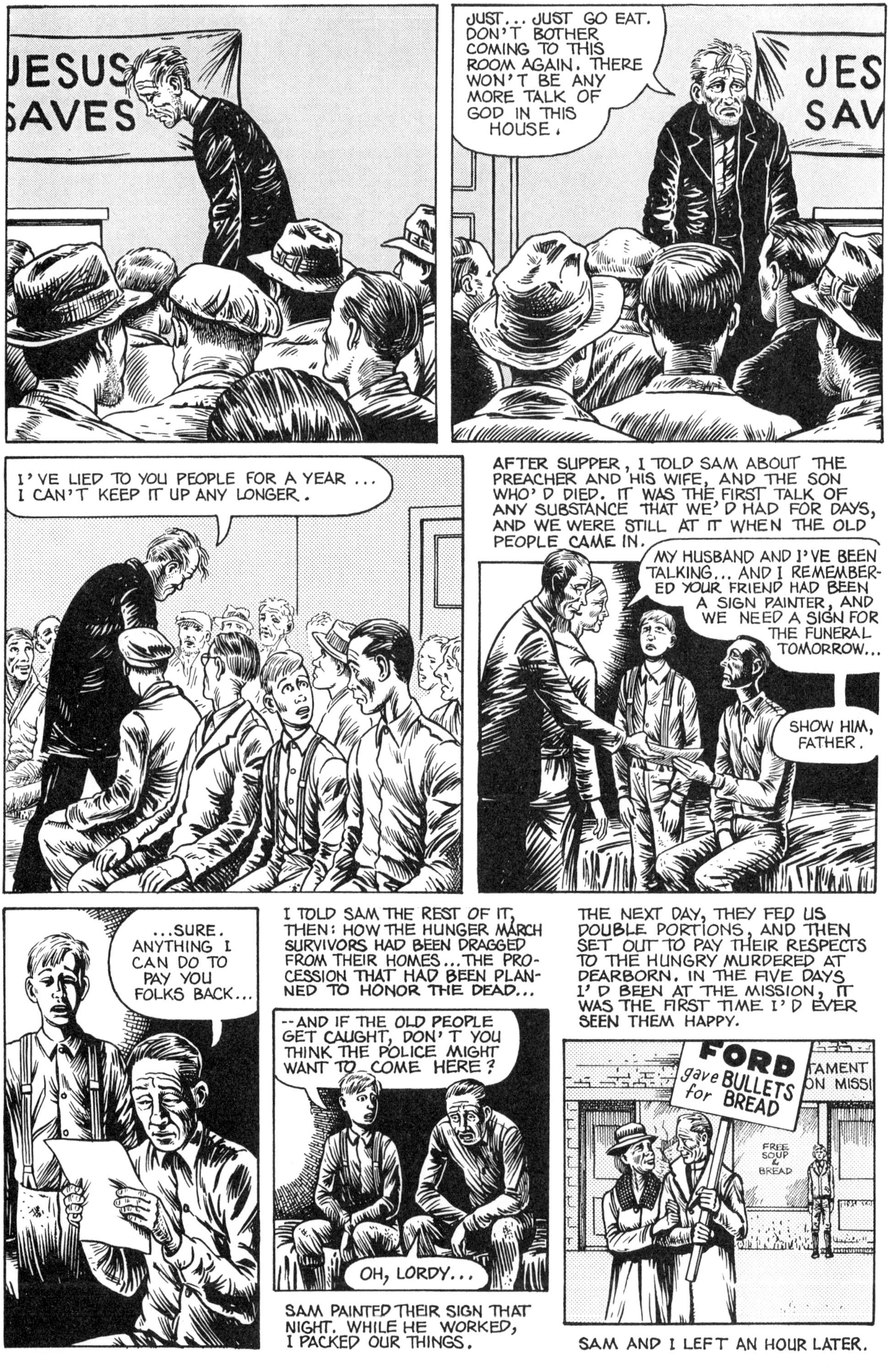
JESUS SAVES
JUST... JUST GO EAT. DON'T BOTHER COMING TO THIS ROOM AGAIN. THERE WON'T BE ANY MORE TALK OF GOD IN THIS HOUSE.
I'VE LIED TO YOU PEOPLE FOR A YEAR ... I CAN'T KEEP IT UP ANY LONGER.
AFTER SUPPER, I TOLD SAM ABOUT THE PREACHER AND HIS WIFE, AND THE SON WHO'D DIED. IT WAS THE FIRST TALK OF ANY SUBSTANCE THAT WE'D HAD FOR DAYS, AND WE WERE STILL AT IT WHEN THE OLD PEOPLE CAME IN.
MY HUSBAND AND I'VE BEEN TALKING... AND I REMEMBERED YOUR FRIEND HAD BEEN A SIGN PAINTER, AND WE NEED A SIGN FOR THE FUNERAL TOMORROW...
SHOW HIM, FATHER.
...SURE. ANYTHING I CAN DO TO PAY YOU FOLKS BACK...
I TOLD SAM THE REST OF IT, THEN: HOW THE HUNGER MARCH SURVIVORS HAD BEEN DRAGGED FROM THEIR HOMES...THE PROCESSION THAT HAD BEEN PLANNED TO HONOR THE DEAD...
--AND IF THE OLD PEOPLE GET CAUGHT, DON'T YOU THINK THE POLICE MIGHT WANT TO COME HERE?
OH, LORDY...
SAM PAINTED THEIR SIGN THAT NIGHT. WHILE HE WORKED, I PACKED OUR THINGS.
THE NEXT DAY, THEY FED US DOUBLE PORTIONS, AND THEN SET OUT TO PAY THEIR RESPECTS TO THE HUNGRY MURDERED AT DEARBORN. IN THE FIVE DAYS I'D BEEN AT THE MISSION, IT WAS THE FIRST TIME I'D EVER SEEN THEM HAPPY.
FORD gave BULLETS for BREAD
TAMENT
ON MISSI
FREE SOUP & BREAD
SAM AND I LEFT AN HOUR LATER.

WE KEPT TO THE SIDE STREETS, CAREFULLY AVOIDING ANY FURTHER BRUSH WITH HISTORY. EVEN AT A DISTANCE, I COULD SEE THAT MORE PEOPLE HAD TURNED OUT THAN HAD MARCHED TO THE FORD PLANT. I TRIED TO PUT THEM OUT OF MY MIND, AND CONCENTRATED ON RETRACING OUR STEPS FROM THE TRAINYARD. BY NIGHTFALL, IT WAS CLEAR THAT SAM WOULD HAVE TO REST.

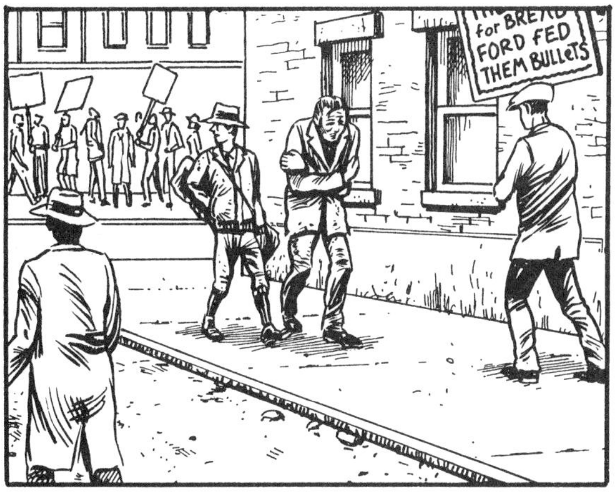
for BREAD
FORD FED
THEM BULLETS

I LISTENED FOR SOUNDS OF VIOLENCE, AND WONDERED FOR WHOM THE NEW WORLD WOULD BEGIN THAT NIGHT. I HEARD THE VIOLENCE SAM WAS DOING TO HIMSELF, AND WONDERED WHEN IT HAD BEGUN FOR HIM.

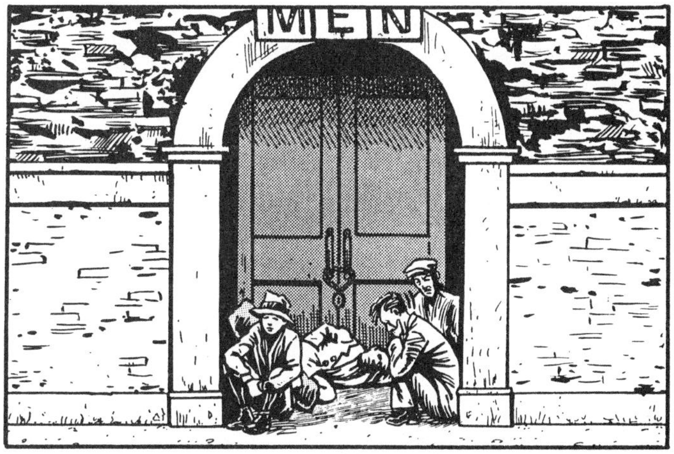
MEN

I THOUGHT OF TWO MEN, ONE WHO HAD A CHURCH AND ONE WHO HAD GOD... I THOUGHT OF THE WORDS MY FATHER HAD WRITTEN IN A BOOK... AND THEN, FOR A FEW HOURS, I THOUGHT OF NOTHING AT ALL.

IT WAS NEARLY DAWN WHEN WE FOUND THE TRAINYARD. SAM'S COUGHING ECHOED LIKE PISTOL SHOTS AROUND THE CARS. I HAD THE FEELING THAT I'D LIVED THIS MOMENT MANY TIMES BEFORE, AND NOT JUST IN MY WAKING HOURS.

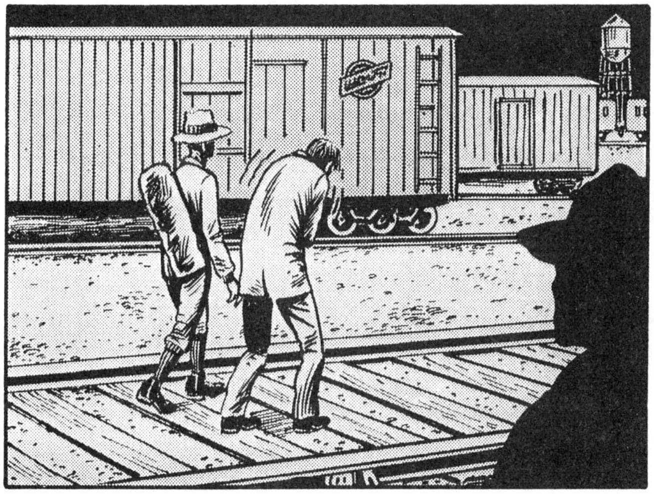

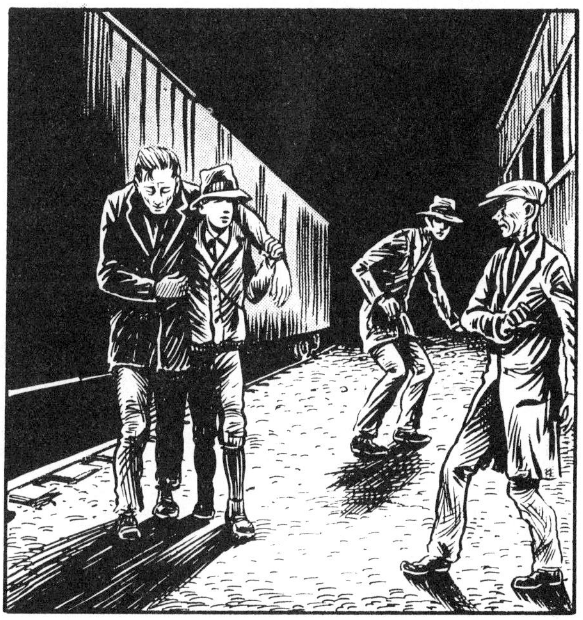

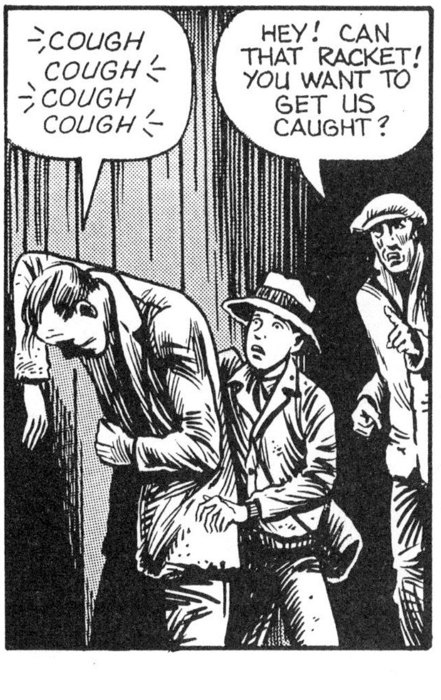
COUGH COUGH COUGH COUGH
HEY! CAN THAT RACKET! YOU WANT TO GET US CAUGHT?

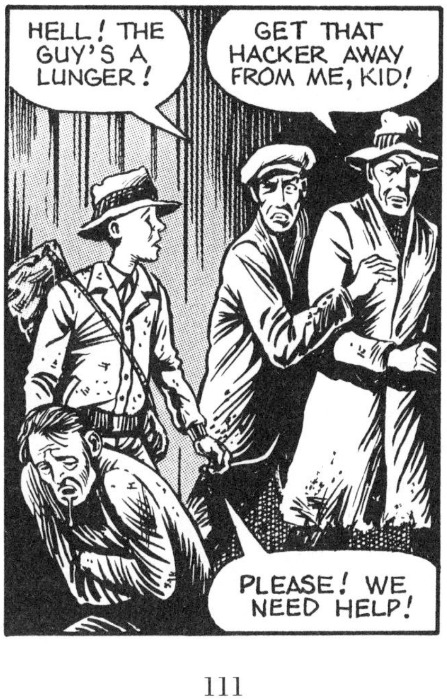
HELL! THE GUY'S A LUNGER!
GET THAT HACKER AWAY FROM ME, KID!
PLEASE! WE NEED HELP!

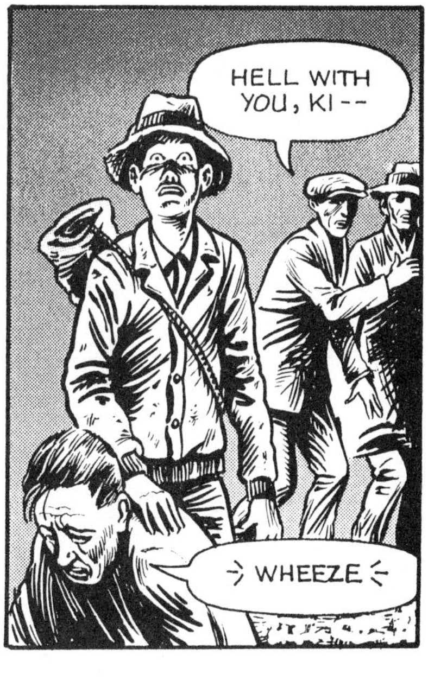
HELL WITH YOU, KI--
WHEEZE

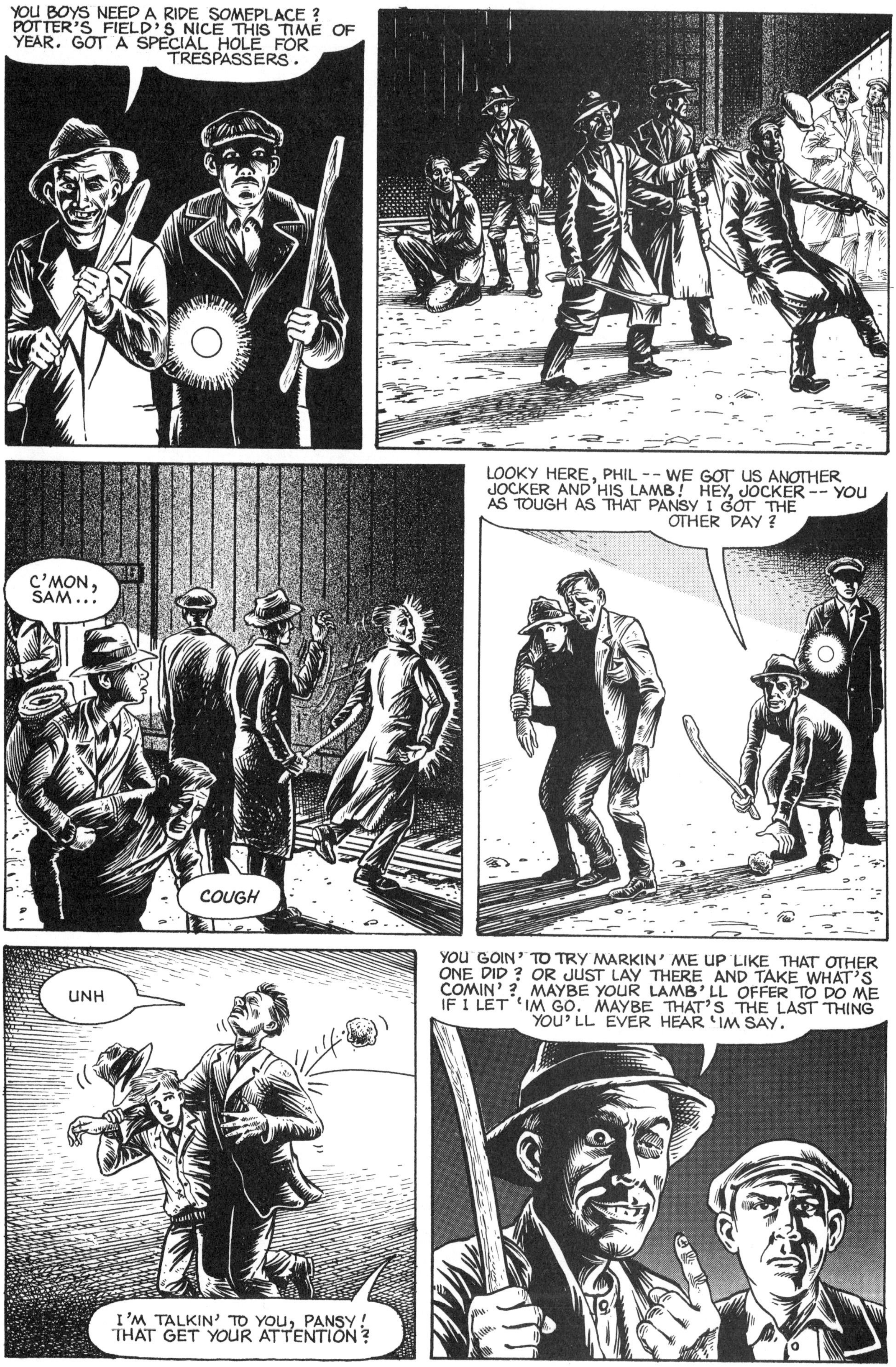
YOU BOYS NEED A RIDE SOMEPLACE? POTTER'S FIELD'S NICE THIS TIME OF YEAR. GOT A SPECIAL HOLE FOR TRESPASSERS.
C'MON, SAM...
COUGH
LOOKY HERE, PHIL -- WE GOT US ANOTHER JOCKER AND HIS LAMB! HEY, JOCKER -- YOU AS TOUGH AS THAT PANSY I GOT THE OTHER DAY?
UNH
I'M TALKIN' TO YOU, PANSY! THAT GET YOUR ATTENTION?
YOU GOIN' TO TRY MARKIN' ME UP LIKE THAT OTHER ONE DID? OR JUST LAY THERE AND TAKE WHAT'S COMIN'? MAYBE YOUR LAMB'LL OFFER TO DO ME IF I LET 'IM GO. MAYBE THAT'S THE LAST THING YOU'LL EVER HEAR 'IM SAY.

I FELT SAM TREMBLING AS HE STRUGGLED FOR BREATH ...I SAW THE MAN APPROACHING... AND I KNEW THAT I HAD STEPPED INTO MY OWN DREAM. AND YET, IT WAS DIFFERENT.

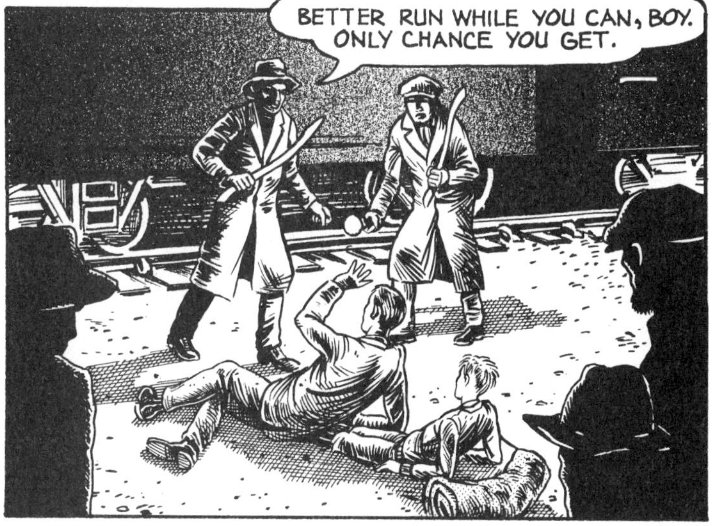
BETTER RUN WHILE YOU CAN, BOY. ONLY CHANCE YOU GET.

UNLIKE MY DREAM, HERE I **COULD** RUN AWAY, AS I'D RUN FROM MY HOME AND FROM JOKER, FROM DEARBORN AND THE MISSION. UNLIKE MY DREAM, HERE I HAD A CHOICE.

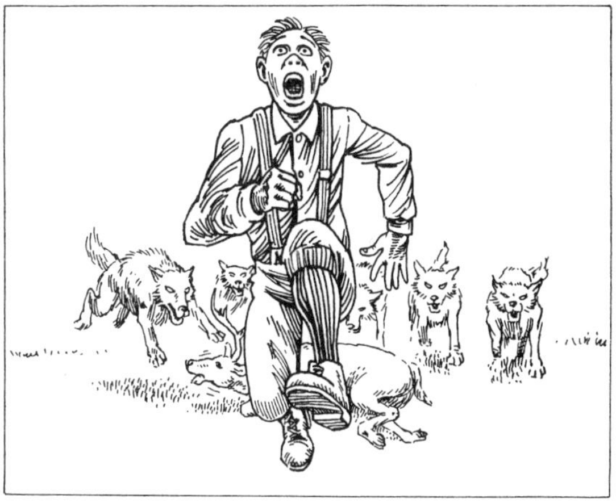

I MADE MY CHOICE...

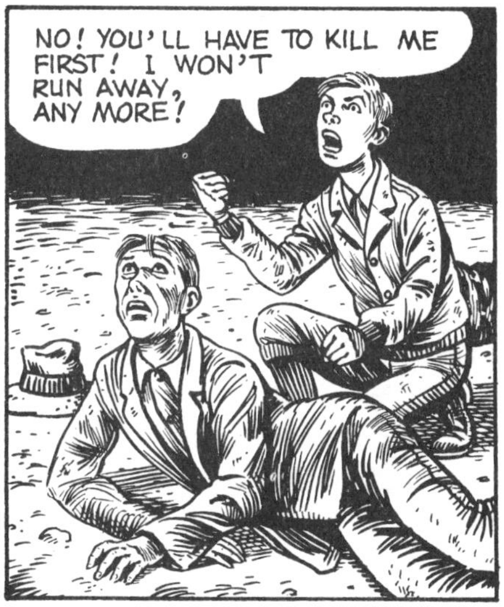
NO! YOU'LL HAVE TO KILL ME FIRST! I WON'T RUN AWAY, ANY MORE!

...AND IN THOSE FINAL GRAY MINUTES BEFORE SUNRISE, WE ENACTED THE MOMENT THAT WOULD INFORM THE REST OF MY LIFE.

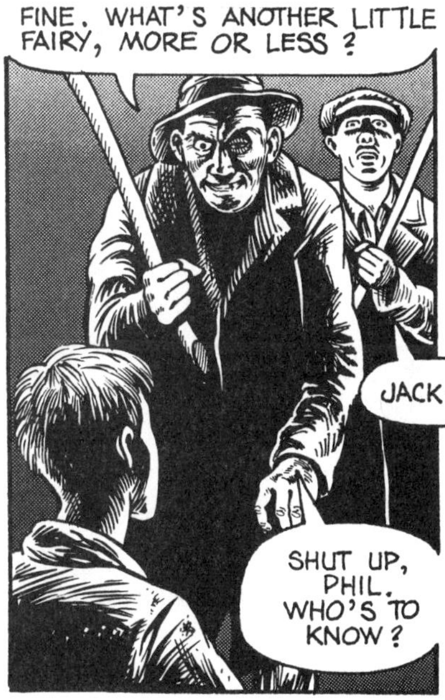
FINE. WHAT'S ANOTHER LITTLE FAIRY, MORE OR LESS?
JACK--!
SHUT UP, PHIL. WHO'S TO KNOW?

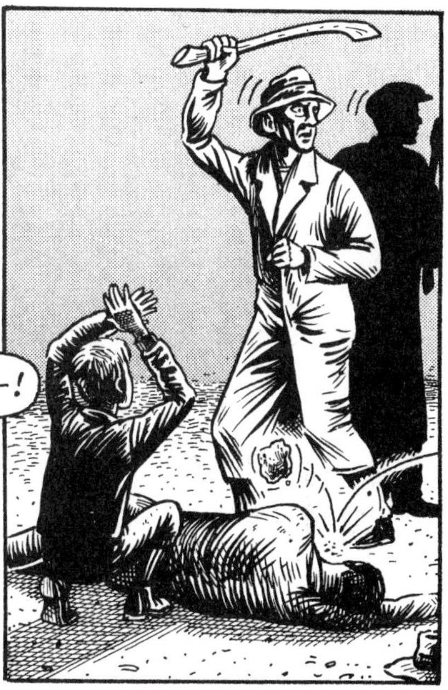

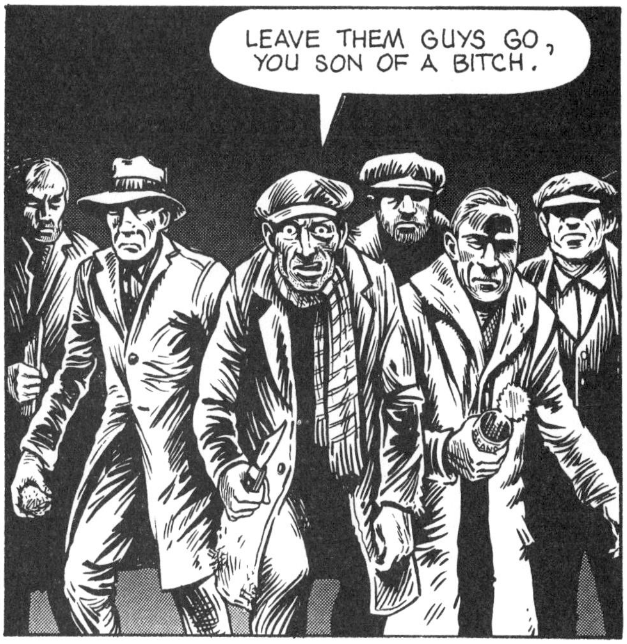
LEAVE THEM GUYS GO, YOU SON OF A BITCH.

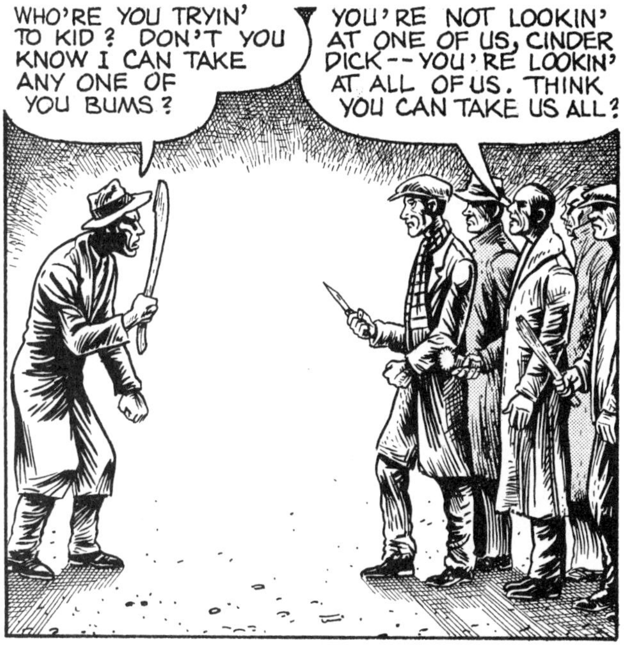
WHO'RE YOU TRYIN' TO KID? DON'T YOU KNOW I CAN TAKE ANY ONE OF YOU BUMS?
YOU'RE NOT LOOKIN' AT ONE OF US, CINDER DICK--YOU'RE LOOKIN' AT ALL OF US. THINK YOU CAN TAKE US ALL?

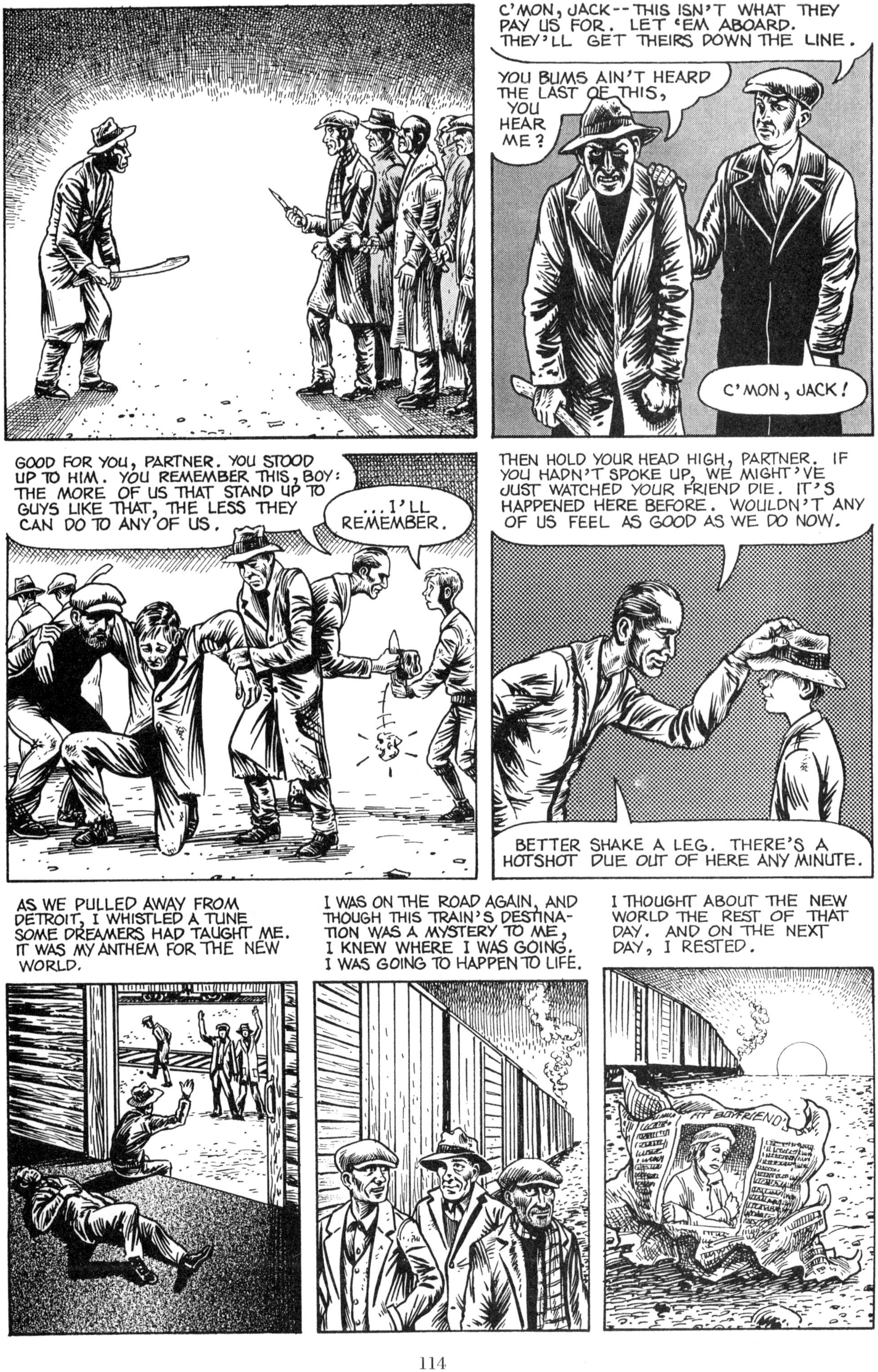
C'MON, JACK--THIS ISN'T WHAT THEY PAY US FOR. LET 'EM ABOARD. THEY'LL GET THEIRS DOWN THE LINE.
YOU BUMS AIN'T HEARD THE LAST OF THIS, YOU HEAR ME?
C'MON, JACK!
GOOD FOR YOU, PARTNER. YOU STOOD UP TO HIM. YOU REMEMBER THIS, BOY: THE MORE OF US THAT STAND UP TO GUYS LIKE THAT, THE LESS THEY CAN DO TO ANY OF US.
...I'LL REMEMBER.
THEN HOLD YOUR HEAD HIGH, PARTNER. IF YOU HADN'T SPOKE UP, WE MIGHT'VE JUST WATCHED YOUR FRIEND DIE. IT'S HAPPENED HERE BEFORE. WOULDN'T ANY OF US FEEL AS GOOD AS WE DO NOW.
BETTER SHAKE A LEG. THERE'S A HOTSHOT DUE OUT OF HERE ANY MINUTE.
AS WE PULLED AWAY FROM DETROIT, I WHISTLED A TUNE SOME DREAMERS HAD TAUGHT ME. IT WAS MY ANTHEM FOR THE NEW WORLD.
I WAS ON THE ROAD AGAIN, AND THOUGH THIS TRAIN'S DESTINATION WAS A MYSTERY TO ME, I KNEW WHERE I WAS GOING. I WAS GOING TO HAPPEN TO LIFE.
I THOUGHT ABOUT THE NEW WORLD THE REST OF THAT DAY. AND ON THE NEXT DAY, I RESTED.

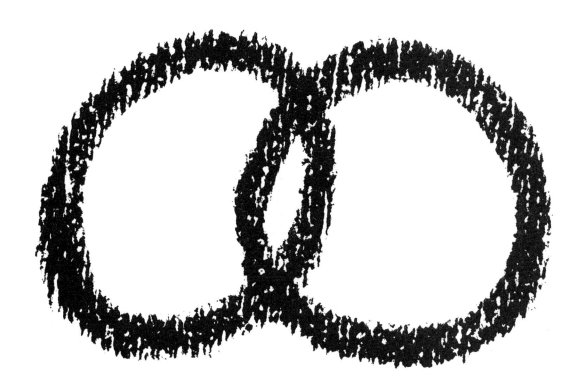

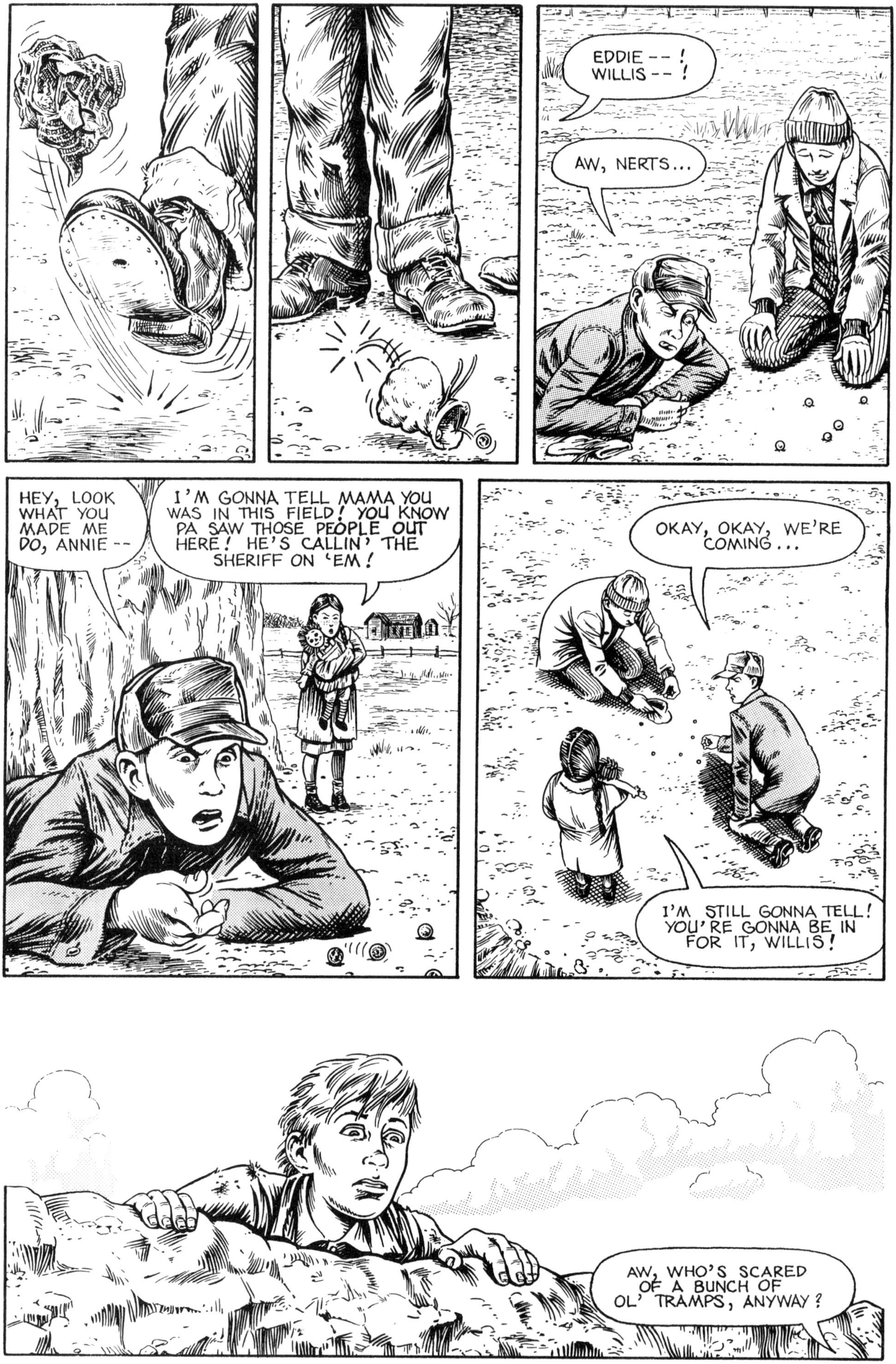
EDDIE -- !
WILLIS -- !
AW, NERTS...
HEY, LOOK WHAT YOU MADE ME DO, ANNIE --
I'M GONNA TELL MAMA YOU WAS IN THIS FIELD! YOU KNOW PA SAW THOSE PEOPLE OUT HERE! HE'S CALLIN' THE SHERIFF ON 'EM!
OKAY, OKAY, WE'RE COMING...
I'M STILL GONNA TELL! YOU'RE GONNA BE IN FOR IT, WILLIS!
AW, WHO'S SCARED OF A BUNCH OF OL' TRAMPS, ANYWAY?

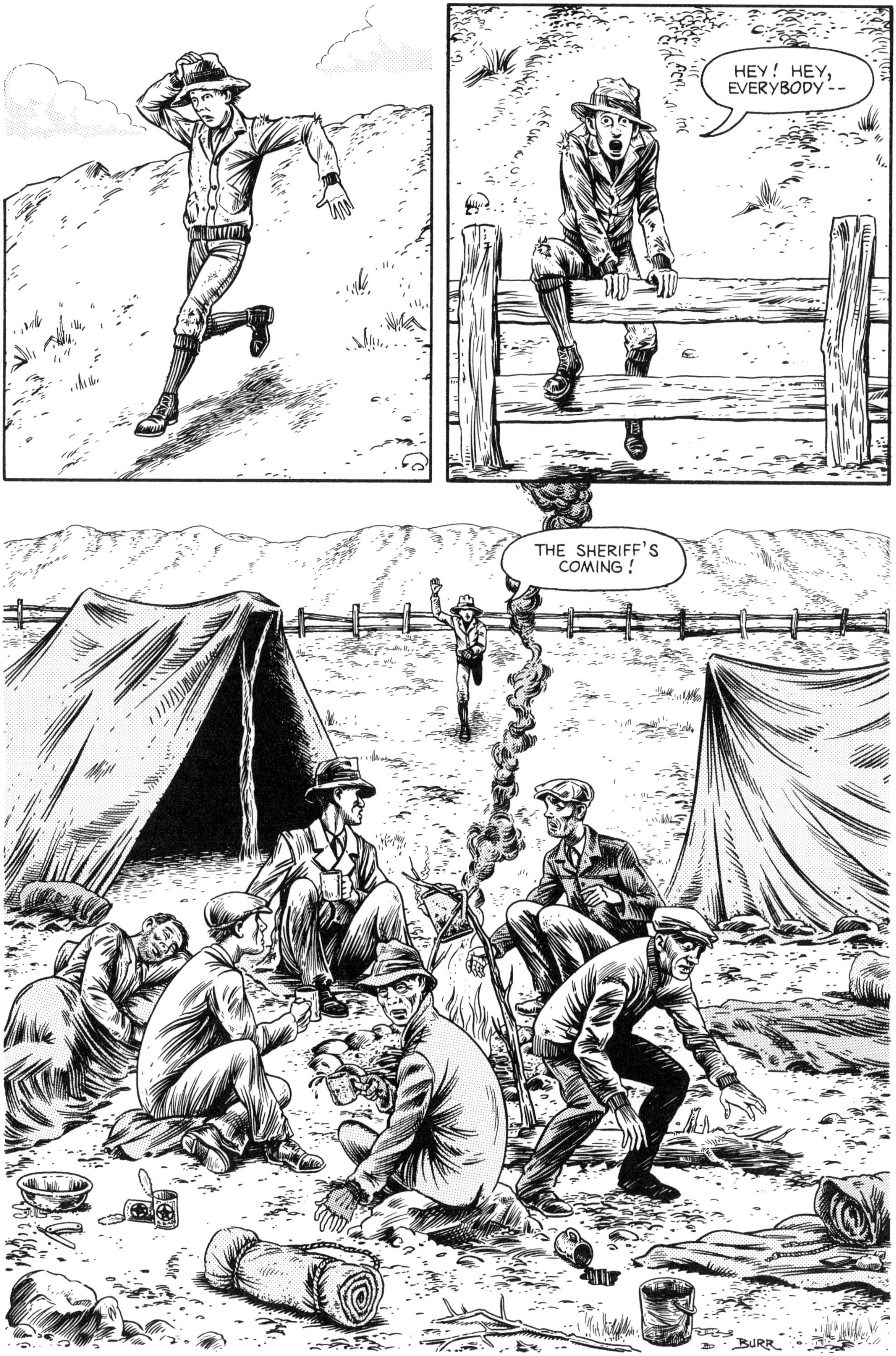
HEY! HEY, EVERYBODY--
THE SHERIFF'S COMING!
BURR

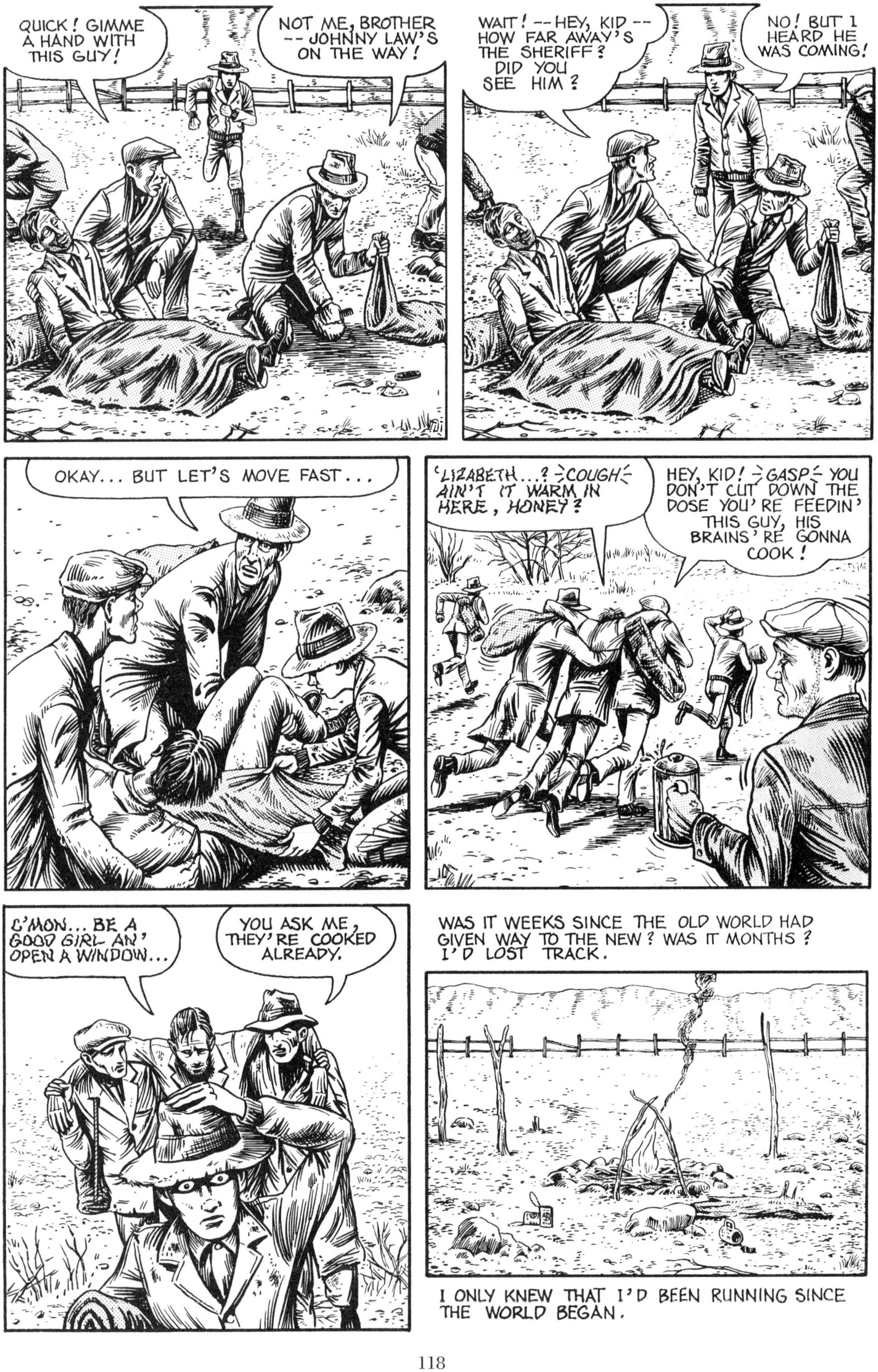
QUICK! GIMME A HAND WITH THIS GUY!
NOT ME, BROTHER -- JOHNNY LAW'S ON THE WAY!
WAIT! -- HEY, KID -- HOW FAR AWAY'S THE SHERIFF? DID YOU SEE HIM?
NO! BUT I HEARD HE WAS COMING!
OKAY... BUT LET'S MOVE FAST...
'LIZABETH...? -COUGH- AIN'T IT WARM IN HERE, HONEY?
HEY, KID! -GASP- YOU DON'T CUT DOWN THE DOSE YOU'RE FEEDIN' THIS GUY, HIS BRAINS'RE GONNA COOK!
C'MON... BE A GOOD GIRL AN' OPEN A WINDOW...
YOU ASK ME, THEY'RE COOKED ALREADY.
WAS IT WEEKS SINCE THE OLD WORLD HAD GIVEN WAY TO THE NEW? WAS IT MONTHS? I'D LOST TRACK.
I ONLY KNEW THAT I'D BEEN RUNNING SINCE THE WORLD BEGAN.

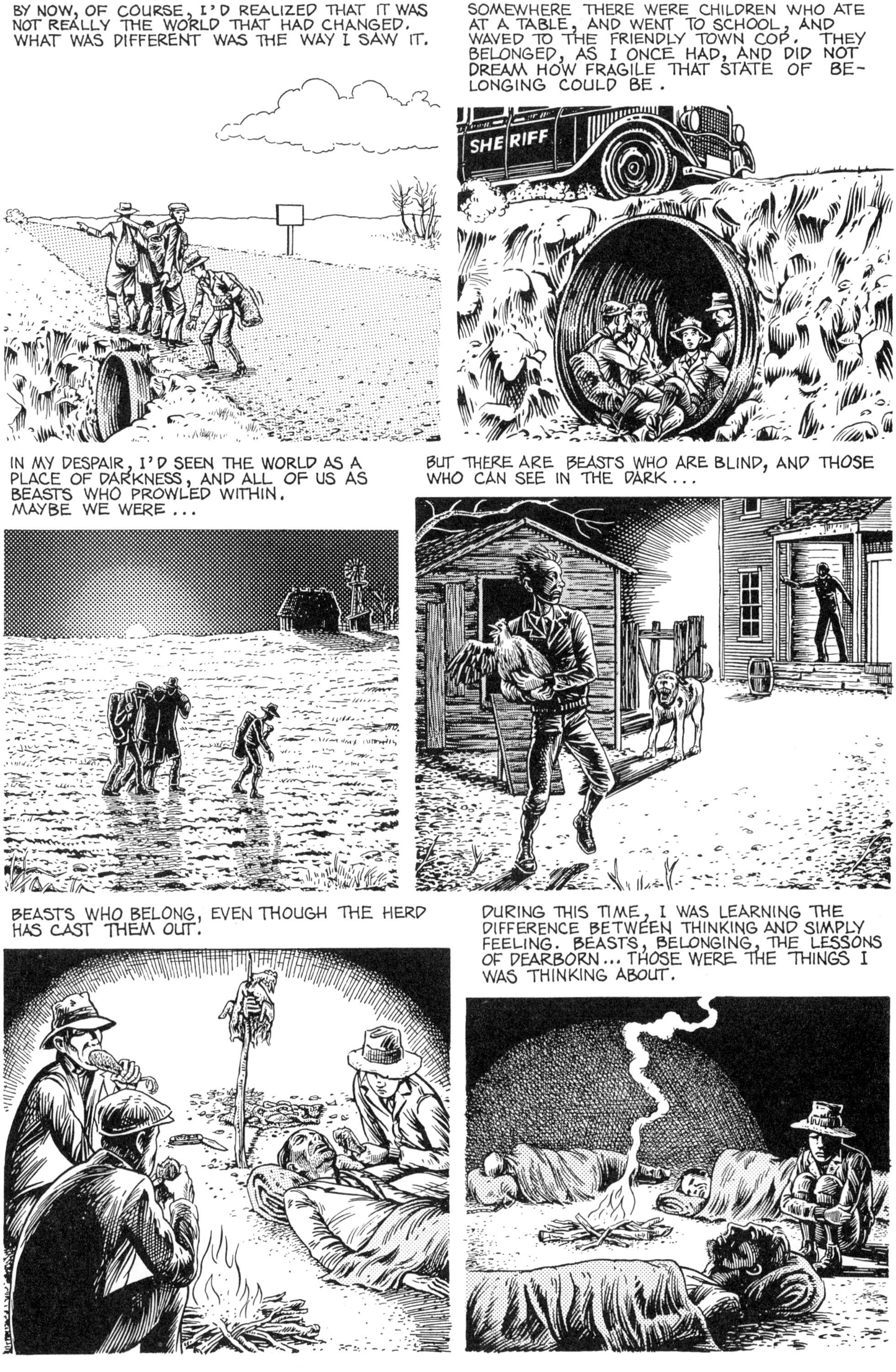
BY NOW, OF COURSE, I'D REALIZED THAT IT WAS NOT REALLY THE WORLD THAT HAD CHANGED. WHAT WAS DIFFERENT WAS THE WAY I SAW IT.
SOMEWHERE THERE WERE CHILDREN WHO ATE AT A TABLE, AND WENT TO SCHOOL, AND WAVED TO THE FRIENDLY TOWN COP. THEY BELONGED, AS I ONCE HAD, AND DID NOT DREAM HOW FRAGILE THAT STATE OF BELONGING COULD BE.
SHERIFF
IN MY DESPAIR, I'D SEEN THE WORLD AS A PLACE OF DARKNESS, AND ALL OF US AS BEASTS WHO PROWLED WITHIN. MAYBE WE WERE...
BUT THERE ARE BEASTS WHO ARE BLIND, AND THOSE WHO CAN SEE IN THE DARK...
BEASTS WHO BELONG, EVEN THOUGH THE HERD HAS CAST THEM OUT.
DURING THIS TIME, I WAS LEARNING THE DIFFERENCE BETWEEN THINKING AND SIMPLY FEELING. BEASTS, BELONGING, THE LESSONS OF DEARBORN... THOSE WERE THE THINGS I WAS THINKING ABOUT.

WHAT'S THAT, KID? COOKIN' UP SOME MORE HOP FOR YOUR PAL?

HIS RIBS ARE HURTING AGAIN. HE NEEDS IT.

ANY O' YOU BOYS GET THE NUMBER O' THAT MULE? ...HEH...–COUGH–

YEAH, HE NEEDS IT BAD.

BETTER DOSE HIM UP QUICK, BEFORE HE REMEMBERS WHAT HIS NAME IS.

HE DOESN'T BREATHE RIGHT IF I DON'T GIVE IT TO HIM! HE HURTS TOO BAD!

I DON'T KNOW WHAT TO DO... I'M SCARED HE'S GOING TO DIE...

I GUESS IT'S YOUR BUSINESS, NOT MINE. -- BUT IF IT WAS ME LAID OUT THERE, IT MIGHT BE WORTH A LITTLE PAIN TO LOOK UP AND SEE A GOOD FRIEND WATCHIN' OVER ME.

'LESS HIS BRAINS IS ALREADY COOKED FOR GOOD, THEN YOU JUST GOT A VEGETABLE THAT HURTS ALL THE TIME.

AND HE SAYS... "HELL, MISTER.... HOW'D YOU 'SPECT A OLD MAN LIKE THAT TO CATCH THAT RABBIT...?"

LET'S GET MOVIN'. WE'VE GOT A TRAIN TO CATCH.

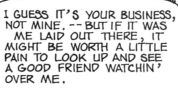

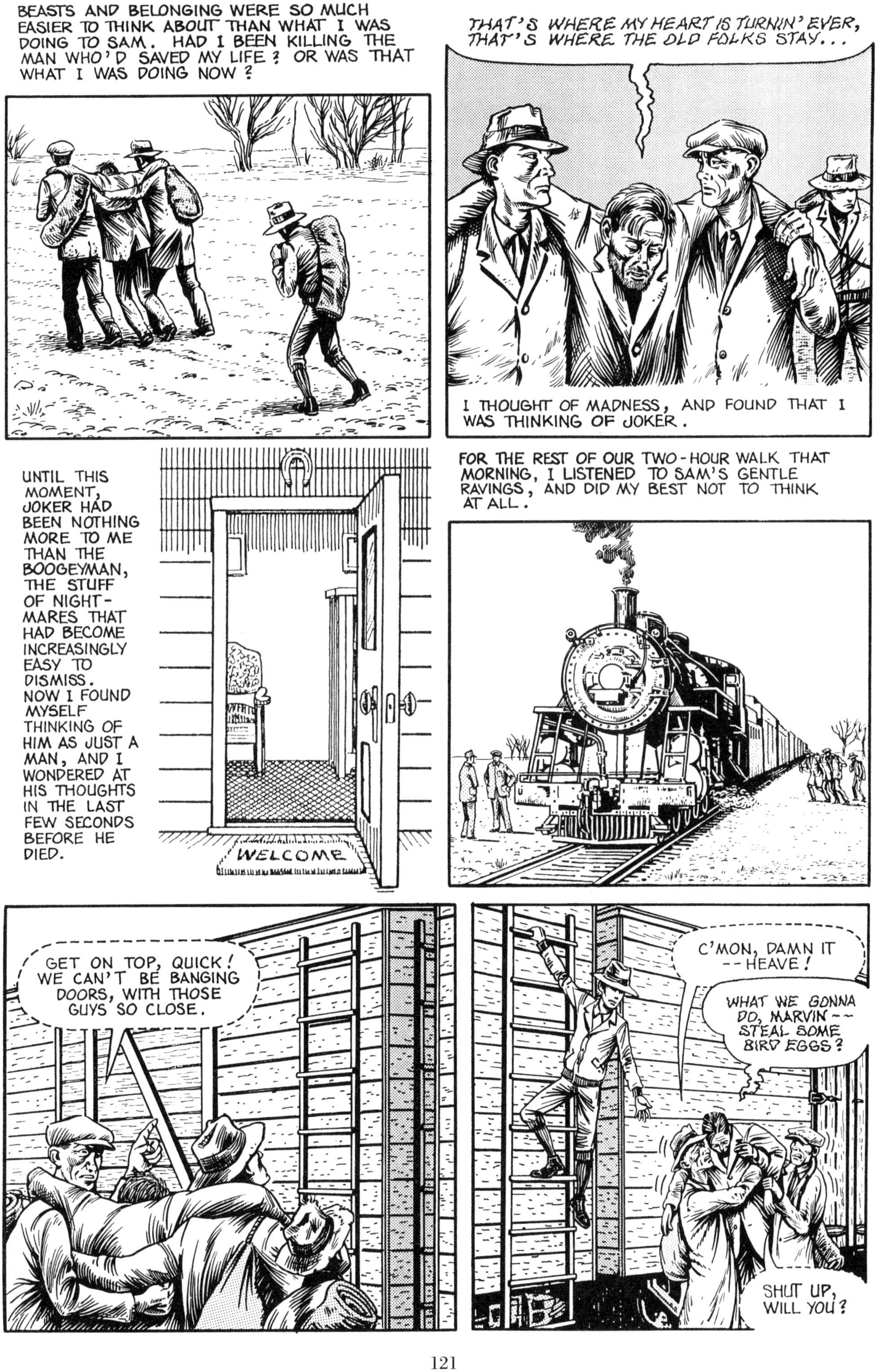
BEASTS AND BELONGING WERE SO MUCH EASIER TO THINK ABOUT THAN WHAT I WAS DOING TO SAM. HAD I BEEN KILLING THE MAN WHO'D SAVED MY LIFE? OR WAS THAT WHAT I WAS DOING NOW?
THAT'S WHERE MY HEART IS TURNIN' EVER, THAT'S WHERE THE OLD FOLKS STAY...
I THOUGHT OF MADNESS, AND FOUND THAT I WAS THINKING OF JOKER.
UNTIL THIS MOMENT, JOKER HAD BEEN NOTHING MORE TO ME THAN THE BOOGEYMAN, THE STUFF OF NIGHT-MARES THAT HAD BECOME INCREASINGLY EASY TO DISMISS. NOW I FOUND MYSELF THINKING OF HIM AS JUST A MAN, AND I WONDERED AT HIS THOUGHTS IN THE LAST FEW SECONDS BEFORE HE DIED.
WELCOME
FOR THE REST OF OUR TWO-HOUR WALK THAT MORNING, I LISTENED TO SAM'S GENTLE RAVINGS, AND DID MY BEST NOT TO THINK AT ALL.
GET ON TOP, QUICK! WE CAN'T BE BANGING DOORS, WITH THOSE GUYS SO CLOSE.
C'MON, DAMN IT --HEAVE!
WHAT WE GONNA DO, MARVIN-- STEAL SOME BIRD EGGS?
SHUT UP, WILL YOU?

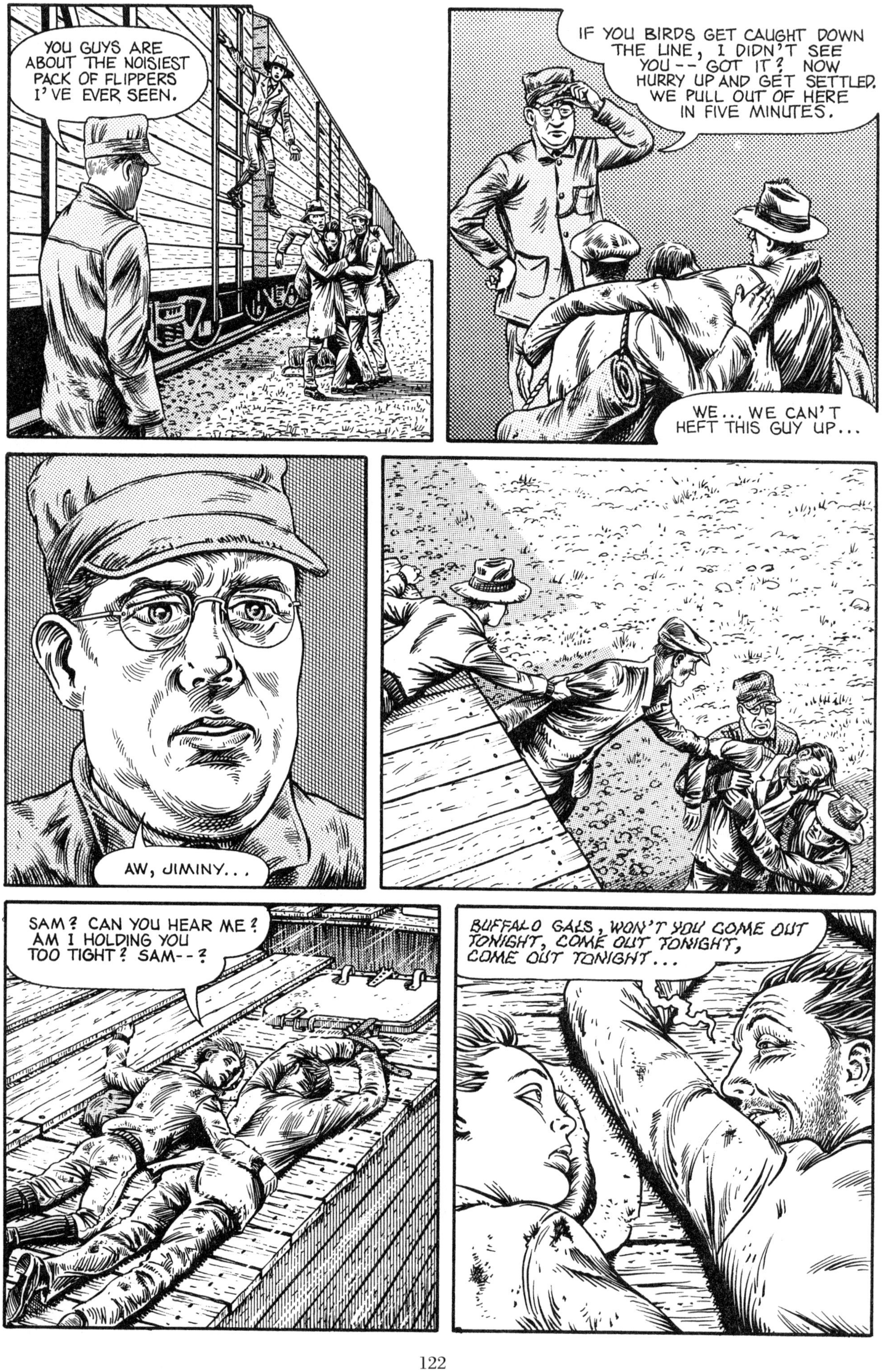
YOU GUYS ARE ABOUT THE NOISIEST PACK OF FLIPPERS I'VE EVER SEEN.
IF YOU BIRDS GET CAUGHT DOWN THE LINE, I DIDN'T SEE YOU -- GOT IT? NOW HURRY UP AND GET SETTLED. WE PULL OUT OF HERE IN FIVE MINUTES.
WE... WE CAN'T HEFT THIS GUY UP...
AW, JIMINY...
SAM? CAN YOU HEAR ME? AM I HOLDING YOU TOO TIGHT? SAM--?
BUFFALO GALS, WON'T YOU COME OUT TONIGHT, COME OUT TONIGHT, COME OUT TONIGHT...

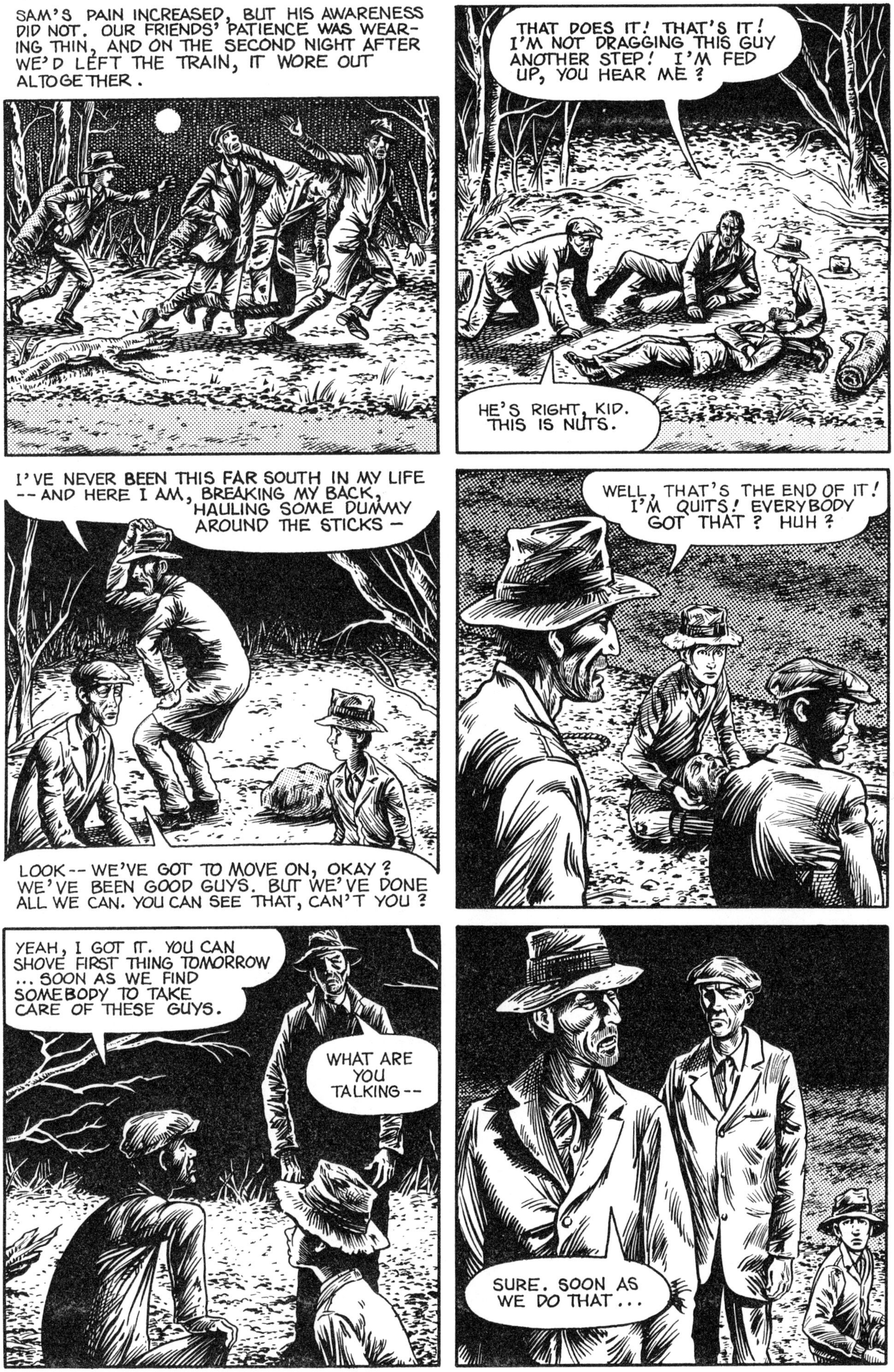
SAM'S PAIN INCREASED, BUT HIS AWARENESS DID NOT. OUR FRIENDS' PATIENCE WAS WEARING THIN, AND ON THE SECOND NIGHT AFTER WE'D LEFT THE TRAIN, IT WORE OUT ALTOGETHER.
THAT DOES IT! THAT'S IT! I'M NOT DRAGGING THIS GUY ANOTHER STEP! I'M FED UP, YOU HEAR ME?
HE'S RIGHT, KID. THIS IS NUTS.
I'VE NEVER BEEN THIS FAR SOUTH IN MY LIFE -- AND HERE I AM, BREAKING MY BACK, HAULING SOME DUMMY AROUND THE STICKS --
LOOK -- WE'VE GOT TO MOVE ON, OKAY? WE'VE BEEN GOOD GUYS. BUT WE'VE DONE ALL WE CAN. YOU CAN SEE THAT, CAN'T YOU?
WELL, THAT'S THE END OF IT! I'M QUITS! EVERYBODY GOT THAT? HUH?
YEAH, I GOT IT. YOU CAN SHOVE FIRST THING TOMORROW ... SOON AS WE FIND SOMEBODY TO TAKE CARE OF THESE GUYS.
WHAT ARE YOU TALKING --
SURE. SOON AS WE DO THAT ...

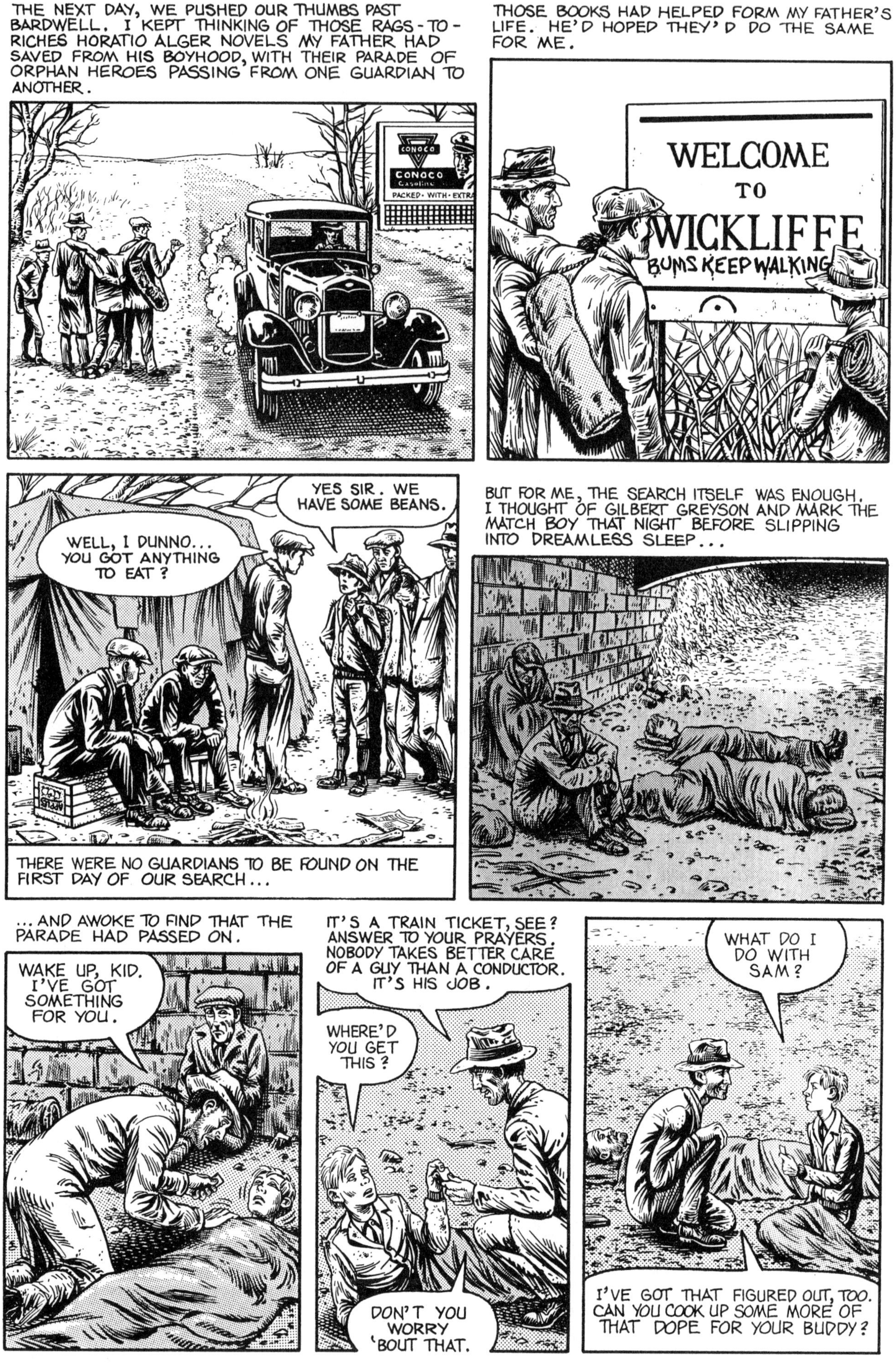
THE NEXT DAY, WE PUSHED OUR THUMBS PAST BARDWELL. I KEPT THINKING OF THOSE RAGS-TO-RICHES HORATIO ALGER NOVELS MY FATHER HAD SAVED FROM HIS BOYHOOD, WITH THEIR PARADE OF ORPHAN HEROES PASSING FROM ONE GUARDIAN TO ANOTHER.
CONOCO
CONOCO Gasoline
PACKED WITH EXTRA
THOSE BOOKS HAD HELPED FORM MY FATHER'S LIFE. HE'D HOPED THEY'D DO THE SAME FOR ME.
WELCOME TO WICKLIFFE
BUMS KEEP WALKING
WELL, I DUNNO... YOU GOT ANYTHING TO EAT?
YES SIR. WE HAVE SOME BEANS.
THERE WERE NO GUARDIANS TO BE FOUND ON THE FIRST DAY OF OUR SEARCH...
BUT FOR ME, THE SEARCH ITSELF WAS ENOUGH. I THOUGHT OF GILBERT GREYSON AND MARK THE MATCH BOY THAT NIGHT BEFORE SLIPPING INTO DREAMLESS SLEEP...
...AND AWOKE TO FIND THAT THE PARADE HAD PASSED ON.
WAKE UP, KID. I'VE GOT SOMETHING FOR YOU.
IT'S A TRAIN TICKET, SEE? ANSWER TO YOUR PRAYERS. NOBODY TAKES BETTER CARE OF A GUY THAN A CONDUCTOR. IT'S HIS JOB.
WHERE'D YOU GET THIS?
DON'T YOU WORRY 'BOUT THAT.
WHAT DO I DO WITH SAM?
I'VE GOT THAT FIGURED OUT, TOO. CAN YOU COOK UP SOME MORE OF THAT DOPE FOR YOUR BUDDY?

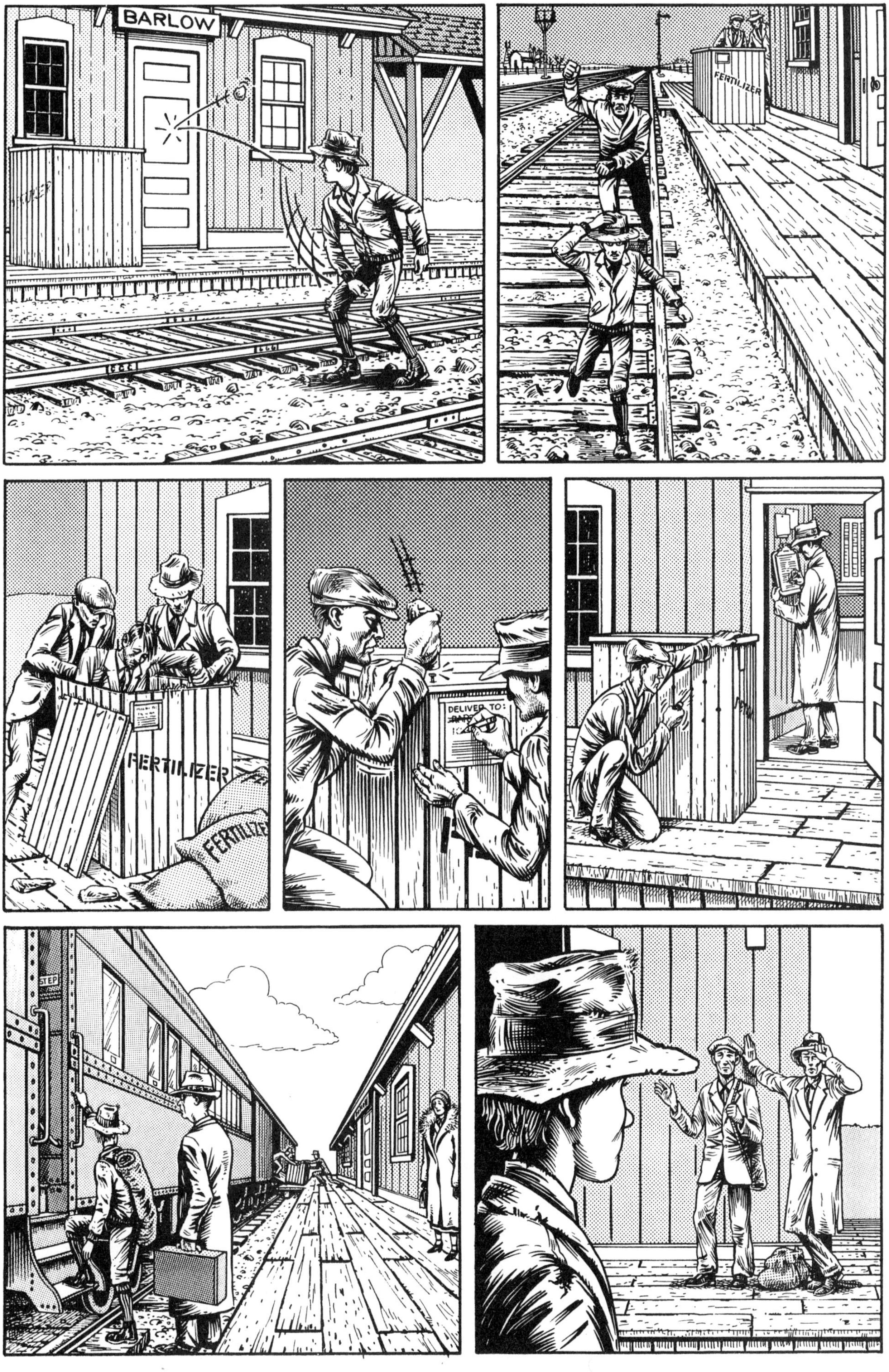

BARLOW
FERTILIZER
FERTILIZER
DELIVER TO:
STEP

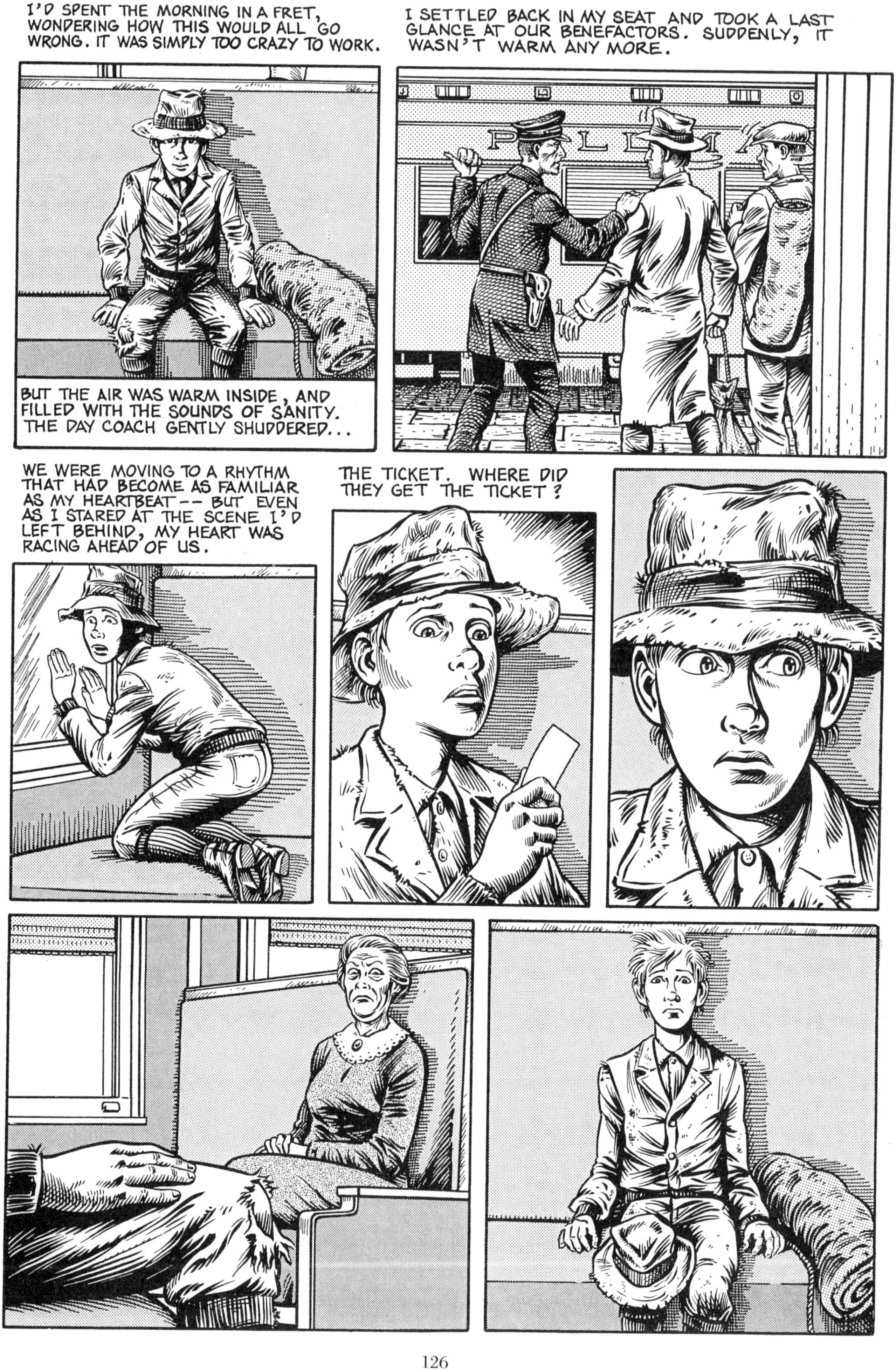
I'D SPENT THE MORNING IN A FRET, WONDERING HOW THIS WOULD ALL GO WRONG. IT WAS SIMPLY TOO CRAZY TO WORK.
BUT THE AIR WAS WARM INSIDE, AND FILLED WITH THE SOUNDS OF SANITY. THE DAY COACH GENTLY SHUDDERED...
I SETTLED BACK IN MY SEAT AND TOOK A LAST GLANCE AT OUR BENEFACTORS. SUDDENLY, IT WASN'T WARM ANY MORE.
WE WERE MOVING TO A RHYTHM THAT HAD BECOME AS FAMILIAR AS MY HEARTBEAT -- BUT EVEN AS I STARED AT THE SCENE I'D LEFT BEHIND, MY HEART WAS RACING AHEAD OF US.
THE TICKET. WHERE DID THEY GET THE TICKET?

"THEY WERE DESPERATE," I TOLD MYSELF. "THEY EMPTIED THEIR POCKETS TO GET US OUT OF THEIR HAIR." BUT HOW DESPERATE HAD THEY BEEN?

THE MORE I CONSIDERED THE QUESTION, THE MORE LURID THE ANSWER BECAME. I KEPT THINKING OF THE COP AT THE DEPOT, FEELING HIS HAND UPON MY SHOULDER, HEARING HIM SNARL IN MY EAR...

TICKET.

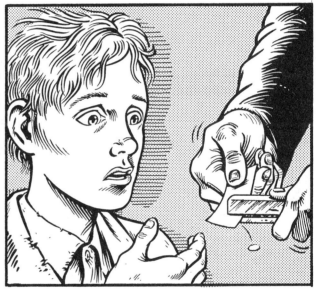

THERE YOU GO, SON. ENJOY YOUR TRIP.

"MOVE ALONG," SNARLED THE VOICE IN MY HEAD; "MOVE ALONG OR I'LL RUN YOU IN."

THE LITANY OF THE SMALL TOWN COP: THAT WAS ALL IT HAD BEEN. NOTHING MORE.

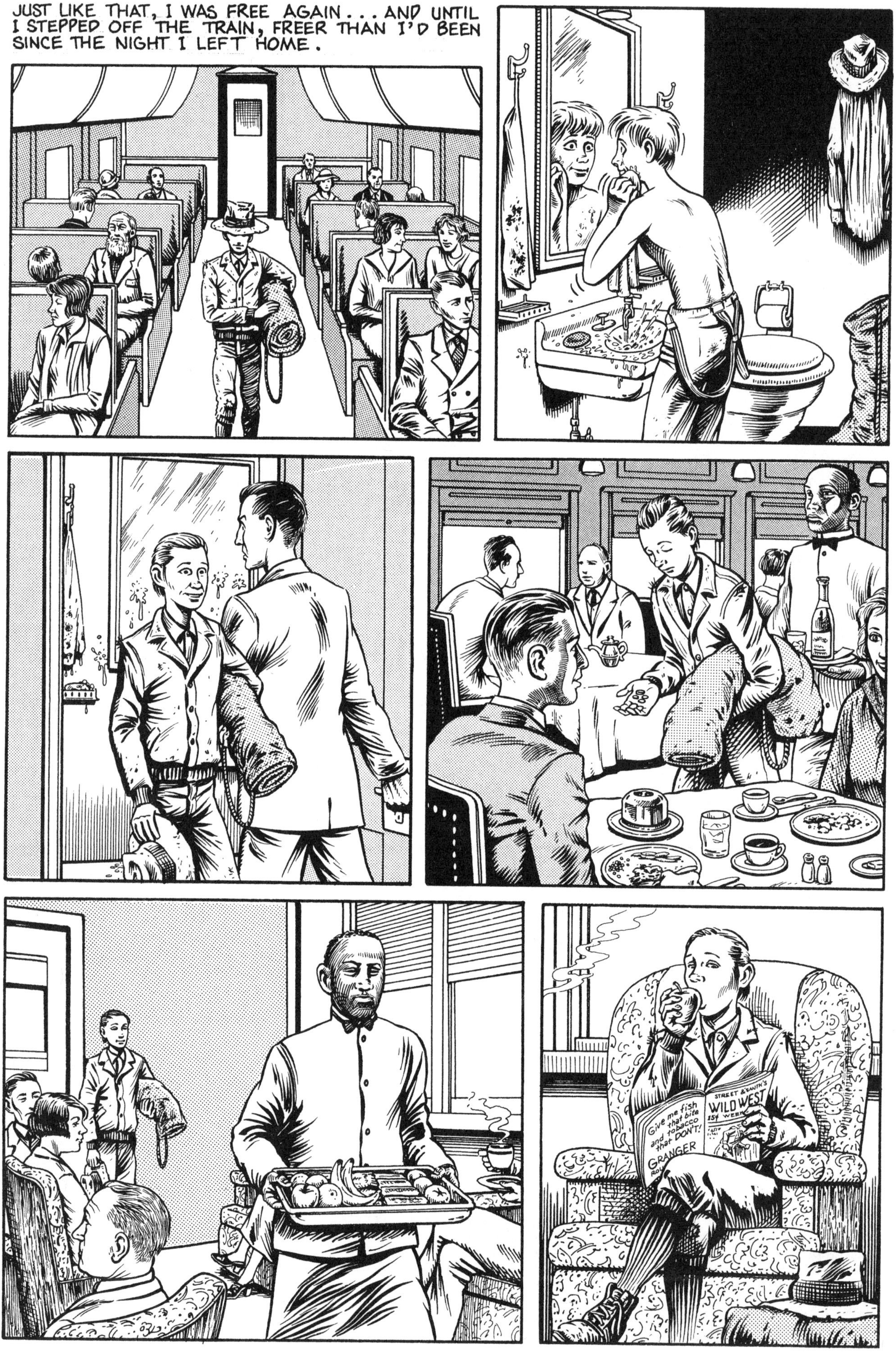
JUST LIKE THAT, I WAS FREE AGAIN . . . AND UNTIL I STEPPED OFF THE TRAIN, FREER THAN I'D BEEN SINCE THE NIGHT I LEFT HOME.
STREET & SMITH'S
WILD WEST
Give me fish that bite and tobacco that DON'T!
GRANGER

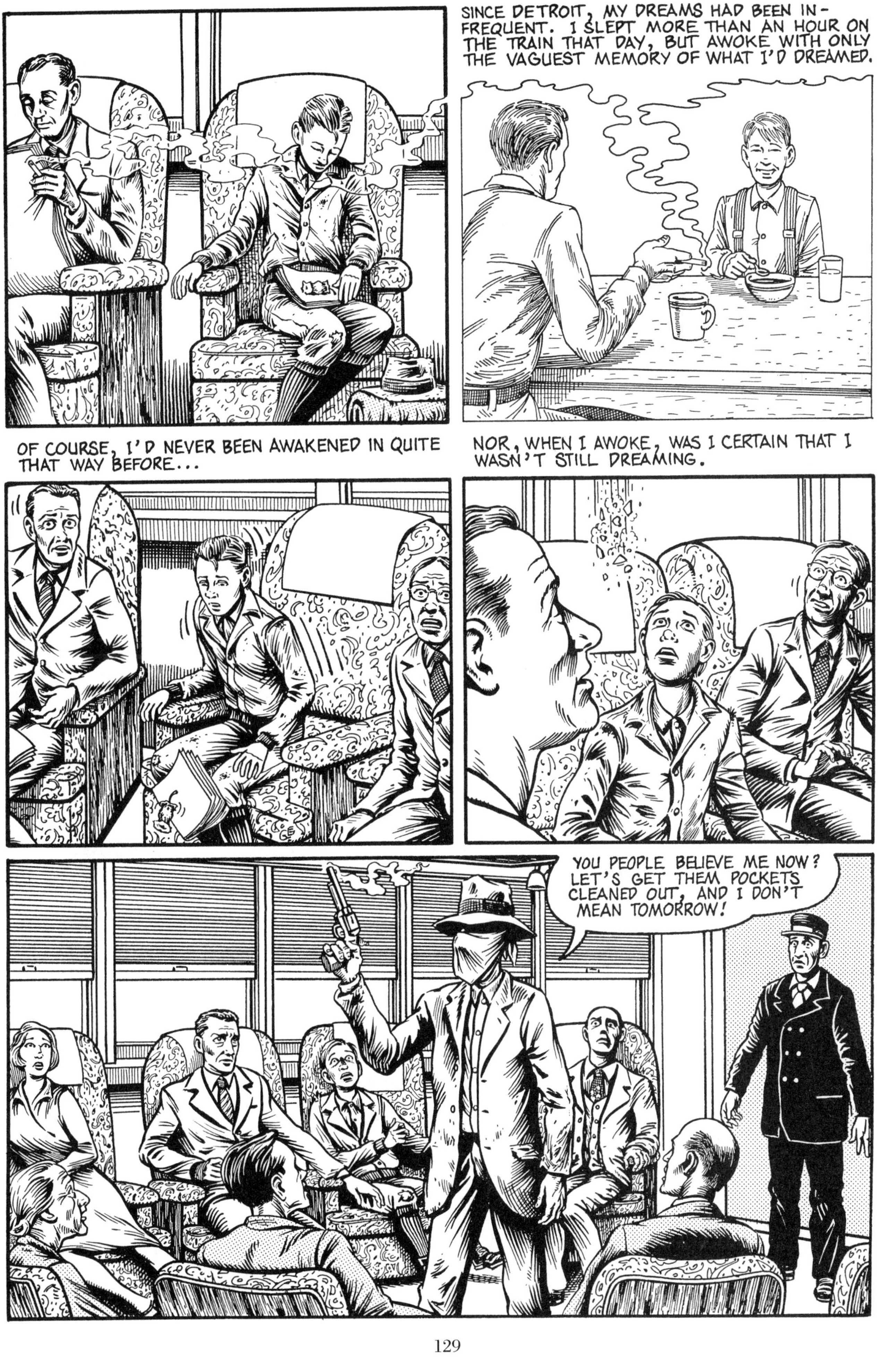
SINCE DETROIT, MY DREAMS HAD BEEN INFREQUENT. I SLEPT MORE THAN AN HOUR ON THE TRAIN THAT DAY, BUT AWOKE WITH ONLY THE VAGUEST MEMORY OF WHAT I'D DREAMED.
OF COURSE, I'D NEVER BEEN AWAKENED IN QUITE THAT WAY BEFORE...
NOR, WHEN I AWOKE, WAS I CERTAIN THAT I WASN'T STILL DREAMING.
YOU PEOPLE BELIEVE ME NOW? LET'S GET THEM POCKETS CLEANED OUT, AND I DON'T MEAN TOMORROW!

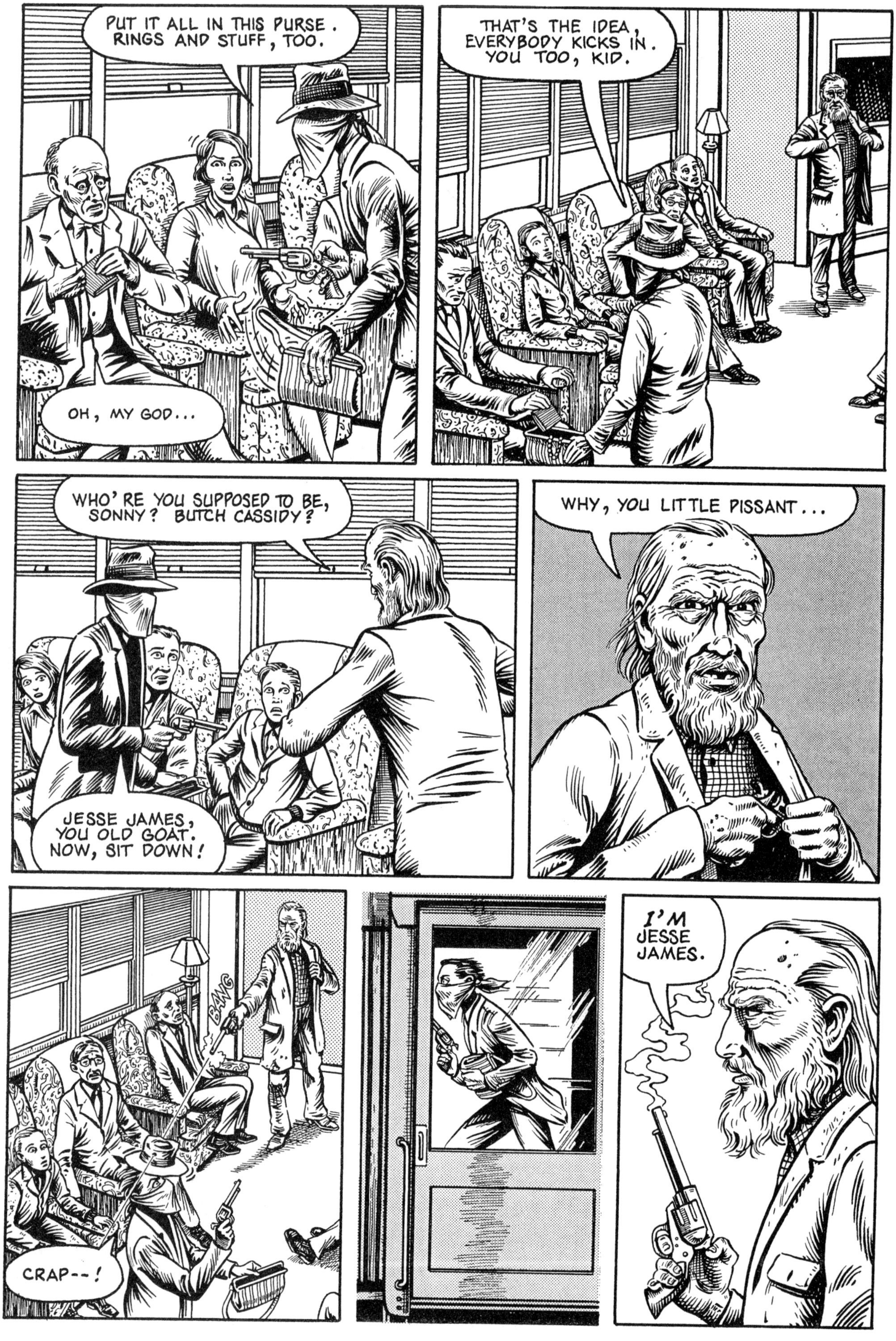
PUT IT ALL IN THIS PURSE. RINGS AND STUFF, TOO.
OH, MY GOD...
THAT'S THE IDEA, EVERYBODY KICKS IN. YOU TOO, KID.
WHO'RE YOU SUPPOSED TO BE, SONNY? BUTCH CASSIDY?
JESSE JAMES, YOU OLD GOAT. NOW, SIT DOWN!
WHY, YOU LITTLE PISSANT...
BANG
CRAP--!
I'M JESSE JAMES.

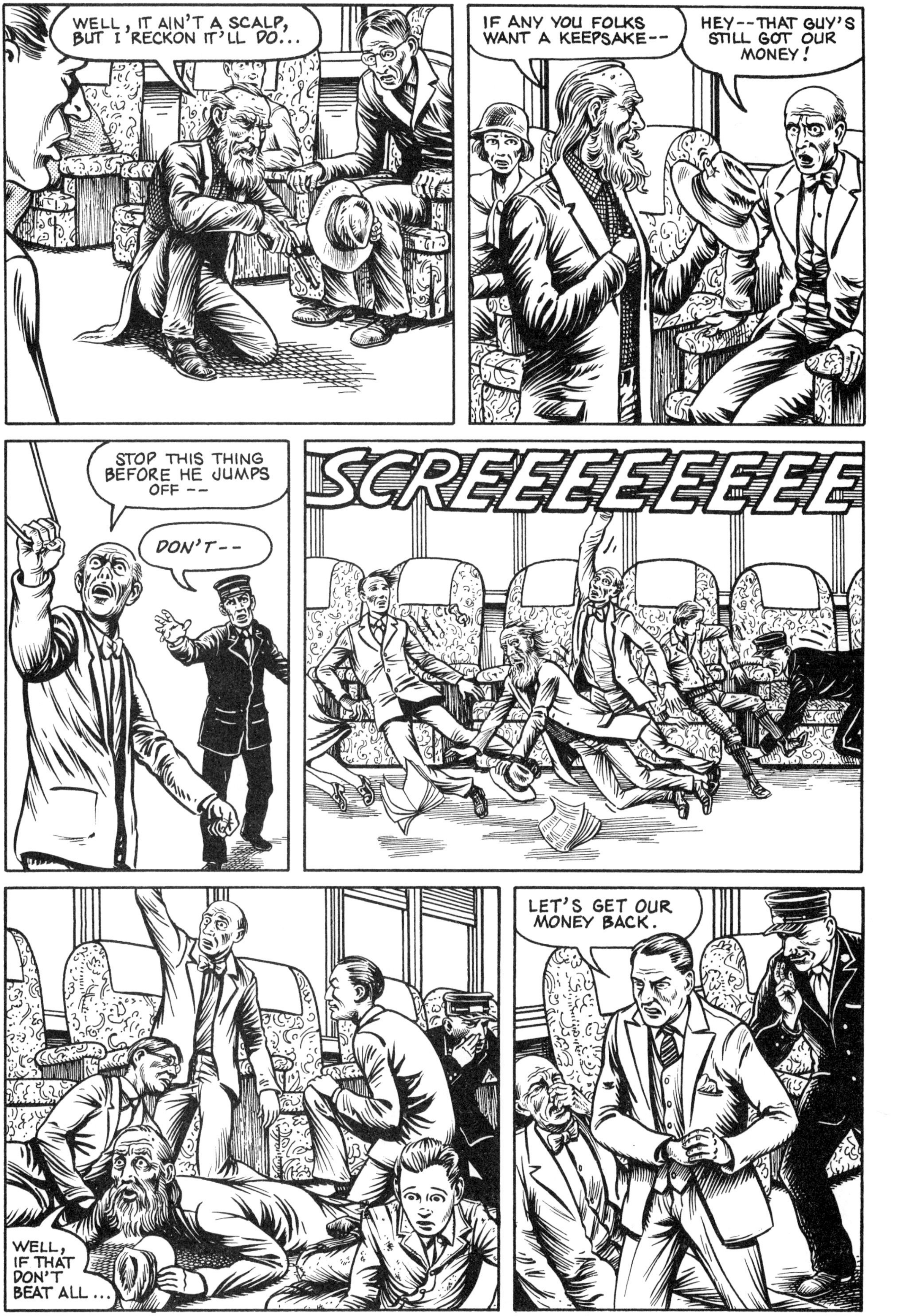
WELL, IT AIN'T A SCALP, BUT I RECKON IT'LL DO...
IF ANY YOU FOLKS WANT A KEEPSAKE--
HEY--THAT GUY'S STILL GOT OUR MONEY!
STOP THIS THING BEFORE HE JUMPS OFF --
DON'T--
SCREEEEEEEEE
WELL, IF THAT DON'T BEAT ALL...
LET'S GET OUR MONEY BACK.

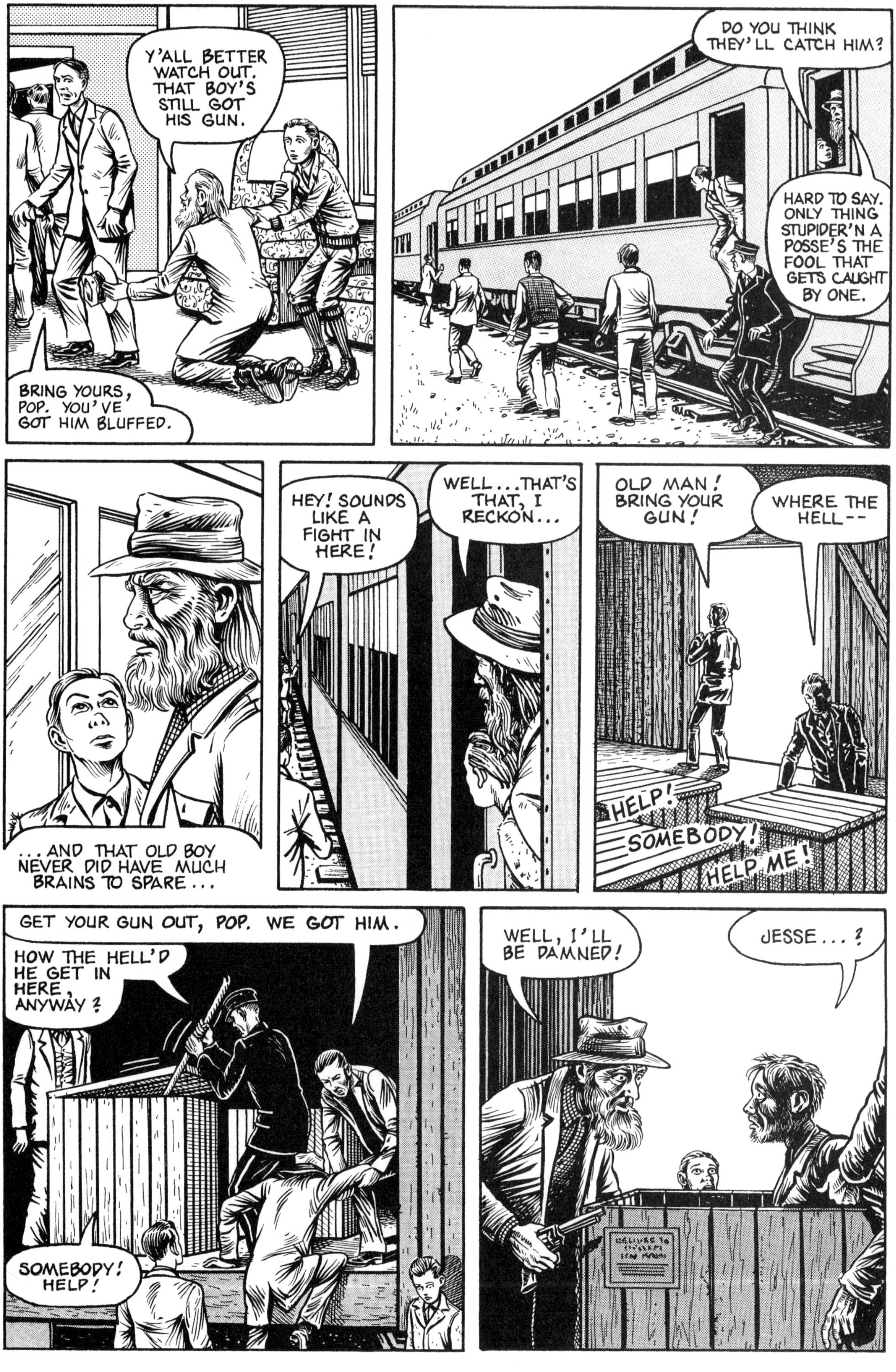
Y'ALL BETTER WATCH OUT. THAT BOY'S STILL GOT HIS GUN.
BRING YOURS, POP. YOU'VE GOT HIM BLUFFED.
DO YOU THINK THEY'LL CATCH HIM?
HARD TO SAY. ONLY THING STUPIDER'N A POSSE'S THE FOOL THAT GETS CAUGHT BY ONE.
...AND THAT OLD BOY NEVER DID HAVE MUCH BRAINS TO SPARE...
HEY! SOUNDS LIKE A FIGHT IN HERE!
WELL...THAT'S THAT, I RECKON...
OLD MAN! BRING YOUR GUN!
WHERE THE HELL--
HELP!
SOMEBODY!
HELP ME!
GET YOUR GUN OUT, POP. WE GOT HIM.
HOW THE HELL'D HE GET IN HERE, ANYWAY?
SOMEBODY! HELP!
WELL, I'LL BE DAMNED!
JESSE...?

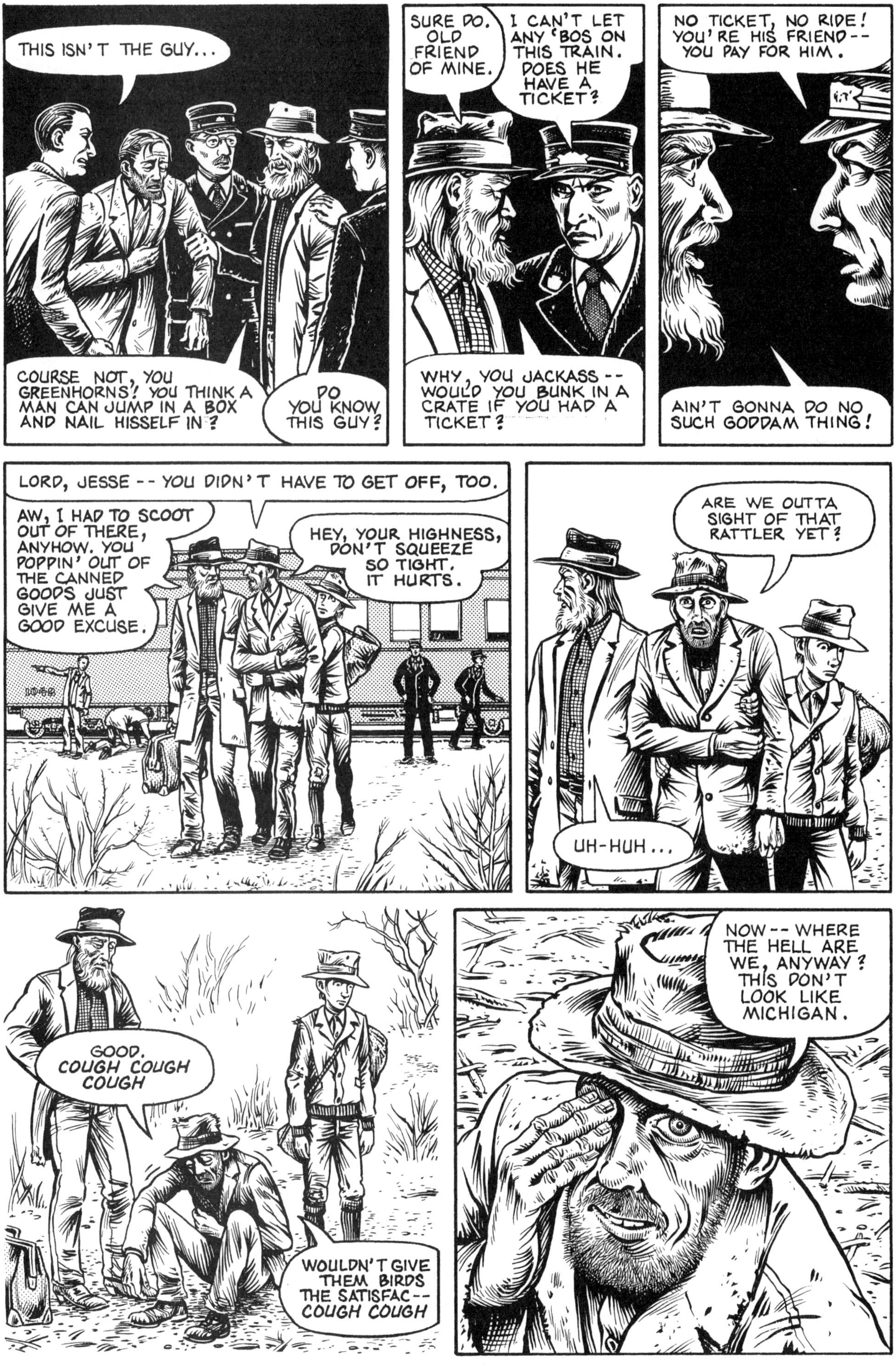
THIS ISN'T THE GUY...
COURSE NOT, YOU GREENHORNS! YOU THINK A MAN CAN JUMP IN A BOX AND NAIL HISSELF IN?
DO YOU KNOW THIS GUY?
SURE DO. OLD FRIEND OF MINE.
I CAN'T LET ANY 'BOS ON THIS TRAIN. DOES HE HAVE A TICKET?
WHY, YOU JACKASS -- WOULD YOU BUNK IN A CRATE IF YOU HAD A TICKET?
NO TICKET, NO RIDE! YOU'RE HIS FRIEND -- YOU PAY FOR HIM.
AIN'T GONNA DO NO SUCH GODDAM THING!
LORD, JESSE -- YOU DIDN'T HAVE TO GET OFF, TOO.
AW, I HAD TO SCOOT OUT OF THERE, ANYHOW. YOU POPPIN' OUT OF THE CANNED GOODS JUST GIVE ME A GOOD EXCUSE.
HEY, YOUR HIGHNESS, DON'T SQUEEZE SO TIGHT. IT HURTS.
ARE WE OUTTA SIGHT OF THAT RATTLER YET?
UH-HUH...
GOOD. COUGH COUGH COUGH
WOULDN'T GIVE THEM BIRDS THE SATISFAC-- COUGH COUGH
NOW -- WHERE THE HELL ARE WE, ANYWAY? THIS DON'T LOOK LIKE MICHIGAN.

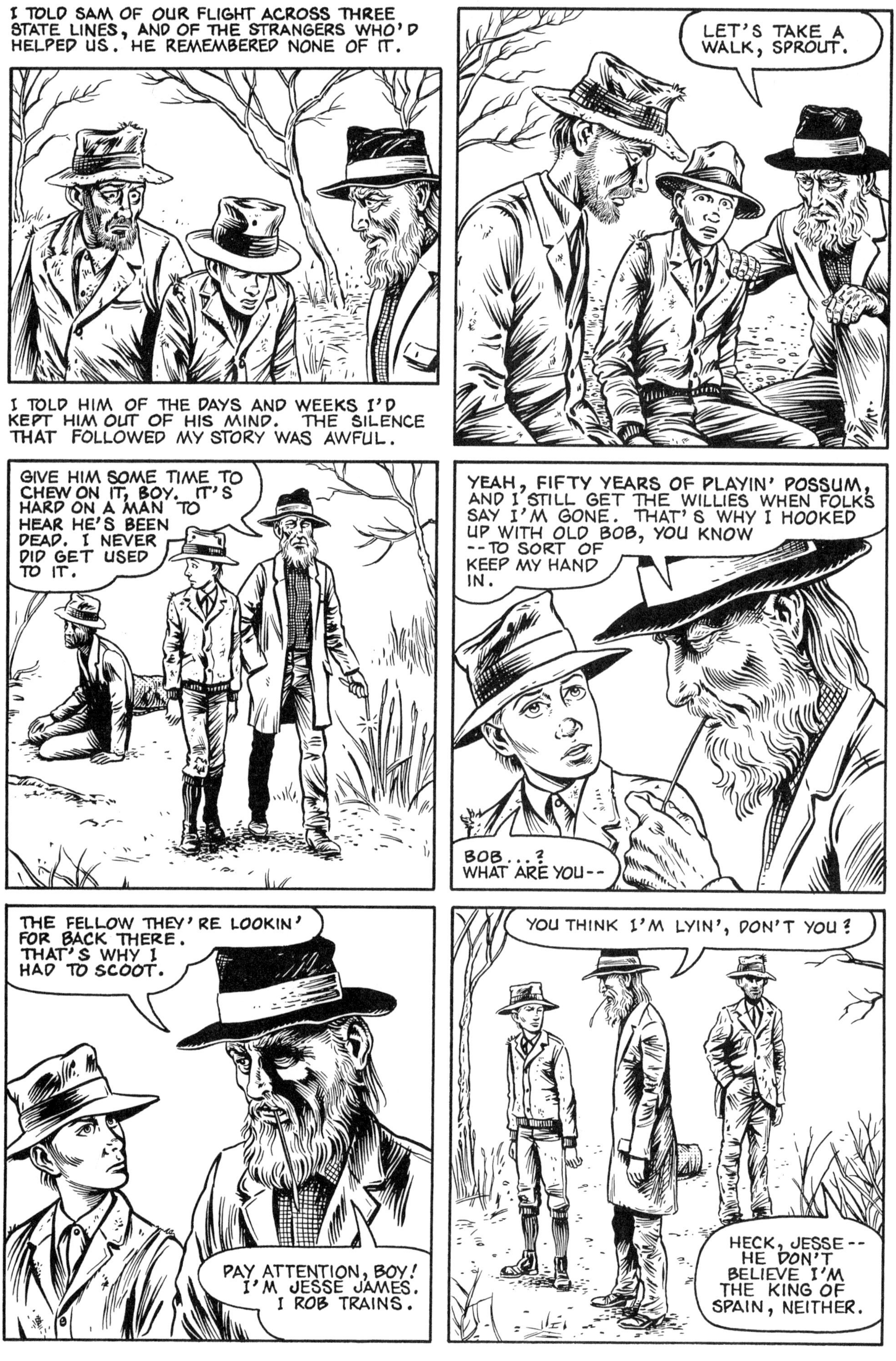
I TOLD SAM OF OUR FLIGHT ACROSS THREE STATE LINES, AND OF THE STRANGERS WHO'D HELPED US. HE REMEMBERED NONE OF IT.
I TOLD HIM OF THE DAYS AND WEEKS I'D KEPT HIM OUT OF HIS MIND. THE SILENCE THAT FOLLOWED MY STORY WAS AWFUL.
LET'S TAKE A WALK, SPROUT.
GIVE HIM SOME TIME TO CHEW ON IT, BOY. IT'S HARD ON A MAN TO HEAR HE'S BEEN DEAD. I NEVER DID GET USED TO IT.
YEAH, FIFTY YEARS OF PLAYIN' POSSUM, AND I STILL GET THE WILLIES WHEN FOLKS SAY I'M GONE. THAT'S WHY I HOOKED UP WITH OLD BOB, YOU KNOW --TO SORT OF KEEP MY HAND IN.
BOB...? WHAT ARE YOU--
THE FELLOW THEY'RE LOOKIN' FOR BACK THERE. THAT'S WHY I HAD TO SCOOT.
PAY ATTENTION, BOY! I'M JESSE JAMES. I ROB TRAINS.
YOU THINK I'M LYIN', DON'T YOU?
HECK, JESSE-- HE DON'T BELIEVE I'M THE KING OF SPAIN, NEITHER.

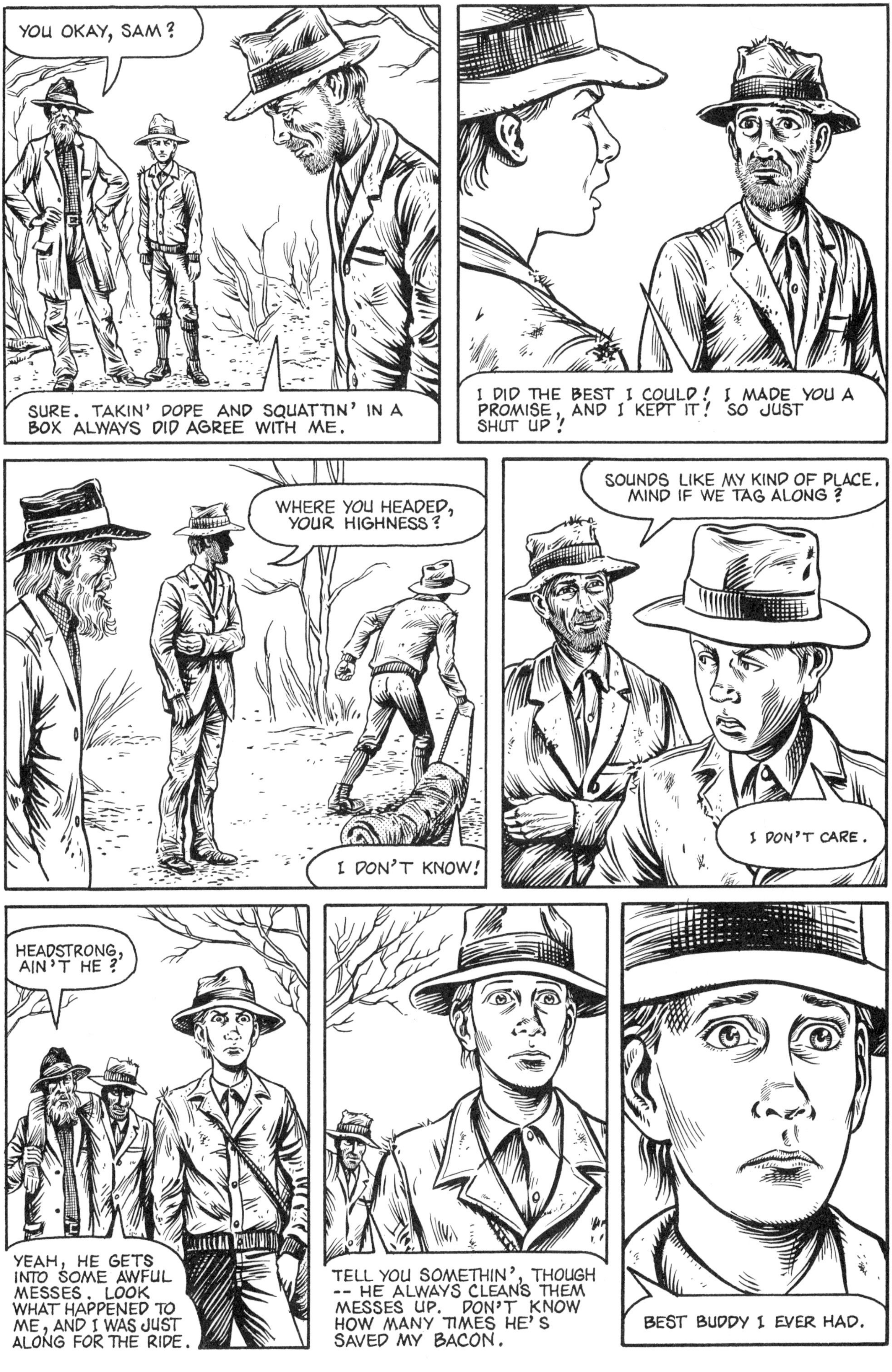

YOU OKAY, SAM?
SURE. TAKIN' DOPE AND SQUATTIN' IN A BOX ALWAYS DID AGREE WITH ME.
I DID THE BEST I COULD! I MADE YOU A PROMISE, AND I KEPT IT! SO JUST SHUT UP!
WHERE YOU HEADED, YOUR HIGHNESS?
I DON'T KNOW!
SOUNDS LIKE MY KIND OF PLACE. MIND IF WE TAG ALONG?
I DON'T CARE.
HEADSTRONG, AIN'T HE?
YEAH, HE GETS INTO SOME AWFUL MESSES. LOOK WHAT HAPPENED TO ME, AND I WAS JUST ALONG FOR THE RIDE.
TELL YOU SOMETHIN', THOUGH -- HE ALWAYS CLEANS THEM MESSES UP. DON'T KNOW HOW MANY TIMES HE'S SAVED MY BACON.
BEST BUDDY I EVER HAD.

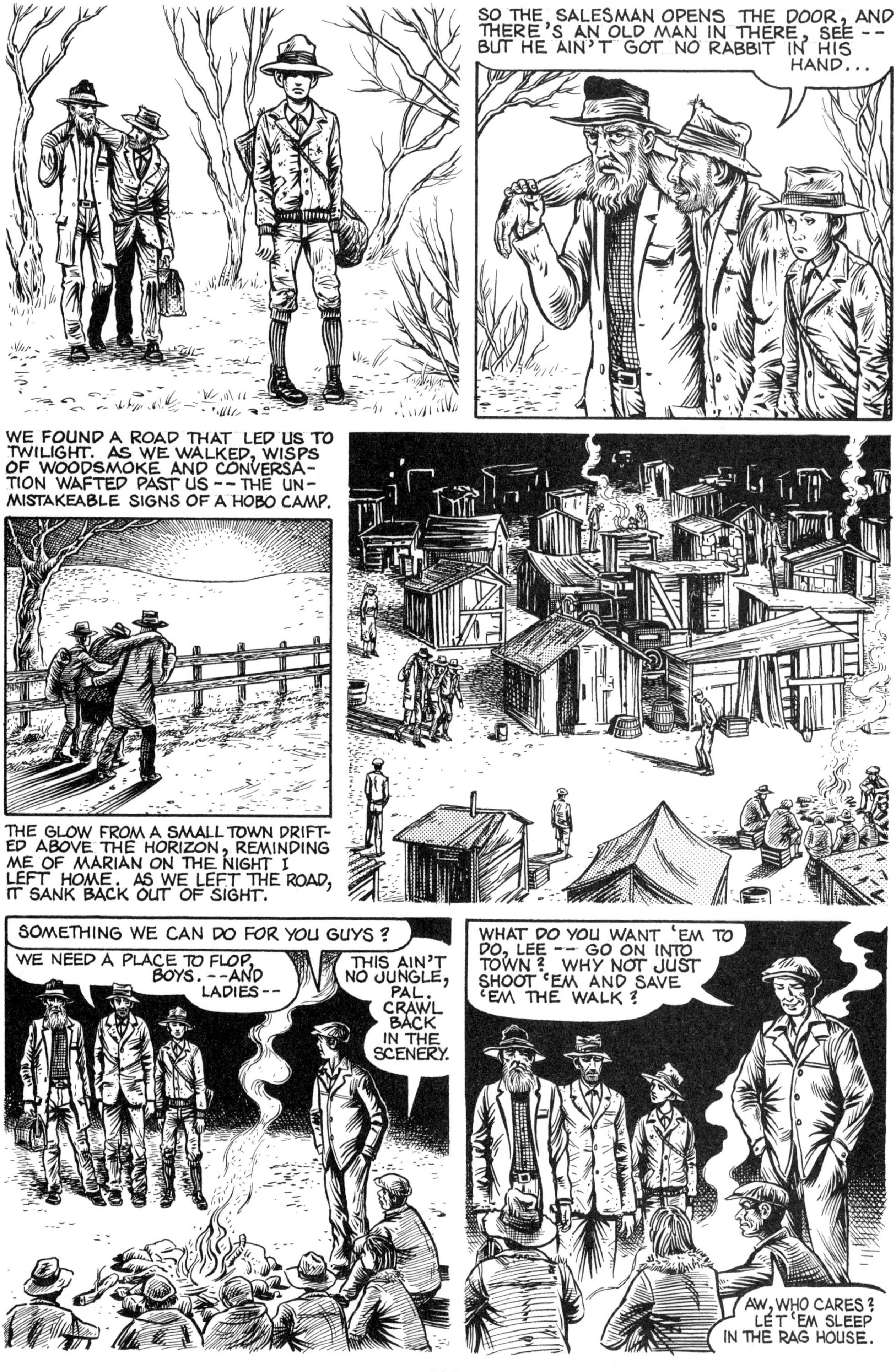
SO THE SALESMAN OPENS THE DOOR, AND THERE'S AN OLD MAN IN THERE, SEE -- BUT HE AIN'T GOT NO RABBIT IN HIS HAND...
WE FOUND A ROAD THAT LED US TO TWILIGHT. AS WE WALKED, WISPS OF WOODSMOKE AND CONVERSATION WAFTED PAST US -- THE UNMISTAKEABLE SIGNS OF A HOBO CAMP.
THE GLOW FROM A SMALL TOWN DRIFTED ABOVE THE HORIZON, REMINDING ME OF MARIAN ON THE NIGHT I LEFT HOME. AS WE LEFT THE ROAD, IT SANK BACK OUT OF SIGHT.
SOMETHING WE CAN DO FOR YOU GUYS?
WE NEED A PLACE TO FLOP, BOYS. --AND LADIES--
THIS AIN'T NO JUNGLE, PAL. CRAWL BACK IN THE SCENERY.
WHAT DO YOU WANT 'EM TO DO, LEE -- GO ON INTO TOWN? WHY NOT JUST SHOOT 'EM AND SAVE 'EM THE WALK?
AW, WHO CARES? LET 'EM SLEEP IN THE RAG HOUSE.

WATCH YOUR STEP -- THIS IS ALL STORAGE, AND WE'RE NOT TOO NEAT ABOUT IT. ANYTHING'S IN THE WAY, JUST SHOVE IT OVER.

IS THIS WHOLE HOUSE CARDBOARD?

CARDBOARD, AND MUD ON THE CRACKS. NO SMOKING, GENTS.

ONE OF THE JUNGLES WE WERE IN HAD A PLACE MADE OUT OF SOUP CANS, ALL FLATTENED OUT --

WELL, THESE HERE ARE THE BOXES THEY CAME IN.

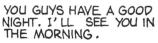

YOU GUYS HAVE A GOOD NIGHT. I'LL SEE YOU IN THE MORNING.

HE SAID WE SHOULDN'T--

HUSH.

SMELL ANYTHING, JESSE?

SURE 'NOUGH. GUN OIL.

YOU PROB'LY WANT TO SNUFF THAT MATCH. HATE TO FIND OUT THEY GOT DYNAMITE OR SOMETHIN' HERE, TOO...

WELL -- PURTY DREAMS, BOYS.

IF THE BEDBUGS BITE, JUST BLOW THEIR HEADS OFF.

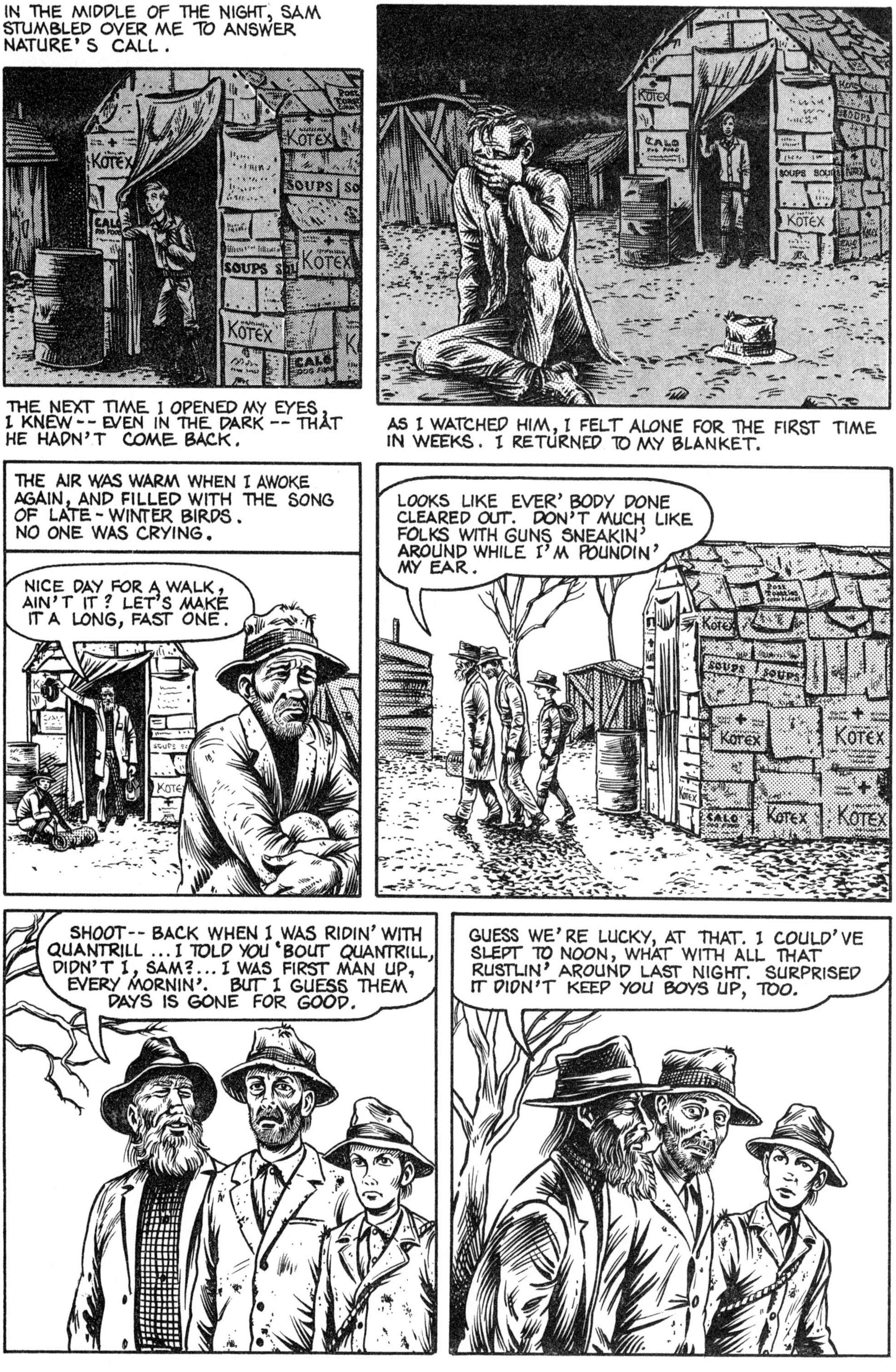
IN THE MIDDLE OF THE NIGHT, SAM STUMBLED OVER ME TO ANSWER NATURE'S CALL.
THE NEXT TIME I OPENED MY EYES, I KNEW -- EVEN IN THE DARK -- THAT HE HADN'T COME BACK.
AS I WATCHED HIM, I FELT ALONE FOR THE FIRST TIME IN WEEKS. I RETURNED TO MY BLANKET.
THE AIR WAS WARM WHEN I AWOKE AGAIN, AND FILLED WITH THE SONG OF LATE-WINTER BIRDS. NO ONE WAS CRYING.
NICE DAY FOR A WALK, AIN'T IT? LET'S MAKE IT A LONG, FAST ONE.
LOOKS LIKE EVER' BODY DONE CLEARED OUT. DON'T MUCH LIKE FOLKS WITH GUNS SNEAKIN' AROUND WHILE I'M POUNDIN' MY EAR.
SHOOT -- BACK WHEN I WAS RIDIN' WITH QUANTRILL ... I TOLD YOU 'BOUT QUANTRILL, DIDN'T I, SAM? ... I WAS FIRST MAN UP, EVERY MORNIN'. BUT I GUESS THEM DAYS IS GONE FOR GOOD.
GUESS WE'RE LUCKY, AT THAT. I COULD'VE SLEPT TO NOON, WHAT WITH ALL THAT RUSTLIN' AROUND LAST NIGHT. SURPRISED IT DIDN'T KEEP YOU BOYS UP, TOO.

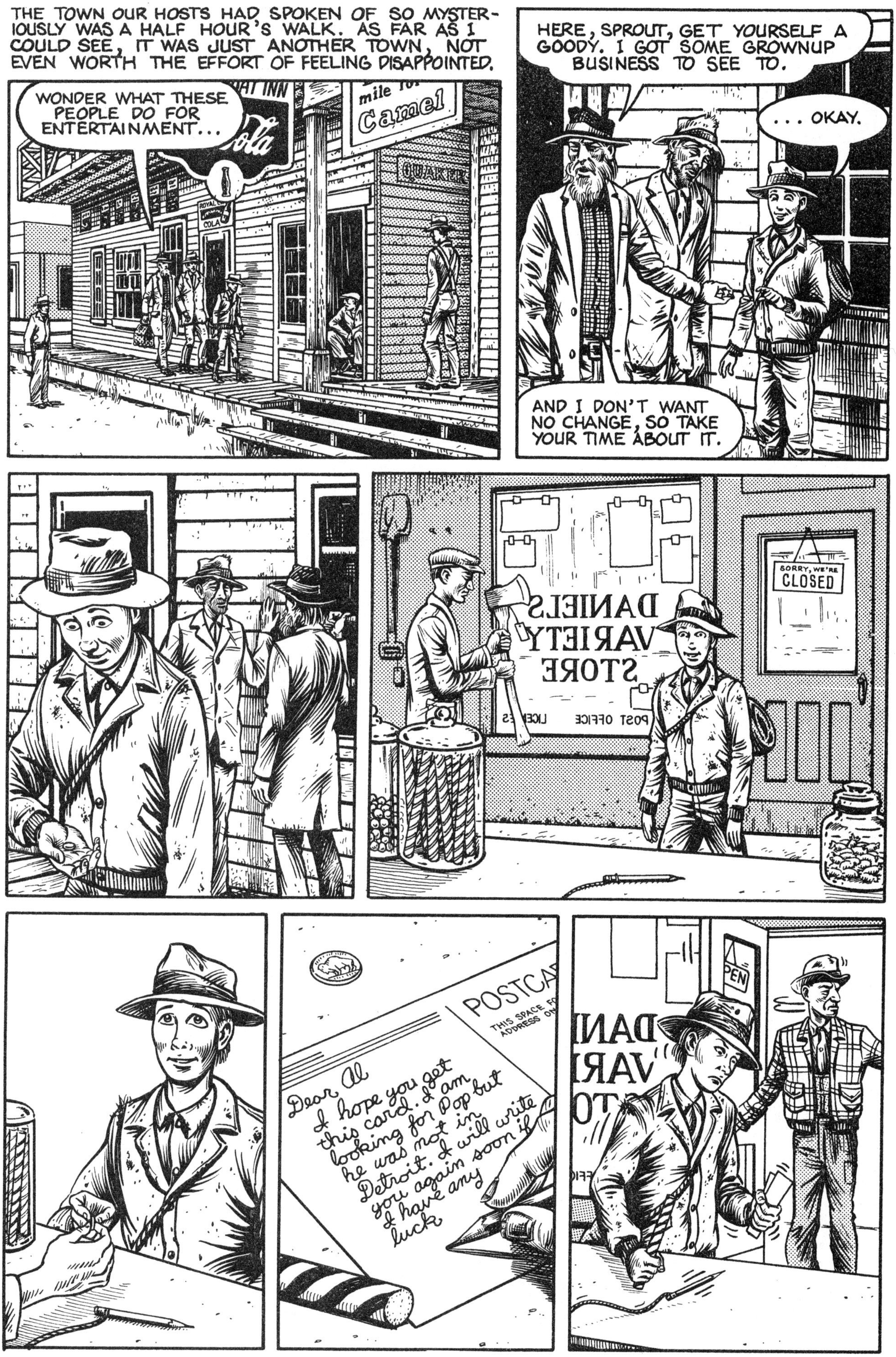
THE TOWN OUR HOSTS HAD SPOKEN OF SO MYSTERIOUSLY WAS A HALF HOUR'S WALK. AS FAR AS I COULD SEE, IT WAS JUST ANOTHER TOWN, NOT EVEN WORTH THE EFFORT OF FEELING DISAPPOINTED.
WONDER WHAT THESE PEOPLE DO FOR ENTERTAINMENT...
mile for
Camel
Cola
QUAKER
HERE, SPROUT, GET YOURSELF A GOODY. I GOT SOME GROWNUP BUSINESS TO SEE TO.
. . . OKAY.
AND I DON'T WANT NO CHANGE, SO TAKE YOUR TIME ABOUT IT.
DANIELS VARIETY STORE
POST OFFICE
SORRY, WE'RE CLOSED
POSTCA
Dear Al
I hope you get this card. I am looking for Pop but he was not in Detroit. I will write you again soon if I have any luck

AIN'T YOU BEEN TOLD TO STAY OUTTA TOWN? ARE YOU PEOPLE STUPID, OR JUST PLAIN CRAZY?

YOU GUESSED IT, FARM BOY -- BUGHOUSE, EVERY ONE OF US.

BOBBY, YOU TAKE THAT FIGHT OUTSIDE! ANYBODY PAYS CASH, IS WELCOME HERE

SURE HE CAN PAY, WITH TWENTY GUYS KICKIN' IN ON EVERY DOLLAR! BUNCHA COMM'NISTS!

MIGHT AS WELL SAVE YOUR MONEY, MISTER. COME NIGHTFALL, YOU REDS'LL BE OFFA THAT LAND.

HAD SAM AND JESSE BEEN IN SIGHT, I MIGHT NOT HAVE FOLLOWED THE "COMMUNIST" -- AFTER ALL, THE LAST TIME I'D DONE SO, I'D FOUND MYSELF IN A WAR. BUT MY CURIOSITY HAD BEEN PIQUED...

WE CAME UPON A CROWD IN THE TOWN SQUARE.

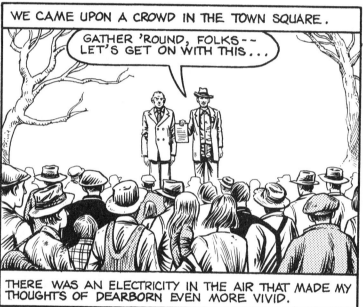

GATHER 'ROUND, FOLKS -- LET'S GET ON WITH THIS...

THERE WAS AN ELECTRICITY IN THE AIR THAT MADE MY THOUGHTS OF DEARBORN EVEN MORE VIVID.

THIS HERE'S A FORECLOSURE AUCTION ON THE LEONARD PLACE. ANYBODY GOT ANY QUESTIONS 'FORE WE START?

YEAH! WHO'S GONNA GET THAT GANG OFF THE LAND, ONCE IT'S SOLD?

LEONARD, HERE, GUARANTEES HE'LL HAVE HIS FRIENDS OFF ONCE THE LAND'S PASSED TO A PROPER OWNER.

THE BANK'S A PROPER OWNER, BUT NO ONE'S MOVED THESE HOOLIGANS --

SHUT UP, HOWARD. THEY'RE LEAVING. THE TOWN'S GOT WHAT IT WANTS.

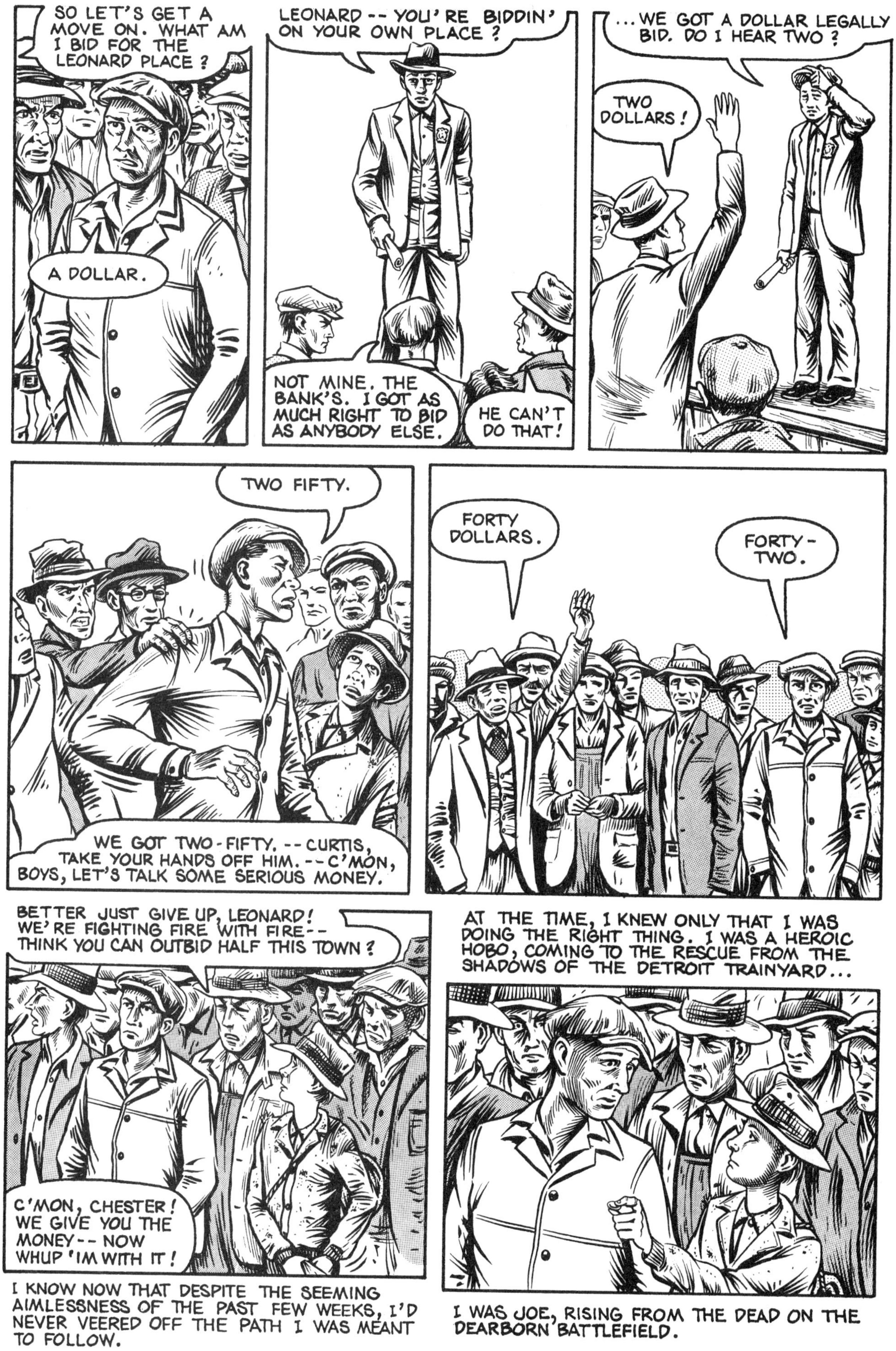
SO LET'S GET A MOVE ON. WHAT AM I BID FOR THE LEONARD PLACE ?
A DOLLAR.
LEONARD -- YOU'RE BIDDIN' ON YOUR OWN PLACE ?
NOT MINE. THE BANK'S. I GOT AS MUCH RIGHT TO BID AS ANYBODY ELSE.
HE CAN'T DO THAT!
... WE GOT A DOLLAR LEGALLY BID. DO I HEAR TWO ?
TWO DOLLARS!
TWO FIFTY.
WE GOT TWO-FIFTY. -- CURTIS, TAKE YOUR HANDS OFF HIM. -- C'MON, BOYS, LET'S TALK SOME SERIOUS MONEY.
FORTY DOLLARS.
FORTY-TWO.
BETTER JUST GIVE UP, LEONARD! WE'RE FIGHTING FIRE WITH FIRE-- THINK YOU CAN OUTBID HALF THIS TOWN ?
C'MON, CHESTER! WE GIVE YOU THE MONEY -- NOW WHUP 'IM WITH IT!
I KNOW NOW THAT DESPITE THE SEEMING AIMLESSNESS OF THE PAST FEW WEEKS, I'D NEVER VEERED OFF THE PATH I WAS MEANT TO FOLLOW.
AT THE TIME, I KNEW ONLY THAT I WAS DOING THE RIGHT THING. I WAS A HEROIC HOBO, COMING TO THE RESCUE FROM THE SHADOWS OF THE DETROIT TRAINYARD...
I WAS JOE, RISING FROM THE DEAD ON THE DEARBORN BATTLEFIELD.

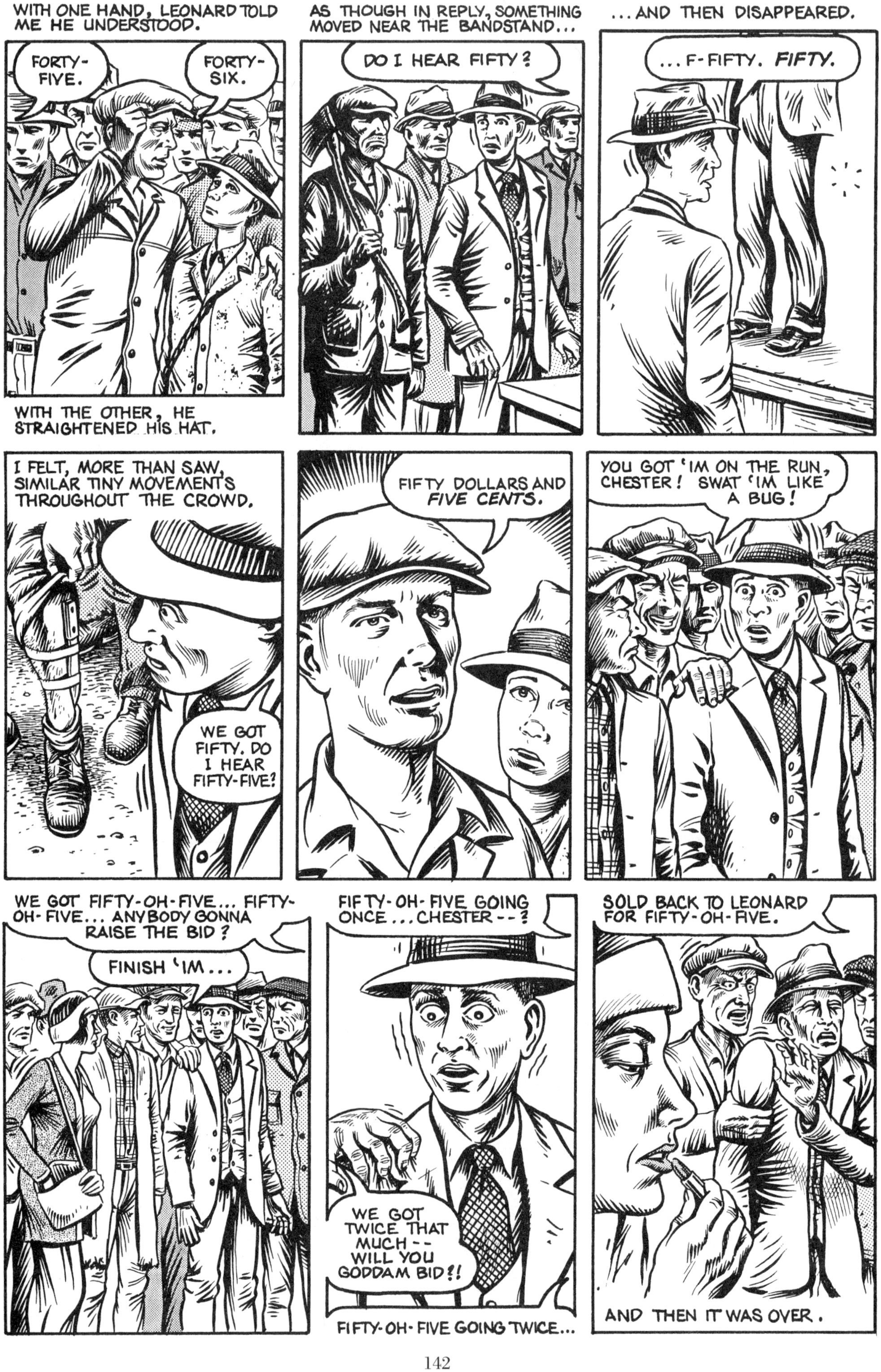

WITH ONE HAND, LEONARD TOLD ME HE UNDERSTOOD.
FORTY-FIVE.
FORTY-SIX.
WITH THE OTHER, HE STRAIGHTENED HIS HAT.
AS THOUGH IN REPLY, SOMETHING MOVED NEAR THE BANDSTAND...
DO I HEAR FIFTY?
...AND THEN DISAPPEARED.
...F-FIFTY. FIFTY.
I FELT, MORE THAN SAW, SIMILAR TINY MOVEMENTS THROUGHOUT THE CROWD.
WE GOT FIFTY. DO I HEAR FIFTY-FIVE?
FIFTY DOLLARS AND FIVE CENTS.
YOU GOT 'IM ON THE RUN, CHESTER! SWAT 'IM LIKE A BUG!
WE GOT FIFTY-OH-FIVE... FIFTY-OH-FIVE... ANYBODY GONNA RAISE THE BID?
FINISH 'IM...
FIFTY-OH-FIVE GOING ONCE... CHESTER--?
WE GOT TWICE THAT MUCH -- WILL YOU GODDAM BID?!
FIFTY-OH-FIVE GOING TWICE...
SOLD BACK TO LEONARD FOR FIFTY-OH-FIVE.
AND THEN IT WAS OVER.

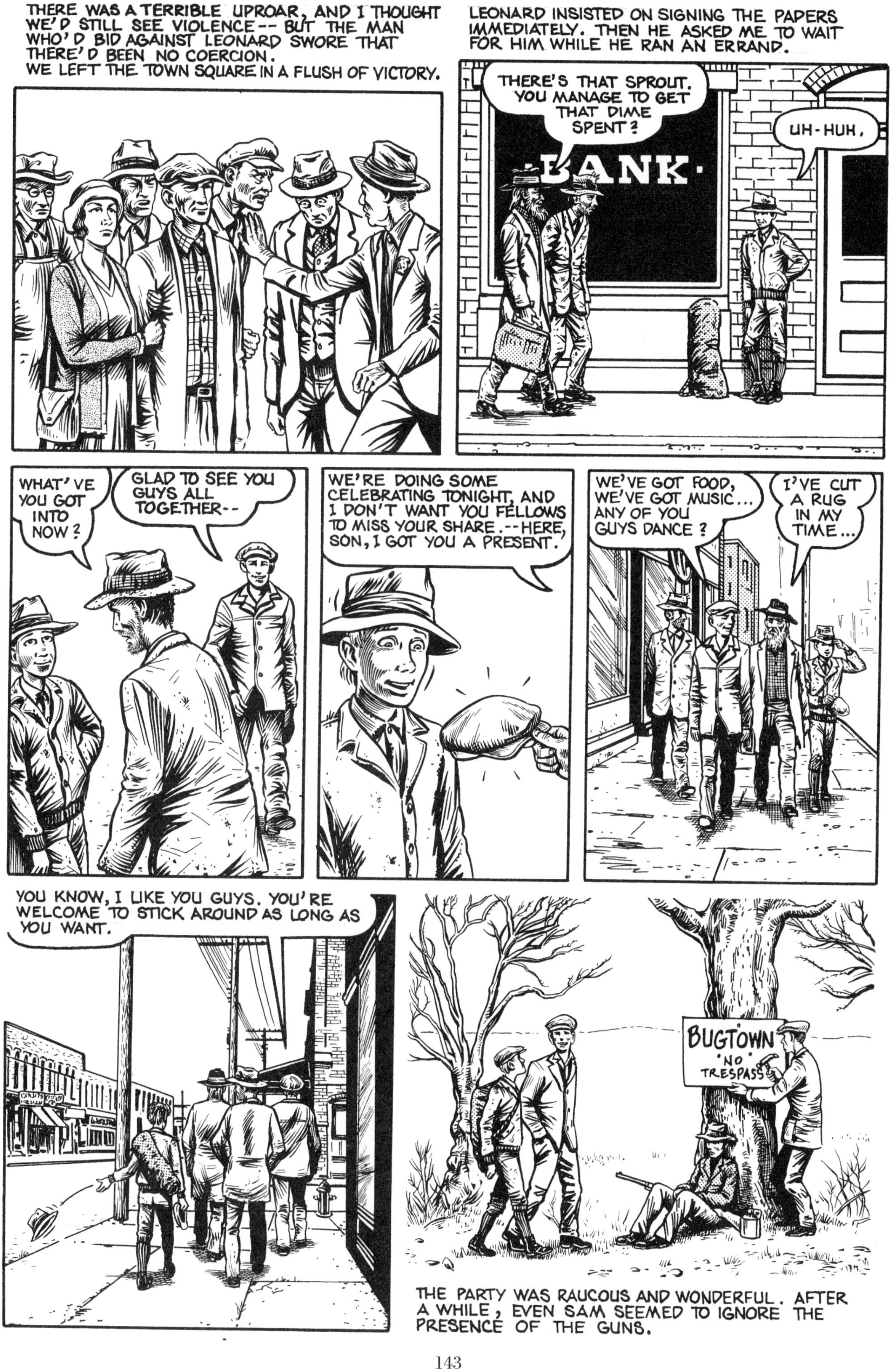
THERE WAS A TERRIBLE UPROAR, AND I THOUGHT WE'D STILL SEE VIOLENCE -- BUT THE MAN WHO'D BID AGAINST LEONARD SWORE THAT THERE'D BEEN NO COERCION.
WE LEFT THE TOWN SQUARE IN A FLUSH OF VICTORY.
LEONARD INSISTED ON SIGNING THE PAPERS IMMEDIATELY. THEN HE ASKED ME TO WAIT FOR HIM WHILE HE RAN AN ERRAND.
THERE'S THAT SPROUT. YOU MANAGE TO GET THAT DIME SPENT?
UH-HUH.
BANK
WHAT'VE YOU GOT INTO NOW?
GLAD TO SEE YOU GUYS ALL TOGETHER--
WE'RE DOING SOME CELEBRATING TONIGHT, AND I DON'T WANT YOU FELLOWS TO MISS YOUR SHARE.--HERE, SON, I GOT YOU A PRESENT.
WE'VE GOT FOOD, WE'VE GOT MUSIC... ANY OF YOU GUYS DANCE?
I'VE CUT A RUG IN MY TIME...
YOU KNOW, I LIKE YOU GUYS. YOU'RE WELCOME TO STICK AROUND AS LONG AS YOU WANT.
BUGTOWN
'NO' TRESPASS
THE PARTY WAS RAUCOUS AND WONDERFUL. AFTER A WHILE, EVEN SAM SEEMED TO IGNORE THE PRESENCE OF THE GUNS.

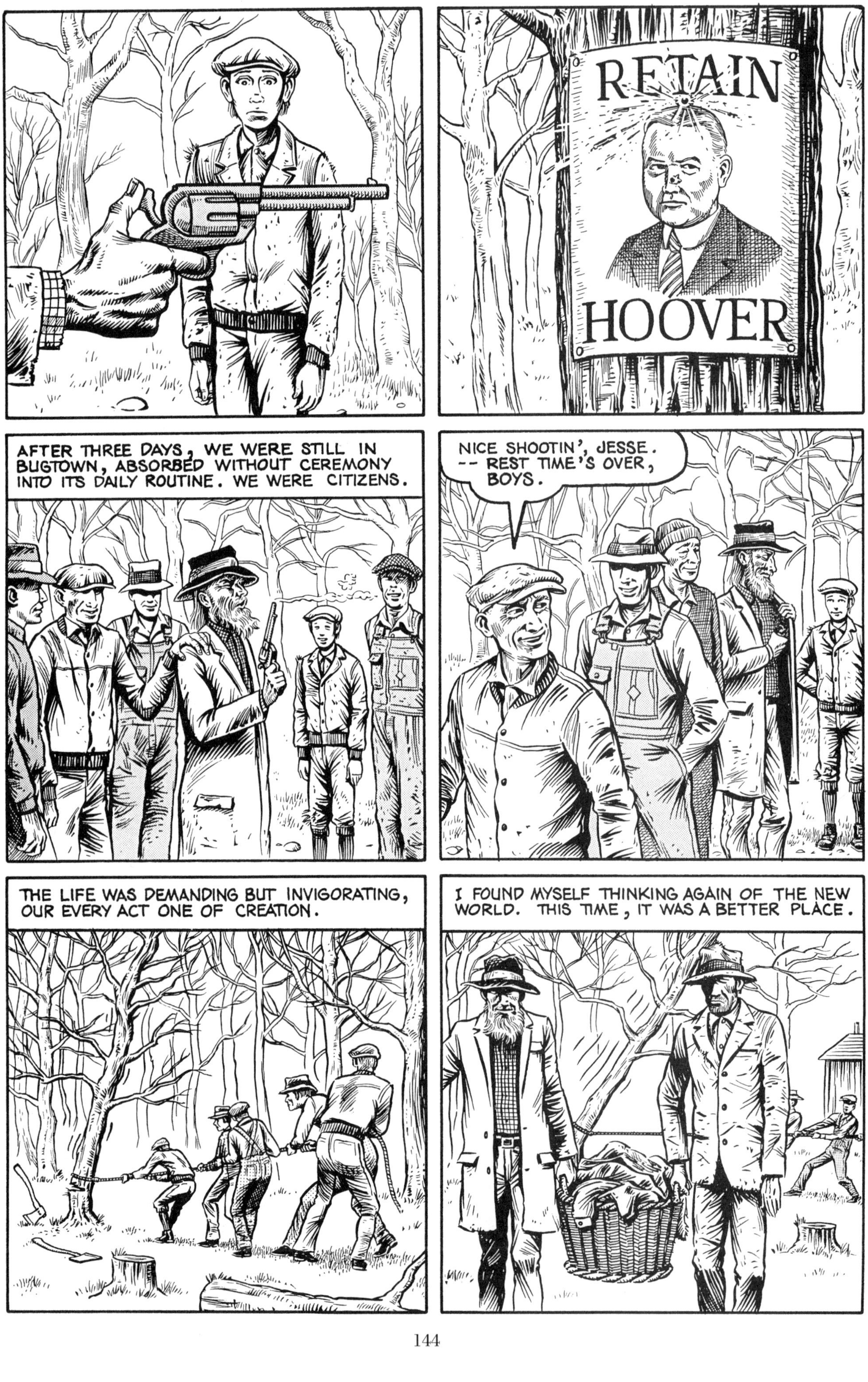
RETAIN
HOOVER
AFTER THREE DAYS, WE WERE STILL IN BUGTOWN, ABSORBED WITHOUT CEREMONY INTO ITS DAILY ROUTINE. WE WERE CITIZENS.
NICE SHOOTIN', JESSE. -- REST TIME'S OVER, BOYS.
THE LIFE WAS DEMANDING BUT INVIGORATING, OUR EVERY ACT ONE OF CREATION.
I FOUND MYSELF THINKING AGAIN OF THE NEW WORLD. THIS TIME, IT WAS A BETTER PLACE.

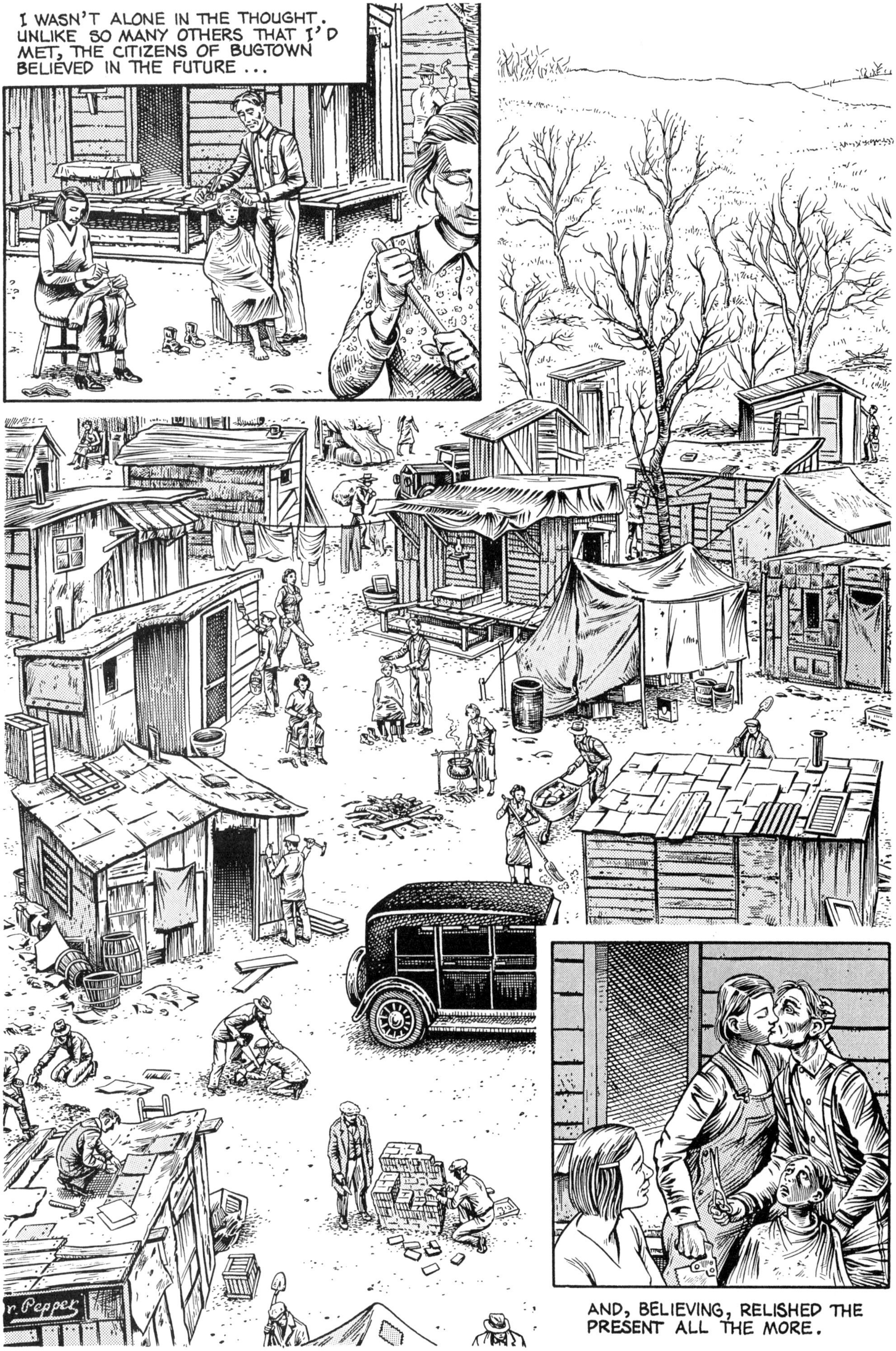
I WASN'T ALONE IN THE THOUGHT. UNLIKE SO MANY OTHERS THAT I'D MET, THE CITIZENS OF BUGTOWN BELIEVED IN THE FUTURE ...
AND, BELIEVING, RELISHED THE PRESENT ALL THE MORE.

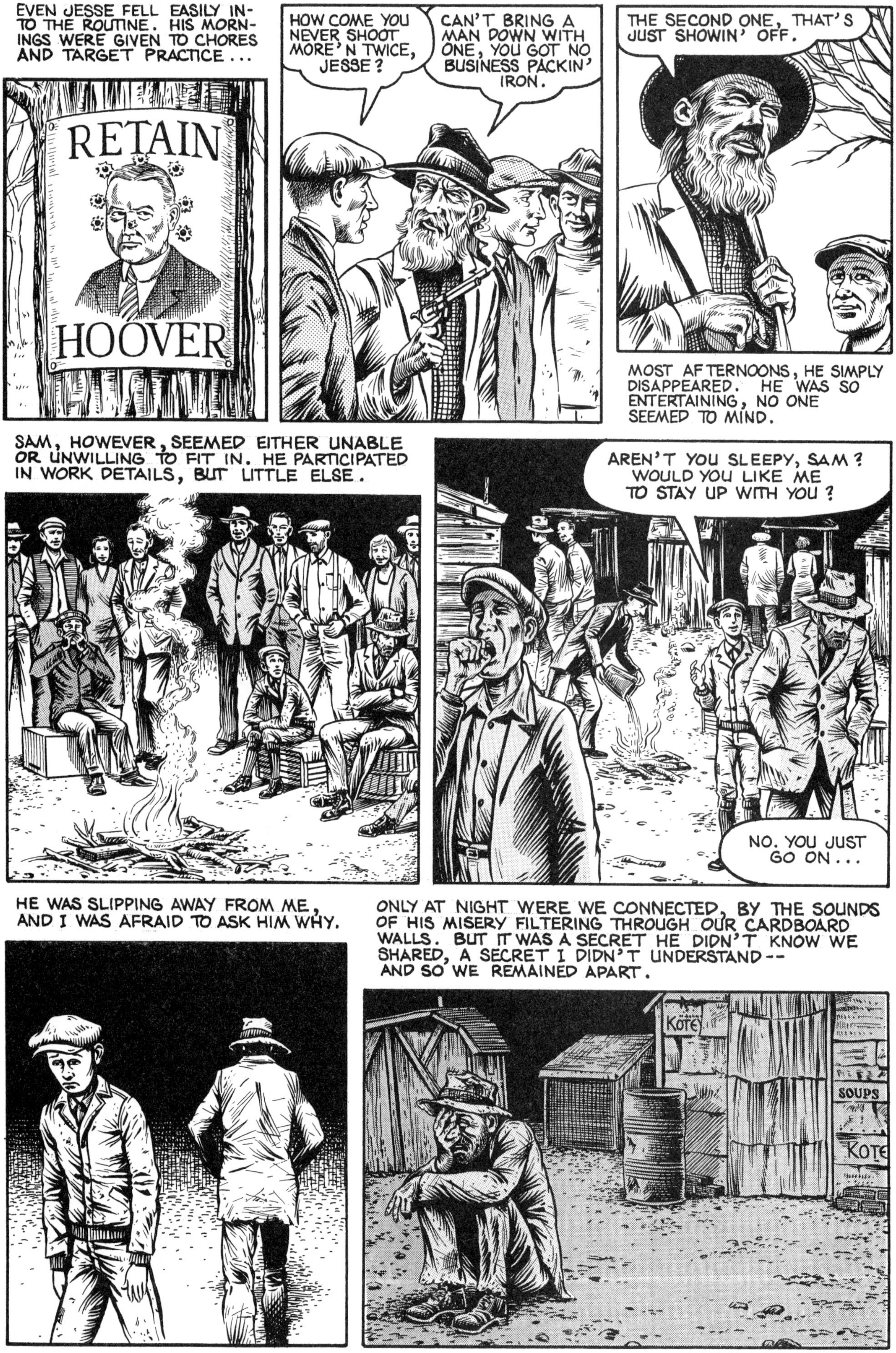
EVEN JESSE FELL EASILY INTO THE ROUTINE. HIS MORNINGS WERE GIVEN TO CHORES AND TARGET PRACTICE...
RETAIN
HOOVER
HOW COME YOU NEVER SHOOT MORE'N TWICE, JESSE?
CAN'T BRING A MAN DOWN WITH ONE, YOU GOT NO BUSINESS PACKIN' IRON.
THE SECOND ONE, THAT'S JUST SHOWIN' OFF.
MOST AFTERNOONS, HE SIMPLY DISAPPEARED. HE WAS SO ENTERTAINING, NO ONE SEEMED TO MIND.
SAM, HOWEVER, SEEMED EITHER UNABLE OR UNWILLING TO FIT IN. HE PARTICIPATED IN WORK DETAILS, BUT LITTLE ELSE.
AREN'T YOU SLEEPY, SAM? WOULD YOU LIKE ME TO STAY UP WITH YOU?
NO. YOU JUST GO ON...
HE WAS SLIPPING AWAY FROM ME, AND I WAS AFRAID TO ASK HIM WHY.
ONLY AT NIGHT WERE WE CONNECTED, BY THE SOUNDS OF HIS MISERY FILTERING THROUGH OUR CARDBOARD WALLS. BUT IT WAS A SECRET HE DIDN'T KNOW WE SHARED, A SECRET I DIDN'T UNDERSTAND -- AND SO WE REMAINED APART.
KOTEX
SOUPS
KOTE

I TURNED TO OTHERS FOR COMPANIONSHIP. AS I GOT TO KNOW THEM, I BEGAN TO UNDERSTAND THEIR DEVOTION TO BUGTOWN.

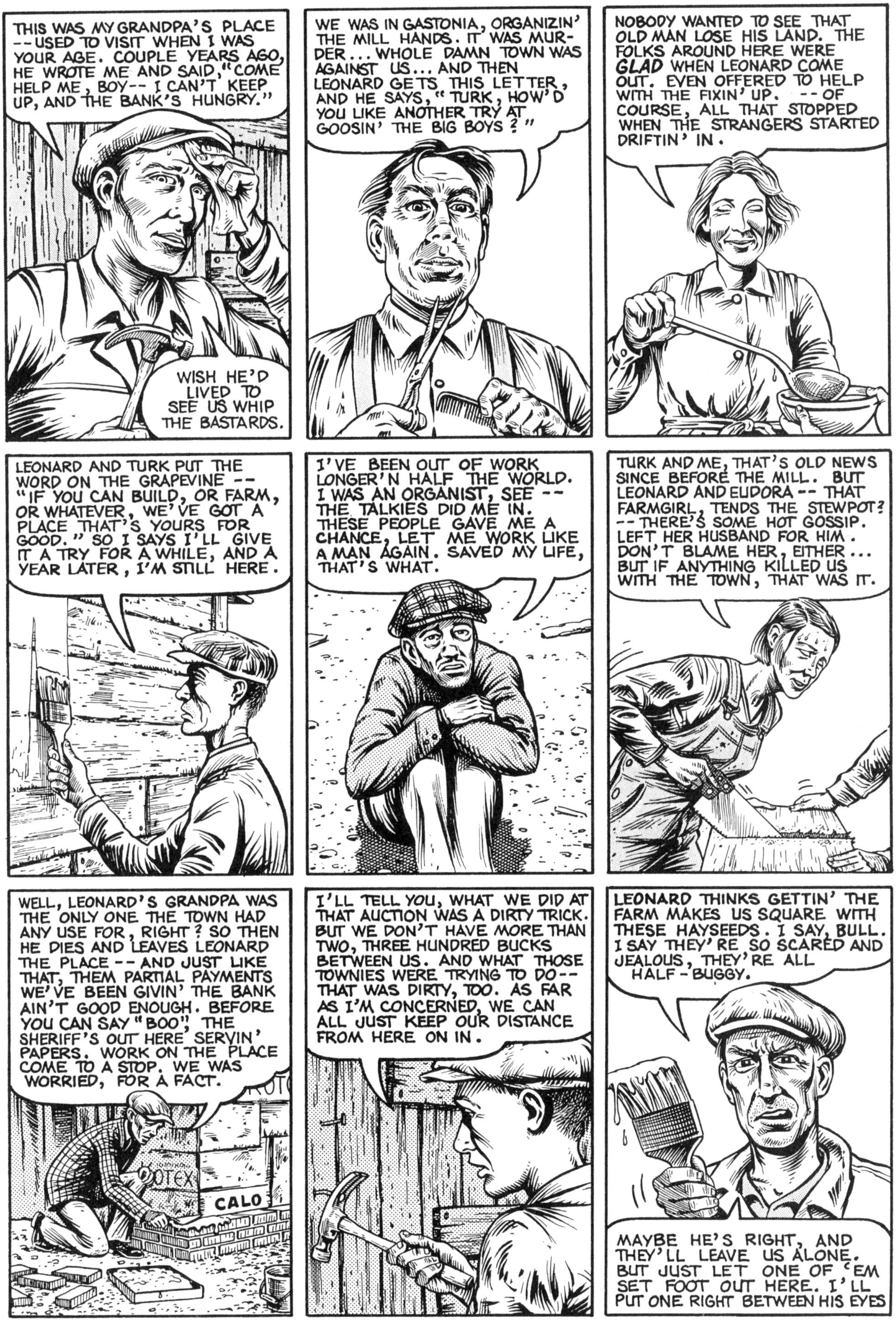
THIS WAS MY GRANDPA'S PLACE --USED TO VISIT WHEN I WAS YOUR AGE. COUPLE YEARS AGO, HE WROTE ME AND SAID, "COME HELP ME, BOY-- I CAN'T KEEP UP, AND THE BANK'S HUNGRY."
WISH HE'D LIVED TO SEE US WHIP THE BASTARDS.
WE WAS IN GASTONIA, ORGANIZIN' THE MILL HANDS. IT WAS MURDER... WHOLE DAMN TOWN WAS AGAINST US... AND THEN LEONARD GETS THIS LETTER, AND HE SAYS, "TURK, HOW'D YOU LIKE ANOTHER TRY AT GOOSIN' THE BIG BOYS?"
NOBODY WANTED TO SEE THAT OLD MAN LOSE HIS LAND. THE FOLKS AROUND HERE WERE GLAD WHEN LEONARD COME OUT. EVEN OFFERED TO HELP WITH THE FIXIN' UP. --OF COURSE, ALL THAT STOPPED WHEN THE STRANGERS STARTED DRIFTIN' IN.
LEONARD AND TURK PUT THE WORD ON THE GRAPEVINE -- "IF YOU CAN BUILD, OR FARM, OR WHATEVER, WE'VE GOT A PLACE THAT'S YOURS FOR GOOD." SO I SAYS I'LL GIVE IT A TRY FOR A WHILE, AND A YEAR LATER, I'M STILL HERE.
I'VE BEEN OUT OF WORK LONGER'N HALF THE WORLD. I WAS AN ORGANIST, SEE -- THE TALKIES DID ME IN. THESE PEOPLE GAVE ME A CHANCE. LET ME WORK LIKE A MAN AGAIN. SAVED MY LIFE, THAT'S WHAT.
TURK AND ME, THAT'S OLD NEWS SINCE BEFORE THE MILL. BUT LEONARD AND EUDORA -- THAT FARMGIRL, TENDS THE STEWPOT? --THERE'S SOME HOT GOSSIP. LEFT HER HUSBAND FOR HIM. DON'T BLAME HER, EITHER... BUT IF ANYTHING KILLED US WITH THE TOWN, THAT WAS IT.
WELL, LEONARD'S GRANDPA WAS THE ONLY ONE THE TOWN HAD ANY USE FOR, RIGHT? SO THEN HE DIES AND LEAVES LEONARD THE PLACE -- AND JUST LIKE THAT, THEM PARTIAL PAYMENTS WE'VE BEEN GIVIN' THE BANK AIN'T GOOD ENOUGH. BEFORE YOU CAN SAY "BOO", THE SHERIFF'S OUT HERE SERVIN' PAPERS. WORK ON THE PLACE COME TO A STOP. WE WAS WORRIED, FOR A FACT.
CALO
I'LL TELL YOU, WHAT WE DID AT THAT AUCTION WAS A DIRTY TRICK. BUT WE DON'T HAVE MORE THAN TWO, THREE HUNDRED BUCKS BETWEEN US. AND WHAT THOSE TOWNIES WERE TRYING TO DO-- THAT WAS DIRTY, TOO. AS FAR AS I'M CONCERNED, WE CAN ALL JUST KEEP OUR DISTANCE FROM HERE ON IN.
LEONARD THINKS GETTIN' THE FARM MAKES US SQUARE WITH THESE HAYSEEDS. I SAY, BULL. I SAY THEY'RE SO SCARED AND JEALOUS, THEY'RE ALL HALF-BUGGY.
MAYBE HE'S RIGHT, AND THEY'LL LEAVE US ALONE. BUT JUST LET ONE OF 'EM SET FOOT OUT HERE. I'LL PUT ONE RIGHT BETWEEN HIS EYES

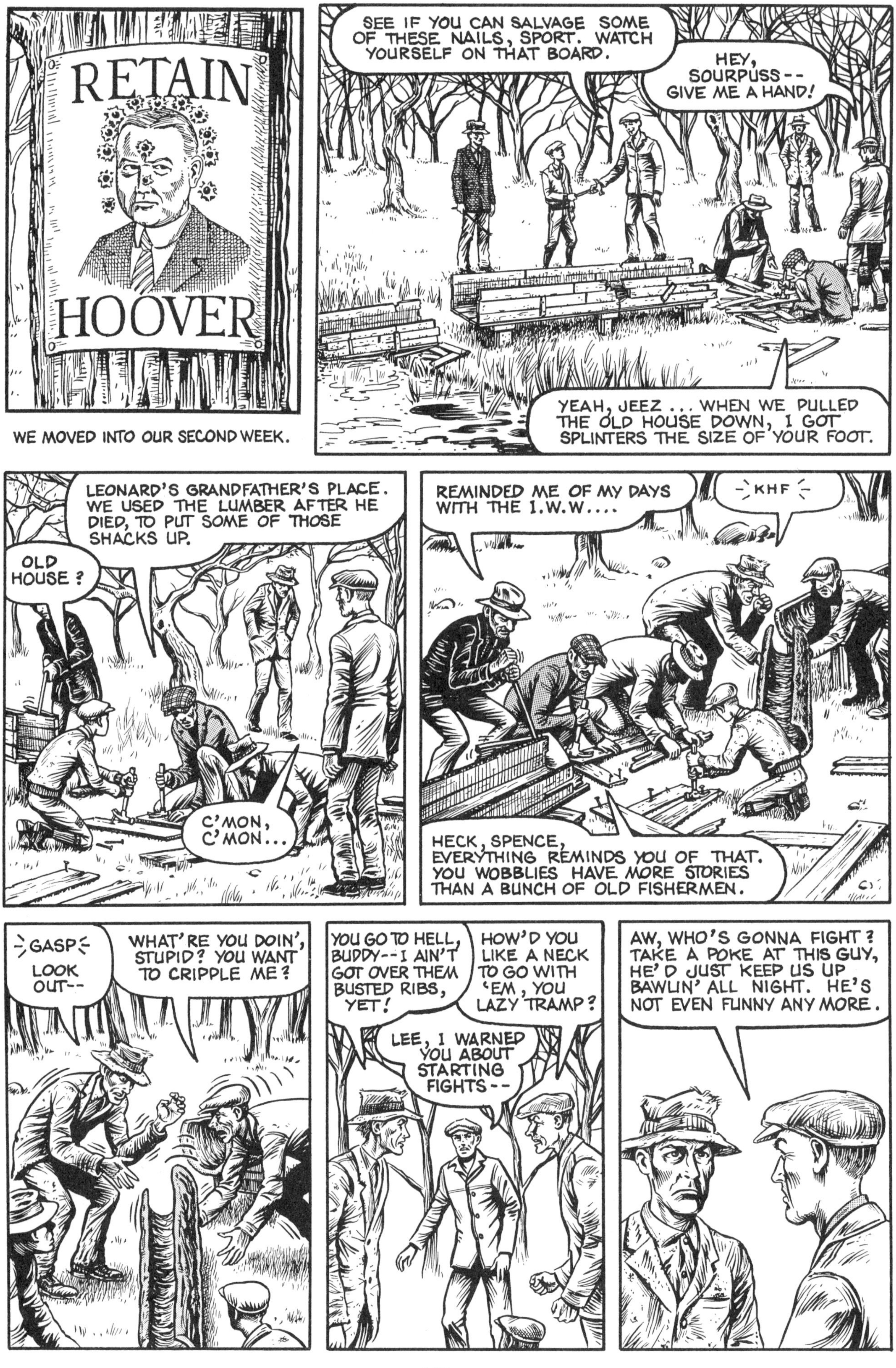
RETAIN
HOOVER
WE MOVED INTO OUR SECOND WEEK.
SEE IF YOU CAN SALVAGE SOME OF THESE NAILS, SPORT. WATCH YOURSELF ON THAT BOARD.
HEY, SOURPUSS-- GIVE ME A HAND!
YEAH, JEEZ ... WHEN WE PULLED THE OLD HOUSE DOWN, I GOT SPLINTERS THE SIZE OF YOUR FOOT.
OLD HOUSE ?
LEONARD'S GRANDFATHER'S PLACE. WE USED THE LUMBER AFTER HE DIED, TO PUT SOME OF THOSE SHACKS UP.
C'MON, C'MON...
REMINDED ME OF MY DAYS WITH THE I.W.W....
KHF
HECK, SPENCE, EVERYTHING REMINDS YOU OF THAT. YOU WOBBLIES HAVE MORE STORIES THAN A BUNCH OF OLD FISHERMEN.
GASP
LOOK OUT--
WHAT'RE YOU DOIN', STUPID? YOU WANT TO CRIPPLE ME?
YOU GO TO HELL, BUDDY--I AIN'T GOT OVER THEM BUSTED RIBS, YET!
HOW'D YOU LIKE A NECK TO GO WITH 'EM, YOU LAZY TRAMP?
LEE, I WARNED YOU ABOUT STARTING FIGHTS--
AW, WHO'S GONNA FIGHT? TAKE A POKE AT THIS GUY, HE'D JUST KEEP US UP BAWLIN' ALL NIGHT. HE'S NOT EVEN FUNNY ANY MORE.

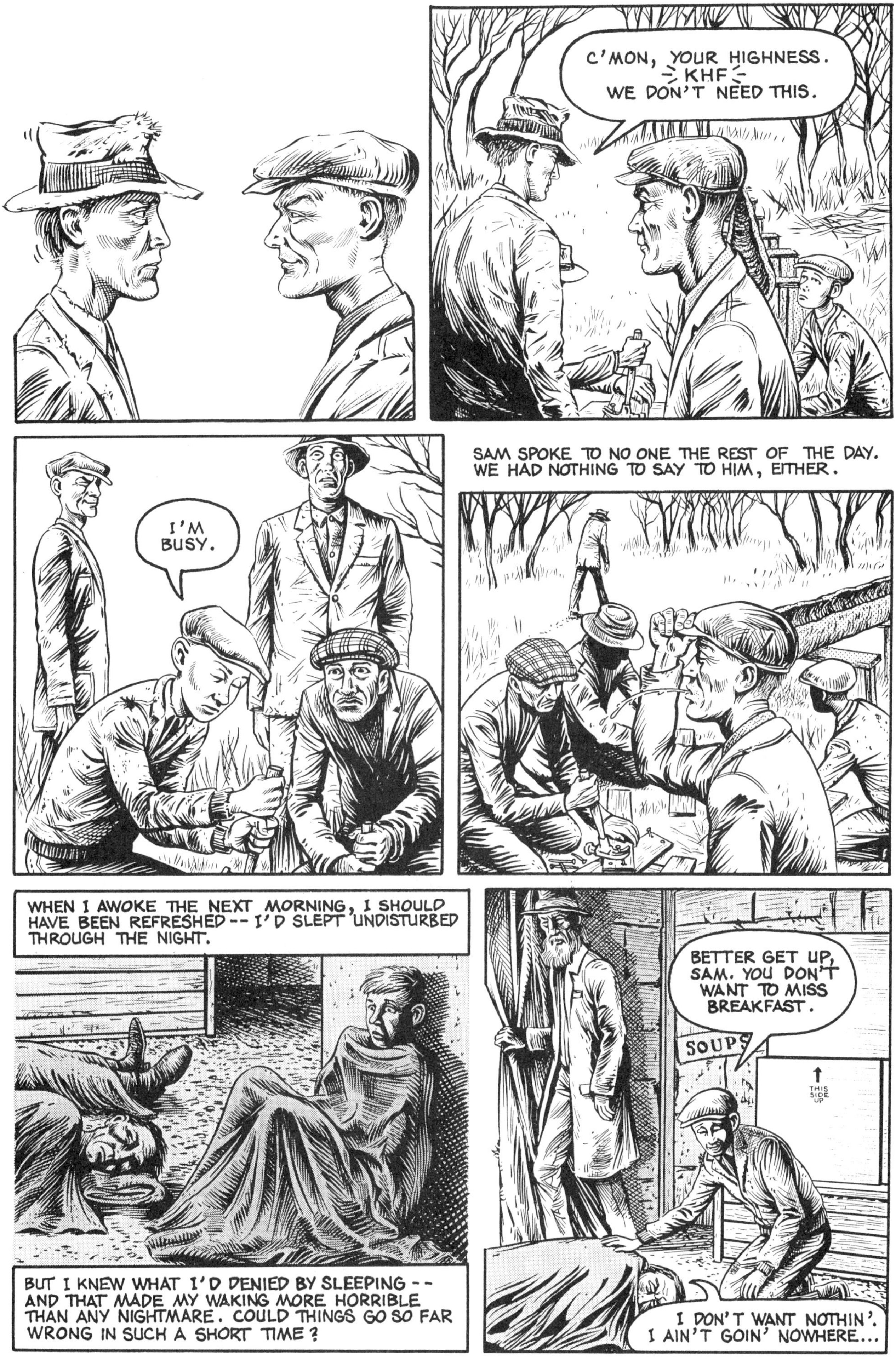

C'MON, YOUR HIGHNESS.
KHF
WE DON'T NEED THIS.
I'M BUSY.
SAM SPOKE TO NO ONE THE REST OF THE DAY. WE HAD NOTHING TO SAY TO HIM, EITHER.
WHEN I AWOKE THE NEXT MORNING, I SHOULD HAVE BEEN REFRESHED -- I'D SLEPT UNDISTURBED THROUGH THE NIGHT.
BUT I KNEW WHAT I'D DENIED BY SLEEPING -- AND THAT MADE MY WAKING MORE HORRIBLE THAN ANY NIGHTMARE. COULD THINGS GO SO FAR WRONG IN SUCH A SHORT TIME?
BETTER GET UP, SAM. YOU DON'T WANT TO MISS BREAKFAST.
SOUPS
THIS SIDE UP
I DON'T WANT NOTHIN'. I AIN'T GOIN' NOWHERE...

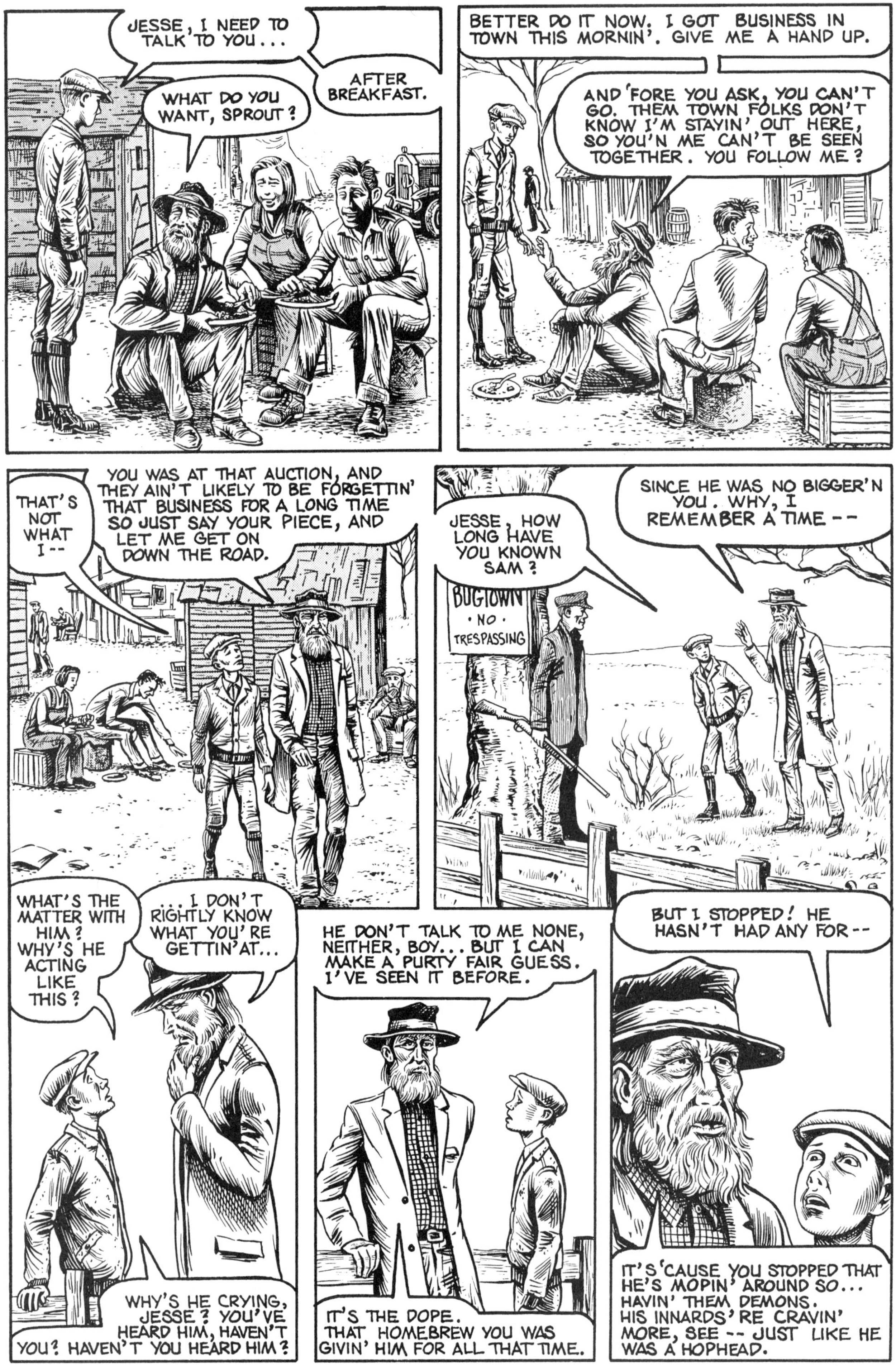
JESSE, I NEED TO TALK TO YOU...
WHAT DO YOU WANT, SPROUT?
AFTER BREAKFAST.
BETTER DO IT NOW. I GOT BUSINESS IN TOWN THIS MORNIN'. GIVE ME A HAND UP.
AND 'FORE YOU ASK, YOU CAN'T GO. THEM TOWN FOLKS DON'T KNOW I'M STAYIN' OUT HERE, SO YOU'N ME CAN'T BE SEEN TOGETHER. YOU FOLLOW ME?
THAT'S NOT WHAT I--
YOU WAS AT THAT AUCTION, AND THEY AIN'T LIKELY TO BE FORGETTIN' THAT BUSINESS FOR A LONG TIME SO JUST SAY YOUR PIECE, AND LET ME GET ON DOWN THE ROAD.
JESSE, HOW LONG HAVE YOU KNOWN SAM?
SINCE HE WAS NO BIGGER'N YOU. WHY, I REMEMBER A TIME --
BUGTOWN
NO
TRESPASSING
WHAT'S THE MATTER WITH HIM? WHY'S HE ACTING LIKE THIS?
... I DON'T RIGHTLY KNOW WHAT YOU'RE GETTIN' AT...
WHY'S HE CRYING, JESSE? YOU'VE HEARD HIM, HAVEN'T YOU? HAVEN'T YOU HEARD HIM?
HE DON'T TALK TO ME NONE, NEITHER, BOY... BUT I CAN MAKE A PURTY FAIR GUESS. I'VE SEEN IT BEFORE.
IT'S THE DOPE. THAT HOMEBREW YOU WAS GIVIN' HIM FOR ALL THAT TIME.
BUT I STOPPED! HE HASN'T HAD ANY FOR --
IT'S 'CAUSE YOU STOPPED THAT HE'S MOPIN' AROUND SO... HAVIN' THEM DEMONS. HIS INNARDS'RE CRAVIN' MORE, SEE -- JUST LIKE HE WAS A HOPHEAD.

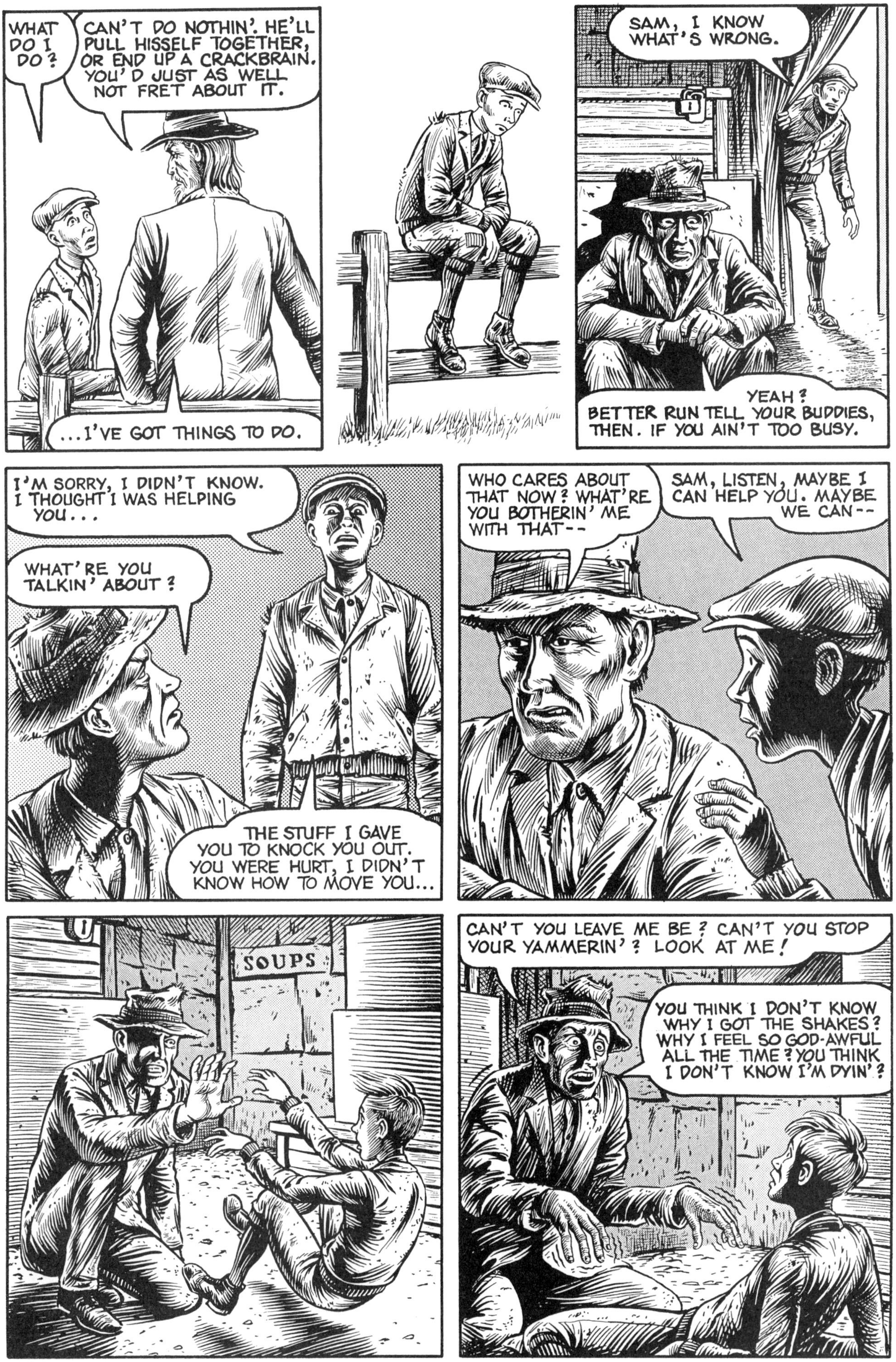
WHAT DO I DO?
CAN'T DO NOTHIN'. HE'LL PULL HISSELF TOGETHER, OR END UP A CRACKBRAIN. YOU'D JUST AS WELL NOT FRET ABOUT IT.
...I'VE GOT THINGS TO DO.
SAM, I KNOW WHAT'S WRONG.
YEAH? BETTER RUN TELL YOUR BUDDIES, THEN. IF YOU AIN'T TOO BUSY.
I'M SORRY, I DIDN'T KNOW. I THOUGHT I WAS HELPING YOU...
WHAT'RE YOU TALKIN' ABOUT?
THE STUFF I GAVE YOU TO KNOCK YOU OUT. YOU WERE HURT, I DIDN'T KNOW HOW TO MOVE YOU...
WHO CARES ABOUT THAT NOW? WHAT'RE YOU BOTHERIN' ME WITH THAT--
SAM, LISTEN, MAYBE I CAN HELP YOU. MAYBE WE CAN--
SOUPS
CAN'T YOU LEAVE ME BE? CAN'T YOU STOP YOUR YAMMERIN'? LOOK AT ME!
YOU THINK I DON'T KNOW WHY I GOT THE SHAKES? WHY I FEEL SO GOD-AWFUL ALL THE TIME? YOU THINK I DON'T KNOW I'M DYIN'?

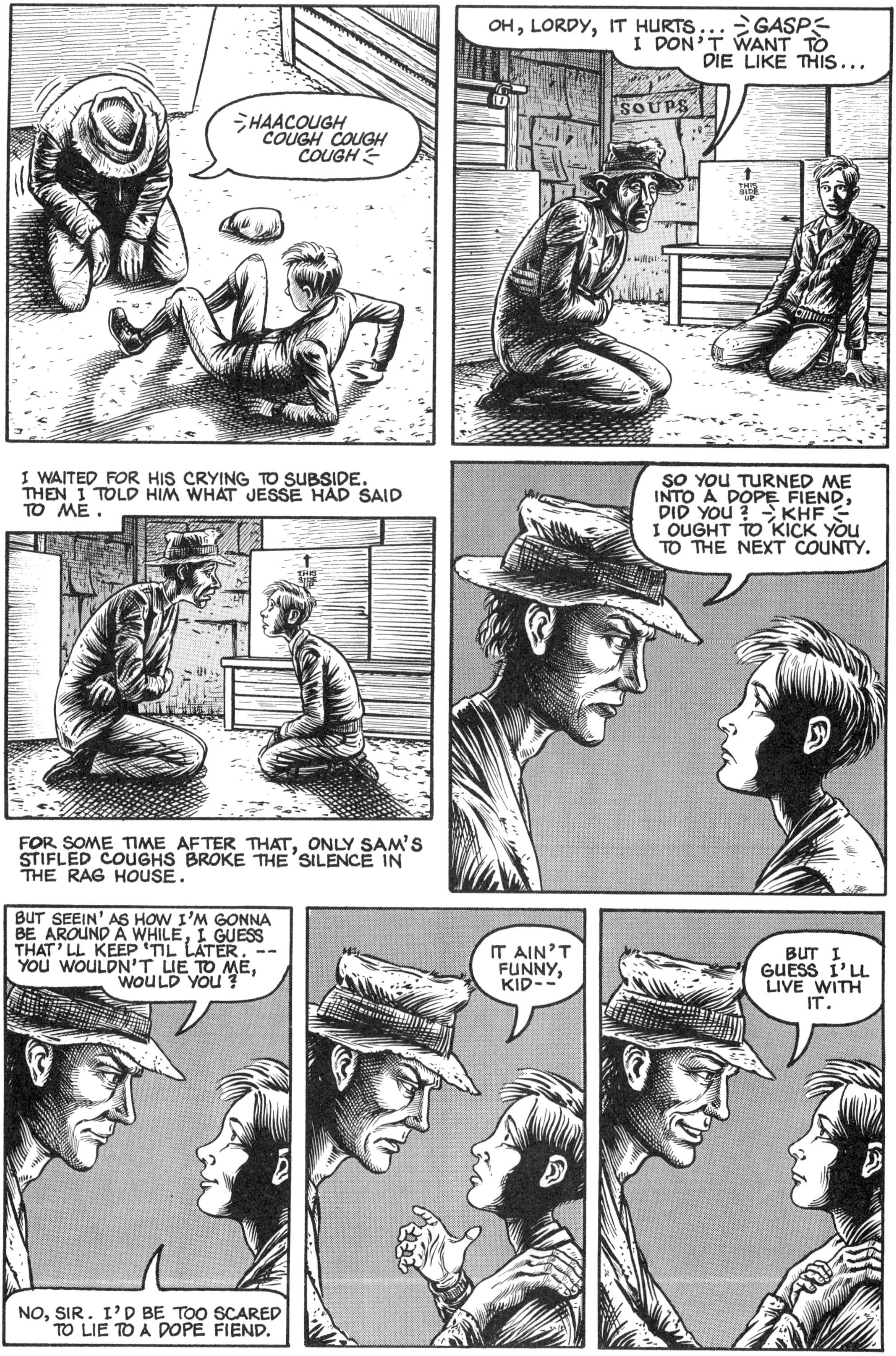
HAACOUGH COUGH COUGH COUGH
OH, LORDY, IT HURTS... GASP I DON'T WANT TO DIE LIKE THIS...
SOUPS
THIS SIDE UP
I WAITED FOR HIS CRYING TO SUBSIDE. THEN I TOLD HIM WHAT JESSE HAD SAID TO ME.
THIS SIDE UP
FOR SOME TIME AFTER THAT, ONLY SAM'S STIFLED COUGHS BROKE THE SILENCE IN THE RAG HOUSE.
SO YOU TURNED ME INTO A DOPE FIEND, DID YOU? KHF I OUGHT TO KICK YOU TO THE NEXT COUNTY.
BUT SEEIN' AS HOW I'M GONNA BE AROUND A WHILE, I GUESS THAT'LL KEEP 'TIL LATER. -- YOU WOULDN'T LIE TO ME, WOULD YOU?
NO, SIR. I'D BE TOO SCARED TO LIE TO A DOPE FIEND.
IT AIN'T FUNNY, KID--
BUT I GUESS I'LL LIVE WITH IT.

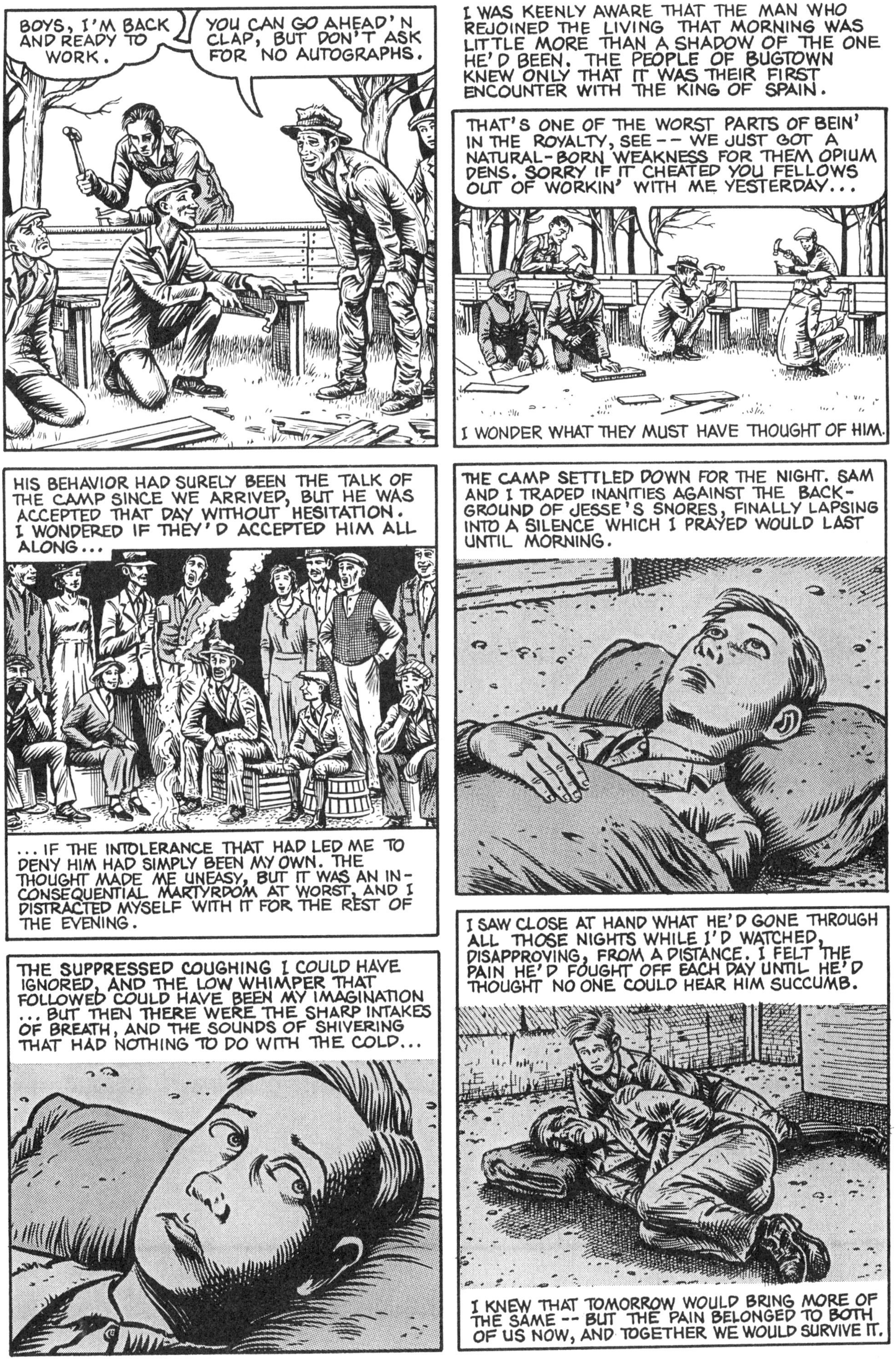
BOYS, I'M BACK AND READY TO WORK.
YOU CAN GO AHEAD'N CLAP, BUT DON'T ASK FOR NO AUTOGRAPHS.
I WAS KEENLY AWARE THAT THE MAN WHO REJOINED THE LIVING THAT MORNING WAS LITTLE MORE THAN A SHADOW OF THE ONE HE'D BEEN. THE PEOPLE OF BUGTOWN KNEW ONLY THAT IT WAS THEIR FIRST ENCOUNTER WITH THE KING OF SPAIN.
THAT'S ONE OF THE WORST PARTS OF BEIN' IN THE ROYALTY, SEE -- WE JUST GOT A NATURAL-BORN WEAKNESS FOR THEM OPIUM DENS. SORRY IF IT CHEATED YOU FELLOWS OUT OF WORKIN' WITH ME YESTERDAY...
I WONDER WHAT THEY MUST HAVE THOUGHT OF HIM.
HIS BEHAVIOR HAD SURELY BEEN THE TALK OF THE CAMP SINCE WE ARRIVED, BUT HE WAS ACCEPTED THAT DAY WITHOUT HESITATION. I WONDERED IF THEY'D ACCEPTED HIM ALL ALONG...
... IF THE INTOLERANCE THAT HAD LED ME TO DENY HIM HAD SIMPLY BEEN MY OWN. THE THOUGHT MADE ME UNEASY, BUT IT WAS AN INCONSEQUENTIAL MARTYRDOM AT WORST, AND I DISTRACTED MYSELF WITH IT FOR THE REST OF THE EVENING.
THE CAMP SETTLED DOWN FOR THE NIGHT. SAM AND I TRADED INANITIES AGAINST THE BACKGROUND OF JESSE'S SNORES, FINALLY LAPSING INTO A SILENCE WHICH I PRAYED WOULD LAST UNTIL MORNING.
THE SUPPRESSED COUGHING I COULD HAVE IGNORED, AND THE LOW WHIMPER THAT FOLLOWED COULD HAVE BEEN MY IMAGINATION ... BUT THEN THERE WERE THE SHARP INTAKES OF BREATH, AND THE SOUNDS OF SHIVERING THAT HAD NOTHING TO DO WITH THE COLD...
I SAW CLOSE AT HAND WHAT HE'D GONE THROUGH ALL THOSE NIGHTS WHILE I'D WATCHED, DISAPPROVING, FROM A DISTANCE. I FELT THE PAIN HE'D FOUGHT OFF EACH DAY UNTIL HE'D THOUGHT NO ONE COULD HEAR HIM SUCCUMB.
I KNEW THAT TOMORROW WOULD BRING MORE OF THE SAME -- BUT THE PAIN BELONGED TO BOTH OF US NOW, AND TOGETHER WE WOULD SURVIVE IT.

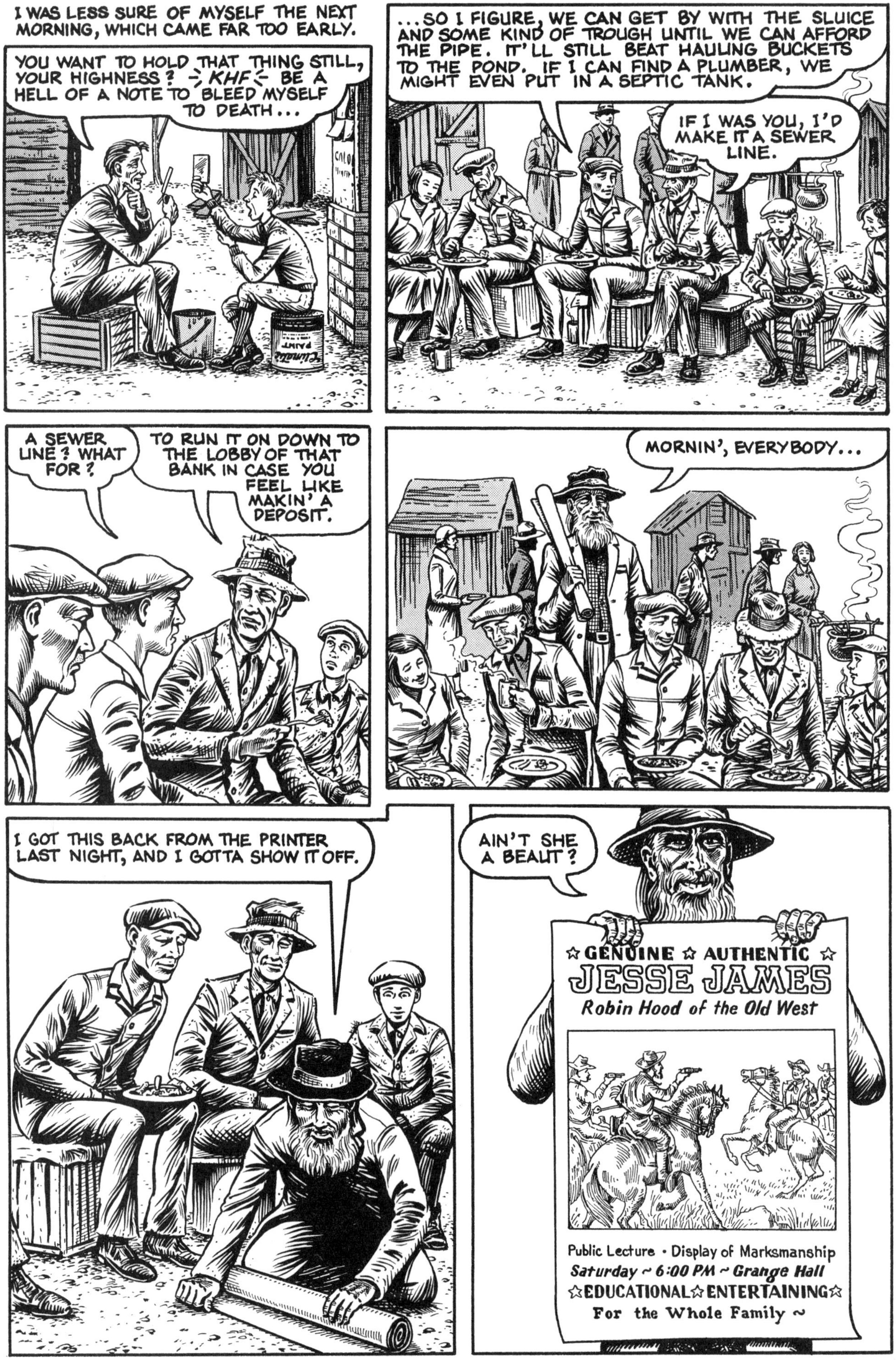
I WAS LESS SURE OF MYSELF THE NEXT MORNING, WHICH CAME FAR TOO EARLY.
YOU WANT TO HOLD THAT THING STILL, YOUR HIGHNESS? KHF BE A HELL OF A NOTE TO BLEED MYSELF TO DEATH...
...SO I FIGURE, WE CAN GET BY WITH THE SLUICE AND SOME KIND OF TROUGH UNTIL WE CAN AFFORD THE PIPE. IT'LL STILL BEAT HAULING BUCKETS TO THE POND. IF I CAN FIND A PLUMBER, WE MIGHT EVEN PUT IN A SEPTIC TANK.
IF I WAS YOU, I'D MAKE IT A SEWER LINE.
A SEWER LINE? WHAT FOR?
TO RUN IT ON DOWN TO THE LOBBY OF THAT BANK IN CASE YOU FEEL LIKE MAKIN' A DEPOSIT.
MORNIN', EVERYBODY...
I GOT THIS BACK FROM THE PRINTER LAST NIGHT, AND I GOTTA SHOW IT OFF.
AIN'T SHE A BEAUT?
☆ GENUINE ☆ AUTHENTIC ☆
JESSE JAMES
Robin Hood of the Old West
Public Lecture • Display of Marksmanship
Saturday ~ 6:00 PM ~ Grange Hall
☆EDUCATIONAL☆ENTERTAINING☆
For the Whole Family ~

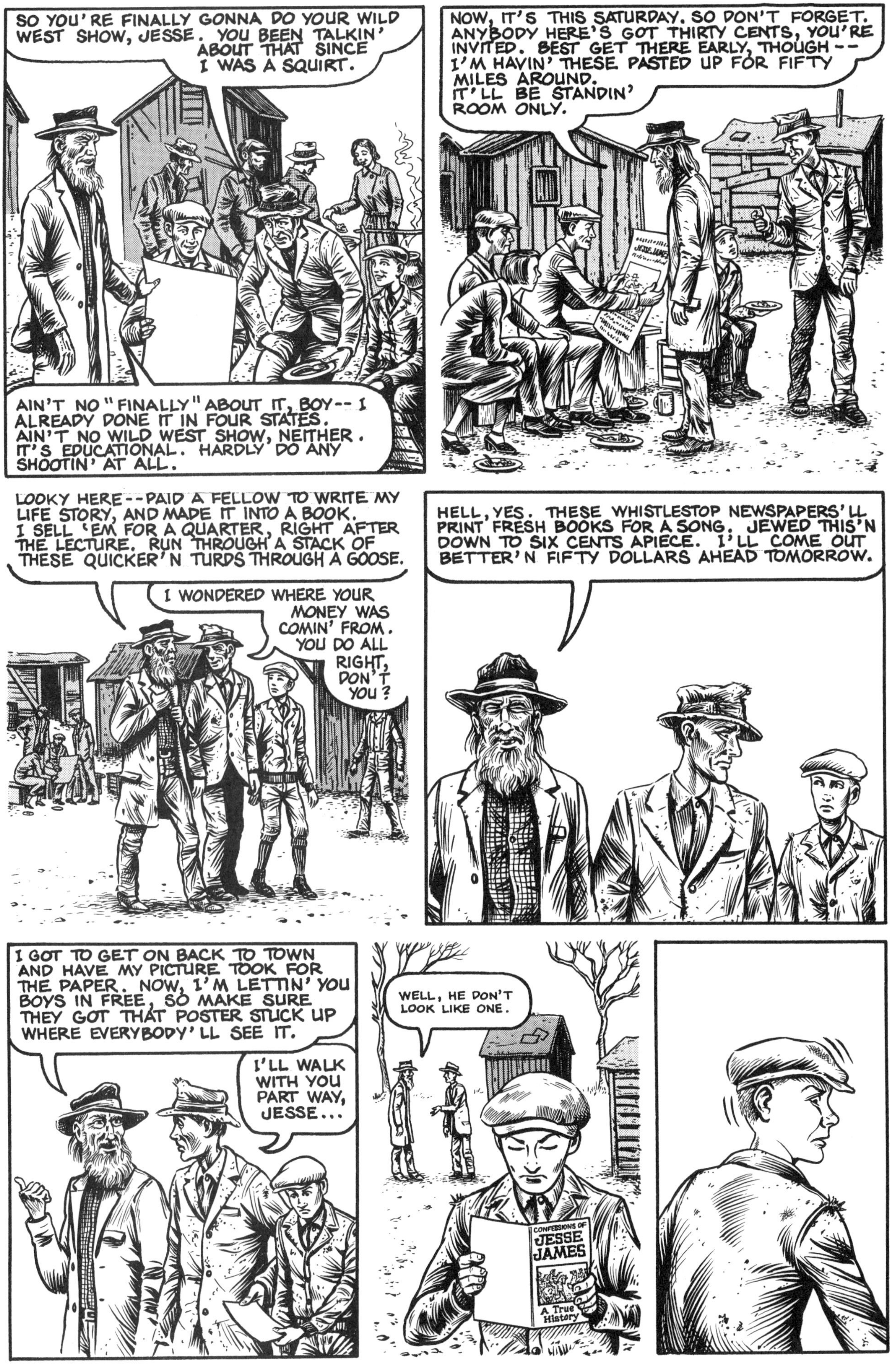
SO YOU'RE FINALLY GONNA DO YOUR WILD WEST SHOW, JESSE. YOU BEEN TALKIN' ABOUT THAT SINCE I WAS A SQUIRT.
AIN'T NO "FINALLY" ABOUT IT, BOY-- I ALREADY DONE IT IN FOUR STATES. AIN'T NO WILD WEST SHOW, NEITHER. IT'S EDUCATIONAL. HARDLY DO ANY SHOOTIN' AT ALL.
NOW, IT'S THIS SATURDAY. SO DON'T FORGET. ANYBODY HERE'S GOT THIRTY CENTS, YOU'RE INVITED. BEST GET THERE EARLY, THOUGH -- I'M HAVIN' THESE PASTED UP FOR FIFTY MILES AROUND. IT'LL BE STANDIN' ROOM ONLY.
LOOKY HERE--PAID A FELLOW TO WRITE MY LIFE STORY, AND MADE IT INTO A BOOK. I SELL 'EM FOR A QUARTER, RIGHT AFTER THE LECTURE. RUN THROUGH A STACK OF THESE QUICKER'N TURDS THROUGH A GOOSE.
I WONDERED WHERE YOUR MONEY WAS COMIN' FROM. YOU DO ALL RIGHT, DON'T YOU?
HELL, YES. THESE WHISTLESTOP NEWSPAPERS'LL PRINT FRESH BOOKS FOR A SONG. JEWED THIS'N DOWN TO SIX CENTS APIECE. I'LL COME OUT BETTER'N FIFTY DOLLARS AHEAD TOMORROW.
I GOT TO GET ON BACK TO TOWN AND HAVE MY PICTURE TOOK FOR THE PAPER. NOW, I'M LETTIN' YOU BOYS IN FREE, SO MAKE SURE THEY GOT THAT POSTER STUCK UP WHERE EVERYBODY'LL SEE IT.
I'LL WALK WITH YOU PART WAY, JESSE...
WELL, HE DON'T LOOK LIKE ONE.
CONFESSIONS OF JESSE JAMES
A True History

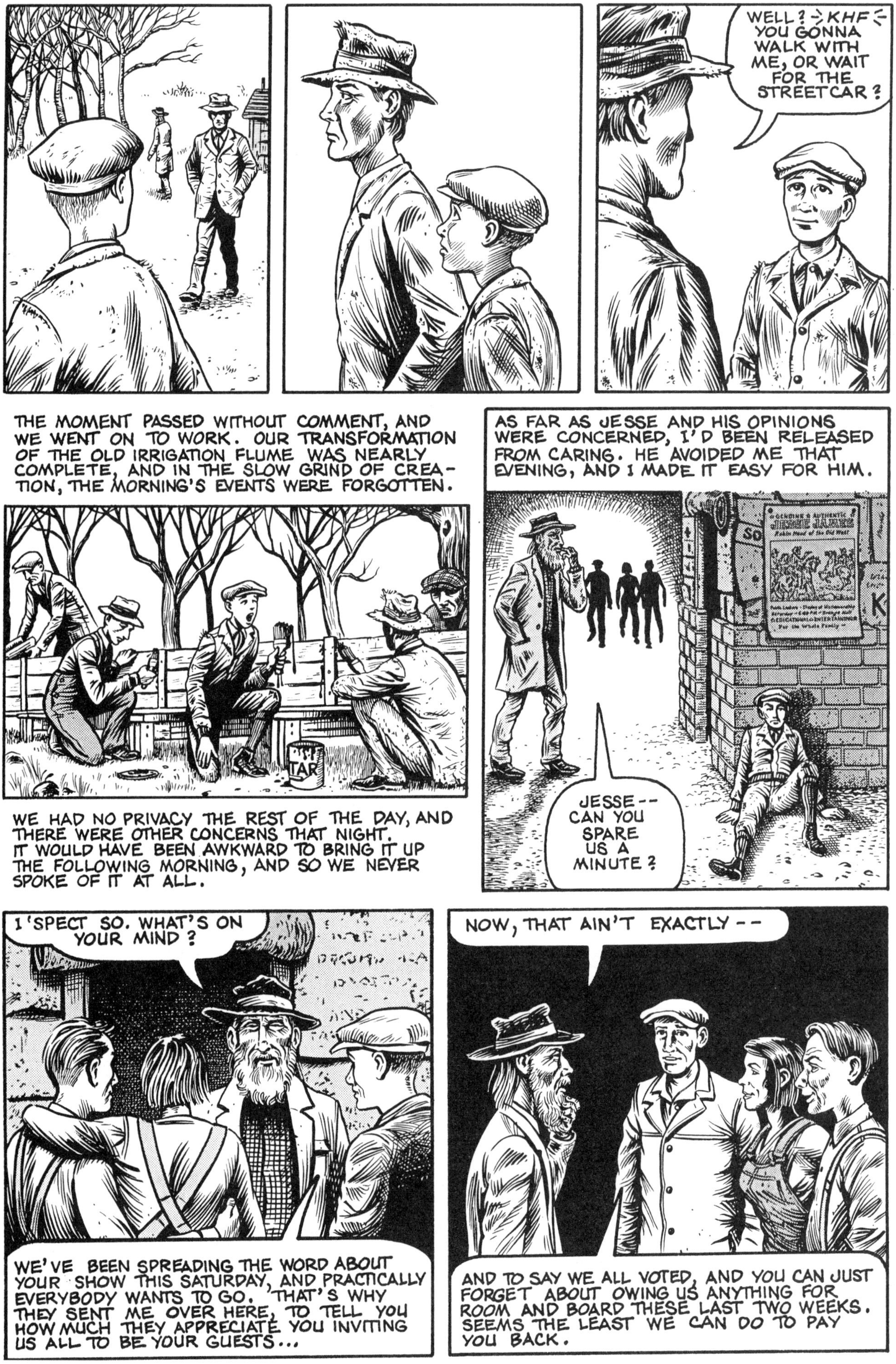
WELL? KHF YOU GONNA WALK WITH ME, OR WAIT FOR THE STREETCAR?
THE MOMENT PASSED WITHOUT COMMENT, AND WE WENT ON TO WORK. OUR TRANSFORMATION OF THE OLD IRRIGATION FLUME WAS NEARLY COMPLETE, AND IN THE SLOW GRIND OF CREATION, THE MORNING'S EVENTS WERE FORGOTTEN.
TAR
WE HAD NO PRIVACY THE REST OF THE DAY, AND THERE WERE OTHER CONCERNS THAT NIGHT. IT WOULD HAVE BEEN AWKWARD TO BRING IT UP THE FOLLOWING MORNING, AND SO WE NEVER SPOKE OF IT AT ALL.
AS FAR AS JESSE AND HIS OPINIONS WERE CONCERNED, I'D BEEN RELEASED FROM CARING. HE AVOIDED ME THAT EVENING, AND I MADE IT EASY FOR HIM.
JESSE-- CAN YOU SPARE US A MINUTE?
I'SPECT SO. WHAT'S ON YOUR MIND?
WE'VE BEEN SPREADING THE WORD ABOUT YOUR SHOW THIS SATURDAY, AND PRACTICALLY EVERYBODY WANTS TO GO. THAT'S WHY THEY SENT ME OVER HERE, TO TELL YOU HOW MUCH THEY APPRECIATE YOU INVITING US ALL TO BE YOUR GUESTS...
AND TO SAY WE ALL VOTED, AND YOU CAN JUST FORGET ABOUT OWING US ANYTHING FOR ROOM AND BOARD THESE LAST TWO WEEKS. SEEMS THE LEAST WE CAN DO TO PAY YOU BACK.
NOW, THAT AIN'T EXACTLY--

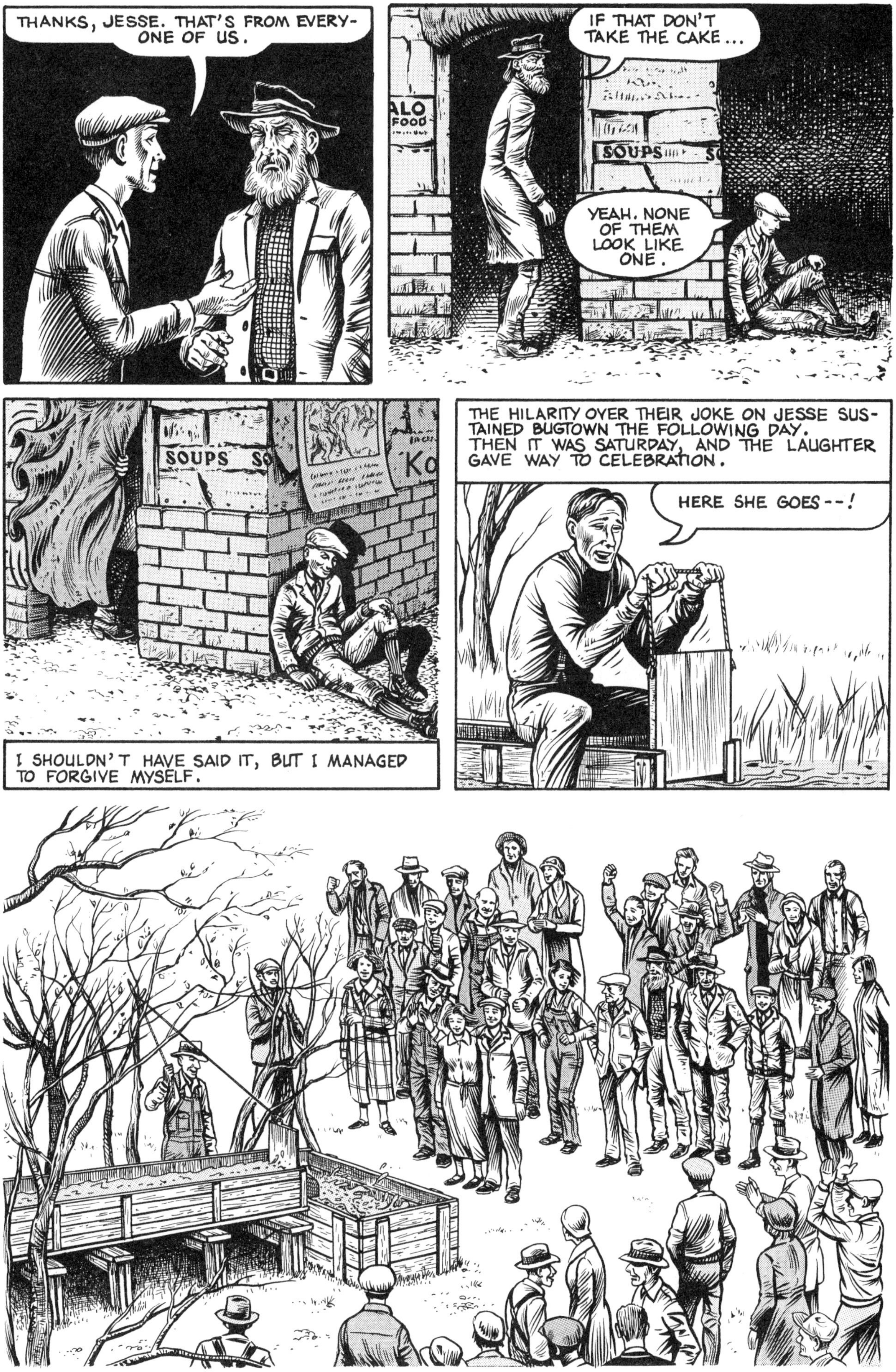

THANKS, JESSE. THAT'S FROM EVERY-ONE OF US.
IF THAT DON'T TAKE THE CAKE...
ALO
FOOD
SOUPS
YEAH. NONE OF THEM LOOK LIKE ONE.
SOUPS
I SHOULDN'T HAVE SAID IT, BUT I MANAGED TO FORGIVE MYSELF.
THE HILARITY OVER THEIR JOKE ON JESSE SUSTAINED BUGTOWN THE FOLLOWING DAY.
THEN IT WAS SATURDAY, AND THE LAUGHTER GAVE WAY TO CELEBRATION.
HERE SHE GOES--!

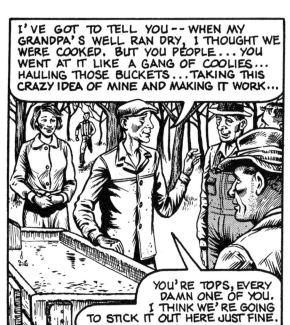

I'VE GOT TO TELL YOU -- WHEN MY GRANDPA'S WELL RAN DRY, I THOUGHT WE WERE COOKED. BUT YOU PEOPLE... YOU WENT AT IT LIKE A GANG OF COOLIES... HAULING THOSE BUCKETS... TAKING THIS CRAZY IDEA OF MINE AND MAKING IT WORK...

YOU'RE TOPS, EVERY DAMN ONE OF YOU. I THINK WE'RE GOING TO STICK IT OUT HERE JUST FINE.

LET'S GO, SPROUT -- THEY CAN WHOOP IT UP FINE ON THEIR OWN. YOU'N ME GOT BUSINESS.

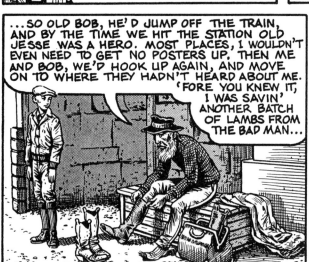

...SO OLD BOB, HE'D JUMP OFF THE TRAIN, AND BY THE TIME WE HIT THE STATION OLD JESSE WAS A HERO. MOST PLACES, I WOULDN'T EVEN NEED TO GET NO POSTERS UP, THEN ME AND BOB, WE'D HOOK UP AGAIN, AND MOVE ON TO WHERE THEY HADN'T HEARD ABOUT ME. 'FORE YOU KNEW IT, I WAS SAVIN' ANOTHER BATCH OF LAMBS FROM THE BAD MAN...

AS JESSE DRONED ON, I KEPT WONDERING WHAT BUSINESS THE TWO OF US COULD POSSIBLY HAVE. BEFORE LONG I'D LOST INTEREST ENTIRELY, AND FELT MYSELF BEING LULLED INTO A STUPOR.

I SAID, SAM TELLS ME I WENT AND HURT YOUR FEELIN'S. THAT RIGHT?

...HUH?

WELL, I HOPE NOT, 'CAUSE I NEVER COULD APOLOGIZE WORTH A DAMN. FINALLY JUST GAVE UP TRYIN' AT ALL. BUT I GOT BETTER THINGS TO DO THAN MISTREAT LITTLE BOYS. I HOPE YOU GOT THE GOOD SENSE TO KNOW THAT.

SURE.

THAT'S FINE. SO IF YOU GOT NO HARD FEELIN'S, MAYBE YOU WON'T MIND GIVIN' ME A HAND TONIGHT WHEN I SHOW OFF MY SHOOTIN'.

NO! I MEAN, IF YOU WANT ME TO...

GOOD. JUST KEEP YOUR HAND STEADY, AND YOU WON'T EVEN KNOW YOU'RE GETTIN' SHOT AT.

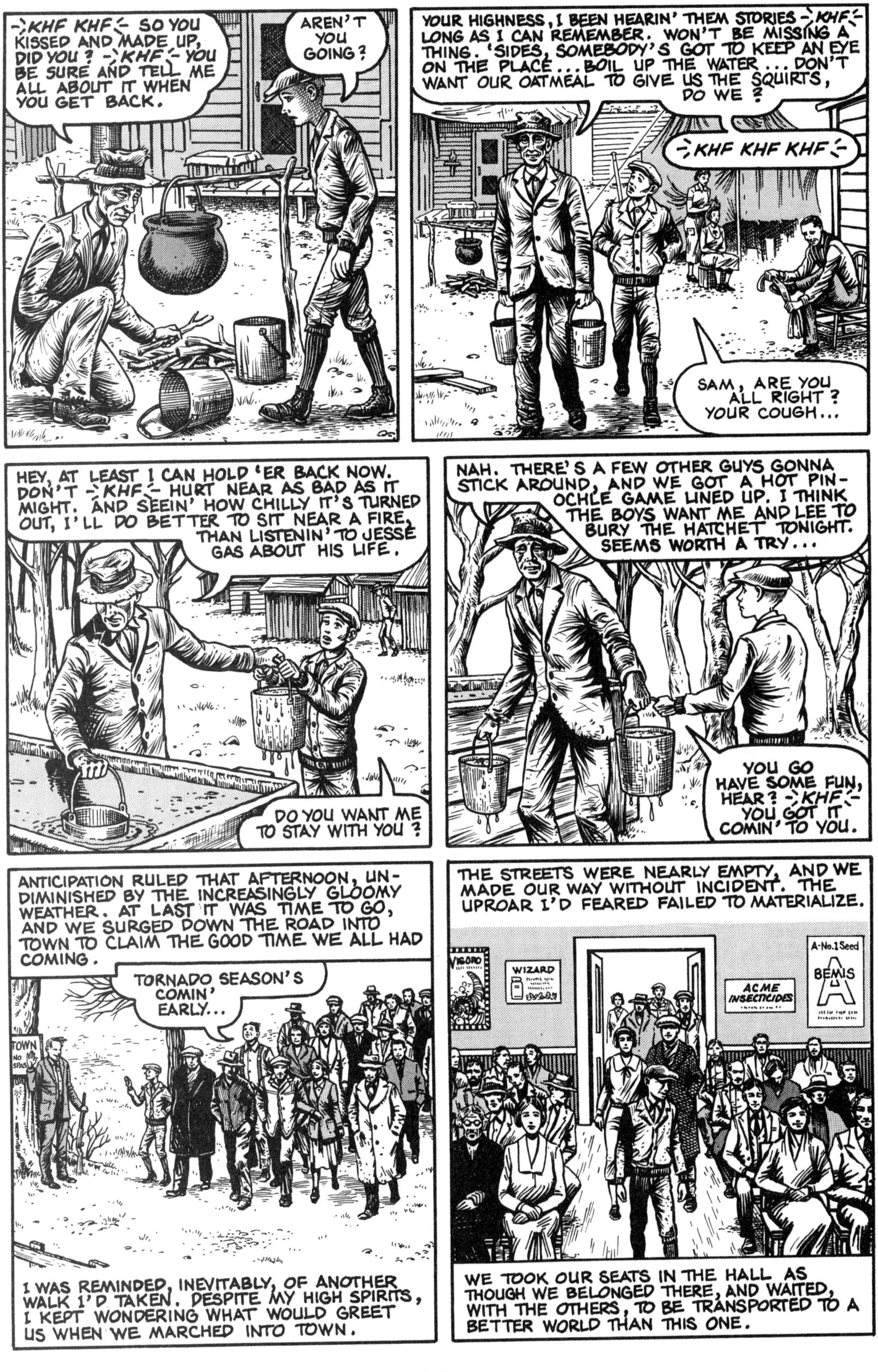
-KHF KHF- SO YOU KISSED AND MADE UP, DID YOU? -KHF- YOU BE SURE AND TELL ME ALL ABOUT IT WHEN YOU GET BACK.
AREN'T YOU GOING?
YOUR HIGHNESS, I BEEN HEARIN' THEM STORIES -KHF- LONG AS I CAN REMEMBER. WON'T BE MISSING A THING. 'SIDES, SOMEBODY'S GOT TO KEEP AN EYE ON THE PLACE... BOIL UP THE WATER... DON'T WANT OUR OATMEAL TO GIVE US THE SQUIRTS, DO WE?
-KHF KHF KHF-
SAM, ARE YOU ALL RIGHT? YOUR COUGH...
HEY, AT LEAST I CAN HOLD 'ER BACK NOW. DON'T -KHF- HURT NEAR AS BAD AS IT MIGHT. AND SEEIN' HOW CHILLY IT'S TURNED OUT, I'LL DO BETTER TO SIT NEAR A FIRE, THAN LISTENIN' TO JESSE GAS ABOUT HIS LIFE.
DO YOU WANT ME TO STAY WITH YOU?
NAH. THERE'S A FEW OTHER GUYS GONNA STICK AROUND, AND WE GOT A HOT PINOCHLE GAME LINED UP. I THINK THE BOYS WANT ME AND LEE TO BURY THE HATCHET TONIGHT. SEEMS WORTH A TRY...
YOU GO HAVE SOME FUN, HEAR? -KHF- YOU GOT IT COMIN' TO YOU.
ANTICIPATION RULED THAT AFTERNOON, UNDIMINISHED BY THE INCREASINGLY GLOOMY WEATHER. AT LAST IT WAS TIME TO GO, AND WE SURGED DOWN THE ROAD INTO TOWN TO CLAIM THE GOOD TIME WE ALL HAD COMING.
TORNADO SEASON'S COMIN' EARLY...
TOWN
I WAS REMINDED, INEVITABLY, OF ANOTHER WALK I'D TAKEN. DESPITE MY HIGH SPIRITS, I KEPT WONDERING WHAT WOULD GREET US WHEN WE MARCHED INTO TOWN.
THE STREETS WERE NEARLY EMPTY, AND WE MADE OUR WAY WITHOUT INCIDENT. THE UPROAR I'D FEARED FAILED TO MATERIALIZE.
WIZARD
ACME INSECTICIDES
A-No.1 Seed
BEMIS
WE TOOK OUR SEATS IN THE HALL AS THOUGH WE BELONGED THERE, AND WAITED, WITH THE OTHERS, TO BE TRANSPORTED TO A BETTER WORLD THAN THIS ONE.

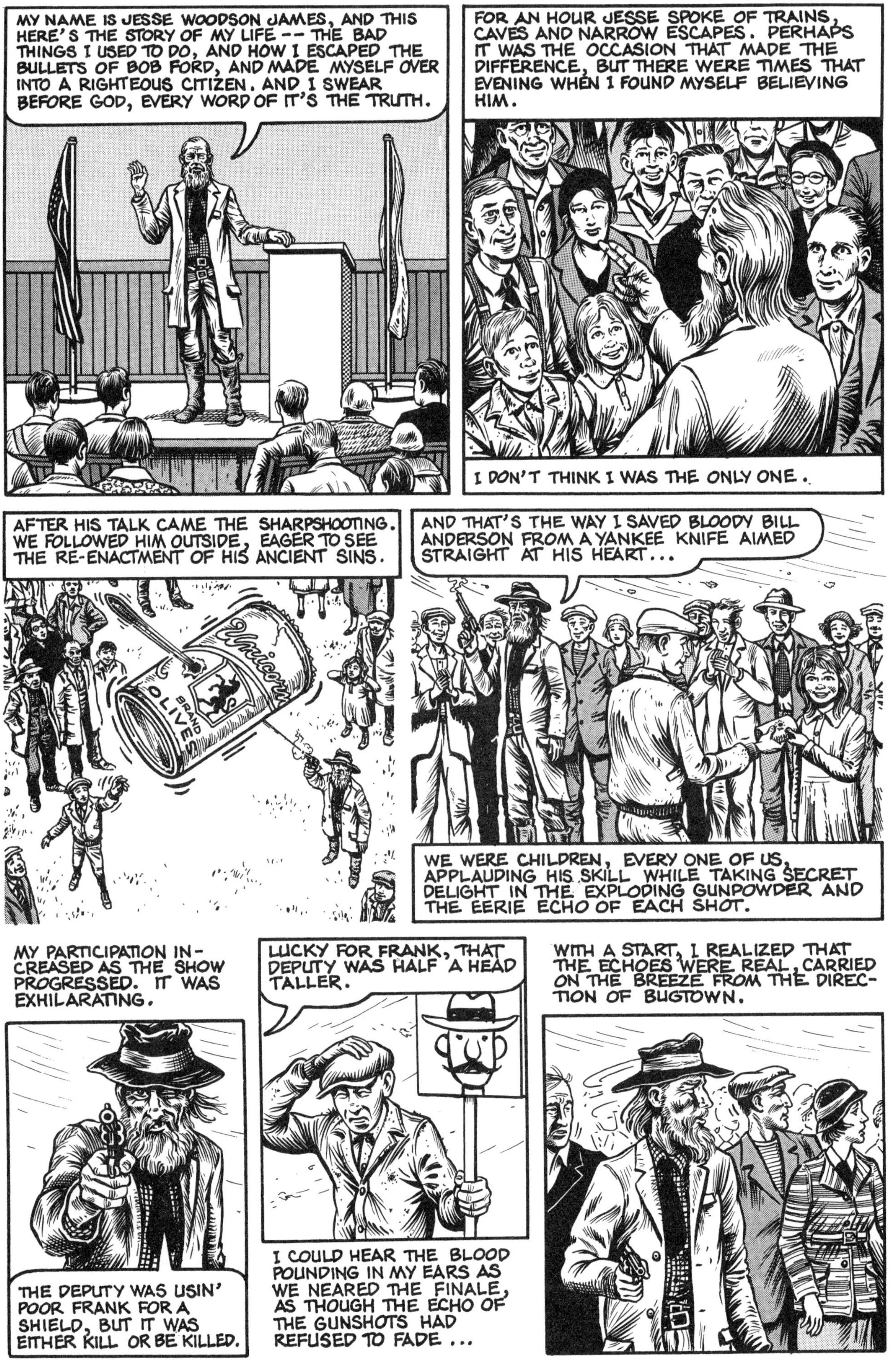
MY NAME IS JESSE WOODSON JAMES, AND THIS HERE'S THE STORY OF MY LIFE -- THE BAD THINGS I USED TO DO, AND HOW I ESCAPED THE BULLETS OF BOB FORD, AND MADE MYSELF OVER INTO A RIGHTEOUS CITIZEN. AND I SWEAR BEFORE GOD, EVERY WORD OF IT'S THE TRUTH.
FOR AN HOUR JESSE SPOKE OF TRAINS, CAVES AND NARROW ESCAPES. PERHAPS IT WAS THE OCCASION THAT MADE THE DIFFERENCE, BUT THERE WERE TIMES THAT EVENING WHEN I FOUND MYSELF BELIEVING HIM.
I DON'T THINK I WAS THE ONLY ONE.
AFTER HIS TALK CAME THE SHARPSHOOTING. WE FOLLOWED HIM OUTSIDE, EAGER TO SEE THE RE-ENACTMENT OF HIS ANCIENT SINS.
Unicorn
BRAND OLIVES
AND THAT'S THE WAY I SAVED BLOODY BILL ANDERSON FROM A YANKEE KNIFE AIMED STRAIGHT AT HIS HEART...
WE WERE CHILDREN, EVERY ONE OF US, APPLAUDING HIS SKILL WHILE TAKING SECRET DELIGHT IN THE EXPLODING GUNPOWDER AND THE EERIE ECHO OF EACH SHOT.
MY PARTICIPATION IN-CREASED AS THE SHOW PROGRESSED. IT WAS EXHILARATING.
THE DEPUTY WAS USIN' POOR FRANK FOR A SHIELD, BUT IT WAS EITHER KILL OR BE KILLED.
LUCKY FOR FRANK, THAT DEPUTY WAS HALF A HEAD TALLER.
I COULD HEAR THE BLOOD POUNDING IN MY EARS AS WE NEARED THE FINALE, AS THOUGH THE ECHO OF THE GUNSHOTS HAD REFUSED TO FADE ...
WITH A START, I REALIZED THAT THE ECHOES WERE REAL, CARRIED ON THE BREEZE FROM THE DIREC-TION OF BUGTOWN.

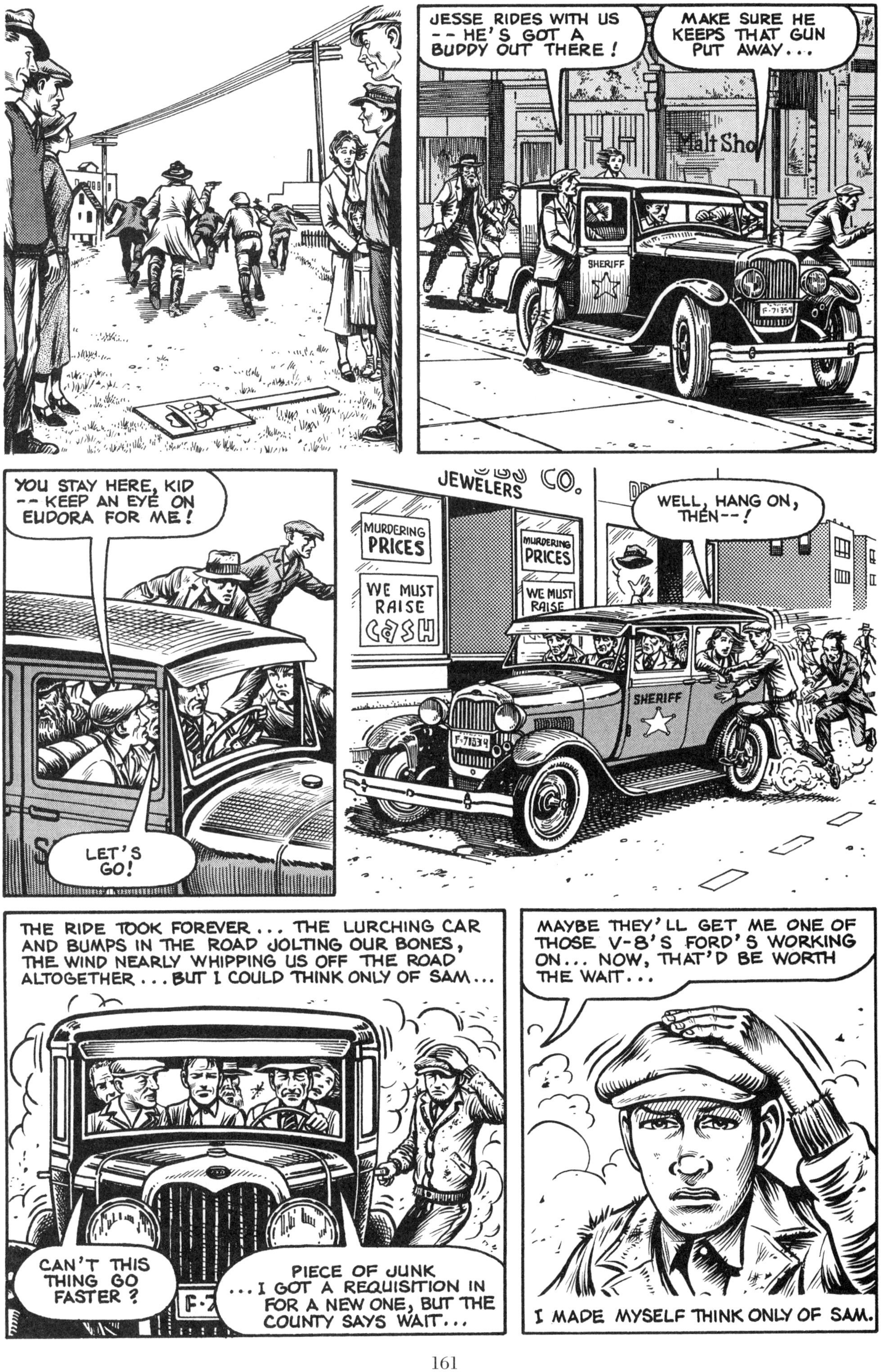
JESSE RIDES WITH US -- HE'S GOT A BUDDY OUT THERE!
MAKE SURE HE KEEPS THAT GUN PUT AWAY...
Malt Sho
SHERIFF
YOU STAY HERE, KID -- KEEP AN EYE ON EUDORA FOR ME!
LET'S GO!
JEWELERS
CO.
MURDERING PRICES
WE MUST RAISE CASH
WELL, HANG ON, THEN--!
SHERIFF
THE RIDE TOOK FOREVER... THE LURCHING CAR AND BUMPS IN THE ROAD JOLTING OUR BONES, THE WIND NEARLY WHIPPING US OFF THE ROAD ALTOGETHER... BUT I COULD THINK ONLY OF SAM...
CAN'T THIS THING GO FASTER?
PIECE OF JUNK ...I GOT A REQUISITION IN FOR A NEW ONE, BUT THE COUNTY SAYS WAIT...
MAYBE THEY'LL GET ME ONE OF THOSE V-8'S FORD'S WORKING ON... NOW, THAT'D BE WORTH THE WAIT...
I MADE MYSELF THINK ONLY OF SAM.

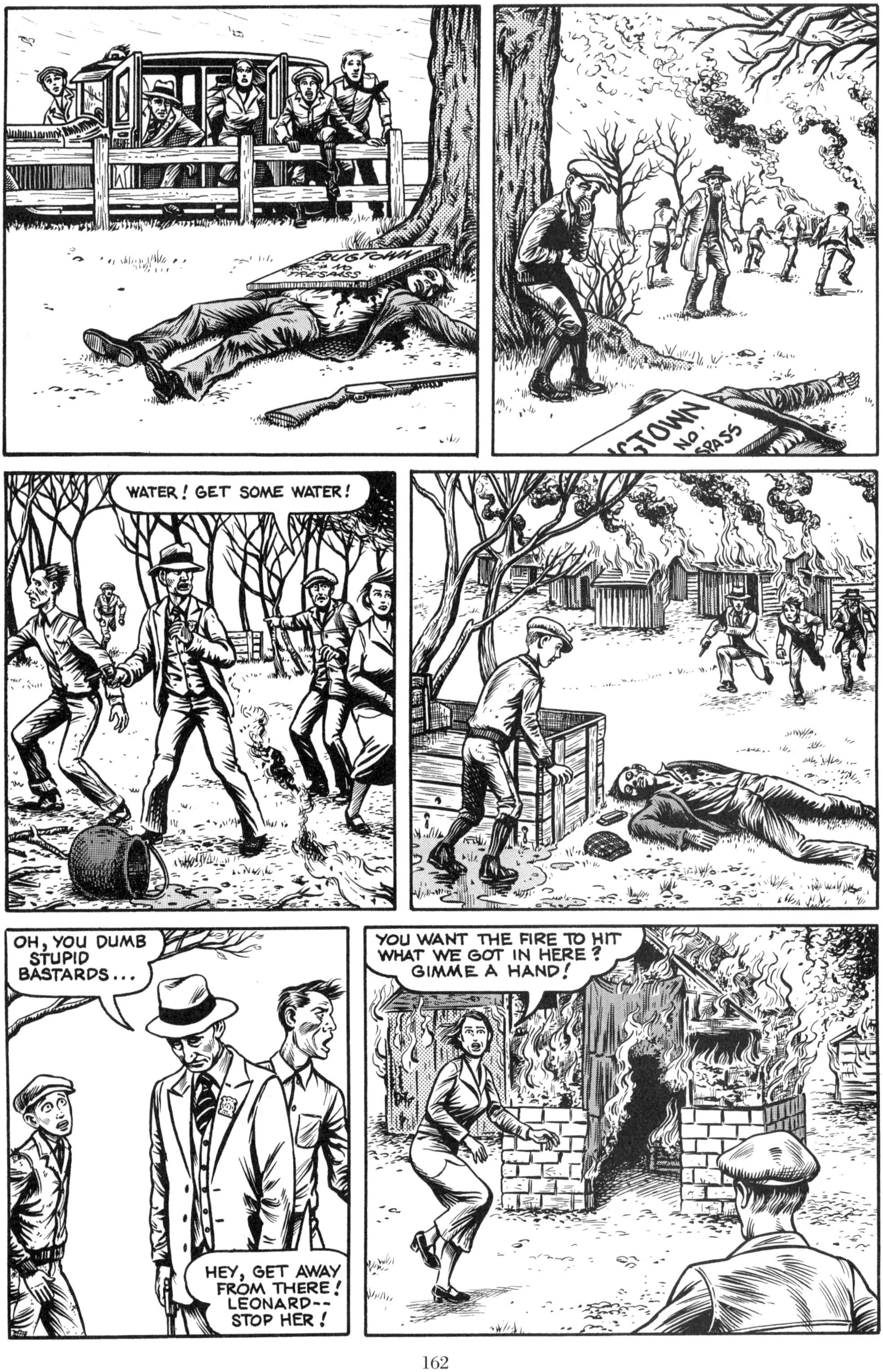
BUGSTOWN NO TRESAASS
WATER! GET SOME WATER!
OH, YOU DUMB STUPID BASTARDS...
HEY, GET AWAY FROM THERE! LEONARD-- STOP HER!
YOU WANT THE FIRE TO HIT WHAT WE GOT IN HERE? GIMME A HAND!

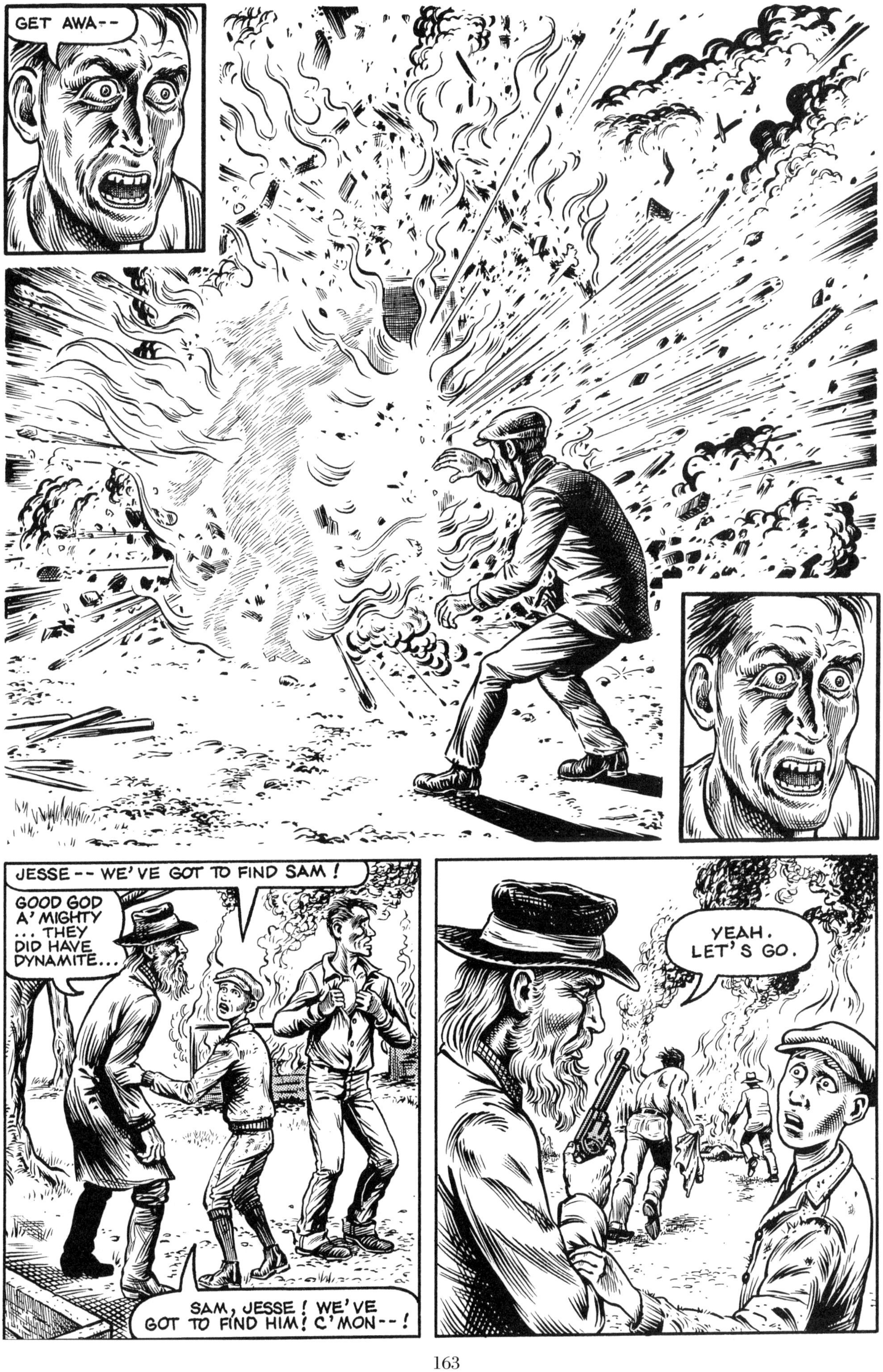
GET AWA--
JESSE-- WE'VE GOT TO FIND SAM!
GOOD GOD A' MIGHTY ... THEY DID HAVE DYNAMITE...
SAM, JESSE! WE'VE GOT TO FIND HIM! C'MON--!
YEAH. LET'S GO.

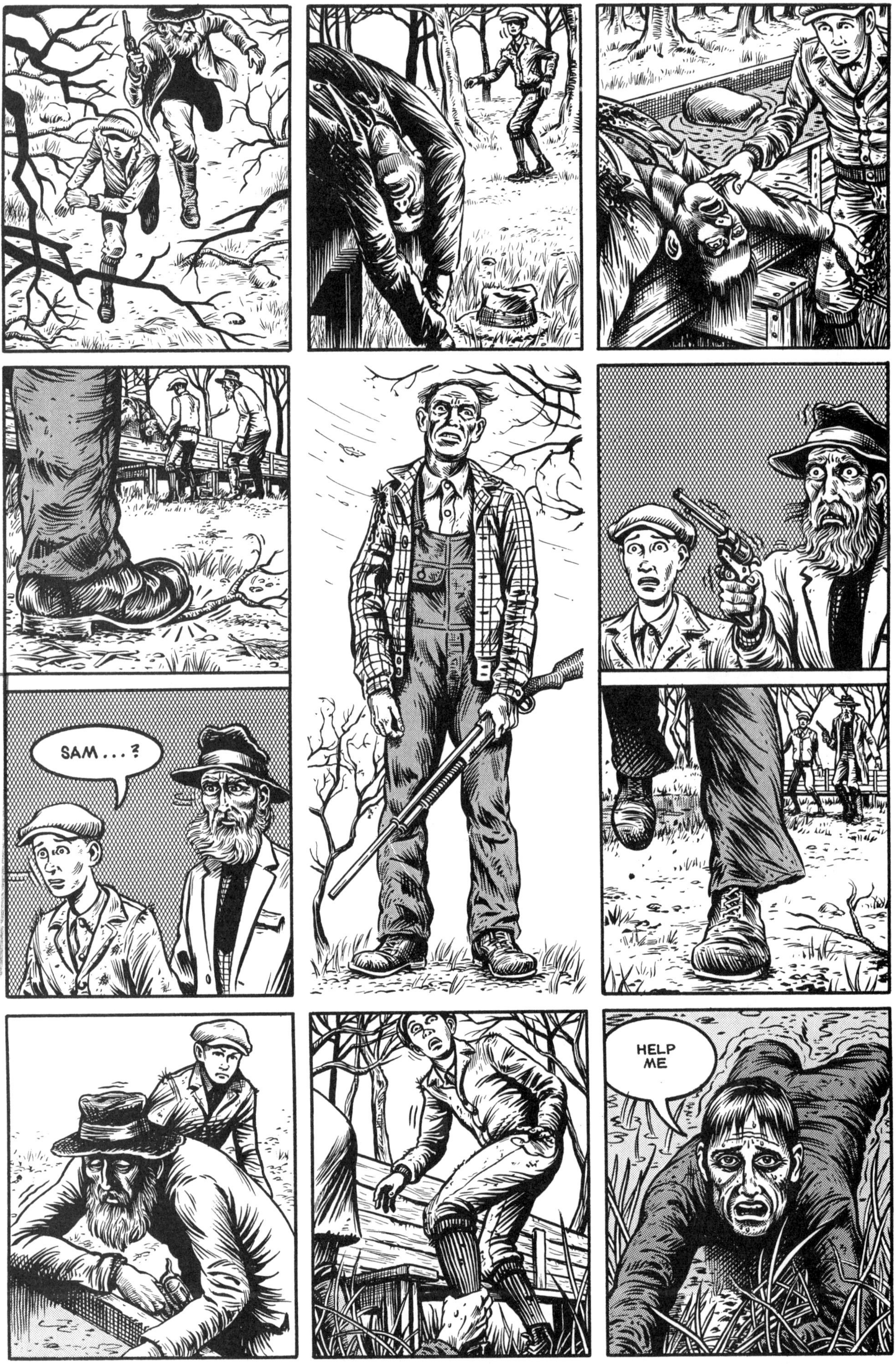
SAM...?
HELP ME

AS WE PULLED HIM FROM THE POND, I WAS GRATE-FUL FOR THE WIND THAT WHIPPED IN MY EARS; IT MUFFLED SAM'S CLOTTED MEWLING. JESSE AND I REMAINED SILENT AND WAITED FOR HIM TO SPEAK --AS THOUGH HE HAD FINALLY BECOME SO FRAGILE THAT EVEN OUR VOICES MIGHT BREAK HIM.

WE COME FOR A JUG HE WAS COOLIN' IN THE WATER ... AND WE HEARD SOMETHIN'... AND THEN HE PUSHED ME IN, AND THEN THERE WAS SHOOTIN'...

AND THEN IT GOT QUIET, AND I STAYED PUT DOWN IN THEM WEEDS... -: COUGH :-... WAITIN' FOR 'EM TO FINISH ME... WONDERIN' WHEN THEY'D DO IT...

THIS SECOND? -- NO.
THIS SECOND? -- NO. NOW...?

SHE WAS GONE BEFORE WE PUT HER OUT -- A PIECE OF BRICK ... I GUESS IT WAS A MERCY.

YOU KNOW WHO DID THIS. WE BOTH KNOW. I'LL GET YOU ALL THE HELP YOU NEED TO BRING 'EM IN.

THE LAST KIND OF HELP I NEED'S A LYNCH PARTY, LEONARD. YOU STAY OUT OF THIS.

THE HELL I WILL! I WANT 'EM ARRESTED, I WANT A TRIAL THIS TOWN'LL NEVER FORGET!

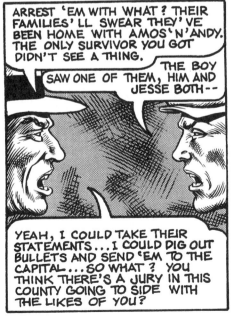

ARREST 'EM WITH WHAT? THEIR FAMILIES'LL SWEAR THEY'VE BEEN HOME WITH AMOS 'N' ANDY. THE ONLY SURVIVOR YOU GOT DIDN'T SEE A THING.

THE BOY SAW ONE OF THEM, HIM AND JESSE BOTH--

YEAH, I COULD TAKE THEIR STATEMENTS... I COULD DIG OUT BULLETS AND SEND 'EM TO THE CAPITAL... SO WHAT? YOU THINK THERE'S A JURY IN THIS COUNTY GOING TO SIDE WITH THE LIKES OF YOU?

DON'T YOU UNDERSTAND? THE GUYS THAT DID THIS ARE HEROES. THEY BURNED OUT THE RAT'S NEST. THAT'S WHAT THE PEOPLE HERE WILL SAY.

AND THEY'RE MY PEOPLE, LEONARD. I'VE GOT TO LIVE WITH THEM ... EVEN IF IT MAKES ME SICK.

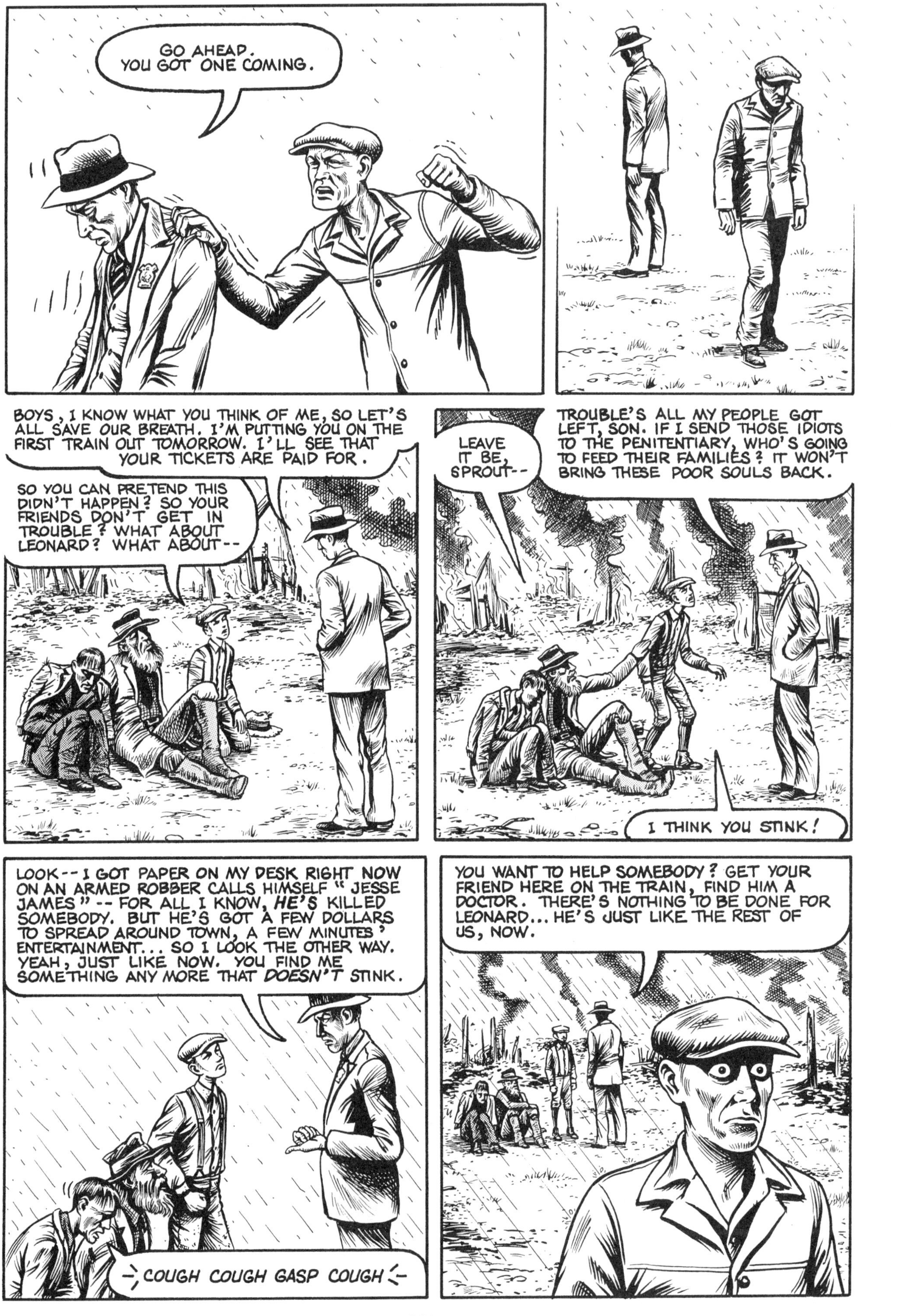
GO AHEAD. YOU GOT ONE COMING.
BOYS, I KNOW WHAT YOU THINK OF ME, SO LET'S ALL SAVE OUR BREATH. I'M PUTTING YOU ON THE FIRST TRAIN OUT TOMORROW. I'LL SEE THAT YOUR TICKETS ARE PAID FOR.
SO YOU CAN PRETEND THIS DIDN'T HAPPEN? SO YOUR FRIENDS DON'T GET IN TROUBLE? WHAT ABOUT LEONARD? WHAT ABOUT--
LEAVE IT BE, SPROUT--
TROUBLE'S ALL MY PEOPLE GOT LEFT, SON. IF I SEND THOSE IDIOTS TO THE PENITENTIARY, WHO'S GOING TO FEED THEIR FAMILIES? IT WON'T BRING THESE POOR SOULS BACK.
I THINK YOU STINK!
LOOK--I GOT PAPER ON MY DESK RIGHT NOW ON AN ARMED ROBBER CALLS HIMSELF "JESSE JAMES"--FOR ALL I KNOW, HE'S KILLED SOMEBODY. BUT HE'S GOT A FEW DOLLARS TO SPREAD AROUND TOWN, A FEW MINUTES' ENTERTAINMENT... SO I LOOK THE OTHER WAY. YEAH, JUST LIKE NOW. YOU FIND ME SOMETHING ANY MORE THAT DOESN'T STINK.
COUGH COUGH GASP COUGH
YOU WANT TO HELP SOMEBODY? GET YOUR FRIEND HERE ON THE TRAIN, FIND HIM A DOCTOR. THERE'S NOTHING TO BE DONE FOR LEONARD... HE'S JUST LIKE THE REST OF US, NOW.

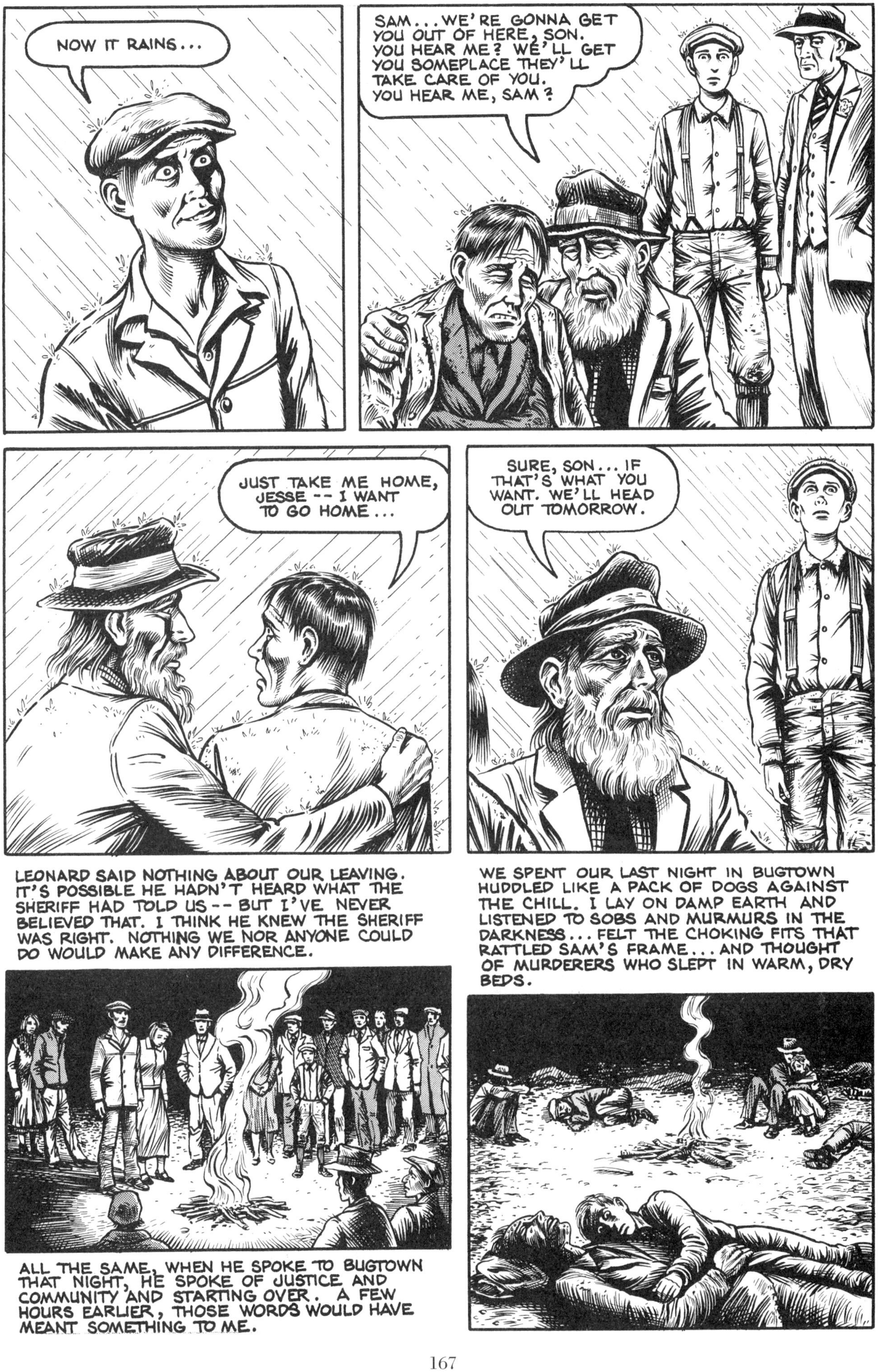
NOW IT RAINS...
SAM... WE'RE GONNA GET YOU OUT OF HERE, SON. YOU HEAR ME? WE'LL GET YOU SOMEPLACE THEY'LL TAKE CARE OF YOU. YOU HEAR ME, SAM?
JUST TAKE ME HOME, JESSE -- I WANT TO GO HOME...
SURE, SON... IF THAT'S WHAT YOU WANT. WE'LL HEAD OUT TOMORROW.
LEONARD SAID NOTHING ABOUT OUR LEAVING. IT'S POSSIBLE HE HADN'T HEARD WHAT THE SHERIFF HAD TOLD US -- BUT I'VE NEVER BELIEVED THAT. I THINK HE KNEW THE SHERIFF WAS RIGHT. NOTHING WE NOR ANYONE COULD DO WOULD MAKE ANY DIFFERENCE.
ALL THE SAME, WHEN HE SPOKE TO BUGTOWN THAT NIGHT, HE SPOKE OF JUSTICE AND COMMUNITY AND STARTING OVER. A FEW HOURS EARLIER, THOSE WORDS WOULD HAVE MEANT SOMETHING TO ME.
WE SPENT OUR LAST NIGHT IN BUGTOWN HUDDLED LIKE A PACK OF DOGS AGAINST THE CHILL. I LAY ON DAMP EARTH AND LISTENED TO SOBS AND MURMURS IN THE DARKNESS... FELT THE CHOKING FITS THAT RATTLED SAM'S FRAME... AND THOUGHT OF MURDERERS WHO SLEPT IN WARM, DRY BEDS.

THE CAMP WAS STILL ASLEEP WHEN WE STOLE AWAY. I AVOIDED LOOKING AT LEONARD, PREFERRING TO REMEMBER HIM AS HE'D BEEN THE NIGHT BEFORE -- STILL DREAMING AGAINST THE ODDS.

THE STENCH OF HIS CHARRED DREAM CLUNG TO OUR CLOTHES FOR DAYS. IN MY MEMORY, IT STILL LINGERS.

AS PROMISED, OUR TICKETS HAD BEEN PAID FOR; WITH THE MONEY SAVED AT THE AUCTION, THE TOWN COULD AFFORD THEM.

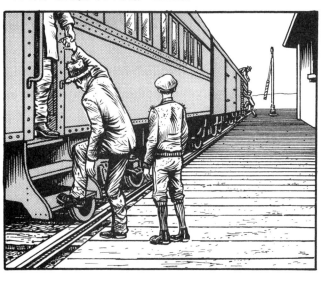

THE RIDE WAS LONG AND CLUMSILY ROUTED, WITH TEDIOUS STOPS BETWEEN CONNECTIONS -- A MODEL OF WHAT MY LIFE HAD BECOME. SMALL WONDER THAT I SPENT SO MANY HOURS THAT DAY GROPING TOWARD CONCLUSIONS ABOUT MYSELF.

AGAIN, I WAS ON THE RUN, FLEEING WHAT I'D ONCE THOUGHT OF AS "ADVENTURE." I'D SINCE LEARNED THAT ADVENTURE WAS WHAT WAS INFLICTED UPON THOSE WHO COULDN'T RUN AND HIDE.

I FELT NO SHAME IN THINKING THAT; IT WAS SIMPLY A FACT I'D LEARNED THROUGH REPEATED EXAMPLE. IT WAS WHAT THE WORLD FORCED US TO DO, EACH IN OUR OWN WAY, IF WE WISHED TO SURVIVE...

AND WHEN WE COULD RUN NO FURTHER, THE WORLD FOUND US IN OUR LONELY HIDING PLACES AND DESTROYED US, ONE BY ONE.

AND YET THERE WERE THOSE WHO WOULD NOT HIDE, WHO SHOUTED OUT, TO THE WORLD, "THIS CANNOT GO ON."

THEY, TOO, WERE DESTROYED... BUT IT WAS AS HUMANITY, NOT FRIGHTENED ANIMALS, THAT THEY MET THEIR END.

AND THERE WERE THE FEW WHO'D LEARNED THE SECRET: THAT BY BANDING TOGETHER, THEY COULD AVOID DESTRUCTION ENTIRELY. THEY COULD EVEN FIGHT BACK.

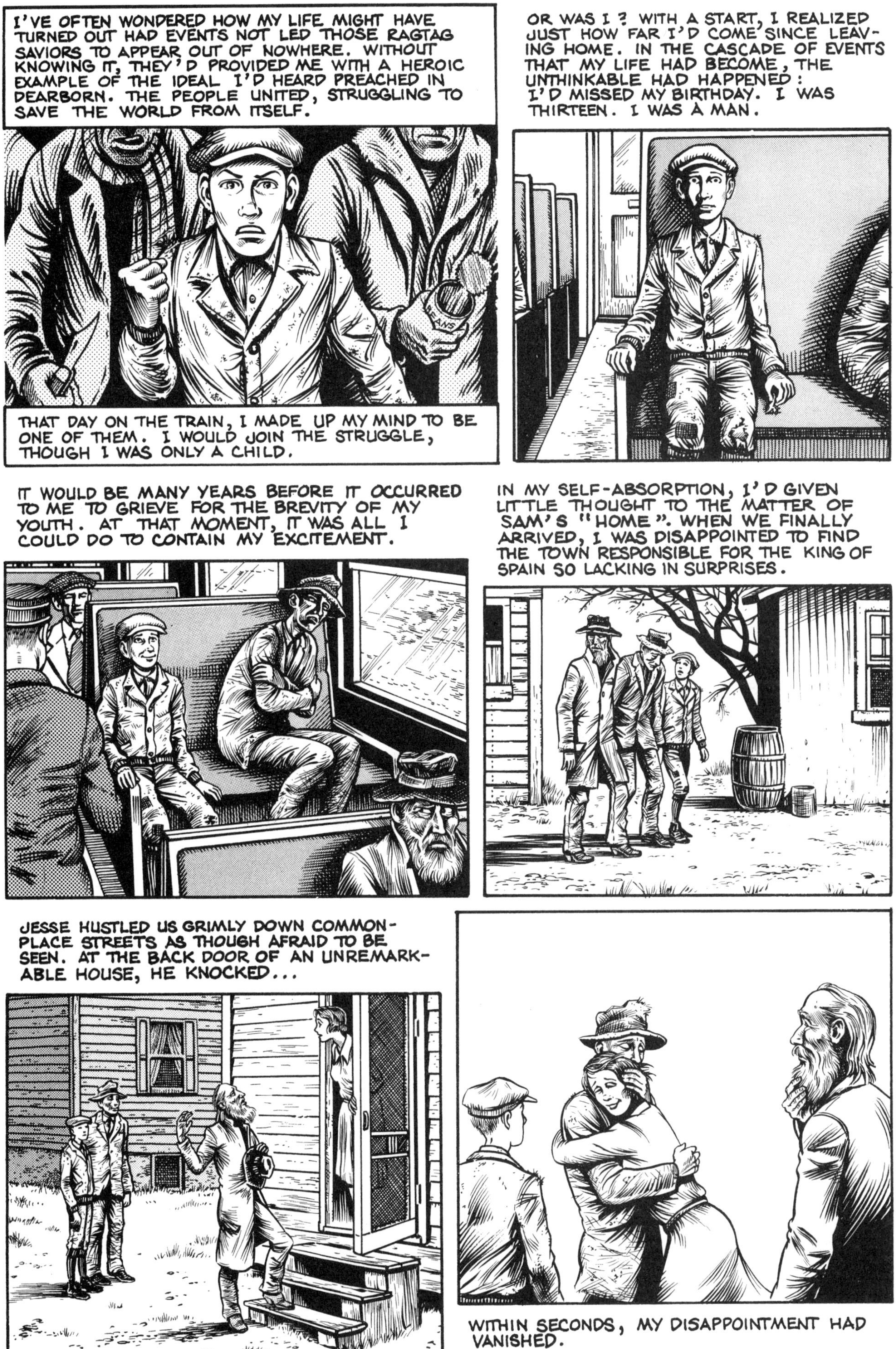
I'VE OFTEN WONDERED HOW MY LIFE MIGHT HAVE TURNED OUT HAD EVENTS NOT LED THOSE RAGTAG SAVIORS TO APPEAR OUT OF NOWHERE. WITHOUT KNOWING IT, THEY'D PROVIDED ME WITH A HEROIC EXAMPLE OF THE IDEAL I'D HEARD PREACHED IN DEARBORN. THE PEOPLE UNITED, STRUGGLING TO SAVE THE WORLD FROM ITSELF.
THAT DAY ON THE TRAIN, I MADE UP MY MIND TO BE ONE OF THEM. I WOULD JOIN THE STRUGGLE, THOUGH I WAS ONLY A CHILD.
OR WAS I ? WITH A START, I REALIZED JUST HOW FAR I'D COME SINCE LEAVING HOME. IN THE CASCADE OF EVENTS THAT MY LIFE HAD BECOME, THE UNTHINKABLE HAD HAPPENED: I'D MISSED MY BIRTHDAY. I WAS THIRTEEN. I WAS A MAN.
IT WOULD BE MANY YEARS BEFORE IT OCCURRED TO ME TO GRIEVE FOR THE BREVITY OF MY YOUTH. AT THAT MOMENT, IT WAS ALL I COULD DO TO CONTAIN MY EXCITEMENT.
IN MY SELF-ABSORPTION, I'D GIVEN LITTLE THOUGHT TO THE MATTER OF SAM'S "HOME". WHEN WE FINALLY ARRIVED, I WAS DISAPPOINTED TO FIND THE TOWN RESPONSIBLE FOR THE KING OF SPAIN SO LACKING IN SURPRISES.
JESSE HUSTLED US GRIMLY DOWN COMMONPLACE STREETS AS THOUGH AFRAID TO BE SEEN. AT THE BACK DOOR OF AN UNREMARKABLE HOUSE, HE KNOCKED...
WITHIN SECONDS, MY DISAPPOINTMENT HAD VANISHED.

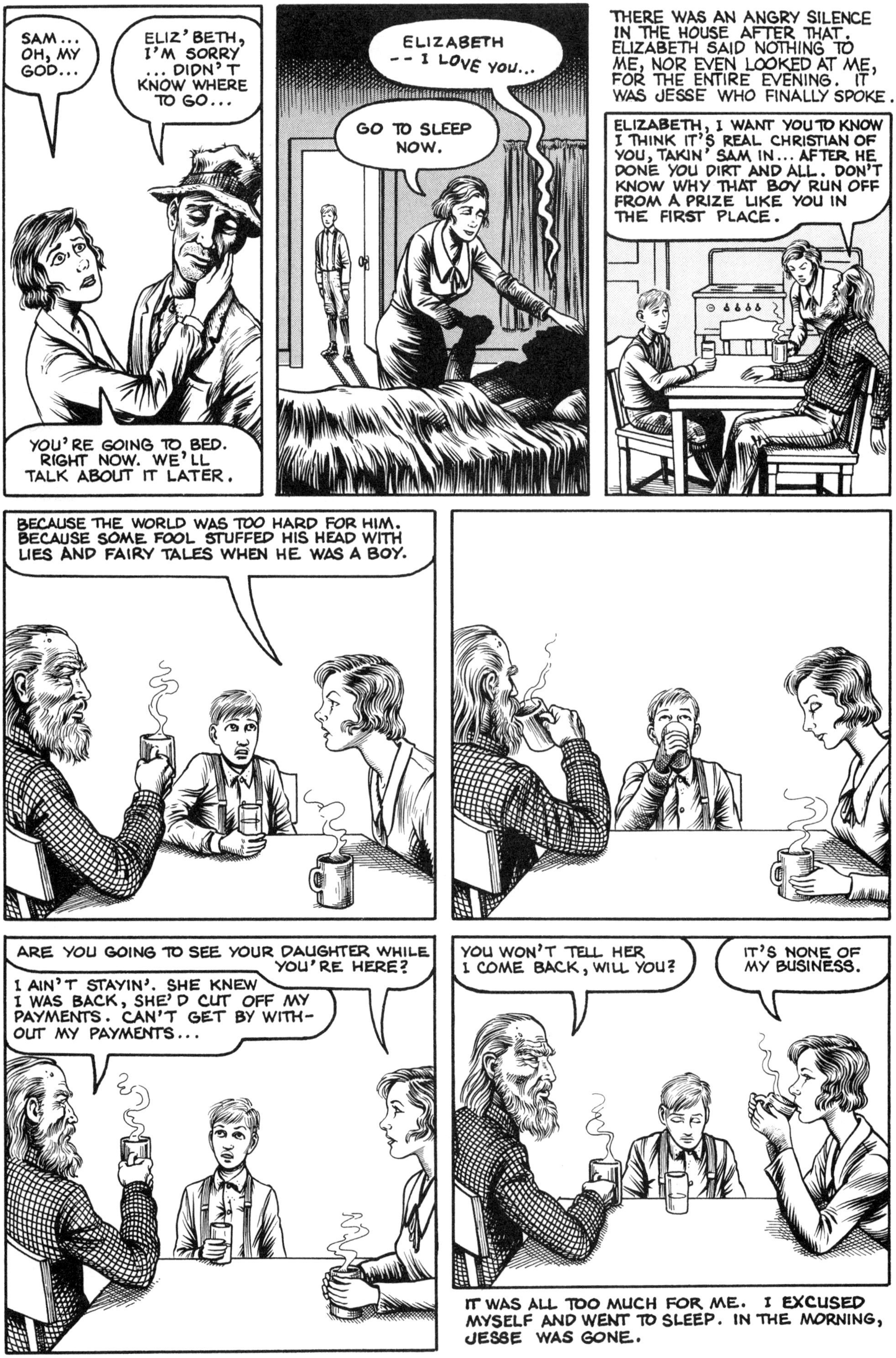
SAM... OH, MY GOD...
ELIZ'BETH, I'M SORRY ... DIDN'T KNOW WHERE TO GO...
YOU'RE GOING TO BED. RIGHT NOW. WE'LL TALK ABOUT IT LATER.
ELIZABETH -- I LOVE YOU...
GO TO SLEEP NOW.
THERE WAS AN ANGRY SILENCE IN THE HOUSE AFTER THAT. ELIZABETH SAID NOTHING TO ME, NOR EVEN LOOKED AT ME, FOR THE ENTIRE EVENING. IT WAS JESSE WHO FINALLY SPOKE.
ELIZABETH, I WANT YOU TO KNOW I THINK IT'S REAL CHRISTIAN OF YOU, TAKIN' SAM IN... AFTER HE DONE YOU DIRT AND ALL. DON'T KNOW WHY THAT BOY RUN OFF FROM A PRIZE LIKE YOU IN THE FIRST PLACE.
BECAUSE THE WORLD WAS TOO HARD FOR HIM. BECAUSE SOME FOOL STUFFED HIS HEAD WITH LIES AND FAIRY TALES WHEN HE WAS A BOY.
ARE YOU GOING TO SEE YOUR DAUGHTER WHILE YOU'RE HERE?
I AIN'T STAYIN'. SHE KNEW I WAS BACK, SHE'D CUT OFF MY PAYMENTS. CAN'T GET BY WITH-OUT MY PAYMENTS...
YOU WON'T TELL HER I COME BACK, WILL YOU?
IT'S NONE OF MY BUSINESS.
IT WAS ALL TOO MUCH FOR ME. I EXCUSED MYSELF AND WENT TO SLEEP. IN THE MORNING, JESSE WAS GONE.

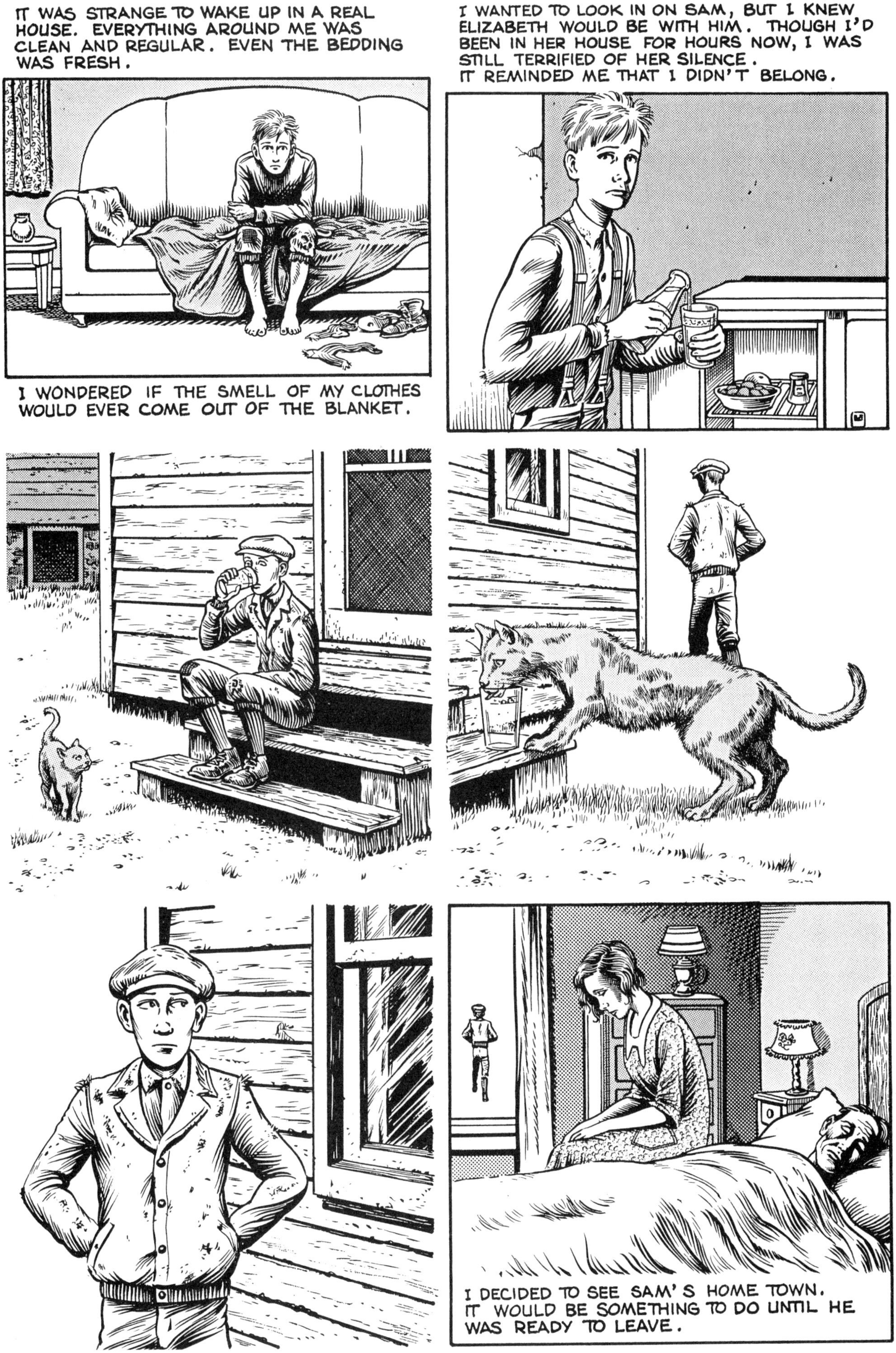
IT WAS STRANGE TO WAKE UP IN A REAL HOUSE. EVERYTHING AROUND ME WAS CLEAN AND REGULAR. EVEN THE BEDDING WAS FRESH.
I WONDERED IF THE SMELL OF MY CLOTHES WOULD EVER COME OUT OF THE BLANKET.
I WANTED TO LOOK IN ON SAM, BUT I KNEW ELIZABETH WOULD BE WITH HIM. THOUGH I'D BEEN IN HER HOUSE FOR HOURS NOW, I WAS STILL TERRIFIED OF HER SILENCE.
IT REMINDED ME THAT I DIDN'T BELONG.
I DECIDED TO SEE SAM'S HOME TOWN.
IT WOULD BE SOMETHING TO DO UNTIL HE WAS READY TO LEAVE.

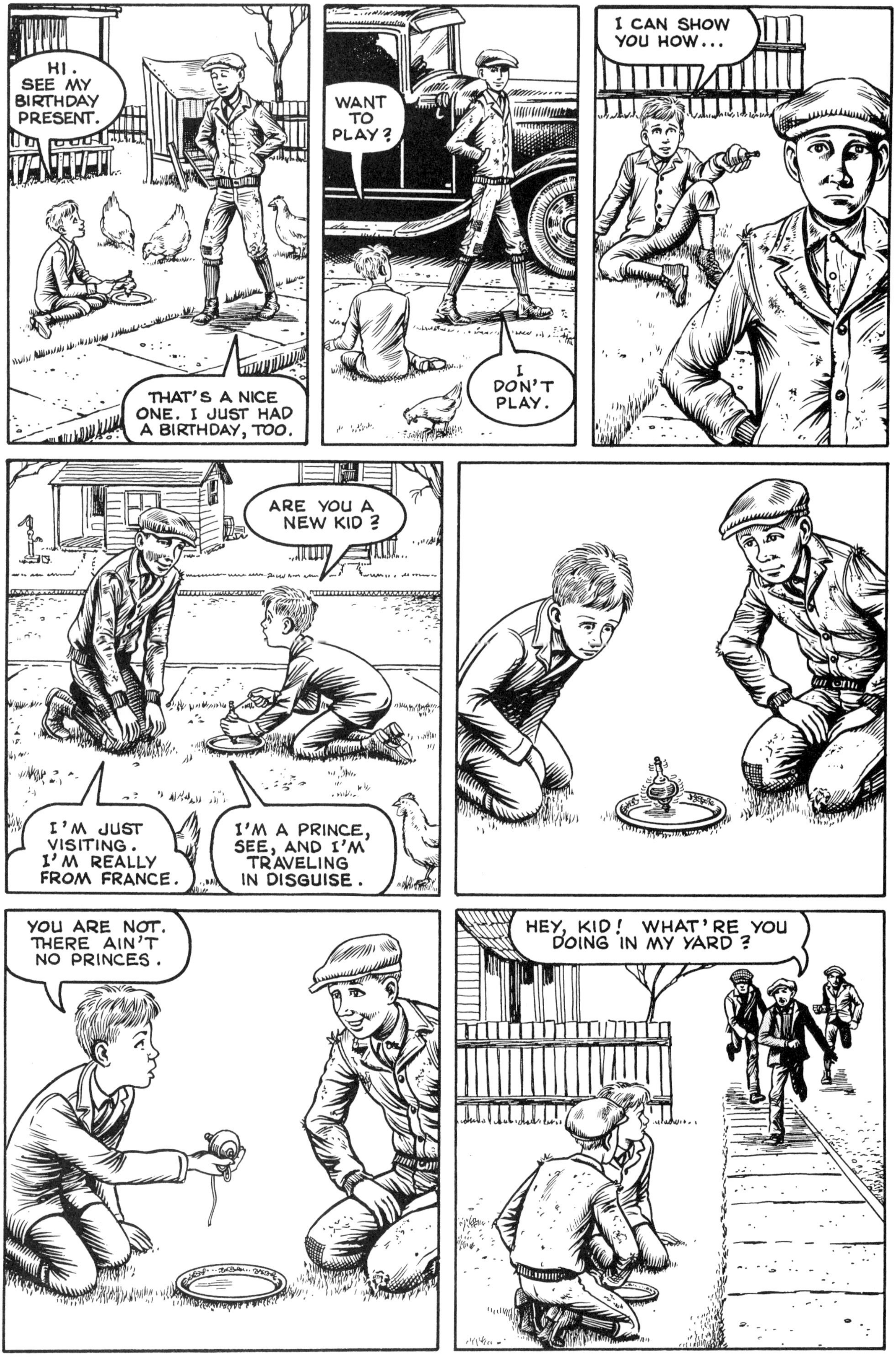
HI. SEE MY BIRTHDAY PRESENT.
THAT'S A NICE ONE. I JUST HAD A BIRTHDAY, TOO.
WANT TO PLAY?
I DON'T PLAY.
I CAN SHOW YOU HOW...
ARE YOU A NEW KID?
I'M JUST VISITING. I'M REALLY FROM FRANCE.
I'M A PRINCE, SEE, AND I'M TRAVELING IN DISGUISE.
YOU ARE NOT. THERE AIN'T NO PRINCES.
HEY, KID! WHAT'RE YOU DOING IN MY YARD?

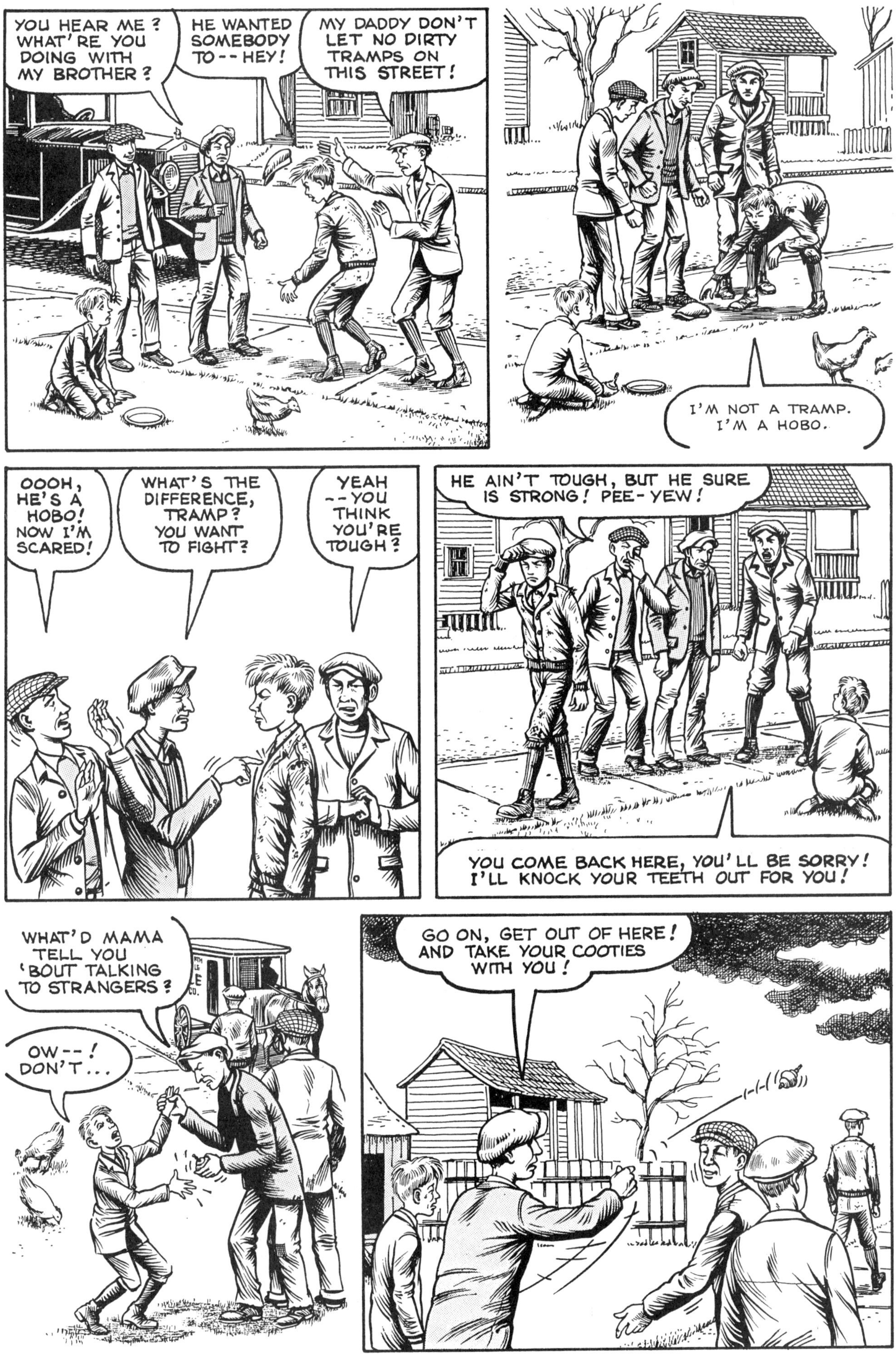
YOU HEAR ME? WHAT'RE YOU DOING WITH MY BROTHER?
HE WANTED SOMEBODY TO--HEY!
MY DADDY DON'T LET NO DIRTY TRAMPS ON THIS STREET!
I'M NOT A TRAMP. I'M A HOBO.
OOOH, HE'S A HOBO! NOW I'M SCARED!
WHAT'S THE DIFFERENCE, TRAMP? YOU WANT TO FIGHT?
YEAH --YOU THINK YOU'RE TOUGH?
HE AIN'T TOUGH, BUT HE SURE IS STRONG! PEE-YEW!
YOU COME BACK HERE, YOU'LL BE SORRY! I'LL KNOCK YOUR TEETH OUT FOR YOU!
WHAT'D MAMA TELL YOU 'BOUT TALKING TO STRANGERS?
OW--! DON'T...
GO ON, GET OUT OF HERE! AND TAKE YOUR COOTIES WITH YOU!

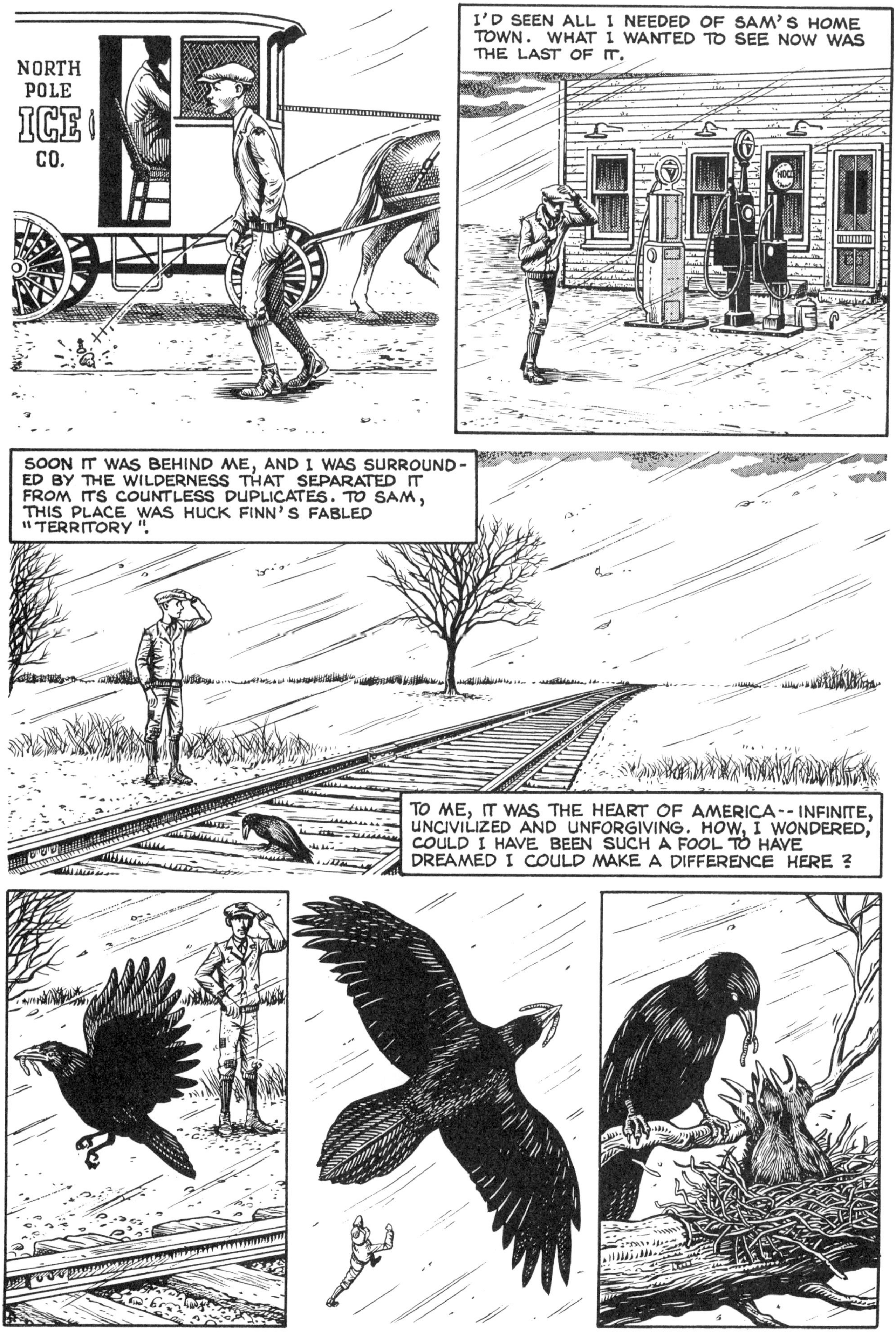
NORTH POLE ICE CO.
I'D SEEN ALL I NEEDED OF SAM'S HOME TOWN. WHAT I WANTED TO SEE NOW WAS THE LAST OF IT.
SOON IT WAS BEHIND ME, AND I WAS SURROUNDED BY THE WILDERNESS THAT SEPARATED IT FROM ITS COUNTLESS DUPLICATES. TO SAM, THIS PLACE WAS HUCK FINN'S FABLED "TERRITORY".
TO ME, IT WAS THE HEART OF AMERICA--INFINITE, UNCIVILIZED AND UNFORGIVING. HOW, I WONDERED, COULD I HAVE BEEN SUCH A FOOL TO HAVE DREAMED I COULD MAKE A DIFFERENCE HERE?

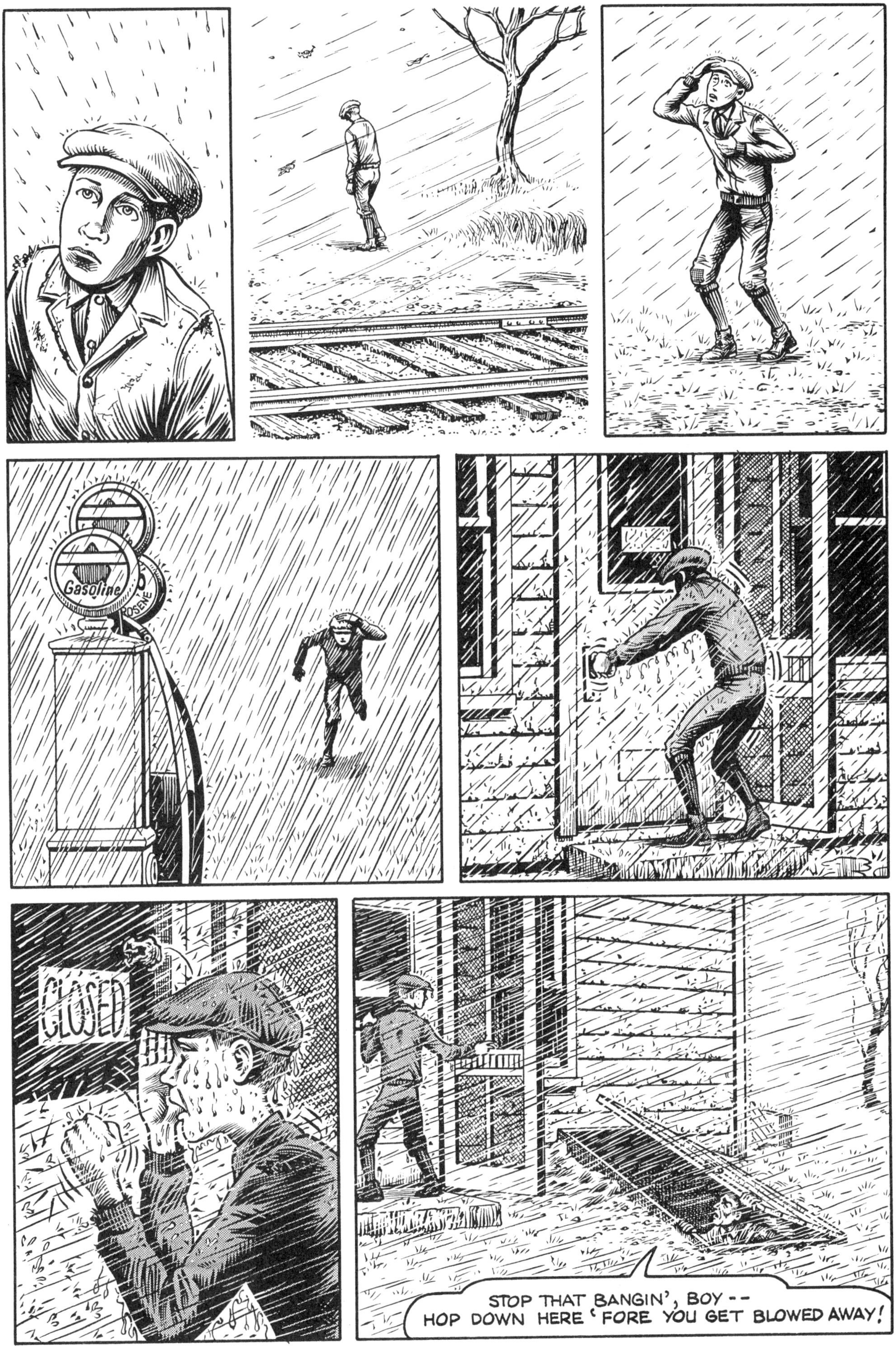
Gasoline
ROSENE
CLOSED
STOP THAT BANGIN', BOY --
HOP DOWN HERE 'FORE YOU GET BLOWED AWAY!

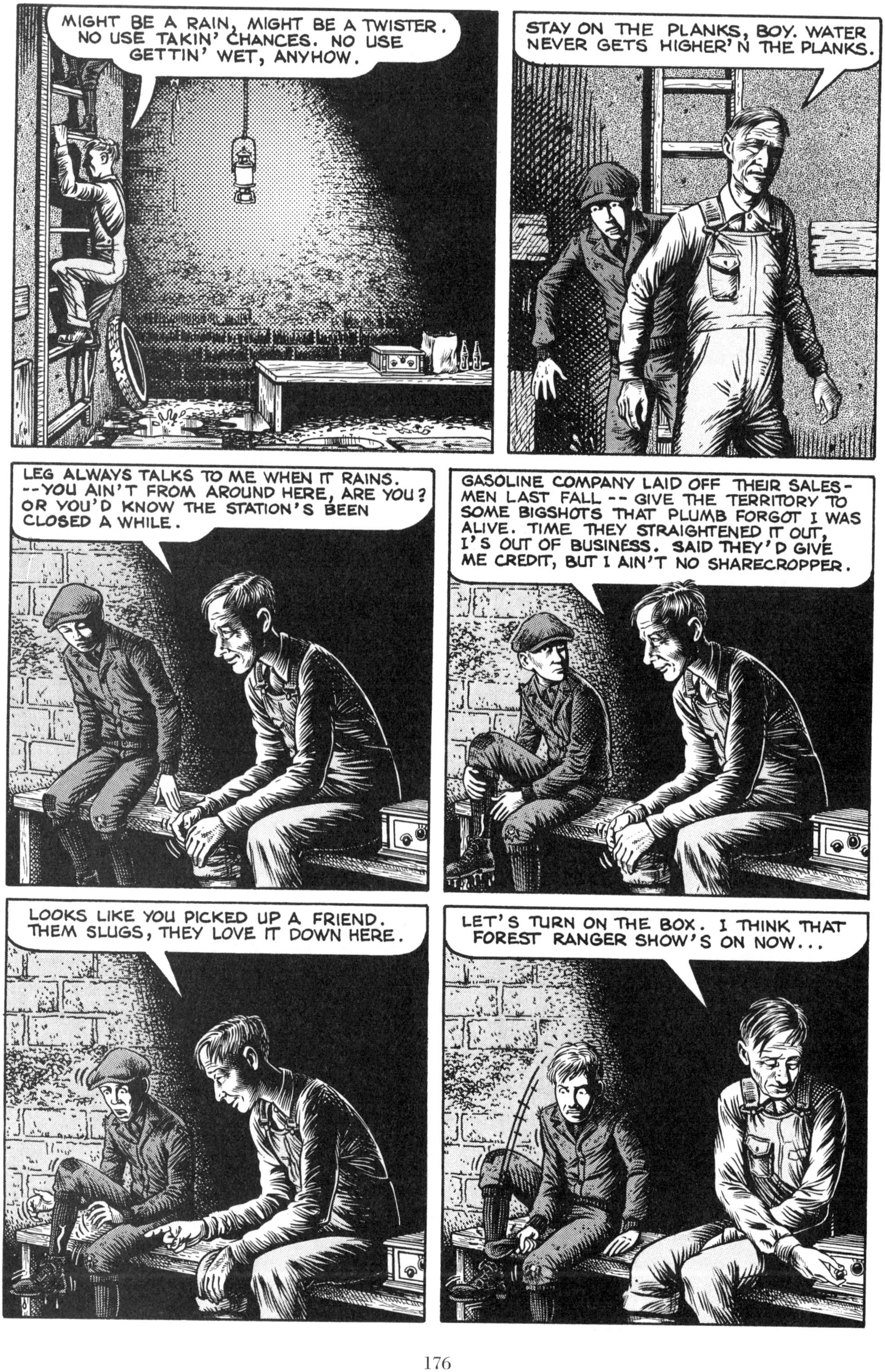
MIGHT BE A RAIN, MIGHT BE A TWISTER. NO USE TAKIN' CHANCES. NO USE GETTIN' WET, ANYHOW.
STAY ON THE PLANKS, BOY. WATER NEVER GETS HIGHER'N THE PLANKS.
LEG ALWAYS TALKS TO ME WHEN IT RAINS. --YOU AIN'T FROM AROUND HERE, ARE YOU? OR YOU'D KNOW THE STATION'S BEEN CLOSED A WHILE.
GASOLINE COMPANY LAID OFF THEIR SALES-MEN LAST FALL -- GIVE THE TERRITORY TO SOME BIGSHOTS THAT PLUMB FORGOT I WAS ALIVE. TIME THEY STRAIGHTENED IT OUT, I'S OUT OF BUSINESS. SAID THEY'D GIVE ME CREDIT, BUT I AIN'T NO SHARECROPPER.
LOOKS LIKE YOU PICKED UP A FRIEND. THEM SLUGS, THEY LOVE IT DOWN HERE.
LET'S TURN ON THE BOX. I THINK THAT FOREST RANGER SHOW'S ON NOW...

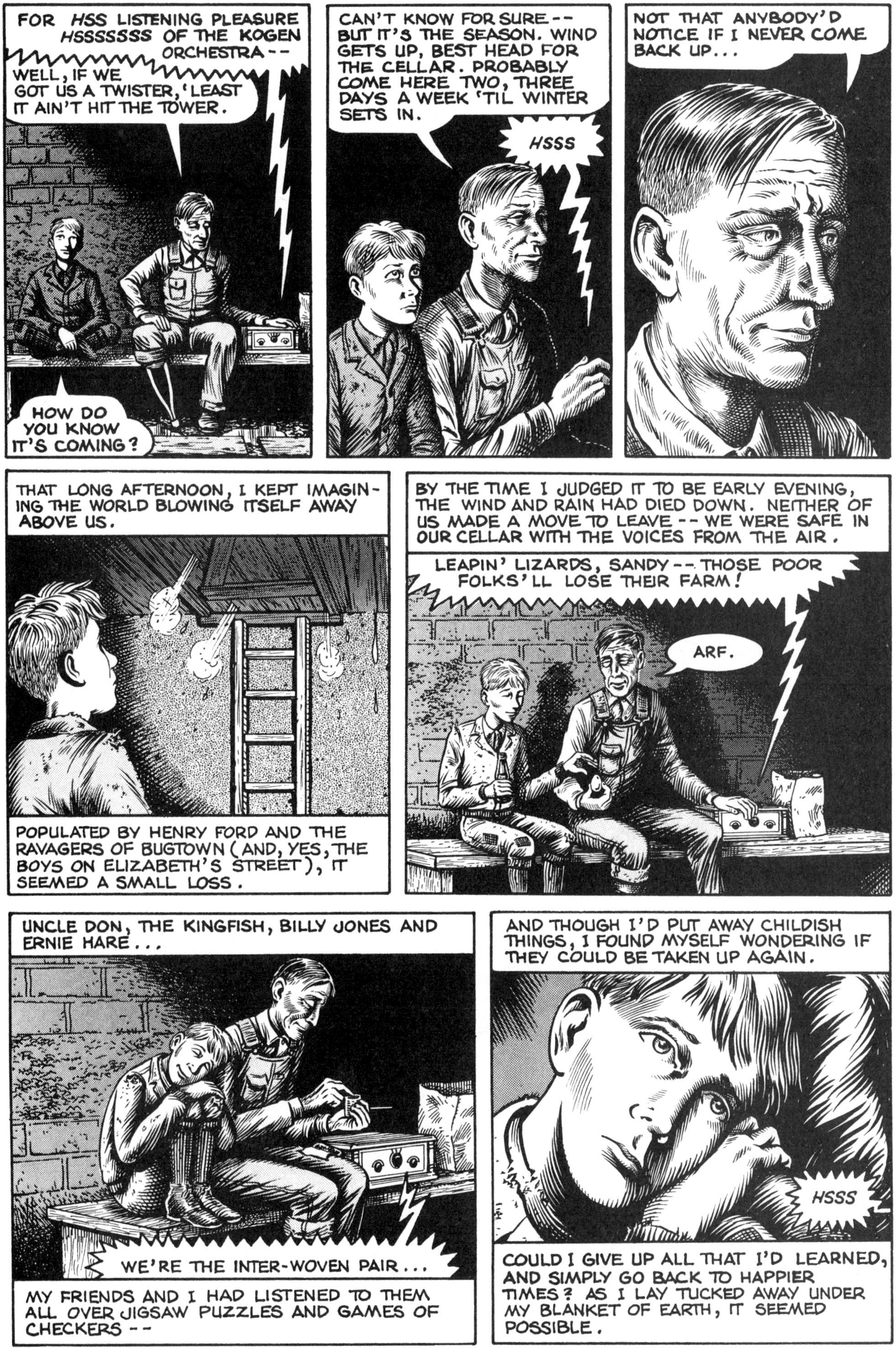
FOR HSS LISTENING PLEASURE HSSSSSSS OF THE KOGEN ORCHESTRA --
WELL, IF WE GOT US A TWISTER, 'LEAST IT AIN'T HIT THE TOWER.
HOW DO YOU KNOW IT'S COMING?
CAN'T KNOW FOR SURE -- BUT IT'S THE SEASON. WIND GETS UP, BEST HEAD FOR THE CELLAR. PROBABLY COME HERE TWO, THREE DAYS A WEEK 'TIL WINTER SETS IN.
HSSS
NOT THAT ANYBODY'D NOTICE IF I NEVER COME BACK UP...
THAT LONG AFTERNOON, I KEPT IMAGINING THE WORLD BLOWING ITSELF AWAY ABOVE US.
POPULATED BY HENRY FORD AND THE RAVAGERS OF BUGTOWN (AND, YES, THE BOYS ON ELIZABETH'S STREET), IT SEEMED A SMALL LOSS.
BY THE TIME I JUDGED IT TO BE EARLY EVENING, THE WIND AND RAIN HAD DIED DOWN. NEITHER OF US MADE A MOVE TO LEAVE -- WE WERE SAFE IN OUR CELLAR WITH THE VOICES FROM THE AIR.
LEAPIN' LIZARDS, SANDY -- THOSE POOR FOLKS'LL LOSE THEIR FARM!
ARF.
UNCLE DON, THE KINGFISH, BILLY JONES AND ERNIE HARE...
WE'RE THE INTER-WOVEN PAIR...
MY FRIENDS AND I HAD LISTENED TO THEM ALL OVER JIGSAW PUZZLES AND GAMES OF CHECKERS --
AND THOUGH I'D PUT AWAY CHILDISH THINGS, I FOUND MYSELF WONDERING IF THEY COULD BE TAKEN UP AGAIN.
HSSS
COULD I GIVE UP ALL THAT I'D LEARNED, AND SIMPLY GO BACK TO HAPPIER TIMES? AS I LAY TUCKED AWAY UNDER MY BLANKET OF EARTH, IT SEEMED POSSIBLE.

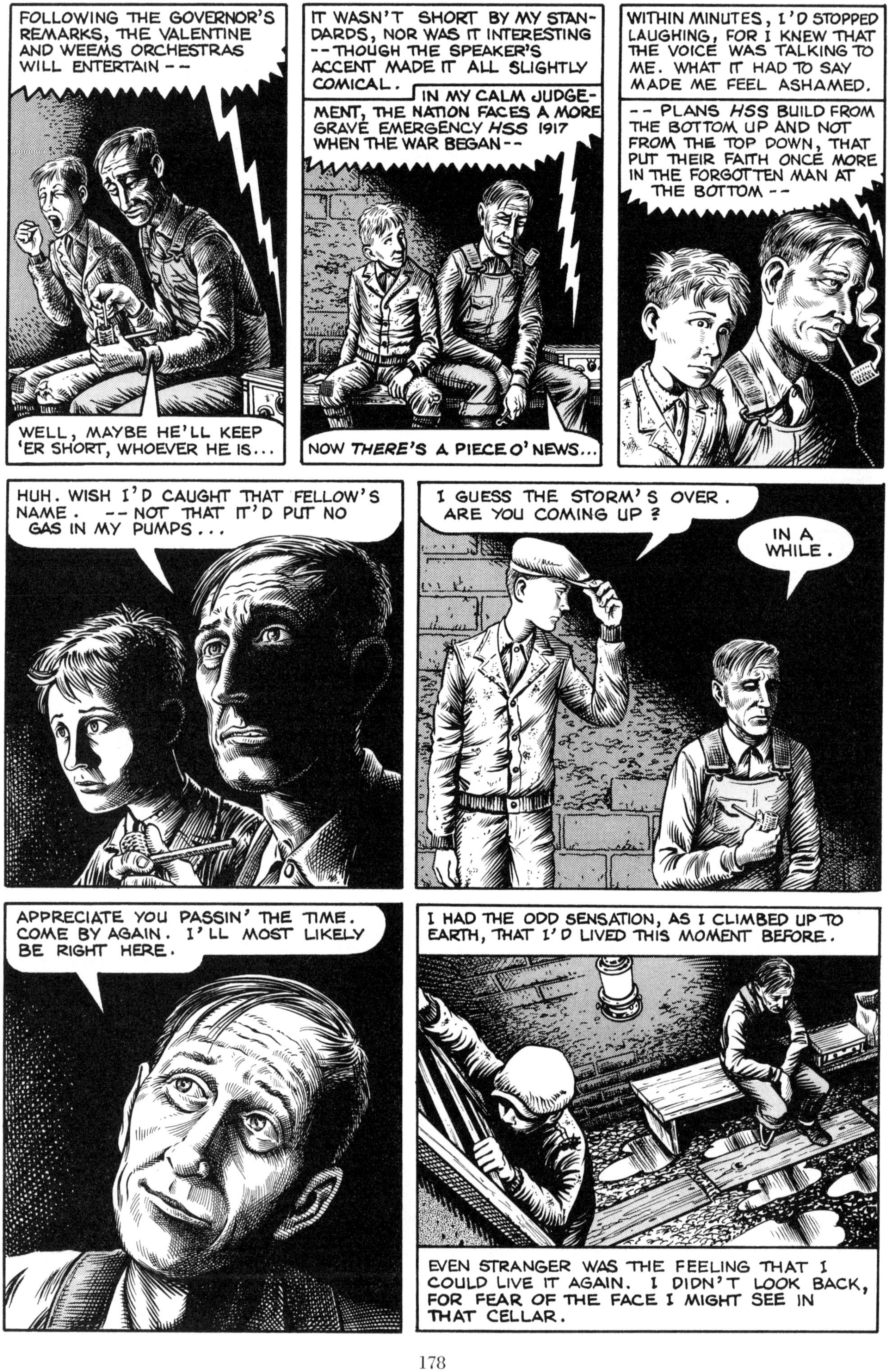

FOLLOWING THE GOVERNOR'S REMARKS, THE VALENTINE AND WEEMS ORCHESTRAS WILL ENTERTAIN --
WELL, MAYBE HE'LL KEEP 'ER SHORT, WHOEVER HE IS...
IT WASN'T SHORT BY MY STANDARDS, NOR WAS IT INTERESTING --THOUGH THE SPEAKER'S ACCENT MADE IT ALL SLIGHTLY COMICAL.
IN MY CALM JUDGEMENT, THE NATION FACES A MORE GRAVE EMERGENCY HSS 1917 WHEN THE WAR BEGAN --
NOW THERE'S A PIECE O' NEWS...
WITHIN MINUTES, I'D STOPPED LAUGHING, FOR I KNEW THAT THE VOICE WAS TALKING TO ME. WHAT IT HAD TO SAY MADE ME FEEL ASHAMED.
-- PLANS HSS BUILD FROM THE BOTTOM UP AND NOT FROM THE TOP DOWN, THAT PUT THEIR FAITH ONCE MORE IN THE FORGOTTEN MAN AT THE BOTTOM --
HUH. WISH I'D CAUGHT THAT FELLOW'S NAME. -- NOT THAT IT'D PUT NO GAS IN MY PUMPS...
I GUESS THE STORM'S OVER. ARE YOU COMING UP ?
IN A WHILE.
APPRECIATE YOU PASSIN' THE TIME. COME BY AGAIN. I'LL MOST LIKELY BE RIGHT HERE.
I HAD THE ODD SENSATION, AS I CLIMBED UP TO EARTH, THAT I'D LIVED THIS MOMENT BEFORE.
EVEN STRANGER WAS THE FEELING THAT I COULD LIVE IT AGAIN. I DIDN'T LOOK BACK, FOR FEAR OF THE FACE I MIGHT SEE IN THAT CELLAR.

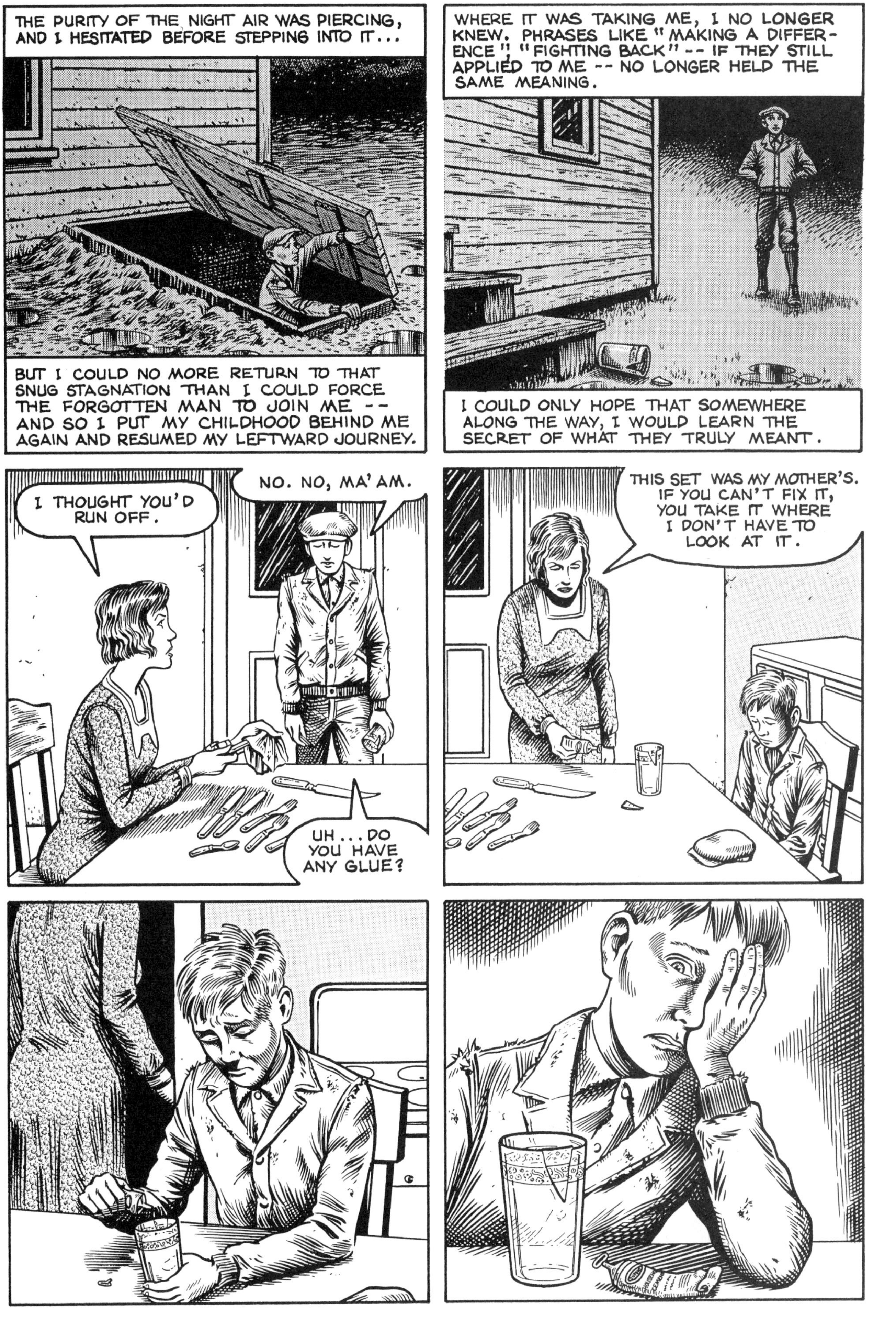
THE PURITY OF THE NIGHT AIR WAS PIERCING, AND I HESITATED BEFORE STEPPING INTO IT...
BUT I COULD NO MORE RETURN TO THAT SNUG STAGNATION THAN I COULD FORCE THE FORGOTTEN MAN TO JOIN ME -- AND SO I PUT MY CHILDHOOD BEHIND ME AGAIN AND RESUMED MY LEFTWARD JOURNEY.
WHERE IT WAS TAKING ME, I NO LONGER KNEW. PHRASES LIKE "MAKING A DIFFERENCE", "FIGHTING BACK" -- IF THEY STILL APPLIED TO ME -- NO LONGER HELD THE SAME MEANING.
I COULD ONLY HOPE THAT SOMEWHERE ALONG THE WAY, I WOULD LEARN THE SECRET OF WHAT THEY TRULY MEANT.
I THOUGHT YOU'D RUN OFF.
NO. NO, MA'AM.
UH... DO YOU HAVE ANY GLUE?
THIS SET WAS MY MOTHER'S. IF YOU CAN'T FIX IT, YOU TAKE IT WHERE I DON'T HAVE TO LOOK AT IT.

ON MY WAY TO THE DOOR, IT CAME TO ME BETWEEN HEARTBEATS : THE SECRET.

"MAKING A DIFFERENCE," "FIGHTING BACK" -- THEY HAD NOTHING TO DO WITH FORCE. THE SECRET WAS TO REMEMBER, AND TO BE REMEMBERED...

TO PIECE TOGETHER THOSE SHARDS OF THE WORLD THAT YOU COULD...

AND HOPE THAT THE DAY WOULD COME WHEN WE COULD PUT IT ALL BACK TOGETHER.

THAT NIGHT, I SLEPT THE SLEEP OF VICTORY.

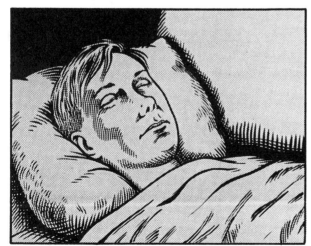

I AWOKE IN A ROOM THAT SMELLED LIKE A CELLAR. THE HOUSE WAS QUIET AS A TOMB. I KNEW THAT I'D MADE MY MARK HERE, TOO.

UNNERVED BY ELIZABETH'S SILENCE, FRIGHTENED BY ITS BITTER ALTERNATIVE, I KEPT TO MYSELF. AROUND NOON, I HEARD VOICES. THEY WERE TALKING ABOUT SAM.

THE EMPHYSEMA'S BAD ENOUGH -- BUT THIS PNEUMONIA... IT'S VERY SERIOUS. THERE'S NOTHING WE CAN DO BUT KEEP HIM IN BED, AND HOPE FOR THE BEST. AND REMEMBER -- SOMETIMES MIRACLES HAPPEN.

HE WAS ASKING FOR YOU. DON'T SAY ANY-THING ABOUT THE PNEUMONIA. HE DOESN'T KNOW.

SIT DOWN, YOUR HIGHNESS. I BEEN DOIN' A LOT OF THINKIN' *GASP* -- WANT TO TALK TO YOU 'BOUT IT...

YOU UNDERSTAND ABOUT ME 'N ELIZABETH... I BEEN LAYIN' HERE THINKIN' 'BOUT WHAT A FOOL I BEEN. I NEARLY LOST HER FOR GOOD. MIGHT NEVER HAVE COME BACK, IF I HADN'T CAUGHT THIS BUG. GUESS IT'S THE BEST THING EVER HAPPENED TO ME.

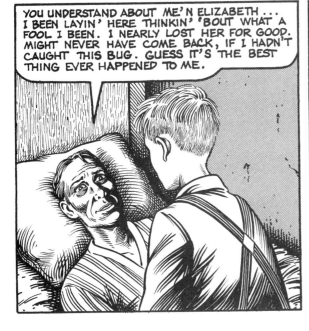

I'M GONNA MARRY HER, IF SHE'LL STILL HAVE ME. FIX THIS PLACE UP... FIX MYSELF UP...

ME AND HER'S TALKED ABOUT THIS, AND WE'D LIKE YOU TO THINK ABOUT STAYIN' HERE WITH US. IT COULD BE LIKE WE WAS ALL A FAMILY. I'D LIKE THAT A LOT.

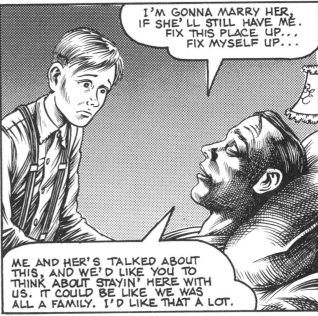

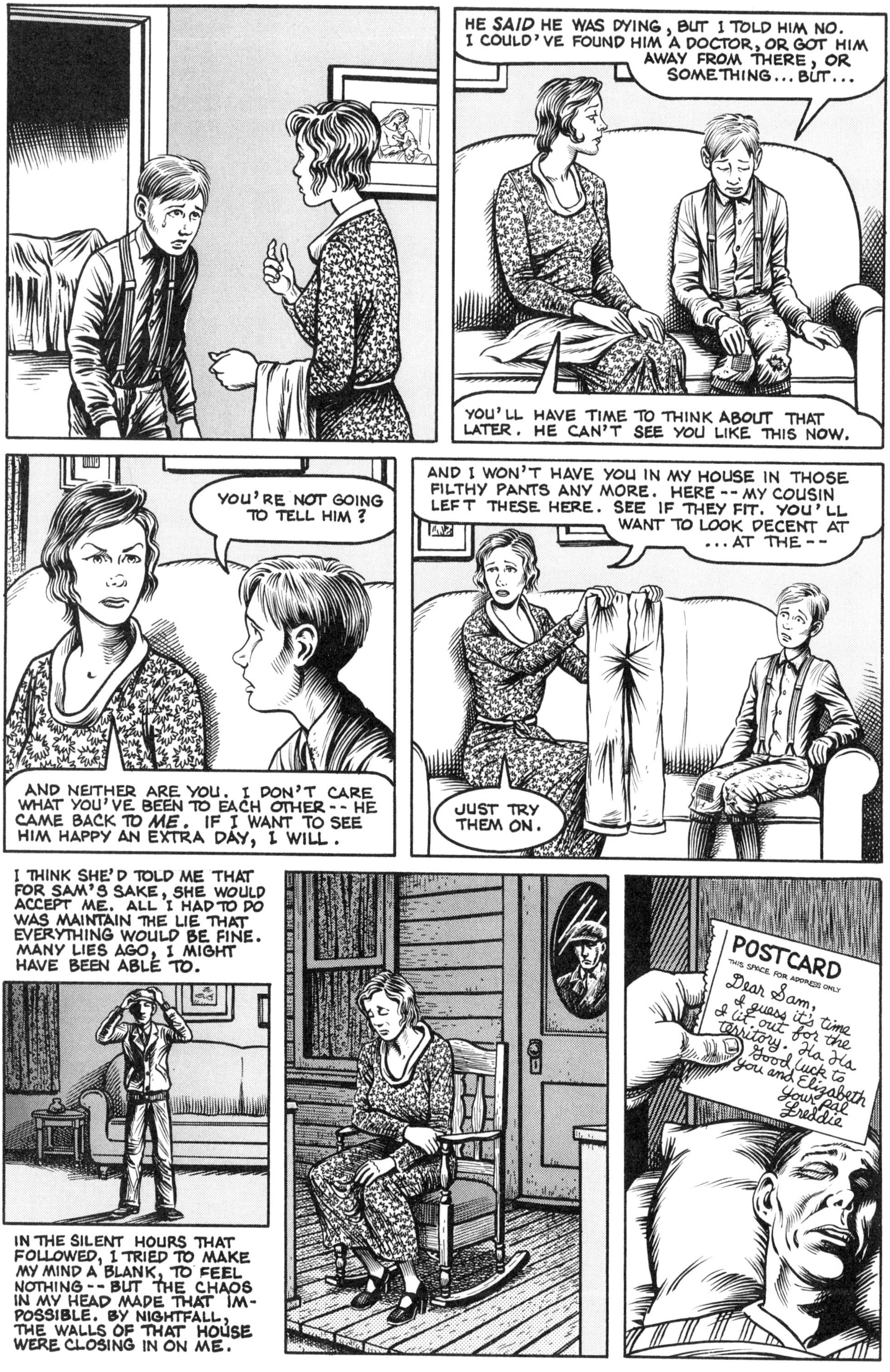
HE SAID HE WAS DYING, BUT I TOLD HIM NO. I COULD'VE FOUND HIM A DOCTOR, OR GOT HIM AWAY FROM THERE, OR SOMETHING... BUT...
YOU'LL HAVE TIME TO THINK ABOUT THAT LATER. HE CAN'T SEE YOU LIKE THIS NOW.
YOU'RE NOT GOING TO TELL HIM?
AND NEITHER ARE YOU. I DON'T CARE WHAT YOU'VE BEEN TO EACH OTHER -- HE CAME BACK TO ME. IF I WANT TO SEE HIM HAPPY AN EXTRA DAY, I WILL.
AND I WON'T HAVE YOU IN MY HOUSE IN THOSE FILTHY PANTS ANY MORE. HERE -- MY COUSIN LEFT THESE HERE. SEE IF THEY FIT. YOU'LL WANT TO LOOK DECENT AT ... AT THE --
JUST TRY THEM ON.
I THINK SHE'D TOLD ME THAT FOR SAM'S SAKE, SHE WOULD ACCEPT ME. ALL I HAD TO DO WAS MAINTAIN THE LIE THAT EVERYTHING WOULD BE FINE. MANY LIES AGO, I MIGHT HAVE BEEN ABLE TO.
IN THE SILENT HOURS THAT FOLLOWED, I TRIED TO MAKE MY MIND A BLANK, TO FEEL NOTHING -- BUT THE CHAOS IN MY HEAD MADE THAT IMPOSSIBLE. BY NIGHTFALL, THE WALLS OF THAT HOUSE WERE CLOSING IN ON ME.
POSTCARD
THIS SPACE FOR ADDRESS ONLY
Dear Sam,
I guess it's time I lit out for the territory. Ha Ha
Good luck to you and Elizabeth
Your pal
Freddie

HM-- ?
COUGH
GASP
COUGH COUGH
COUGH COUGH
THE CHAOS IN MY HEAD CONTINUED. I'D BE HEARING IT FOR A LONG TIME TO COME.
SOMETIME AFTER THAT, I HAD A DREAM . . .
FROM :
DETROIT, MICH
TO :
MARIAN, CALIF
YMHA will call

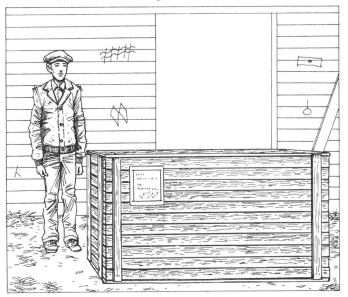

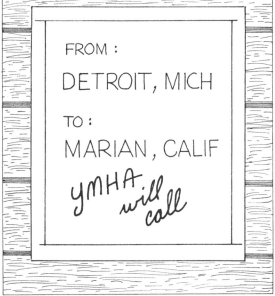

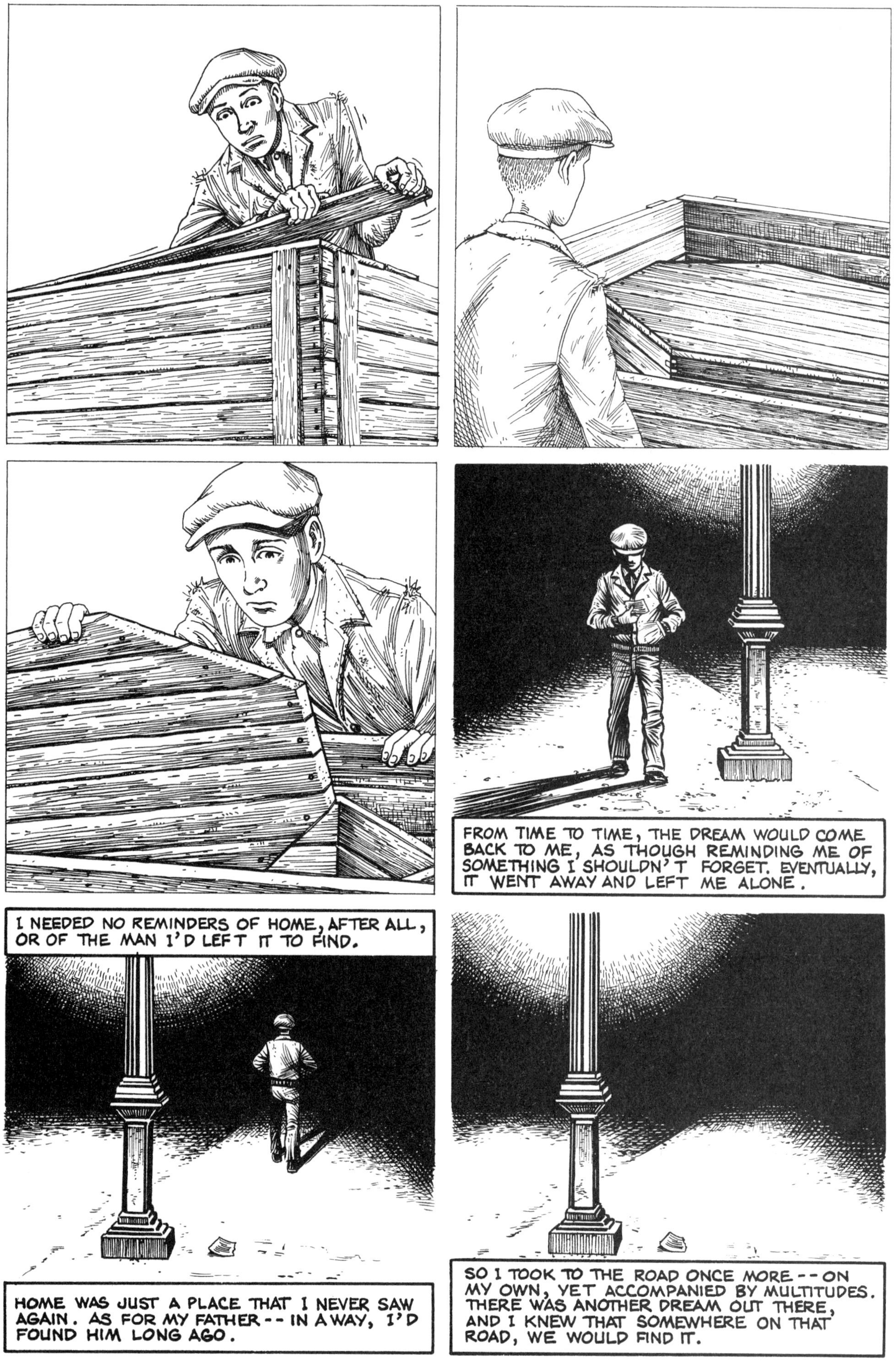
FROM TIME TO TIME, THE DREAM WOULD COME BACK TO ME, AS THOUGH REMINDING ME OF SOMETHING I SHOULDN'T FORGET. EVENTUALLY, IT WENT AWAY AND LEFT ME ALONE.
I NEEDED NO REMINDERS OF HOME, AFTER ALL, OR OF THE MAN I'D LEFT IT TO FIND.
HOME WAS JUST A PLACE THAT I NEVER SAW AGAIN. AS FOR MY FATHER -- IN A WAY, I'D FOUND HIM LONG AGO.
SO I TOOK TO THE ROAD ONCE MORE -- ON MY OWN, YET ACCOMPANIED BY MULTITUDES. THERE WAS ANOTHER DREAM OUT THERE, AND I KNEW THAT SOMEWHERE ON THAT ROAD, WE WOULD FIND IT.

8. Sept. 08 Amazon 12.74 105542